SOCIAL PSYCHOLOGY AND EVALUATION

Social Psychology and Evaluation

EDITED BY

Melvin M. Mark
Stewart I. Donaldson
Bernadette Campbell

THE GUILFORD PRESS
New York   London

To Kurt Lewin, Donald Campbell, Peter Rossi,
and their followers,
who toil at the intersection of social psychology and evaluation
in service of social betterment

© 2011 The Guilford Press
A Division of Guilford Publications, Inc.
72 Spring Street, New York, NY 10012
www.guilford.com

Printed in the United States of America

This book is printed on acid-free paper.

Last digit is print number: 9   8   7   6   5   4   3   2   1

Library of Congress Cataloging-in-Publication Data

Social psychology and evaluation / edited by Melvin M. Mark, Stewart I.
Donaldson, Bernadette Campbell.
     p.   cm.
   Includes bibliographical references and index.
   ISBN 978-1-60918-212-0 (pbk.: alk. paper) — ISBN 978-1-60918-213-7
(hardcover: alk. paper)
   1. Social psychology—Methodology.   2. Evaluation.   I. Mark, Melvin M.
II. Donaldson, Stewart I. (Stewart Ian)   III. Campbell, Bernadette.
   HM1033.S6423 2011
   302.01—dc22
                                                            2011010212

Preface

A staple of both epic literature and pulp fiction is the existence of separate plot lines that intertwine. This book examines two real-life plot lines that have already intertwined in certain ways. The chapters in this book tell the story of the two plot lines to date. But we hope and believe that the story is not over. Part of the impetus of this book is to try to motivate readers to help write the rest of this real-life story.

One of the plot lines involves social psychology, a traditional subfield of psychology and sociology. An important stream in social psychology's history consists of efforts to apply its theory and research in ways that help solve social problems. Another plot line in this book involves the evaluation of programs, policies, and practices. The very existence of evaluation as a field is premised on notions such as the belief that better programs can be built, and more effective programs can be retained, if systematic evidence is collected about program operations and effects.

The plot lines of social psychology and of evaluation have already intersected in important ways. For example, social psychology was one of the sources of human capacity during evaluation's growth spurt in the Great Society period of United States history. As another example, theories from social psychology have informed the development of conceptual models of programs in the practice of evaluation. However, we believe the final chapter has not been written. That is, in the future, a larger and more productive integration of these two plot lines is possible. We look forward to the sequel, so to speak.

We thank the authors of the chapters in this volume for their interest in the project, for their thoughtful products, and for their patience with us. Thanks, too, to Chris Gamble and Jen Mills, who coauthored a conference paper with Melvin Mark that foreshadowed parts of Chapter 1. A special thanks to C. Deborah Laughton of The Guilford Press, who is in important ways a partner with and advocate for the authors and editors with whom she works.

Contents

PART I

Background, History, and Overview

EDITORS' INTRODUCTORY COMMENTS
TO CHAPTER 1

In this introductory chapter, the volume editors explore the relationship between social psychology and the evaluation of programs, policies, and practices. They discuss the historical relationship, including the role of a set of major figures whose work involves both fields. The current status of the relationship is also examined. Today, the authors suggest, the primary form of intersection involves "program theory." A program theory is a conceptual model of how and why a social intervention is expected to bring about its anticipated benefits. In many domains of social and educational interventions, social psychological research and theory underlies program theories.

As Mark, Donaldson, and Campbell indicate, however, there are several other potential benefits for both evaluation and social psychology that are far from fully realized. Whether these benefits are achieved will depend on the future of the relationship between social psychology and evaluation. The authors of Chapter 1 consider three alternative futures, clearly preferring one over the others.

In Appendix 1.1, they also review several of the concepts and terms related to research methodology that are used throughout the volume.

The Past, the Present, and Possible Futures of Social Psychology and Evaluation

Melvin M. Mark
Stewart I. Donaldson
Bernadette Campbell

Consider the following four scenarios:

> Staff members of an international assistance agency are developing a new program. It is intended to help women in a traditional culture develop the ability to insist on safe sex practices with their (often unfaithful) partners. In developing the program, the staff members refer to the literature on behavior change and build a plan for the program that draws on concepts such as social norms and self-efficacy.

> Members of a research firm are hired to evaluate the effectiveness of a workplace-based program that was put in place to reduce employees' unhealthy behaviors (and ultimately to improve health and reduce health care costs). In designing the evaluation, the researchers discuss theories of interpersonal influence and behavior change processes to help them identify shorter-term outcomes to measure. The researchers also look at summaries from research on the best ways to get valid self-reports about behavior (such as diet and exercise) that takes place over time.

> A researcher interested in theories of negotiation is asked to help with and study a contentious process in the person's local school district. The school is trying to implement a policy to "mainstream" children

with serious disabilities into regular classrooms. While observing meetings with various interested parties, the researcher realizes that traditional academic research on negotiation has left out an important factor—the degree to which participants identify with multiple interest groups in the negotiation (like the teacher who is also the mother of a special needs student).

The United States Government Accountability Office (GAO) is often asked to study the implementation and effectiveness of government programs and policies. When hiring new staff members, the GAO seeks new PhDs with skills in research design, understanding of behavior change theories, and the ability to measure attitudes and behaviors.

All four of these scenarios, and many others described throughout this book, involve the intersection of social psychology, on the one hand, and the evaluation of social programs, policies, and practices, on the other. The historical linkages between these two areas are noteworthy. For example, Kurt Lewin, one of the most important figures in the history of social psychology, carried out what we would call evaluations. A prominent example involves his work in developing and evaluating efforts to modify food choices during World War II (Lewin, 1947, 1948). Later, in the 1960s and 1970s, the United States saw rapid growth in the practice of evaluation. This expansion largely took place during the Great Society, when the birth of new social and educational programs (such as Head Start) was accompanied by mandates to evaluate them. Among the leading figures during that growth spurt in evaluation were social psychologists such as Don Campbell and Peter Rossi (Shadish, Cook, & Leviton, 1991), whose roots in social psychology and contributions to evaluation are described shortly.

The current volume explores various aspects of the relationship between social psychology and evaluation. This includes discussion and examples of how beneficial the relationship can be. The volume also identifies ways the social psychology–evaluation relationship has not yet fulfilled its promise and ways this relationship might fruitfully be enhanced in the future.

This chapter introduces and overviews the social psychology–evaluation relationship. After providing definitions of both fields, we briefly review how this relationship developed and how it has changed over the years. We offer our views on the relationship as it currently stands. We close the chapter by speculating about alternative futures for the social psychology–evaluation relationship. This includes steps that we believe might be taken to help bring about a more beneficial relationship, both for evaluation and for social psychology. An appendix to the chapter provides a selective review of research methods used in evaluation and of a few key concepts from social psychology; this appendix serves as a kind of glossary for many of the concepts and terms used throughout the volume.

Social Psychology, and Evaluation, Defined

Numerous definitions of social psychology have been offered through the years. Many have described social psychology as the scientific study of the way the thoughts, feeling, or actions of an individual are affected by the real or implied presence of others. Other definitions focus on the interplay between the individual and the group. In part, what the field of social psychology is can be inferred from the topics that its members study. Social psychology has long addressed a wide range of topics, such as person perception, interpersonal attraction, helping, aggression, and prejudice and stereotyping.

Many of the topics addressed by social psychology are relevant to evaluation, as well as to the design of the programs, policies, and practices that are evaluated. Social psychological topics of interest to evaluation include the general processes that affect behavior change; attitude change and persuasion; the effects of perceived norms; biases that can affect human judgment; individual and collective decision making; and interpersonal and intergroup processes.

Social psychology has roots in both sociology and psychology, with most social psychologists trained in psychology departments. Social psychologists are interested in developing and testing theories. They do so both to better understand social psychological phenomena (so-called basic research) and to apply research and theory to address social problems (so-called applied research). In fact, much of social psychology through the years has defied categorization in terms of basic versus applied. For example, researchers have striven both to enhance understanding of fundamental social psychological processes and to address issues of societal import, such as obedience to authority (Milgram, 1974), failure to help others (Darley & Latané, 1968), and prejudice and discrimination (Dovidio, Glick, & Rudman, 2005).

Social psychologists employ a wide range of methods, including an increasing array of complex statistical procedures. However, it appears that psychological social psychologists, at least as represented in the major mainstream journals, tend primarily to use randomized experiments, in which participants are assigned at random, as by the flip of a fair coin or a random number program, to one of two or more conditions (e.g., to a positive or negative mood induction). These experiments are typically conducted in laboratory settings with introductory psychology students as study participants (Cook & Groom, 2004). As noted later in this chapter, an increased relationship between social psychology and evaluation could help overcome some of the limitations that arise from these methodological predispositions.

Like social psychology, evaluation has been defined in various ways. Perhaps the most common definition today, popularized by Michael

Scriven (1991), defines evaluation as the systematic determination of the merit, worth, or significance of something. For example, is a school-based pregnancy prevention program worthwhile? Is it worthy, metaphorically speaking, of a grade of A, or B, or perhaps an F? Another kind of definition, popularized by Peter Rossi and his colleagues (e.g., Rossi, Lipsey, & Freeman, 2004), describes evaluation as the application of social science research methods to the study of social programs or policies, in order to improve understanding and guide action. A typical illustration would be the use of a well-designed experiment to see whether the pregnancy prevention program in fact led to fewer pregnancies, with the hope that the findings would inform policy makers who make choices about school-based programs.

A wide range of methods is used in evaluation. The choice of methods should depend in part on the purpose of the evaluation (as well as other considerations, such as the pragmatics of budget and timeframes). Two of the common purposes of evaluation are formative—that is, the evaluation is intended to help improve the thing being evaluated—and summative— that is, the evaluation is intended to generate a bottom-line judgment about the thing being evaluated (Scriven, 1967). For example, a summative evaluation might be undertaken to help program staff improve the program, perhaps by identifying ways of doing a better job of implementing it and by getting more of those who are eligible to participate. The evaluator in this example might engage in direct observation of the program, along with interviews of program staff, clients, and prospective clients. Alternatively, a summative evaluation might be conducted in order to inform public officials about whether to fund the expansion of a pilot program that currently is operating at only a few sites. In this case, the evaluator might carry out an experiment or other kind of study to see what effect, if any, the program has on the outcomes of interest. Many other possibilities exist in terms of evaluation methods, as is illustrated throughout this volume.

Before turning to a brief history of the relationship between social psychology and evaluation, a note about terminology is needed. To this point, we have often referred to "the evaluation of program, policies and practices," rather than simply to "evaluation." There are two reasons we have used this long phrase, with one reason coming from social psychology and the other from evaluation. First, for social psychologists, the concept of attitude refers to the degree an individual likes or dislikes something—that is, to an individual's evaluative judgment about some object. In social psychology, the term *evaluation* is sometimes used to refer to these individual-level attitudes or evaluative judgments. To be clear, we are not focused on these individual-level evaluations, but rather on systematic research studies that contribute to sensible evaluative judgments about policies, programs, and practices. Second, evaluators recognize that in principle it is possible to evaluate anything. Product evaluation and personnel evaluation are two other broad areas of evaluation practice, for example. By referring to the evaluation of programs, policies, and practices, we explicitly restrict the focus of the book. In particular, we are referring to systematic evaluation of programs, policies, and practices. For the most part, we ignore the evaluation of personnel, products, or anything other than programs, policies, or practices. Stylistically, to continually repeat this trilogy, "programs, policies, and practices," would soon be redundant, if not outright irritating. Usually, then, for the sake of simplicity we and the other contributors to the volume refer simply to "evaluation," even though we mean the systematic evaluation of programs, policies, and practices. Likewise, for simplicity's sake we will often refer to the "program" being evaluated, rather than the "program, policy, or practice."

A Brief and Selective History[1]

Even a brief review of noteworthy historical connections between social psychology and evaluation cannot ignore the role of Kurt Lewin. Lewin is widely recognized as a central figure in the development of social psychology. Indeed, he is considered by many to be the founder, or father, of modern social psychology. Rooted in Gestalt psychology, which maintained that the whole is different than the sum of its parts, Lewin's "field theory" emphasized the dynamic interaction between the individual and the social context within which the individual's behavior occurs. In social psychology, Lewin is credited, among other things, for initiating the study of group dynamics, for stimulating the work that led to balance theory, dissonance, and attribution theory, and for highlighting the value of integrating so-called basic and applied research.

Lewin had an unwavering commitment to blending theory and practice—he once said, "Research that produces nothing but books will not suffice" (Lewin, 1946). Lewin's contributions to the field of evaluation are not as widely recognized as his contributions to social psychology, but they are important. Indeed, Lewin's work foreshadowed many developments that took years to take root in evaluation. For example, Lewin's focus on using theory in any applied research was an intellectual predecessor to the attention to program theory in much of evaluation practice today (see Chen, 1990, and Donaldson & Crano, Chapter 5, this volume). Lewin's attention to social context presaged growing concern for context in contemporary evaluation (Rog, 2009), including attention to identifying for whom and in which settings a program is effective (e.g., Pawson & Tilley, 1997).

Perhaps the contribution to evaluation for which Lewin is most widely credited centers on what he named "action research." Defined broadly, action research is the process by which practitioners (perhaps aided by a researcher) attempt to study their problems scientifically in order to guide, correct, and evaluate their decisions and actions (Corey, 1953). Lewin's legacy of action research has persisted more in related fields other than in (psychological) social psychology. These include organizational development, community psychology, and education. Drawing on these fields and on Lewin and his colleagues' original work, action research has historically been and increasingly today is a key influence for some approaches to evaluation. In terms of evaluation, action research is often cited and sometimes used by those interested in *improving* programs and practices, that is, formative evaluation, rather than conducting a summative, bottom-line test of their effectiveness (e.g., Rogers & Williams, 2006). Several contemporary evaluation scholars acknowledge Lewin's direct influence in their theorizing. Without going into detail here, the heritage of action research can be seen in several approaches to evaluation, including Fetterman's (1998) empowerment evaluation, Rothman's (1997) action evaluation, practical participatory evaluation (Cousins & Whitmore, 1998), and developmental evaluation (Patton, 2008).

Lewin's action research spanned a broad range of topics, several of which are relevant to evaluation. Take but one prominent example. During World War II, the U.S. Defense Department commissioned Lewin, along with Margaret Mead and dozens of other prominent social scientists in the United States, to help solve a potential food shortage. Much of the domestic meat supply was being shipped abroad to feed soldiers and allies, creating concern about a shortage of protein for domestic consumption. Government officials thought they could solve this problem by getting Americans to eat so-called variety meats or organ meats, such as hearts, brains, intestines, and heads. Lewin and others were asked to figure out how to get Americans to eat organ meat and enjoy it. In his successful studies, Lewin found that the key to changing the eating habits of individuals was first to change the perspectives and practices of the group (Lewin, 1947, 1948). Lewin subsequently applied this mechanism to efforts to address other social problems, including prejudice, criminal behavior, and work productivity (Lewin, 1948).

In this work, Lewin foreshadowed theory-driven evaluation and its cousins. In short, theory-driven evaluation involves identifying the processes by which a program should have its effects, and using this model to guide evaluation activities. Theory-driven evaluation is described in more detail in chapters that follow, especially Donaldson and Crano (Chapter 5). This relationship between Lewin and theory-driven evaluation should not be surprising. After all, Lewin (1951) was the source of the oft-repeated quote, "There's nothing as practical as a good theory."

In sum, Kurt Lewin not only founded modern social psychology but also had a formative impact on the field of evaluation. Indeed, we would argue that his impact on evaluation was greater than is generally recognized. In part, this is because his contributions largely occurred before evaluation existed as a distinct area of practice. In addition, Lewin's contributions to evaluation are underestimated because many of them have been indirect. That is, they have taken place by way of Lewin's influence on others who in turn influenced evaluation.

More evident to many evaluators is the influential role of Donald Campbell as well as various of his associates at the Northwestern University (Oral History Project Team; Miller, King, Mark, & Stockdill, 2003). Although Campbell is known to most evaluators for his methodological contributions, such as the detailing of quasi-experimental designs and the taxonomy of kinds of validity (see Appendix 1.1), he was a notable social psychologist. His wide-ranging work included research and theory on prejudice, ethnocentrism, and intergroup relations (e.g., Campbell, 1965, 1967), interpersonal perception, including the biasing effects of one's own attitudes (Miller, Campbell, Twedt, & O'Connell, 1966), the intergenerational transmission of norms (Jacobs & Campbell, 1961), and attitude measurement (e.g., Campbell, 1950). In evaluation, in addition to being a persuasive advocate of experimental and quasi-experimental methods, Campbell was also instrumental in bringing a number of colleagues and students (and some of their colleagues and students) into the field of evaluation. For those interested in more detail, Shadish, Cook, and Leviton (1991) offer a thorough analysis of Campbell's theory of and contributions to evaluation.

Campbell was among the people who indirectly brought some of Lewin's influence to evaluation. While Campbell was a graduate student at Berkeley, he took three courses from Lewin (who was visiting professor), including a small seminar on Lewin's theories (Campbell, 1988). Like Lewin, Campbell was drawn to the integration of theory and application. However, the theory Campbell brought to evaluation was not program-specific theory about how behavior change can be achieved in a particular case. Rather, Campbell brought to evaluation a broader theory of human knowledge processes, of the biases that can affect the informal evaluations people make of a program, and of methodological theory that could be brought to bear to reduce biases in evaluation. It was a theory that supported the use of experimental and quasi-experimental research designs to evaluate programs, so as to avoid the erroneous conclusions that could otherwise arise when attempting to estimate the effects of a program.

Another important kind of intersection between social psychology and evaluation is personified by Peter Rossi, who represented the link between more sociological social psychology and evaluation. A sociologist, Rossi came from the "social problems" approach to social psychology. The issues that Rossi studied during his highly productive career include homelessness (e.g., Rossi, 1989), social welfare (e.g., Rossi, 1998), public perceptions of criminal sentences (Rossi & Berk, 1997), crime, public subsidies, and recidivism (Rossi, Berk, & Lenihan, 1980), and gun control (Wright & Rossi, 1994). For Rossi, attention to evaluation was a relatively simple extension of his other work as an applied social researcher. Among Rossi's many contributions to evaluation are his best-selling textbook (now Rossi, Lipsey, & Freeman, 2004) and his advocacy of theory-driven evaluation in articles and chapters with Huey Chen (which preceded Chen's widely cited, 1990, book on the topic). Shadish, Cook, and Leviton (1991) provide a detailed discussion of Rossi's theory of and contributions to evaluation, and they credit him with developing a model of the different types of evaluation that should be undertaken under varying circumstances.[2]

Although it would be possible to examine the intersection of social psychology and evaluation through many individuals and institutions beyond Lewin, Campbell, and Rossi, we will turn our brief historical review to another question. That is, was it purely historical accident, or was there something more meaningful that led to the interplay that occurred between social psychology and evaluation?

Certainly, it appears that aspects of happenstance were involved. For example, the nature of food shortages on the home front in World War II led to Lewin being asked to develop and evaluate interventions to change eating patterns. In the case of Campbell, both he (Campbell, 1984) and Shadish et al. (1991) have told the story of how Campbell came to be involved in evaluation—by accident. E. A. Suchman (1967) wrote a seminal book on evaluation that highlighted Campbell and Stanley's (1966) work on experimental and quasi-experimental design and on internal and external validity. After Suchman's book, Campbell was widely sought as an expert in evaluation. Suchman, his book, and its aftermath essentially pulled Campbell into the field of evaluation.

If happenstance sometimes contributed to a *particular* connection between social psychology and evaluation, there were also sound reasons that made the *general* connection compelling. For example, Suchman's book may have pulled Campbell into the field, but Campbell did not drag his heels and resist. Rather, he quickly became a major, senior figure in evaluation. Perhaps this social psychologist entered the field of evaluation because there are many sensible reasons for an intersection between social psychology and evaluation.

- There is a good fit between the methodological and measurement skills of social psychologists and many of the practice needs of evaluation (with Suchman's attention to Campbell and his experimental and quasi-experimental design work being but one important example).
- Another kind of fit exists, in terms of the motivation for joining a research community. Many people in social psychology were drawn to the field because of applied interests and the concern for social betterment. This motivation was quite compatible with doing evalu-

ation, with its potential consequences including program improvement and the selection of more effective programs.

- Social psychological change processes underlie many if not most social programs and policies. As a result, social psychologists have a head start in thinking about program theory—that is, the underlying rationale as to how and why the program is expected to operate.

- Pragmatically, career options were needed at a time period when graduate training in social psychology was growing beyond the capacity of the traditional, mostly academic job market to offer positions to newly trained professionals.

Given the compatibility between social psychology and evaluation, and perhaps especially given the desirability of a new employment pathway for growing numbers of PhDs, many social psychologists and other applied social scientists moved into evaluation during the 1960s and 1970s. Despite the forces that attracted social psychologists to evaluation, however, the link between the two declined sharply in the 1980s. This decline appears to be attributable largely to two factors. First, budget cuts of the early Reagan administration resulted not only in the elimination or reduction of many social programs. These cuts also seriously set back the then-growing field of evaluation (Shadish et al., 1991, p. 27). At the very least, the Reagan era budget cuts probably stemmed the inflow of young social psychologists (and others) into the previously growing field of evaluation.

We believe a second factor also contributed to a weakened relationship between evaluation and social psychology: the so-called cognitive revolution in social psychology (e.g., Fiske & Taylor, 1984). The social cognition movement had several features that increased the distance between social psychology and evaluation. Specifically, the social cognitive movement served to decrease the status and frequency of applied research in mainstream social psychology; focus social psychologists on "cold" cognitive processes, which in general may be less relevant to social issues and social programs than are "warmer" motivational and affective processes; increase use of methods from cognitive psychology, such as response time and recall measures, which are not as applicable to evaluation as is the measurement of attitudes and behaviors; and lead to corresponding changes in graduate training in ways that meant newly trained social psychologists had skills that were less appropriate for work in evaluation (skills in measuring response time not being too relevant for evaluation, for instance). The budget cuts under Reagan can probably be credited for disrupting the early relationship between social psychology and evaluation. However, the social cognitive revolution may have helped preclude a speedy resumption of the relationship from occurring later on, when funding for social programs and evaluation picked up again.

The split between social psychology and evaluation was of sufficient magnitude that some people left the field in which they had been trained. For example, in his chapter with Manuel Riemer (Chapter 4), Leonard Bickman describes his separation from social psychology during many years of doing evaluation. Others drifted from mainstream social psychology, doing applied research and evaluation in a content area such as health or criminal justice. Today seems ripe for a strengthening of the relationship. As an example, despite his having left social psychology earlier, Bickman and his co-author Riemer detail their use of social psychological theory and research findings in constructing an intervention. In Chapter 13, Johnson, Smoak, and Boynton describe the benefits of a stronger integration of the applied research and evaluation in health psychology with the theory building and testing of more basic social psychology. Before examining the promise of the future, however, let's consider the present a bit more.

The Present

In principle, the relationship between social psychology and evaluation can be bidirectional. Each side can profit from the other, perhaps equally. However, our strong sense is that today evaluation draws substantially more from social psychology than it gives back. Most notably, social psychology provides a set of theories and concepts that translate into theories of the program, policy, or practice being evaluated. Other kinds of exchanges, in either direction, are not as frequent.

Consider the "program theory" connection. Since the early heyday of evaluation in the United States, most evaluators have become far more attentive to program theory, that is, to the assumptions that underlie the program, policy, or practice being evaluated. In contrast, the Great Society days provided many examples of what are now called "black box" evaluations. That is, the program was treated as a black box into which the evaluator did not peek. A Campbell-styled evaluation would tell you, for example, *whether* Head Start resulted in increased test scores, but not *why*. Nor would a black box evaluation even tell you what the Head Start program actually consisted of, in terms of the specific activities that children experienced. As a result, when a program did not work, the evaluation gave no information as to why it was ineffective. Was some aspect of the underlying rationale simply wrong? Was the underlying rationale sound, but implementation poor? Black box evaluations didn't give guidance as to what to try next when the program didn't work. When programs did work, there was no learning about underlying processes that might guide action in other settings. Indeed, without understanding more about what the program actually consisted of and how it worked, it was dubious to generalize evaluation findings to other settings.

Over time, evaluators have learned to give considerable attention to the (usually implicit) model specifying why the program is expected to make a difference. There are several, somewhat overlapping ways that evaluators have tried to capture the rationale that underlies a program, policy, or practice. These are sometimes combined under the broad umbrella of "theories of change."

One approach is to build a "logic model." In practice, logic models consist of listings of inputs (the resources that go into a program), activities (the things a program does, such as offer certain services), outputs (how many people receive which services), and short-term, intermediate, and long-term outcomes. A well-constructed logic model represents a string of if-then relationships that, if they prove to be true, will result in program success. Consider a simplified (and theoretically not very compelling example). If the resources are available, then the program activities will occur. If services are offered, many people will receive them. If people receive the services, then their attitudes will change (a short-term outcome). If attitudes change, then the targeted behavior will change (an intermediate outcome). And if their behavior changes, then their health will improve (a long-term outcome). Although this kind of if-then logic should underlie a logic model, in practice these models are typically presented as lists of resources, activities, and so on, with little if any attention to the expected causal linkages

As the term is generally used, a "program theory" lays out the expected causal connections between program activities, intermediate outcomes, and long-term outcomes. Program theories are typically presented graphically, with arrows showing the expected causal pathways from certain activities to specific intermediate to long-term outcomes. This volume shows many examples of program theories, including Figures 2.2, 3.1, and 4.3.

Evaluators often begin their work by helping to uncover or make explicit the program theory. Often this involves working with program staff and other interested parties (stakeholders), as well as reviewing program documents and observing program operations. Increasingly, evaluators are taking a more active role, playing a part in the initial development and the reformulation of explicit program theories (Coryn, Noakes, Westine, & Schröter, in press; Donaldson, 2007; Patton, 2008; Renger & Titcomb, 2002). Whether the evaluator's role is to uncover the program theories implicit in stakeholders' minds or to contribute more actively to program theory, concepts from social psychology and related disciplines play a large role in many program theories. This should be not surprising, for theories of the kind associated with Al Bandura and Icek Ajzen were designed as general theories of behavior change. The use of these theories for program design and evaluation is described and illustrated in the next two chapters, by Bandura and Ajzen, respectively. The use of social psychological theory to inform program theory is discussed in many other chapters in this book, including all of the chapters in Part II and several in Part IV.

This particular connection, with social psychological theories informing program theory, is a major contribution of social psychology to evaluation. This is not to say that social psychology is the only field whose theories can inform program theory—but it is one major source. To trained social psychologists, this contribution of their theories to the applied work of evaluation may seem rather natural and unsurprising. On the other hand, to those unfamiliar with social psychology, the way that social psychological theory can inform program design and program theory is fairly impressive. In our experience, in many program and policy areas, social psychology will largely be foreign territory to program designers, program staff, and most stakeholders—who will have an everyday understanding of many concepts of the field, such as attitudes and norms, but often will not have formal training in the relevant theory and research. In such circumstances, having an evaluator who is well versed with social psychological theory and research can lead to program theories that are better grounded in the research base of social psychology.

In short, the behavior change theories from social psychology can have considerable benefit for program design and for theory-driven program evaluation. We hasten to add, however, that social psychological theory is probably not sufficient in and of itself. Indeed, several of this book's early chapters both describe the value of social psychological theory and point to the need for other kinds of theories or models for guidance. The need commonly exists, for example, for guidance that can aid in the translation of abstract social psychological concepts into concrete program activities. Bandura illustrates this need nicely in his discussion of how to translate the general concepts from his theory into specific scenes for the characters in a radio or TV serial. Need also often exists for guidance about such things as how to integrate a new program or practice into the ongoing routines of an organization, how to ensure high-quality implementation, and how to facilitate sustainability or maintenance of the program over time. Reimer and Bickman illustrate several of these considerations. In short, then, social psychology is likely to provide a good general map as to how a program is supposed to change behavior and other outcomes, while other kinds of theories and knowledge might be useful for such matters as making the program appropriate to the context in which it is being implemented and making it sustainable.

In summary, social psychological theory can play an important role in the major evaluation tasks for articulating and testing sound program theory. Notably, there are other important ways that social psychology can enhance evaluation. Practicing evaluators face a range of challenges, and social psychology potentially can contribute solutions to many of these. For instance, a classic concern in evaluation involves "evaluation use" (e.g., whether evaluation findings are used by policy makers in their decisions or affect stakeholders' understandings of the problem or its potential solutions). The large social psychological literature on attitude change and persuasion is quite relevant to the topic of evaluation use, as discussed by Fleming in Chapter 8. As that chapter suggests, applying the literature on persuasion to evaluation holds potential both for understanding and for increasing use (see also Mark & Henry, 2004).

To take another example, social psychological literatures such as those on negotiation and accountability can offer considerable insight into stakeholder processes and dialogue in evaluation. See Campbell and McGrath in Chapter 13 for more discussion of these topics. Similarly, Donaldson, Gooler, and Scriven (2002), Taut and Brauns (2003), and Stevahn and King (2009) have drawn on the social psychological literature on evaluation apprehension and test anxiety to illuminate the anxiety that stakeholders often have about evaluation and to discuss ways to alleviate this anxiety. Tindale and Posavac in Chapter 7 offer a related discussion about increasing trust among those involved with evaluation, drawing on the literature in interpersonal relations. Sanna, Panter, Cohen, and Kennedy (Chapter 6) draw on the social psychological literature on judgment biases, specifically time-related or temporal biases, to address several potential challenges in program design and evaluation. As another example, Schwarz and Oyserman (2001; see also Chapter 9, this volume) describe the implications for evaluation of research on the cognitive and social psychological processes that are involved in answering survey and self-report questions. Our view is that, although several articles and chapters have mined the social psychological literature for its insights for practical challenges in evaluation, much more could be done. Part III of this book includes several efforts to extend social psychology's contributions to specific challenges of evaluation practice.

Contributions can and should also take place in the other direction. That is, evaluations from many areas of practice should have implications for social psychological research and theory. In some instances, such as evaluations of a variety of health-related interventions, relevant findings have made their way back into social psychology and related literatures. Indeed, in some areas of public health and health psychology, little if any distinction is made between evaluation and other forms of research. For the most part, however, lessons from evaluation have not been consolidated and fed back into social psychology. Each chapter in Part IV focuses on a particular area of practice in which evaluation findings have, or could, feed back into social psychology. For example, Johnson, Johnson, and Stevahn (Chapter 11) detail how evaluations of cooperative learning programs and other educational interventions have had important implications for the social psychological literature on cooperation and competition. Cialdini, Goldstein, and Griskevicius (Chapter 10) discuss what social psychologists can learn from evaluations of environmental interventions. Johnson, Dove, and Boynton (Chapter 12) contend that evaluation and other applied research can profitably be tied back more strongly to mainstream social psychology.

Lessons from evaluation need not come solely from evaluation findings. Sometimes the lessons can be conceptual, taking place even before evaluation findings are in. For instance, attempts to apply social psychology to evaluation can demonstrate gaps in social psychological theory and research. In one example, Campbell and Mark (2006) applied the concept of accountability to interactions between evaluation stakeholders with different interests. Application to this aspect of evaluation revealed a gap in the accountability literature. Specifically, the accountability literature in social psychology had focused on whether or not a person perceived he or she was accountable to others. In considering the evaluation process, Campbell and Mark saw that the practical issue instead often was *to whom* a stakeholder participating in evaluation processes felt he or she was accountable. As this example shows, social psychology can benefit from considering evaluation other than by actual evaluation findings. That is, Campbell and Mark conducted an experiment apart from any program evaluation, to test the effect of different forms of accountability on the quality of stakeholder interactions. We believe that increased involvement in research on evaluation may benefit social psychology as much as or more than evaluation findings per se.

In summary, the current relationship between social psychology and evaluation can be characterized as follows. First, social psychological research and theory is often drawn on when evaluators attempt to discover or build a program theory. This is a noteworthy contribution. Second, social psychology is occasionally used as a source of potential answers to the challenges evaluators face in practice, such as how to deal with the anxiety that the stakeholders in an evaluation may feel. We believe that social psychology could be applied far more extensively to the varied practice challenges of evaluation. Third, in principle social psychology should be able to benefit from evaluation, but this direction of contribution has largely been limited to a few areas such as cooperation and competition. In some instances, evaluation findings themselves should be of interest, while in other cases social psychology might be integrated with research on evaluation.

Alternative Futures for the Social Psychology–Evaluation Intersection

Going beyond the past and the present, we want to briefly explore alternative possible futures for the relationship between social psychology and evaluation. Of course, one possibility is that the connection between social psychology and evaluation will dissipate in the future. Perhaps it is wishful thinking, but we judge this to be the least likely future direction. The value of social psychological theories to program theory seems strong and likely at least to persist. A variant on this scenario could take place, though. That is, the presence of people in evaluation who were trained in social psychology could decline by attrition, even as others draw on social psychological theories as a source of sound program theory.

In another, quite feasible future, the relationship between social psychology and evaluation will remain much as it is. That is, social psychology will continue to contribute substantially to the development of program theory. Occasionally evaluators will draw on specific aspects of the social psychological literature as a guide to a particular challenge in evaluation practice (e.g., reducing anxiety about being evaluated). In a few select areas, findings from evaluation may feed back into the social psychological literature, identifying gaps or enhancing the validity of findings by examining a social psychological question in a real-world setting. There may even be occasional emigrants, individuals trained as social psychologists who move to a career in evaluation. But in this possible future, most of the fertile ground at the intersection of these two fields, as at present, will go unexplored.

In yet another alternative future, the relationship between these two fields will be enhanced. This would have several potentially important benefits, several of which we have alluded to already.

- Theory-driven evaluation would benefit from the continued and increased importation of theory and findings from social psychology for the purpose of developing sound program theory.

- In return, social psychology's theory and evidence base would be strengthened by (a) assessing its fit and its modification when translated into program theory and (b) the findings from real-world evaluations that test aspects of social psychological theory.

- Evaluation practice would be strengthened by the importation of social psychological research and theory that is applicable to a wide array of challenges that arise in the conduct of evaluation. Examples include challenges in guiding interactions among stakeholders who vary in power, developing and maintaining trust, and measuring behaviors that take place repeatedly over time, to name but a few. Social psychology should be able to help address such practice-based challenges, as illustrated in several of the chapters that follow.

- Social psychologists interested in evaluation could help meet the need for more systematic study of evaluation (Mark, 2008). For instance, social psychologists might be well positioned to study evaluation influence and use (Mark & Henry, 2004), leading to a better knowledge base to guide evaluators' actions. As another example, rather than simply import lessons from social psychology about how to engender trust, an experiment could be conducted to study the presumed lesson in an evaluation context.

- This future would allow tests of selected social psychological hypotheses in the real-world settings of evaluations. For example, most of the past research on empathy and power has been conducted in artificial laboratory settings. Dialogue between members of different stakeholder groups offers a more realistic setting for such research, and is important in its own right. The often artificial settings and restricted participant populations of social psychology studies are a cause for criticism (Cook & Groom, 2004). The criticism involves both construct validity (i.e., concern about whether the lab experiment is studying the real phenomenon, such as cooperation) and external validity (i.e., concern about whether the findings can be generalized elsewhere). These criticisms would largely be muted for social psychological research coming from evaluation contexts.

- Both fields would be strengthened by the opportunities for joint training.

- Recently trained social psychologists, especially those with a good grounding in evaluation, can help meet what appears to be an expanding market for evaluation (American Psychological Association, 2005).

- Theory generation in social psychology would be improved. In the Campbell and Mark (2006) example, it became apparent to these researchers that the social psychological literature had generally treated accountability as an either/or, with the person either being accountable or not. In contrast, within stakeholder situations in evaluation, the issue instead often seemed to be *to whom* the stakeholder felt accountable. As this example suggests, the real-life crucible of evaluation practice should help in the development of better, more comprehensive theories.

Fortunately, we believe that conditions may be conducive to a resurgence of interest in evaluation among social psychologists. Relative to the early days of the social cognitive revolution, there has been a return to the historically strong interest in applied work within social psychology, which would seem to bode well for involvement with evaluation. In addition, the continued growth of theory-driven evaluation has reduced the distance between social psychology and evaluation. As we noted previously, much program theory is social psychological in nature. Moreover, the theory-driven approach to evaluation blurs the distinction between basic and applied research because basic theory is tested in the context of the applied work of evaluation. This should increase the overlap between social psychology and at least those evaluations that involve tests of program theory based in social psychology. Perhaps less powerful than the program theory connection but still potentially important is the continuing need for guidance regarding the challenges that arise in the practice of evaluation—and many of these are fundamentally social psychological in nature. For example, challenges involving power, stereotyping, and negotiation arise when evaluators work with representatives from multiple stakeholder groups to plan an evaluation. Testing hypotheses from social psychology in the context of these practice challenges should not only provide better guidance to evaluators, but also help quell criticisms about the artificiality and questionable validity of much social psychological research. Finally, the pragmatics of employment trends—with limited job opportunities in traditional academic areas of basic social psychology, but a strong market in evaluation and applied social psychology (Donaldson & Berger, 2006; Donaldson & Christie, 2006)—should make the strengthened connection between social psychology and evaluation more appealing to many, including graduate students in social psychology.

We return in the final chapter to some ideas about strengthening the future relationship between social psychology and the evaluation of programs, policies, and practices. For the moment, suffice it to say that the future of this relationship may in fact depend on some of the readers of this book.

APPENDIX 1.1.
Overview of Selected Methods and Concepts

This appendix is provided to serve as an introduction to and review of several concepts and terms that are used elsewhere in this volume. Our focus here is on research methods. Numerous other concepts and terms are described in the chapters and in the introductions to the chapters.

We begin with a question. How does one evaluate the merit and worth of a program? Scriven (1991) has offered a kind of general logic for evaluation. In short, it involves (1) identifying criteria of merit, (2) defining standards of performance on those criteria, (3) measuring performance, and (4) synthesizing across the multiple criteria to generate a bottom-line judgment. This logic applies widely. For example, in evaluating midsize cars, one would initially identify criteria of merit, such as gas mileage, safety in a head-on collision, legroom, and so on. You would then determine standards for each of the criteria (e.g., you might rate gas mileage relative to other midsize cars, but for safety, you might set a minimum performance for a crash test). You would measure performance on the various criteria, such as road tests to calculate gas mileage and crash tests to assess safety. And you could then combine across criteria, leading you to recommend some cars over others.

In the case of programs, one of Campbell's insights is that the things people care about, the criteria of merit, typically involve the program's effects on certain valued outcomes. In evaluating Head Start or other preschool programs, people care about such things as whether the program causes improvements in children's readiness for school, their social skills, and so on. In evaluating HIV/AIDS prevention program, people care about whether the program causes a reduction in unsafe sex practices and in the number of new HIV/AIDS cases. In short, the criteria of merit that people generally care about for programs, policies, and practices are their outcomes, the effects they have. Further, although the topic is worthy of more discussion than we will give it here, the performance standards of interest are usually relative. For example, how much better is the school readiness of children who have participated in Head Start than those who did not? How effective is one preschool program relative to others?

Ah, then, how can performance be measured? Imagine that you were going to evaluate Head Start decades ago, when there were few preschool programs and nearly all other children had home-based care, commonly with their mothers. Imagine too that you had a set of measures, such as knowledge of the alphabet, ability to count, and so on. Perhaps you might consider measuring children's performance before and after they participated in Head Start. Of course, this would be problematic. The children would be older after a year of Head Start, and simply because they were older they would probably do better even if Head Start was completely ineffective. (Campbell labeled this sort of problem as the "validity threat" of **maturation**.) You might think instead, let me find a group of kids the same age as my Head Start graduates and measure them at the same point in time. If Head Start was effective, you might think, the Head Start graduates should outperform the comparison group that did not participate in the program. Again, there's a problem. The kind of kids that ended up in Head Start may differ from those who did not. If so, these preexisting differences, not Head Start, might be responsible for any group differences on the measures (Campbell used the term **selection** to refer to problems like this). In fact, Head Start was restricted to children from families with low incomes, so the comparison group is likely to differ on income and other indicators of socioeconomic status. Hmm, you might say, let me try **matching**, that is to say, to find for each Head Start participant a child who did not attend Head Start but whose family has a similar income. The problem is that there may still be other differences that your matching didn't take care of. For example, for two families with similar incomes, perhaps the family with the Head Start participant is more interested in education or has better connections in the community.

Problems such as maturation and selection are known as threats to **internal validity**. In a program evaluation context, internal validity refers to the accuracy of inferences about the effect of the program on the outcome variables of interest. If you simply measured kids before and after Head Start, your evaluation would have serious internal validity problems. Concerns about internal validity threats, and the inadequacy of simple approaches such as matching, is why evaluators such as Campbell and his followers (Campbell Collaboration, 2009) advocate the use of **randomized experiments**. In a randomized experiment, individuals (or other units) are assigned at random, essentially by the flip of a coin or some other random process, to groups. For example, you might use a computer program that generates random numbers to assign children either to Head Start or to a comparison group. Because the groups that result are equivalent (within certain statistical limits), randomized experiments provide a fair test of the performance of a program—though other problems can arise. In evaluation, randomized experiments are often referred to as **randomized controlled trials**, or **RCTs**.

Randomized experiments are not always feasible. It may be impractical or unethical to assign children at random to a program, for example. In such circumstances, a **quasi-experiment**—Campbell's term for an approximation of an experiment—may be the best alternative. There exists a wide range of quasi-experiments, some close to the randomized experiment in terms of internal validity, others far weaker. We will not cover the entire array here. Rather, we note that there has been a trend toward integrating quasi-experimental design with increasingly sophisticated statistical analysis. One development along these lines, referred to in several chapters of this volume, is the use of **propensity scores**. In essence, propensity scores are a form of matching on steroids. Multiple matching variables are combined statistically into a single index. (More technically, this index is created by conducting a logistic regression using the variables to predict membership in the program rather than the comparison group. The index thus captures the propensity to be in the program group, and it is used to match similar treatment and comparison group members).

As noted previously, internal validity refers to the accuracy of inferences about the effect of the program on outcome variables of interest. As Campbell and his colleagues pointed out, internal validity is not the only kind of validity one worries about in experiments and other studies that are used to estimate the effects of an intervention. **External validity** refers to the accuracy of inferences about other persons, places, and settings than those observed in the evaluation. Put differently, external validity involves the generalizability of the evaluation findings, including generalizability to the future. **Construct validity** refers to the accuracy of the abstract labels that are used to identify the treatment and outcomes. For example, there is a construct validity problem if you refer to "Head Start" as the causal variable, when the real reason that participants in the program condition outperformed the comparison group is that they received two nutritious meals a day while at Head Start. In this instance, perhaps the treatment should instead be labeled as "nutritional supplementation."

Experiments do not in and of themselves solve external and construct validity problems. To the contrary, in some instances conducting an RCT may create external validity problems. For example, perhaps only very unusual kinds of families will consent to having their children randomly assigned to conditions in an evaluation. If so, there would be a tradeoff between internal and external validity. Skillful evaluation practice involves efforts to choose the best methods in the face of tradeoffs. Often the best approach, if resources allow, is to use different methods over time.

Increasingly, both experimental and quasi-experimental evaluations include procedures that can help strengthen external and construct validity in a single evaluation study. Tests of **moderation** assess whether a program is equally effective for different types of clients or across different circumstances. For example, you might test to see whether Head Start works better for boys or girls, or whether it is equally beneficial in urban, suburban, and rural settings. (For those trained in an analysis of variance framework, tests of moderation involve a statistical interaction.) With tests of **mediation**, one traces the steps in a program theory to see whether, for example, change in the hypothesized short-term outcomes appear to be responsible for change in the longer-term outcomes. For instance, in an evaluation of Head Start, program theory might suggest that initial improvement in both prereading skills and attention span will mediate longer-term academic performance. Various kinds of statistical procedures, such as structural equation modeling, can be used to estimate meditational models. Tests of moderation can contribute to external validity by showing the conditions under which the program is effective. Tests of mediation can enhance construct validity by clarifying what the processes are by which the program has its effects.

Even so, to the extent possible it is desirable not to rely on a single evaluation when making high-stakes decisions. **Meta-analysis** is a way of putting together the findings from multiple evaluations. Meta-analytic procedures allow you, for example, to combine statistically the estimated effects of Head Start from dozens of Head Start evaluations. Meta-analysis can also allow you to test for moderation, for example, by comparing the effects of Head Start from evaluations in urban areas, relative to the effects in rural areas, thus strengthening external validity.

Meta-analysis requires the computation of an **effect size estimate** for each of the individual studies that is included. Head Start evaluations might use slightly different measures of reading readiness, for example, and these would have to be put into a common metric to be combined and compared. A common and relatively simple effect size estimate is computed by subtracting the average comparison group score from the average treatment group score (e.g., how much better does the Head Start group do on reading readiness?); this figure is then divided by the pooled standard deviation (a measure of how spread out scores are within the treatment and within the comparison group). Meta-analyses typically give an average effect size combining across the multiple studies. There are general guidelines for whether an effect size is large or small, but it is generally advisable to make a judgment of size in the context of the specific program area.

There are many methods other than those reviewed in this brief Appendix. This includes a wide range of quasi-experimental designs, a similarly wide range of qualitative methods, descriptive methods such as sample surveys, and mixed method designs that integrate qualitative and quantitative methods. All of these methods have a proper role in evaluation, depending on the purpose of an evaluation, the stage and other characteristics of the program to be evaluated, the resources available and the time and other pragmatic constraints, and how much is already known. This Appendix has focused primarily on the methods that are presented, sometimes without much explanation, in other chapters in this volume. We hope the Appendix will help readers who needed general background to these methods.

NOTES

1. Portions of this and some subsequent sections in this chapter draw on Mark, Gamble, and Mills (2005).

2. In light of Lewin's seminal contributions, it is interesting to note that both Campbell and Rossi did work early in their careers on topics that echoed those of Lewin's earlier studies. Like Lewin, Rossi early on did research for the armed forces on changing food attitudes (Armed Forces Food and Container Institute, 1958). Leadership was another area in which Lewin did what we would consider to be evaluation, particularly in the evaluation of different types of leadership practices (Lewin, Lippitt, & White, 1939). Campbell also did research on leadership, specifically leadership in the Navy (described in Campbell, 1984). And the dots connect: Campbell apparently generated some of his ideas about quasi-experimentation while thinking about the effects of a given leader. The rotation of officers in and out of particular military units in theory offered a way to try to estimate a leader's effects on unit performance.

REFERENCES

American Psychological Association. (2005). *Non-academic careers for scientific psychologists: Interesting careers in psychology.* Retrieved October 15, 2010, from *www.apa.org/science/nonacad_careers.html.*

Armed Forces Food and Container Institute. (1958). *Study of the bases for changing food attitudes* (Official investigator, Peter H. Rossi). Chicago: Quartermaster Food and Container Institute for the Armed Forces, Research and Engineering Command, Quartermaster Corps, U.S. Army.

Campbell, B., & Mark, M. M. (2006). Toward more effective stakeholder dialogue: Applying theories of negotiation to policy and program evaluation. *Journal of Applied Social Psychology, 2834–2863.*

Campbell Collaboration. (2009). Available at *www.campbellcollaboration.org.*

Campbell D. T. (1950). The indirect assessment of social attitudes. *Psychological Bulletin, 47,* 15–38.

Campbell, D. T. (1965). Ethnocentrism and other altruistic motives. In D. Levine (Ed.), *Nebraska Symposium on Motivation* (pp. 283–311). Lincoln: University of Nebraska Press.

Campbell, D. T. (1967). Stereotypes and the perception of group differences. *American Psychologist, 22,* 817–829.

Campbell, D. T. (1969). Ethnocentrism of disciplines and the fishscale model of omniscience. In M. Sherif (Ed.), *Problems of interdisciplinary relationships in the social sciences* (pp. 328–348). Chicago: Aldine.

Campbell, D. T. (1984). Can we be scientific in applied social science? *Evaluation Studies Review Annual,* 26–48.

Campbell, D. T. (1988). Perspectives on a scholarly career. In D. T. Campbell & E. S. Overman (Eds.), *Methodology and epistemology for social science: Selected papers* (pp. 1–26). Chicago: University of Chicago Press.

Campbell, D. T., & Stanley, J. C. (1966). *Experimental and quasi-experimental designs for research.* Chicago: Rand McNally.

Chen, H. T. (1990). *Theory-driven evaluations.* Newbury Park, CA: Sage.

Cook, T. D., & Groom, C. (2004). The methodological assumptions of social psychology: The mutual dependence of substantive theory and method choice. In C. Sansone, C. C. Morf, & A. T. Panter (Eds.), *The Sage handbook of methods in social psychology* (pp. 19–44). Thousand Oaks, CA: Sage.

Corey, S. (1953). *Action research to improve school practice.* New York: Teachers College.

Coryn, C., Noakes, L. A., Westine, C. D., & Schröter, D. C. (in press). A systematic review of theory-driven evaluation practice from 1990 to 2009. *American Journal of Evaluation.*

Cousins, J. B., & Whitmore, E. (1998). Framing participatory evaluation. In E. Whitmore (Ed.), *New directions for evaluation: No. 80. Understanding and practicing participatory evaluation* (pp. 5–23). San Francisco: Jossey-Bass.

Darley, J. M., & Latané, B. (1968). Bystander intervention in emergencies: Diffusion of responsibility. *Journal of Personality and Social Psychology, 8,* 377–383.

Donaldson, S. I. (2007). *Program theory-driven evaluation science: Strategies and applications.* Mahwah, NJ: Erlbaum.

Donaldson, S. I., & Berger, D. E. (2006). *The rise and promise of applied psychology in the 21st century.* In S. I. Donaldson, D. E. Berger, & K. Pezdek (Eds.), *Applied psychology: New frontiers and rewarding careers* (pp. 3–23). Mahwah, NJ: Erlbaum.

Donaldson, S. I., & Christie, C. A. (2006). *Emerging career opportunities in the transdiscipline of evaluation science* (pp. 243–259). In S. I. Donaldson, D. E. Berger, & K. Pezdek (Eds.), *Applied psychology: New frontiers and rewarding careers.* Mahwah, NJ: Erlbaum.

Donaldson, S. I., Gooler, L. E., & Scriven, M. (2002). Strategies for managing evaluation anxiety: Toward a psychology of program evaluation. *American Journal of Evaluation, 23,* 261–273.

Dovidio, J. F., Glick, P. G., & Rudman, L. (Eds.). (2005). *On the nature of prejudice: Fifty years after Allport.* Malden, MA: Blackwell.

Fetterman, D. (1998). Empowerment evaluation: Collaboration, action research, and a case example. Available at *www.aepro.org.*

Fiske, S. T., & Taylor, S. E. (1984). *Social cognition.* New York: Random House.

Jacobs, R. C., & Campbell, D. T. (1961). The perpetuation of an arbitrary tradition through several generations of a laboratory microculture. *Journal of Abnormal and Social Psychology, 62,* 649–658.

Lewin, K. (1946). Action research and minority problems. *Journal of Social Issues, 2,* 34–46.

Lewin, K. (1947). Frontiers in group dynamics: II. Channels of group life; social planning and action research. *Human Relations, 1,* 143–153.

Lewin, K. (1948). Group decision and social change. In T. M. Newcomb & E. L. Hartley (Eds.), *Readings in social psychology* (pp. 330–341). New York: Henry Holt. [Reprinted in M. Gold (Ed.), *The complete social scientist: A Kurt Lewin reader* (pp. 265–284). Washington, DC: American Psychological Association, 1999.

Lewin, K. (1951). *Field theory in social science: Selected theoretical papers* (D. Cartwright, Ed.). New York: Harper & Row.

Lewin, K., Lippitt, R., & White, R. K. (1939). Patterns of aggressive behavior in experimentally created "social climates." *Journal of Social Psychology, 10,* 271–299.

Mark, M. M. (2008). Building a better evidence-base for evaluation theory. In P. R. Brandon & N. L. Smith (Eds.), *Fundamental issues in evaluation* (pp. 111–134). New York: Guilford Press.

Mark, M. M., Gamble, C., & Mills, J. (2005). *Social psychology and evaluation: The past, the present, and alternative possible futures.* Paper presented at the joint meeting of the American Evaluation Association and the Canadian Evaluation Society, Toronto.

Mark, M. M., & Henry, G. T. (2004). The mechanisms and outcomes of evaluation influence. *Evaluation, 10,* 35–57.

Milgram, S. (1974). *Obedience to authority: An experimental view.* New York: HarperCollins.

Miller, N., Campbell, D. T., Twedt, H., & O'Connell, E. J. (1966). Similarity, contrast and complementarity in friendship choice. *Journal of Personality and Social Psychology, 3,* 3–12.

Miller, R., King, J., Mark, M., & Stockdill, S. (2003). The oral history of evaluation, Part I. Reflections on the chance to work with great people: An interview with William Shadish. *American Journal of Evaluation, 24*, 261–272.

Patton, M. Q. (2008). *Utilization-focused evaluation* (4th ed.). Beverly Hills, CA: Sage.

Pawson, R., & Tilley, N. (1997). *Realistic evaluation.* London: Sage.

Renger, R., & Titcomb, A. (2002). A three-step approach to teaching logic models. *American Journal of Evaluation, 23*(4), 493–503.

Rog, D. (2009, November). *Toward context-sensitive evaluation practice.* Presidential Address presented at the American Evaluation Association, Orlando, Florida.

Rogers, P., & Williams, R. (2006). Evaluation for practice improvement and organizational learning. In I. Shaw, J. Greene, & M. M. Mark (Eds.), *Handbook of evaluation* (pp. 76–97). London: Sage.

Rossi, P. H. (1989). *Down and out in America: The origins of homelessness.* Chicago: University of Chicago Press.

Rossi, P. H. (1998). *Feeding the poor: Assessing federal food aid.* Washington, DC: AEI Press.

Rossi, P. H., & Berk, R. A. (1997). *Just punishments: Federal guidelines and public views compared.* New York: De Gruyter.

Rossi, P. H., Berk, R. A., & Lenihan, K. J. (1980). *Money, work, and crime: Experimental evidence.* New York: Academic Press.

Rossi, P. H., Lipsey, M. W., & Freeman, H. E. (2004). *Evaluation: A systematic approach* (7th ed.). Newbury Park, PA: Sage.

Rothman, J. (1997). Action evaluation and conflict resolution: In theory and practice. *Mediation Quarterly, 15*, 119–131.

Schwarz, N., & Oyserman, D. (2001). Asking questions about behavior: Cognition, communication, and questionnaire construction. *American Journal of Evaluation, 22*, 127–160.

Scriven, M. (1967). The methodology of evaluation. In R. W. Tyler, R. M. Gagne, & M. Scriven (Eds.), *Perspectives on curriculum evaluation* (pp. 39–83). Chicago: Rand McNally.

Scriven, M. (1991). *Evaluation thesaurus* (4th ed.). Thousand Oaks, CA: Sage.

Shadish, W. R., Cook, T. D., & Leviton, L. C. (1991). *Foundations of program evaluation: Theories of practice.* Newbury Park, CA: Sage.

Stevahn, L., & King, J. (2009). *Needs assessment phase 3: Taking action for change.* Newbury Park, CA: Sage.

Suchman, E. A. (1967). *Evaluative research: Principles and practice in public service and social action programs.* New York: Sage.

Taut, S., & Brauns, D. (2003). Resistance to evaluation: A psychological perspective. *Evaluation, 9*, 247–264.

Wright, J. D., & Rossi, P. H. (1994). *Armed and considered dangerous: A survey of felons and their firearms.* New York: de Gruyter.

EDITORS' CONCLUDING COMMENTS
TO CHAPTER 1

In the rest of this book, the editors provide comments before and after each chapter. In general, the introductory comments will highlight key points of the upcoming chapter. In some cases, the introduction will also explain new terms or concepts that are used but not explained by chapter authors. The postchapter comments, for the most part, pose questions the editors would like readers to consider, or they reflect on selected themes of the chapter, or both.

PART II

Social Psychological Theories as Global Guides to Program Design and Program Evaluation

EDITORS' INTRODUCTORY COMMENTS TO CHAPTER 2

In the upcoming chapter, Albert Bandura summarizes his approach to social cognitive theory. More central to this book, he also illustrates its application to the design and evaluation of programs. Bandura's work has been widely influential in psychology. Among the features of Bandura's theory is the idea that people's behavior is regulated by such processes as (1) their setting of goals, (2) the motivation they feel associated with goal achievement, (3) their evaluation of their own efforts toward the goals, (4) the resulting satisfaction or dissatisfaction, and (5) their perception of the social rewards associated with goal achievement. Bandura concisely explains these and other aspects of his social cognitive theory. He also illustrates his theory and its application in the context of several interventions that were designed to improve individual health-related behaviors, as well as a few larger "macrosocial" applications targeted at multiple behaviors and wide audiences.

In recent years, program evaluators have increasingly been concerned about the theory of change that underlies—or at least, *should* underlie—the programs they are evaluating. As noted in Chapter 1, this attention to program theory arose partly because, if a program is built on a sound theory about how it is supposed to achieve its goals, then the program should be more likely to be effective. And a theory such as Bandura's, having been well tested and successful in multiple areas of behavior change, offers considerable promise as the foundation for effective programs. The idea of program theory in evaluation has also become popular because, with a well-articulated theory of how the program should work, one can design a better evaluation of the program. For example, imagine a program that is intended to change health-related behavior in part because it increases participants' self-perception that they are capable of the behaviors required to manage a chronic disease. In such a case, the evaluation might fruitfully measure this kind of self-perception, called self-efficacy. Knowing whether this and other steps along the program theory change as expected is useful, either in understanding why the program is effective or in figuring out what to do if it is not.

In addition to his social cognitive theory, Bandura points to the importance of having a "translational model." Social cognitive theory, like other theories from social psychology, offers guidance into the kinds of factors involved in behavior change. It is a general theory, applicable to a variety of circumstances. A translational model complements such a general theory of behavior change. A translational model, as the term suggests, can help guide the translation from a general theory to the details of a specific intervention, implemented in nuts and bolts terms, and intended to affect people and their behaviors of interest, in a particular culture, with specific norms.

CHAPTER 2

The Social and Policy Impact of Social Cognitive Theory

Albert Bandura

When I entered the field of psychology, behaviorism was the reigning theory. It located the causes and regulators of human behavior in the workings of environmental forces. According to behaviorism, conditioning (through paired association) invests environmental stimuli with positive and negative valences. Response consequences, whether rewarding or punishing, shape and control behavior. These conditioning effects were said to occur automatically and below the level of awareness.

Some subspecialties of psychology, principally clinical and to some extent developmental and social psychology, embraced psychoanalytic theory, which had become well entrenched not only professionally but culturally as well. Contrary to behaviorism, psychodynamic theories placed the causes of behavior in psychic forces working within the individual. These inner forces took the form of impulses and complexes operating mainly unconsciously. To circumvent defense mechanisms, researchers and clinicians used surreptitious projective tests to reveal the hidden motivators. People were asked to tell what they saw in inkblots, make up stories to ambiguous pictures, free associate to words, or respond to other types of ambiguous stimuli.

The behavioristic line of theorizing was eventually outmodel by the advent of the cognitive revolution, which documented the centrality of cognitive processes in human functioning. Psychodynamic theorizing also fell out of favor, with growing evidence that it neither had predictive value nor fared any better in therapeutic utility. In many clinical practices, pills supplanted psychosocial changes for the problems of everyday life.

I started my work on social cognitive theory in the early 1960s, when the field of psychology was beginning to undergo transformative changes regarding the determinants of human behavior and the mechanisms governing personal and social change (Bandura & Walters, 1963). Within this theoretical framework, human self-development, adaptation, and change are realized through triadic reciprocal causation (Bandura, 1986). In this transactional view of self and society, (1) personal factors, in the form of cognitive, affective, and biological processes, (2) the way in which one behaves, and (3) environmental events all operate as interacting determinants that influence each other bidirectionally (see Figure 2.1). Social cognitive theory is founded in an agentic perspective (Bandura, 1986, 2001a). To be an agent is to influence intentionally one's functioning and the course of environmental events. People are contributors to their life circumstances, not just products of them. This is why the exercise of personal influence is part of the determining conditions within the triadic interplay shown in Figure 2.1.

Before reviewing some of the applications of social cognitive theory to program evaluation and especially program design, I briefly present the major principles of the theory on which the applications are founded. A more detailed exposition is available elsewhere (Bandura, 1986, 2005, 2006a).

A comprehensive theory of human behavior must explain how people acquire cognitive and behavioral competencies, as well as how people motivate and regulate their behavior in managing their everyday life. Regarding the acquisition of competencies, there are two basic modes of learning. People learn (1) by experiencing the effects of their actions, and (2) through the power of social modeling. Direct experience is a tough teacher. Trial-and-error learning is not only an exceedingly tedious process, but also hazardous when mistakes can have costly or injurious consequences. Moreover, the constraints of time, resources, and mobility impose severe limits

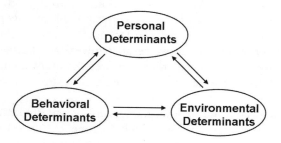

FIGURE 2.1. Schematization of triadic reciprocal determination of human functioning in social cognitive theory.

on the situations and activities that can be directly explored in service of new knowledge. Fortunately, people have evolved an advanced capacity for observational learning that enables them to shortcut the trial-and-error process. They expand their knowledge and competencies through information that is conveyed by modeled behavior and the accompanying consequences (Bandura, 1986; Rosenthal & Zimmerman, 1978).

Modeling influences can have strong motivational effects as well. When people see similar others gain desired results by their actions, they develop positive incentive motivation. In contrast, seeing others punished for certain actions creates negative expectations that serve as disincentives. Moreover, people are easily aroused by the emotional expressions of others. They learn to fear the things that frightened others, to dislike what repulsed them, and to like what gratified them. The behavior of others also serves as a social prompt that activates, channels, and supports modeled styles of behavior.

The types of models that predominate in a given social milieu determine which human qualities, from among many alternatives, are selectively promoted. During the course of their daily lives, people have direct contact with only a small sector of the physical and social environment. Consequently, their conceptions of social reality, on which they base many of their actions, are heavily influenced by vicarious experiences—what they read, see, and hear—rather than through direct experiences. Media portrayals of human nature, social relations, and the norms and structure of society thus shape the public consciousness.

Much of the observational learning is based on the models in one's immediate environment. However, with the revolutionary advances in communications technologies in contemporary society, ideas, values, belief systems, and lifestyles are socially transmitted via the extensive modeling in the symbolic environment. This enables people to transcend the confines of their lived environment. Unlike learning by doing, which requires shaping the actions of each individual through repeated consequences, in observational learning a single model can transmit new ways of thinking and behaving simultaneously to vast populations in widely dispersed locales.

It is one thing to learn new styles of behavior. It is another to motivate oneself to put them into practice and to regulate one's efforts, especially in the face of tough challenges and adversities. Another distinctive human characteristic is the capability for self-directedness through self-regulation. Most human behavior, being purposive, is regulated by thought projected into the future. People set goals for themselves, anticipate the likely consequences of prospective actions, and plan courses of action and strategies that are likely to produce desired outcomes and avoid detrimental ones. Through exercise of forethought, people motivate themselves and guide their actions anticipatorily.

Human behavior is extensively regulated by its effects. These effects include material costs and benefits, social approval or disapproval, and self-evaluative positive and negative reactions. Behavior patterns that produce positive outcomes are readily adopted and used, whereas those that bring unrewarding or punishing outcomes are generally discarded. But external consequences are not the only kind of outcomes that influence human behavior. The self-regulation of motivation, affect, and action operates partly through personal standards and evaluative reactions to one's own behavior (Bandura, 1991). Because people care about their self-regard, they respond evaluatively to their own behavior. They seek self-satisfaction by fulfilling valued goals. They intensify their efforts by experiencing discontent with substandard performances. And they respond self-disapprovingly for conduct that violates their standards. The ability to bring visualized futures and anticipated outcomes to bear on current activities promotes purposeful and foresightful behavior. When projected over a long time course on matters of value, a forethoughtful perspective provides direction, coherence, and meaning to one's life.

People are not only agents of action. They also are self-examiners of their own functioning. They reflect on their personal efficacy, on the soundness of their thoughts and actions, and on the meaning of their pursuits, and they make corrective adjustments if necessary. The metacognitive capability to reflect upon oneself and the adequacy of one's thoughts and actions is the most distinctly human characteristic.

Among the types of cognitive activities that affect human functioning, none are more central or pervasive than people's beliefs in their ability to influence events that affect their lives. Efficacy beliefs exert their diverse effects through cognitive, motivational, emotional, and decisional processes. Efficacy beliefs affect whether individuals think optimistically or pessimistically, in self-enhancing or self-debilitating ways. They play a central role in the self-regulation of motivation through goal challenges and outcome expectations. It is partly on the basis of efficacy beliefs that people choose what challenges to undertake, how much effort to expend in the endeavor, how long to persevere in the face of obstacles and failures, and whether failures are motivating or demoralizing.

Efficacy beliefs also shape people's outcome expectations—whether they expect their efforts to produce favorable outcomes or adverse ones. In addition, efficacy beliefs determine how opportunities and impediments are viewed. People of low efficacy are easily convinced of the futility of effort in the face of difficulties. They quickly give up trying. Those of high efficacy view impediments as surmountable through the development of requisite competencies and perseverant effort. Those with high efficacy stay the course in the face of difficulties and remain resilient to adversity. Moreover, efficacy beliefs affect the quality of emotional life and vulnerability to stress and depression. It is natural to feel despondent following setbacks and failures on matters of import. It is belief in one's recovery efficacy that supports the effort needed to restore one's emotional well-being.

And last, but not least, efficacy beliefs determine the choices people make at important decision points. By choosing their environments people can have a hand in what they become. Beliefs of personal efficacy can, therefore, play a key role in shaping the course that lives take by influencing the types of activities and environments people choose. In self-development through choice processes, personal destinies are shaped by the selection of environments that are known to cultivate valued potentialities and life-styles. A factor that influences choice behavior can profoundly affect the course that lives take. This is because the social influences that operate in the selected environments continue to promote certain competencies, values, and lifestyles.

Social cognitive theory distinguishes among three modes of agency: individual, proxy, and collective efficacy. In personal agency exercised individually, people bring their influence to bear on their own functioning and on environmental events. However, in many spheres of functioning, people do not have direct control over conditions that affect their lives. They exercise proxy agency by influencing others who have the resources, knowledge, and means to act on their belief to secure the outcomes they desire. People do not live their lives in individual autonomy. Many of the things they seek are achievable only by working together through interdependent effort. In the exercise of collective agency, they pool their knowledge, skills, and resources, and act in concert to shape their future.

With this brief review of social cognitive theory as background, the sections that follow present some applications of the theory. Examples are given both at the individual and macrosocial levels. One of the large-scale applications centers on the development of models for health promotion and disease prevention of wide reach and high effectiveness. The other major application is designed to reduce some of the most urgent global problems. For several of the applications, the mechanisms through which the programs produce their effects are described. These applications highlight the potential of social cognitive theory for program design and evaluation (Chen, 2005).

Health Promotion Systems Founded on Self-Regulation Principles

Recent years have witnessed divergent trends in the field of health. On the one hand, we are pouring massive resources into medicalizing the ravages of detrimental health habits. On the other hand, the conception of health is shifting from a disease model to a health model. This newer conception emphasizes health promotion rather than disease management only. It is just as meaningful to speak of levels of vitality and healthfulness as of degrees of impairment and debility.

Health promotion should begin with goals, not means (Nordin, 1999). If health is the goal, biomedical interventions are not the only means to achieve it. The quality of health is heavily influenced by lifestyle habits. Thus, people can exercise some measure of control over the state of their health. To stay healthy, people should exercise, reduce dietary fat, refrain from smoking, keep blood pressure down, and develop effective ways of managing stressors. By managing their health habits, people can live longer, healthier, and retard the process of aging. Self-management is good medicine. If the huge benefits of these few habits were put into a pill, it would be declared a scientific milestone in the field of medicine. However, health habits neither are commercially marketable nor offer a quick fix. So health gatekeepers are disinclined to write behavioral prescriptions.

As a result, current health practices focus heavily on the medical supply side. The growing pressure on health systems is to reduce, ration, and delay health services to contain health costs. The days for the supply-side health system are limited, however. People are living longer. This creates more time for minor dysfunction to develop into chronic diseases. The social cognitive approach, rooted in an agentic model of health promotion, focuses on the demand side (Bandura, 2000a, 2004). It promotes effective self-management of health habits that keep people healthy through their lifespan. Psychosocial factors influence whether the extended lifespan is lived efficaciously or with debility, pain, and dependence (Fries & Crapo, 1981; Fuchs, 1974). Aging populations will force societies to redirect their efforts from supply-side practices to demand-side remedies. Otherwise, nations will be swamped with staggering health costs that consume valuable resources needed for national programs.

Model of Self-Regulation

As noted previously, the capacity for self-regulation is one of the core properties of human agency. Individuals continuously preside over their own behavior. Therefore, skill in self-management is a key personal resource in the development and successful maintenance of healthful habits. Regardless of whether other factors are available as guides and motivators to behavior change, they are unlikely to produce lasting change unless individuals develop the means to exercise control over their motivation and health behavior.

Health habits are not changed by an act of will. Health habits require the exercise of motivational and self-regulatory skills. Self-management operates through a set of psychological subfunctions that must be developed and mobilized for self-directed change. To regulate their health practices, people have to monitor their behavior and its cognitive and situational determinants. Self-monitoring serves a self-diagnostic function, identifying changes that need to be made. Self-monitoring also provides the information needed for setting realistic goals, evaluating one's progress toward them, and adjusting the level of challenge.

People motivate themselves and guide their behavior by the goals they set and by their self-evaluative reactions to their performances. Personal goals, rooted in a value system, enlist self-investment in the activities one undertakes. Once people commit themselves to certain goals, they seek self-satisfaction from fulfilling them. Discontent with substandard performances leads people to intensify their efforts. Long-term goals set the course of personal change. But long-term goals are too distant to override the many competing influences on current behavior. Short-term goals provide the guides, strategies, and motivators for the changes needed in the here and now. To enhance and sustain motivation, people have to adopt attainable subgoals and receive enabling feedback.

Another subfunction of effective self-management involves enlisting self-motivators and social supports for one's self-management efforts. Goals are translated into efficacious action when self-incentives and tangible benefits are conditional on performance accomplishments. In the case of tangible self-motivators, people get themselves to do things they would otherwise put off or avoid altogether by making tangible rewards conditional on given performance attainments. Self-evaluative reactions to one's performances serve as even more influential guides and regulators of one's behavior. People strive to do what gives them self-satisfaction and self-worth, and they refrain from behaving in ways that breed self-dissatisfaction—an observation relevant to the design of interventions for health problems.

Health Promotion through Self-Management

Social cognitive theory, specifically knowledge of the major subfunctions of self-regulation and their self-efficacy underpinning, has informed the development of self-management models that promote habits conducive to health and reduce detrimental habits. The self-management model devised by DeBusk and collaborators combines self-regulatory principles with computer-assisted implementation (DeBusk et al., 1994). This self-regulatory system equips participants with the skills and personal efficacy needed to exercise self-directed change. It includes exercise programs to build cardiovascular capacity and produce other health benefits, nutrition programs to reduce risk of heart disease and cancer, weight reduction programs, and smoking cessation programs. One can add stress management programs to reduce the wear and tear on the body by everyday stressors. For each risk factor, individuals are provided with detailed guides on how to achieve and maintain behavior that will promote health.

Health promotion and risk reduction programs are often structured in ways that are costly, cumbersome, and minimally effective. The net result is minimal prevention and costly remediation. Advances in interactive technologies now enable us to promote health in an individualized way to large numbers of people efficiently and inexpensively using this self-management model. A single program implementor, assisted by the computerized system, can oversee the behavioral changes of hundreds of participants concurrently. Figure 2.2 portrays the structure of the self-management system. Participants monitor the behavior they seek to change. They set short-range attainable subgoals to motivate and guide their efforts. They receive detailed feedback of progress as further guides and motivators for self-directed change. The system is structured in this way based on knowledge that self-motivation requires *both* goal challenges and performance feedback (Bandura, 1991). That is, for self-motivation to persist one needs both to have goals and to know how one is doing.

At selected intervals, the computer generates and mails to participants individually tailored guides for self-directed change. These guides provide attainable subgoals for progressive change. The participants mail performance cards to the implementor on the changes they have achieved and on their perceived efficacy for the next cycle of self-directed change. Efficacy ratings identify areas of vulnerability and difficulties that foretell likely relapse. The computerized feedback portrays graphically the progress patients are making toward each of their subgoals, along with their month-to-month changes, and suggests strategies on how to surmount identified difficulties. The program implementor maintains telephone contact with the participants, if necessary, and is available to provide them extra guidance and support should they run into difficulties. The implementor also serves as the liaison to medical personnel who are called upon when their expertise is needed.

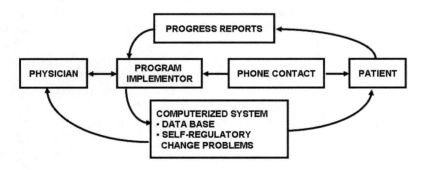

FIGURE 2.2. Computer-assisted self-regulatory system for fostering habits that promote health and reducing those that impair it.

The social utility of health promotion programs can be enhanced by a stepwise implementation model. In the self-management model, the level and type of interactive guidance can be tailored to people's self-management capabilities and to their motivational preparedness to achieve the desired changes. The first level includes people with high efficacy and positive outcome expectations. They can succeed with minimal guidance to accomplish the changes they seek. Individuals at the second level have self-doubts about their efficacy and the likely benefits of their efforts. They make half-hearted efforts to change and are quick to give up when they run into difficulties. They need additional support and guidance by interactive means to see them through tough times. Much of the guidance can be provided through tailored print, telephone consultation, or the Internet. Individuals at the third level believe that their health habits are beyond their personal control, are easily convinced of the futility of effort, and are highly skeptical of the value of behavioral changes. They need a great deal of personal guidance in a structured mastery program. Progressive successes build these individuals' belief in their ability to exercise control and bolster their staying power in the face of difficulties and setbacks.

The preventive value of the self-management model was initially tested in a cholesterol reduction program conducted with employees with elevated cholesterol levels drawn from work sites. One nutritionist administered the program for many participants. They reduced their consumption of saturated fat and lowered their serum cholesterol (see Figure 2.3). They achieved an even larger risk reduction if their spouses took part in the dietary change program at no extra cost. The more room for change in nutritional habits, the greater the cholesterol reduction. The findings point toward a summative, "bottom-line" evaluation of the utility of the self-management model, based on its contribution to beneficial behavioral change.

Further studies attest to the efficacy of the self-management system in reducing plasma cholesterol (Clark et al., 1997). Adding counseling by a dietitian to the self-regulatory system does not produce any further treatment gains (DeBusk et al., 1999). The achieved cholesterol reductions are sustained over time. The self-monitoring component of the self-management system also provides an effective way of differentiating (1) the patients most likely to benefit from dietary treatment because of unhealthy eating habits from (2) those with hyperlipidemia despite having a healthy diet, who thus require lipid-lowering drug therapy. Approximately 40% of the participants lowered their cholesterol by dietary means alone, thus being spared the costs and side effects of medications.

Another source of health risks is the consumption of a lot of foods high in sodium. Sodium intake is linked to hypertension in people who are sensitive to this mineral, a sensitivity that increases with age as the body loses some of its efficiency. Left unchecked, hypertension increases risk of stroke, heart disease, and kidney failure. Sodium-reduction programs can

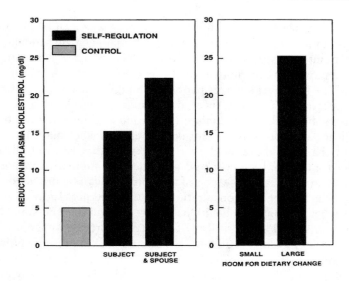

FIGURE 2.3. Levels of reduction in plasma cholesterol achieved with the self-regulation system. The panel on the left summarizes the mean cholesterol reductions achieved in applications in the workplace by participants who used the self-management system either by themselves, along with their spouses, or did not receive the system to provide a control baseline. The right panel presents the mean cholesterol reductions achieved with the self-management system by participants whose daily cholesterol and fat intake were high or relatively low at the outset of the program.

lower blood pressure sufficiently to reduce the need for antihypertensive medication or to discontinue it altogether (Whelton et al., 1998), especially if combined with other lifestyle changes (Reid et al., 1994).

West and collaborators demonstrated the effectiveness of the self-management system in helping patients with heart disease to cut back on their level of sodium intake (West et al., 1999). Foods high in sodium content were targeted for the dietary change. Training in self-management significantly enhanced patients' perceived self-efficacy to adopt a low sodium diet. Patients not only reduced their sodium intake to the recommended target level, they also maintained the dietary change stably over time. And efficacy appeared to play a role in the behavior change. At each successive point in the self-change program, the stronger the perceived self-regulatory efficacy, the greater the reduction in sodium intake. The findings point to self-regulatory efficacy as a mediator of the self-management system's effects. That is, changes in efficacy appear to be the process by which the intervention leads to dietary change. As theory-driven evaluation tells us, identifying mediational processes can be valuable for several reasons, including greater confidence in translating a model to new settings and problems (Chen, 2005).

Some patients cannot achieve sufficient control over their blood pressure solely by dietary and other lifestyle habit changes. They require anti-hypertensive medication. Controlling blood pressure with drugs presents major challenges because nonadherence with prescribed medications is an endemic problem (Rudd, 1997). This is doubly so with nonsymptomatic disorders, where neither the benefits of taking medication regularly nor the detrimental health effects of nonadherence are noticeable. People are reluctant to stick to bothersome drug routines that have no easily noticeable health benefits, but cause some unpleasant side effects. Medical non-adherence not only poses health risks, but may lead physicians to prescribe stronger medications or initiate more drastic interventions in response to the seeming failure of the prescribed treatment.

In randomized controlled studies, Rudd and his collaborators (2004) found that hypertensive patients who received drug therapy via the self-management system received better management of their medication, achieved higher adherence to it, and reduced their systolic and diastolic blood pressure more than did patients who received the usual physician care.

Haskell used the self-management system to promote lifestyle changes in patients suffering from coronary artery disease (Haskell et al., 1994). The targeted risk factors included smoking, exercise, weight, nutrition, and, if necessary, lipid-lowering drug treatment. At the end of four years, those receiving the usual medical care by their physicians showed no change or a worsening of their condition. In contrast, those aided in self-management of health habits achieved substantial reductions in risk factors. They lowered their intake of dietary fat, lost weight, lowered their bad cholesterol and triglycerides, and raised their good cholesterol, exercised more, and increased their cardiovascular capacity. The program also altered the physical progression of the disease. Those receiving the self-management program had 47% less buildup of plaque on artery walls, a higher rate of reversal of arteriosclerosis, and fewer hospitalizations for coronary heart problems and cardiac deaths over time.

Most patients who suffer heart attacks continue the bad health habits that put them at risk. They receive intensive treatment in the hospital but little help following discharge in changing behavioral risk factors. The success of the self-regulatory system was compared against the standard medical postcoronary care to reduce morbidity and mortality in postcoronary patients (DeBusk et al., 1994). The project included nearly 600 postcoronary patients from five hospitals. Among the risk factors were cholesterol, smoking, and physical exercise. The differences in cardiovascular risk factors after one year of postcoronary care are summarized in Figure 2.4. The self-regulatory system is more effective in reducing risk factors and increasing functional cardiovascular capacity than the standard medical care. These preventive health benefits were gained at minimal cost. A single implementor, usually a nurse trained to implement the system, provided the intensive case management to large numbers of patients concurrently.

The self-management model combines the high individualization of the clinical approach with the large-scale applicability of the public health approach. The system is well received by patients for several reasons. It is individually tailored to their needs. It provides them with continuing personalized guidance and informative feedback that enables them to exercise considerable control over their own change. It is a home-based program that does not require any special facilities or equipment. It is not constrained by time and place. It can serve large numbers of people simultaneously, without requiring attendance at group meetings that usually have high drop-out rates. It provides valuable health-promoting services at low cost.

In this kind of application, the computer is used mainly as a tool to guide self-directed change through goal setting, aid in managing troublesome situations, and provide feedback on progress. Linking the interactive aspects of this self-management model to the Internet can vastly expand its reach and availability, while also boosting its health promotive power by providing a ready means to enlist social support and strategic guidance when needed. The amount and form of personalized guidance can be tailored to recipients' needs. Much needed improvements in risk reduction and health promotion can be realized by creative coupling of self-regulatory knowledge with the disseminative and instructive power of online implementation, as discussed later in more detail.

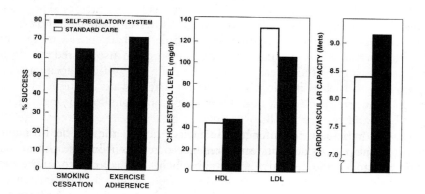

FIGURE 2.4. Changes in coronary risk factors of patients during the first year after acute myocardial infarction, depending on whether they received the usual medical care or training in self-management of health habits. Drawn from data in DeBusk et al. (1994).

The interactive capabilities of electronic technologies are also being creatively enlisted for health promotion in children. Interactive video games are used to raise children's perceived efficacy and enable them to manage chronic health conditions (Lieberman & Brown, 1995). For instance, in a video role-playing game, diabetic children win points depending on how well they understand the diabetic condition and regulate the diet, insulin, and blood sugar levels of two wacky diabetic pachyderms. The elephants set out to retrieve diabetic supplies snatched by pesky enemy critters in a diabetes summer camp. The better they manage the meals, blood glucose, and insulin dosage to stay in the safe zone of the elephants, the more stolen insulin they recover. Results show that children quickly become experts in how to manage diabetes (Brown et al., 1997). The interactive role playing raises the children's self-care efficacy. They talk more freely about their diabetes and their feelings about it. They adopt dietary and insulin practices to keep their blood sugar level under control. In the Brown et al. study they reduced urgent doctor visits for diabetes emergencies by 77% after 6 months, while the children in the control group decreased their self-care and increased emergency doctor visits by 7%.

Another intervention, this one for asthmatic children, involved learning how to manage their condition by helping an asthmatic dinosaur, named Bronchiasaurus, stay strong and healthy while on a risky mission battling the evil Tyrannosaurus Rex who riddles the environment with allergens. Children learn to manage their character's asthma by avoiding asthma triggers, keeping the air free of respiratory irritants, tracking peak flow, and taking medication (Lieberman, 2001). The role-playing simulation, in which asthmatic children gained experience in managing a character's asthma, raised the children's own self-efficacy for asthma self-care. In contrast, comparison group children, who simply watched an instructive video on how to manage asthma, were if anything less self-efficacious. The role-playing simulation also improved children's self-efficacy for talking to parents and peers about asthma and increased their knowledge about asthma self-care and how to avoid asthma triggers.

Another interactive video game discourages children from smoking. A daring surgeon enters the body in microscopic size with lasers to repair the damage done to save the smoker's life. He clears phlegm from the bronchial tubes, removes tar deposits and precancerous cells from the throat and lungs, removes plaque and a deadly blood clot in the arteries, and enters the brain to conquer nicotine addiction. The children become experts in the harmful effects of smoking. In the words of one child, "I didn't know it caused all those diseases." They lose any appetite for smoking. All this is but the beginning in the creative use of the interactive video technology to promote childhood health.

Self-Management of Chronic Diseases

The self-management of chronic diseases provides another example of translating self-regulatory theory to effective implementation models. The weight of disease is shifting from acute to chronic maladies that are the major source of disability. Such diseases do not lend themselves well to biomedical approaches devised primarily for acute illness. The treatment of chronic disease must focus on self-management of physical conditions over time. The goal is to retard the biological progression of impairment to disability and to improve the quality of life of people with chronic disease. Holman and Lorig (1992) devised a prototypic model for the self-management of chronic diseases.

In this model, people are taught cognitive pain control techniques, self-relaxation, and proximal goal setting, combined with self-incentives as motivators to increase level of activity. They are also taught problem-solving and self-diagnostic skills for monitoring and interpreting changes in their health status, as well as skills for locating community resources and managing medication programs. How health care systems deal with clients can alter their sense of efficacy in ways that either support or undermine their restorative efforts (Bandura, 2000b). Lorig's model therefore teaches patients how to take greater initiative for their health care and dealings with health personnel. These capabilities are developed through modeling of self-management skills, guided mastery practice, and informative feedback.

The effectiveness of this self-management approach was tested with patients suffering from arthritis. The program is implemented in convenient community settings in a group format by implementors who suffer similar physical impairments but surmount them in their daily life. Their modeled successes in prevailing over physical debility both inspire participants and provide them with instructive guides and incentives for personal change. The program greatly increases patients' efficacy in exercising some control over their physical condition. The higher their perceived self-efficacy, the less they are disabled by their arthritis, the less pain they experience, and the greater the reduction they achieve in inflammation in their joints (O'Leary, Shoor, Lorig, & Holman, 1988). Patients who believe they can do something about their physical condition are also less depressed and less stressed.

In a 4-year follow-up, arthritic patients who had the benefit of the self-management program displayed increased efficacy to manage their condition, reported a reduction in pain of almost 20%, and showed a slower biological progression of their disease. They also decreased their use of medical services by 43% over the 4-year period. These changes represent huge reductions in health costs with large health benefits. People's sense of efficacy at the end of the self-management program predicts the level of health benefits. In tests of alternative mediating mechanisms, neither increases in knowledge nor behavioral enactments are appreciable predictors of health functioning (Lorig, Chastain, Ung, Shoor, & Holman, 1989; Lorig, Seleznick, et al., 1989). Again, these findings help identify the mechanisms by which the self-management program operates, which can be useful to others who design related interventions in other settings or for different health conditions.

Different types of chronic diseases present many similar problems on how to manage pain, overcome impediments created by physical impairments, maintain self-sufficiency and exercise control over medical services to achieve the best results. The self-management approach, therefore, serves as a generic model that can be adapted to different chronic diseases. Indeed, this model produces similar health benefits for people suffering from heart disease, lung disease, and stroke as well as arthritis (Lorig, Sobel, et al., 1999). Compared to nontreated controls, those who had the benefit of the self-management program made greater use of cognitive symptom management and reported better health, less fatigue, disability, and distress over their physical condition, and fewer limitations on their everyday lives and role activities. They also had fewer hospitalizations, and those requiring hospitalization had shorter stays. If special components that address problems unique to particular chronic diseases were added to the generic model, health benefits might increase.

The generic self-management model devised by Lorig lends itself readily to widespread applications. It can be adapted with supplementary components to different chronic diseases (Lorig, Sobel, et al., 1999). It promotes improvements in health among ethnic participants such as Spanish-speaking ones suffering from arthritis (Lorig, González, & Ritter, 1999) and those at risk for diabetes (Lorig, Ritter, & González, 2003; Lorig, Ritter, & Jacquez, 2005). Major HMOs have adopted this model and integrated it into their mainstream health care systems (Lorig & Holman, 2003; Lorig, Hurwicz, Sobel, & Hobbs, 2006).

The model is being widely disseminated internationally as well. England has adopted it as part of its National Health Service. The National Health Board of Denmark is considering integrating it into their health system. It is being widely applied in Australia, where it is central to their chronic disease management policy. In a randomized controlled trial in China involving diverse chronic conditions (Dongbo et al., 2003), the generic self-management program achieved the same types of health benefits as in other cultural milieus. It raised self-regulatory efficacy, fostered health-promoting behavior, improved health status, and reduced hospitalizations. The generalizability of a self-regulatory model to health promotion is further verified by Clark and her colleagues in a randomized controlled trial in school-based applications in China for children with asthma (Clark, Gong, et al., 2005). It improved asthma management in the home, reduced hospitalization and school absenteeism, and helped academic performance. Future tests will further probe the generalizability of the program.

Internet-Based Health Promotion Systems

Vast populations worldwide have no access to services that promote health and early modification of habits that jeopardize health. For example, high smoking rates worldwide foreshadow a massive global cancer epidemic. We need to develop implementational models of global reach that are readily adaptable to diverse ethnic populations. Psychosocial health programs, implemented via interactive Internet-based systems, enable people worldwide to exercise some control over their health, wherever they may live, at a time of their own choosing, at little cost. People at risk for health problems typically ignore preventive or remedial health services even if they have access to the services. But Internet-delivered guidance is a promising delivery modality because it is readily accessible independent of time and place, highly convenient, and flexible, and it also provides a feeling of anonymity.

A growing body of evidence based on randomized controlled trials attests to the potential of online self-management programs. Consider some examples. Anorexia and bulimia are serious health problems among adolescent girls and young women. In a series of studies by Taylor and collaborators, young women who had the benefit of Internet-based guidance reduced dissatisfaction with their weight and body shape and altered dysfunctional attitudes. The program also prevented the onset of eating disorders in women at risk of developing such disorders (Taylor et al., 2006; Taylor, Winzelberg, & Celio, 2001). Lorig has adopted her arthritis self-management program for implementation through the Internet (Lorig, Ritter, Laurent, & Plant, 2006). The online program produces similar health benefits to those achieved in group applications. Change in perceived self-efficacy at 6 months predicted health status outcomes at one year. This online model improves health in other chronic medical conditions as well (Lorig, Ritter, Dost, et al., 2008; Lorig, Ritter, Laurent, & Plant, 2008). People worldwide could now have access to an effective health self-management program.

Muñoz has developed an Internet-based model of global reach to help people quit smoking. They are taught how to take the steps to quit smoking, what to do in case of relapse, and how to refuse offered cigarettes (Muñoz et al., 2006). He is testing globally the online self-management model in randomized controlled trials. When participants log in, they are assigned to different versions of the program. This will allow components to be identified that can further enhance the effectiveness of the generic self-management models. The quit rate for the online self-management model compares favorably to nicotine replacement. Other evidence indicates that depression is positively related to smoking. If a component on self-management of depressive mood is added to the basic model, it raises quit rates in smokers who suffer from depression. Adding incentives and follow-up guidance also raise quit rates.

The medical gatekeepers of health services are ill-equipped to promote health by psychosocial means. They have neither the expertise nor the time to enable and guide their clients to reduce their weight, quit smoking, exercise, stay off alcohol and drugs, and improve their ability to manage stressors. To achieve results, physicians would have to assess their clients' social realities, have good strategies to offer for personal change, manage resistances, gauge progress and readjust strategies accordingly, and motivate patients to stick with their efforts through failures and setbacks. Not surprisingly, physicians report a low sense of efficacy to alter detrimental health habits (Hyman, Maibach, Flora, & Fortmann, 1992). Physicians give up trying what they doubt they can change. For lack of an alternative, either physicians do not address the problems or they substitute pills for behavior change.

Evidence-based self-management systems can provide physicians with the option of behavioral prescriptions to online programs of demonstrated effectiveness. If online self-management programs are proven more effective in randomized controlled trials than the usual medical service or drug regimens, then behavioral prescriptions should be instituted as a regular part of health care systems. To date, societal efforts to get people to adopt healthful practices rely heavily on public health campaigns. However, these population-based approaches promote changes mainly in people who already have high perceived self-regulatory efficacy and positive expectations that the prescribed changes will improve their health. There is only so much that large-scale health campaigns can do on their own, regardless of whether they are tailored or generic. But public health campaigns could provide a convenient way, at low cost, for linking people to interactive Internet systems that can provide them with the intensive, personalized guidance they need. There is much conceptual and empirical work to be done on how to enhance the level, timing, and quality of online interactivity. A further extension of research efforts is to determine the optimal blend of online and face-to-face interactivity for individuals at different levels of changeability and at different phases of change.

Macrosocial Applications Addressing Urgent Global Problems

The most ambitious applications of social cognitive theory are aimed at abating some of the most pressing global problems. Soaring population growth is an ecologically consequential global problem of massive proportions. It is destroying the ecosystems that sustain life, degrading the quality of life, and draining resources needed for national development. The problem is especially severe in less developed nations, which are doubling their populations at an accelerating rate (Figure 2.5). Shifts in population from rural to urban areas are creating megacities with millions of people living under squalid conditions struggling to survive with scarcities of food, fresh water, and basic sanitation, medical services, and other necessities of life. As Cleland and collaborators (2006) explain, promotion of family planning is unique in the scope of its benefits. It reduces the cycle of poverty, decreases maternal and child mortality, liberates women for personal development by relieving the burden of excessive childbearing, contributes to achievement of universal primary education, and aids environmental sustainability by stabilizing the planet's population, which is headed for a 40% increase in the next 50 years.

Whatever reductions in greenhouse gasses are achieved by changing consumptive habits will be swamped by a 40% increase in the number of consumers worldwide. In the consideration of remedies for rising global warming, the ponderous population elephant in the room strangely goes unnoticed.

The global ecosystem cannot sustain burgeoning populations and high consumption of finite natural resources. By wielding powerful technologies that amplify control over the environment, humans are producing hazardous global changes of huge magnitude—deforestation, desertification, global warming, glacial melting, flooding of low-lying coastal regions,

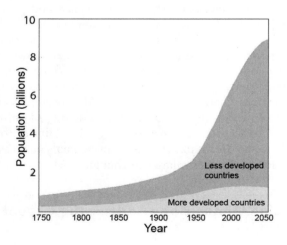

FIGURE 2.5. Population growth in developed and less developed countries. From Population Reference Bureau (1998). Copyright 1998 by Population Reference Bureau. Reprinted by permission.

topsoil erosion and sinking of water tables in the major food-producing regions, depletion of fisheries, and degradation of other aspects of the earth's life-support systems. Expanding economies are fueling consumptive growth by billions of people, which will intensify competition for the earth's vital resources and overwhelm efforts to secure an environmentally and economically sustainable future. Through collective practices driven by a foreshortened perspective, humans may be well on the road to outsmarting themselves into irreversible ecological crises.

Another widespread problem is the pernicious gender inequality in familial, educational, health, and social life. In many societies women are subjugated and denied their liberty, dignity, and opportunities to develop their talents. The demands of our new information era favor intelligence over brawn. Given that women constitute approximately half of population, societies that marginalize or subjugate women undermine their nation's social, technological, and economic viability by neglecting this vast human resource. Fostering the talents and social rights of women provides nations with powerful leverage for national development and renewal. The same is true for ethnic minorities.

Some societies present unique problems that require special social themes tailored to their cultural practices. Approximately 130 million women in Africa are subjected to the brutal genital mutilation procedure. In our change program, Muslim clerics explain that these practices are not sanctioned by their religion. As another example, in the African nation of Mali, child traffickers trick impoverished parents with large families to give up children under the promise that they will receive good care and send money home. They are then sold for slave labor under inhumane conditions. Some are sold for the sex trade. Traffickers also sell orphans of parents who died of AIDS. The spreading AIDS epidemic is another mounting global problem with devastating societal consequences.

Sociocognitive Model for Effecting Societywide Changes

Long running serial dramas serve as the principal vehicle for promoting personal and social changes related to this long list of interrelated social problems. These productions bring life to people's everyday struggles and the consequences of different social practices. The storylines speak ardently to people's fears, hopes, and aspirations for a better life. They inform, enable, motivate, and guide viewers for personal and social changes that can alter the course of their lives. The dramatic productions are not just fanciful stories. They dramatize the realities of people's everyday lives and the impediments with which they struggle. The enabling dramas help viewers to see a better life and provide the strategies and incentives that enable them to take the steps to achieve it. The storylines model family planning, women's equality, degrading dowry systems, spousal abuse, environmental conservation, AIDS prevention, and a variety of life skills. Hundreds of episodes get people emotionally engaged in the evolving lives of the models and identify with them.

There are three major components to this social cognitive approach to fostering societywide changes (Bandura, 2001b). The first component is a theoretical model. It specifies the determinants of psychosocial change and the mechanisms through which they produce their effects. This knowledge provides the guiding principles. The second component is a translational and implementational model. It converts theoretical principles into an innovative operational model, and it specifies the content, strategies of change and their mode of implementation. Miguel Sabido (1981), a creative playwright and producer, devised the translational model based on the verified modeling principles from our early research on social modeling (Bandura, 1962). The third component is a social diffusion model on how to promote adoption of psychosocial programs in diverse cultural milieus. Population Communications International (PCI) and the Population Media Center (PMC) serve as the global diffusion mechanisms (Poindexter, 2004; Ryerson, 1999). These two nonprofit organizations raise funds from various sources, including the UN population fund, private foundations, and individual donors, to cover production costs. They provide the nations' media personnel with the instructive guidance and technical assistance needed to create engrossing serial dramas tailored to the particular cultural milieus. This creative process involves a close collaborative partnership with the host country's production teams.

Major scientific progress and achievement of widespread social changes require pooling the knowledge and innovative expertise of diverse disciplines. In the macrosocial approach under discussion, social cognitive theory provided the theoretical model (Bandura, 1986, 1997), Miguel Sabido devised the generic translational and implemental model (Sabido, 1981, 2002), and Poindexter (2004) and Ryerson (1994) designed the social diffusion model.

Cultural and Value Analyses

These are not social programs foisted on nations by outsiders in pursuit of their self-interest. The dramatic serials are created only on invitation by countries seeking help with intractable problems. The host production team, drawing on a wide variety of sources, including public health systems, religious organizations, women's groups, and other constituencies, identity unique cultural life conditions, social practices, and prevailing values, and itemize the types of changes the dramatizations should address. These data provide the culturally relevant information for developing realistic characters and engrossing functional plotlines. Once a program is aired, producers monitor how viewers perceive the characters, with whom they are identifying, how they view the obstacles and the dramatized options, and the types of futures they envision.

The value issues are cast in concrete real-life terms of detriments and benefits of particular lifestyles. The tangible values embody respect for human dignity and equitable familial, social, health and educational opportunities that support common human aspirations. The dramatizations are thus grounded in the internationally endorsed human values codified in United Nations covenants and resolutions. The dramatized options, and how they affect the course of life, help people make informed choices to improve their lives.

Elements of Enabling Serials

Four basic principles guide the construction of the dramatic serials: social modeling, vicarious motivators, engagement, and environmental supports.

Social Modeling

The first principle enlists the power of social modeling for personal and social change. When audience members see people similar to themselves change their lives for the better, it not only conveys strategies for how to change, it also raises viewers' sense of efficacy that they too can succeed. Viewers come to admire and are inspired by characters in their likenesses who struggle with difficult obstacles and eventually overcome them.

Three types of contrasting models are used to highlight the personal and social effects of different styles of behavior. The episodes include positive models portraying beneficial lifestyles. Other characters personify negative models exhibiting detrimental views and lifestyles. Transitional models are shown transforming their lives by discarding detrimental styles of behavior in favor of beneficial ones. Viewers are especially prone to draw inspiration from, and identify with, transforming models by seeing them surmount adverse life circumstances similar to their own.

Vicarious Motivators

The second principle guiding the dramatic productions is the use of vicarious motivators as incentives for change. Unless people see the modeled lifestyle as improving their welfare, they have little incentive to adopt it. The personal and social benefits of the favorable practices, and the costs of the detrimental ones, are vividly portrayed. Seeing beneficial outcomes instills outcome expectations that serve as positive incentives for change, whereas detrimental outcomes create negative outcome expectations that function as disincentives.

When social change is attempted, it typically challenges power relations and the entrenched societal practices supported by individuals who have a vested interest in preserving adverse behavior. Successes do not come easy. To change their lives for the better, people have to challenge adverse traditions and inequitable constraints. They must be prepared for the obstacles they are likely to encounter. There are several ways of building resilience to impediments through social modeling. Prototypical problem situations and effective ways of overcoming them are modeled. People are taught how to manage setbacks by modeling how to recover from failed attempts. They are shown how to enlist guidance and social support for personal change from self-help groups and other agencies in their localities. Seeing others succeed through perseverant effort also boosts staying power in the face of obstacles.

Attentional and Emotional Engagement

To change deeply held beliefs and social practices, people must develop strong emotional bonding to enabling models who exemplify a vision of a better future and realistic paths to it. Plotlines that dramatize viewers' everyday lives and functional solutions get them deeply involved. They form emotional ties to models who speak to their hopes and aspirations. Unlike brief exposures to media presentations that typically leave most viewers untouched, ongoing engagement in the evolving lives of the models provides numerous opportunities to learn from them and to be inspired by them.

In a radio serial drama in India, with a listenership of about 25 million, a mother challenges restrictive cultural norms for her daughter Taru and promotes her education. Taru inspired formerly illiterate teenagers who had no access to education to become avid readers and pursue their schooling. Here is an example of Taru's powerful impact on teenage listeners: "There are moments when I feel that Taru is directly talking to me, usually at night. She is telling me, 'Usha, you can follow your dreams.' I feel she is like my elder sister ... and giving me encouragement." Modeling the educational practices of Taru's mother, one of the viewers created a school for illiterate women. Several teenage girls started a school for poor children, who attend classes around the village water well. The teenagers fight for social justice and gender equality and fight against class discrimination and forced teenage marriage. Their efforts alter community norms to fit the changing times.

In another serial drama in India, 400,000 viewers sent letters supporting, advising, or criticizing the various models in the drama. In a serial in Tanzania, women spotted a negative role model at a market and drove him out under a rain of tomatoes and mangos. In Brazil, 10,000 people showed up for the filming of the marriage of two of the characters in a serial drama.

Environmental Supports

Motivating people to change has little value if they are not provided with appropriate resources and environmental supports to realize those changes. Enlisting and creating environmental supports is an additional aid designed to expand and sustain the changes promoted by the media. To achieve both levels of change, the dramatic productions are designed to operate through two pathways. In one pathway, the serials promote changes by informing, enabling, motivating, and guiding viewers in ways congruent with social cognitive theory. However, people are socially situated in interpersonal networks (Bandura, 2006b; Rogers & Kincaid, 1981). Therefore, in the second, socially mediated pathway, media influences are used to connect viewers to social networks and community settings. These places provide continued personalized guidance, as well as natural incentives and social supports for desired changes. Behavioral and valuational changes are promoted within these social milieus. Epilogues, delivered by culturally admired figures, provide contact information to relevant community services and support groups.

Global Applications

Many media-based applications of the sociocognitive model have been implemented globally in Africa, Asia, and Latin America, promoting personal and societywide changes that better the lives of millions of people. Some of these applications and formal evaluations of their effects are summarized briefly in the sections that follow. These applications have been extensively reviewed elsewhere in greater detail (Bandura, 2002b; Singhal, Cody, Rogers, & Sabido, 2004).

Literacy is vital for personal and national development. To reduce widespread illiteracy, the Mexican government launched a national self-study program. People who were skilled at reading were urged to organize small self-study groups in which they would teach others how to read using primers developed for this purpose. Although a good idea, it enlisted few takers. So Sabido created a year-long serial with daily episodes to reach, enable, and motivate people to enlist in the program. A popular performer was cast in the role of the literate model. She recruits a diverse set of characters to represent the different segments of the population with problems of illiteracy. As noted previously, assumed similarity enhances the power of social modeling.

A prior interview survey revealed several personal barriers that dis-suaded people from enrolling in the literacy program. Many people believed that they lacked the capabilities to master such a complex skill. Others believed that reading skills could be acquired only when one is young. Still others felt that they were unworthy of having an educated person devote their time to helping them learn to read. These self-dissuading misbeliefs were modeled by the various characters in the dramatic series and corrected by the mentor as she persuaded them that they possessed the capabilities to succeed. As this example illustrates, general knowledge of the social cogni-tive theory will not suffice. Successful translation requires local, contextual knowledge of the specific barriers to high efficacy. This is an important les-son for those who seek to use social science theory in program design and formative evaluation.

The episodes included humor, conflicts, and engrossing discussions of the subjects being read. Characters were shown struggling in the initial phases of learning, then gaining progressive mastery, along with self-pride in their accomplishments. To provide vicarious motivators to pursue the self-education program, the dramatic series depicted the substantial ben-efits of literacy both for personal development and for national efficacy and pride. One of the epilogues, given by an admired movie star, informed viewers about the national self-education program and encouraged them to take advantage of it. The next day, 25,000 people showed up at the distri-bution center to enroll in the self-study program.

Millions of viewers watched this series faithfully. Compared to non-viewers, viewers of the dramatic series were much more informed about the national literacy program and expressed more positive attitudes about help-ing one another to learn. Enrollment in the literacy program was relatively low in the year before the televised series, under 100,000, but rose abruptly during the year of the series to nearly a million (Sabido, 1981). As people develop a sense of efficacy and competencies that enable them to exercise better control over their lives, they serve as models, inspiration, and even tutors for others in the circles in which they travel. In the year following the televised series, over 400,000 people enrolled in the self-study literacy program.

Another serial drama in Mexico promoted family planning to help break the cycle of poverty, which is heightened by a high rate of unplanned childbearing. The storyline centers on the lives of married sisters. The ben-eficial family life of a small family was contrasted with the experiences of one sister burdened by a huge family living in impoverishment and hope-lessness. Much of the drama focused on a married daughter and her family living in her parents' despairingly crowded and destitute environment. She already has two children and is pregnant with the third. She is in marital conflict and distress over her desire to have a voice in her family life and to stop having more babies, which she realizes would condemn her family to an impoverished life without ability to care adequately for them. The young couple served as the transition model. As the drama unfolds, this couple is shown gaining control over their family life with the help of a family planning center, bringing about meaningful changes in their family life. In epilogues, viewers were informed about family planning services.

Compared to nonviewers, heavy viewers were more likely to link lower childbearing to social, economic, and psychological benefits (Sabido, 1981). They also developed a more positive attitude toward helping others plan their family. Family planning centers reported a 32% increase in new contraceptive users over the number for the previous year. People reported that the televised program was the impetus for consulting the health clinics. National sales of contraceptives rose from low in the baseline years to a substantial increase in the year the program was aired (see Figure 2.6).

Efforts to reduce the rate of population growth must address not only the strategies and benefits of family planning, but also the role and status of women in societies in which they are treated subserviently. In some societies, the equity problems stem from machismo dominance; in others, from marriage and pregnancy at the onset of puberty with no say in the choice of husband or the number and spacing of children; and in still others from dispossession by polygamous marriages. Exploiting the cultural preference

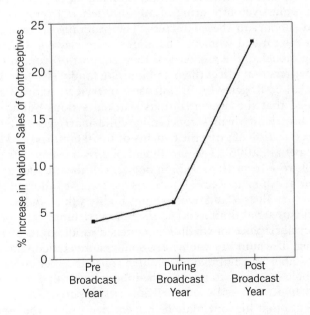

FIGURE 2.6. National sales of contraceptives in the two years preceding the serial drama promoting family planning and during the year it was broadcast. Drawn from data in Sabido (1981).

for sons in India, radiologists offer cheap ultrasound tests to identify female fetuses, some of which are then aborted. This practice is producing a growing imbalance of females to males that will have huge long-term societal consequences.

India has passed the 1 billion mark and is on the brink of surpassing China as the most populous nation in the world. At the present fertility rate, the population will double to 2 billion in 40 years. A serial in India was designed to raise the status of women, as well as to promote a smaller family norm. It addressed a variety of themes about family life in the context of broader social norms and practices (Singhal & Rogers, 1999). The subthemes devoted particular attention to elevating the status of women in family, social, and economic life; educational opportunities and career options for women; son preference and gender bias in child rearing; the detriment of dowry requirements; choice in spouse selection, teenage marriage and parenthood; spousal abuse; family planning to limit family size; youth delinquency; and community development. Some of the characters personified positive role models for gender equality; others were proponents of the traditional subservient role for women; and still others were transitional models. A famous Indian film actor reinforced the modeled messages in epilogues.

The series was immensely popular, enjoying the top viewership on television and a massive outpouring of 400,000 letters from viewers offering advice and support to the characters. The programs fostered more equitable attitudes toward women. The more aware viewers were of the messages being modeled, the greater was their support of women's freedom of choice in matters that affect them and limiting family size (Brown & Cody, 1991; Singhal & Rogers, 1999). Intensive interviews with village inhabitants revealed that the dramatizations sparked serious public discussions about the broadcast themes concerning child marriages, dowry requirements, the education of girls, the benefits of small families, and other social issues (Papa et al., 2000). The enrollment of girls in elementary and junior high schools rose from 10 to 38% in one year of the broadcasts.

The serial drama in Kenya illustrates the creative tailoring of storylines to key cultural values. Land ownership is highly valued in Kenya. A major storyline in this serial drama linked the impoverishing effect of large families to the inheritance of land. The contrast modeling centered on two brothers, one of whom has one wife, a son, and several daughters, whereas the other brother has multiple wives, nine sons, and even more daughters. They squabble over how to pass on the inherited family farm to their next generation. In Kenya, only sons can inherit property. The monogamous brother argues that his lone male heir is entitled to half the land, whereas the polygamous brother insists on dividing the farm into ten small plots which would provide, at best, a marginal subsistence for all. In another concurrent plotline, a teacher pleads with parents, who want their young daughter to quit school, be circumcised, and married off to an arranged partner, to allow her to continue the education she desperately desires.

The serial drama, which was broadcast via radio to reach rural areas, was the most popular program on the air, attracting 40% of the Kenyan population each week. Contraceptive use increased by 58%, and desired family size declined 24%. A survey of women who came to health clinics reported that the radio series helped to persuade their husbands to allow them to seek family planning. Quantitative analyses included multiple statistical controls (Westoff & Rodriguez, 1995), including life-cycle status, number of wives and children, and a host of socioeconomic factors such as ethnicity, religion, education, occupation, and urban-rural residence.

The impact of media exposure on adoption and consistent use of new methods of contraception is shown in Figure 2.7. Because people could not be assigned at random to listen to all, some, or none of the radio series, the evaluation examined the relationship between the level of exposure and subsequent use of contraceptives. The social impact of the dramatizations increased with increased exposure. The media effect remained after applying the multiple statistical controls. Internal analyses of the evaluation surveys further revealed that the media influence was a major factor in raising motivation to limit birthrate and adopt contraception practices.

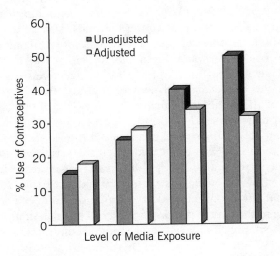

FIGURE 2.7. Percentage of women adopting contraceptive methods depending on the amount of exposure to family planning communications in the media. The white bars represent the level of contraceptive use after controlling for the women's demographic and socioeconomic characteristics and a host of other potential determinants. From Westoff and Rodriguez (1995). Copyright 1995 by the Guttmacher Institute. Reprinted by permission.

Stronger evidence of the effectiveness of serial dramas was possible in Tanzania, which contains regions with separate radio transmitters. This provided a unique opportunity for a quasi-experimental comparison of the effectiveness of the serial dramas to a nonbroadcast region, coupled with a delayed treatment design. The population of Tanzania is 36 million, the fertility rate is 5.6 children per woman, and the doubling time for the population at the current rate is 25 years. No economic development can cope with this soaring population.

Following a pretreatment phase, the serial drama was broadcast by radio in one major region of the country, with the other region serving as the control. The program targeted both family planning and sexual practices that increase vulnerability to infection with the AIDS virus. At the outset, the populace was well informed about contraception and AIDS prevention and was not negatively disposed toward such practices. They had access to contraceptive methods and family planning clinics. But they did not translate these attitudes into action. When other influences conflict with personal attitudes, people can find reasons not to act on their attitudes or justify exemptions to them. The problem was neither informational nor attitudinal, but motivational. The dramatic series provided the impetus for change.

Compared to the control region, the serialized dramatizations raised viewers' perceived efficacy to determine their family size, decreased the desired number of children, increased the ideal age of marriage for women, increased approval of family planning methods, stimulated spousal communication about family size, and increased use of family planning services and adoption of contraceptive methods (Rogers et al., 1999). Figure 2.8 shows the mean number of adopters of contraceptive methods per clinic over time in the broadcast and control regions. Both regions increased slightly and at the same rate during the three-year prebroadcast period. In the second phase, the adoption rate increased only slightly in the control region, but at an abrupt and pronounced rate in the broadcast region. This pattern of effects was replicated when the serial was later broadcast in the initial control region, with a sharp abrupt increase in that region. The replication of effects across regions provides further support for the conclusion that the program made a genuine difference. The fertility rate declined more in the 2-year period of the serial dramas than in the previous 30 years, without any change in socioeconomic conditions and little change in death rate (Vaughan, 2003). The quasi-experimental design, as shown in Figure 2.8, provides considerable confidence in the evaluative conclusion that the serial drama brought about these beneficial changes.

As in the Kenya findings, the more often people listened to the broadcasts, the more the married women talked to their spouses about family planning and the higher the rate of adoption of contraceptive methods. These diverse effects remained after multiple controls were made for other

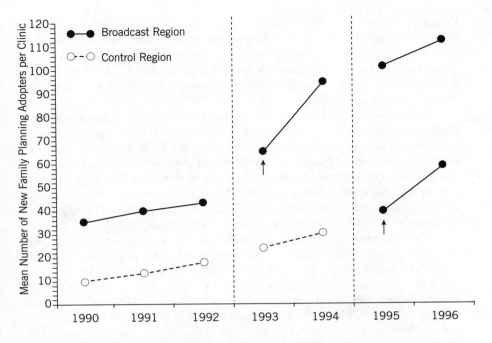

FIGURE 2.8. Mean number of new family planning adopters per clinic in the Ministry of Health Clinics in the broadcast region and those in the control region. The values to the left of the dotted line are adoption levels prior to the broadcast: The values between the dotted lines are adoption levels when the serial was aired in the broadcast region but not in the control region; the values to the right of the dotted line are the adoption levels when the serial was aired in both the broadcast region and previous control region. Drawn from data in Rogers et al. (1999).

potential determinants, including exposure to other radio programs with family planning and AIDS contents, prebroadcast levels and changes in education, increased access to family planning clinics, radio ownership, and rural-urban differences.

Seventeen segments of the series were included to prevent the spread of the AIDS virus. A particular problem was the transmission of AIDS heterosexually by long-distance truckers at truck stop hubs with hundreds of prostitutes. About 60% of the prostitutes and about a third of the truck drivers are infected. The common belief was that AIDS is transmitted by mosquitoes. Some of the males believed that condoms caused infection, that having sexual intercourse with a virgin would cure AIDS, and that sex with young girls is safe because they are unlikely to be infected. The program quickly debunked the false beliefs.

In the contrast modeling, the negative trucker character engages in risky sex with multiple partners; the positive model adopts safer sex practices and cuts back on the number of partners; and the transitional model begins with risky practices but adopts safer ones. The truckers using the safer practices try unsuccessfully to talk their friend into changing his risky ways. He refuses. His wife fears that she will get infected. The community pools its resources to set up the wife in a business. She leaves her husband, who eventually gets infected and dies of AIDS.

Compared to residents in the control region, those in the broadcast region increased belief in their personal risk of HIV infection through unprotected sexual practices, talked more about HIV infection, reduced the number of sexual partners, and increased condom use (Vaughan, Rogers, Singhal, & Swalehe, 2000). The number of condoms distributed annually by the National AIDS program remained low in the control region, increased substantially in the broadcast region, and increased significantly in the control region after exposure later to the broadcast.

A serial drama in Ethiopia also addressed the widespread AIDS problem. Compared to their baseline status and to that of nonviewers, viewers were more informed on how to determine their HIV status, and they were more likely to get a blood test for their HIV status (Figure 2.9). Knowing one's serostatus fosters adoption of safer-sex practices (McKusick, Coates, Morin, Pollack, & Hoff, 1990). To augment the impact of the serial drama, the truckers and sex workers were provided audiocassettes focused on AIDS prevention. They lined up eagerly for each new episode.

Like the other serial dramas, the radio serial in Sudan had multiple intersecting plotlines. These included the benefits of family planning to

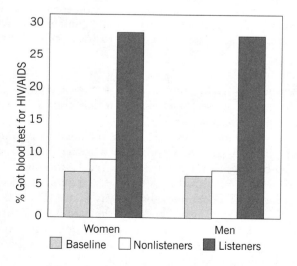

FIGURE 2.9. Impact of the serial drama on motivating viewers to test their serostatus. Data from Ryerson (2006).

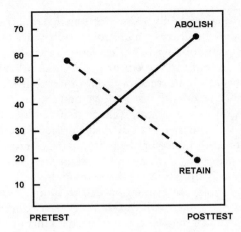

FIGURE 2.10. Reversal of the social norm from favoring genital mutilation to abolishing this brutal procedure. Data from Ryerson (2006).

limit the number of children and their spacing, educational opportunities for daughters, the injustice of forced marriage and risks of early childbearing, domestic violence, embroilment in drug activities leading to a life of crime and narcotics, and prevention of HIV infection. A special theme centered on the devastating consequences of the widespread practice of genital mutilation. In the dramatization, Muslim clerics disapproved of such practices as being without religious justification. As the storyline unfolds, the dangers and deadly consequences of this practice are portrayed. Figure 2.10 testifies to the strong social impact of the serial drama. It reversed the social norm from favoring this brutal practice to widespread support for abolishing it.

Cross-Cultural Generalizability

A contentious dualism pervades the field of cultural psychology, pitting autonomy against interdependence, individualism against collectivism, and human agency against social structure. It is widely claimed that Western theories lack generalizability to non-Western cultures. I have reviewed elsewhere evidence on the exercise of agency in cultural context that calls into question these dualistic views (Bandura, 2002a). One must distinguish between inherent capacities, on the one hand, and how culture shapes these potentialities into diverse forms, on the other. For example, modeling is an essential mode of learning, regardless of the culture in which one resides. Modeling is a universalized human capacity. But what is modeled, how modeling influences are socially structured, and the purposes they serve varies in different cultural milieus. Similarly, a resilient sense of efficacy has generalized functional value regardless of whether one resides in an individualistically oriented culture or a collectivistically oriented one. In short, there is a cultural commonality in basic agentic capacities and mechanisms of operation, but diversity in the culturing of these inherent capacities. In this dual-level conception, universality is not incompatible with the idea of cultural plurality. The evidence just reviewed on the cross-cultural applications of social cognitive theory to promote societywide changes attests to the generalizability of the theory to diverse cultural milieus.

Thoughtful program development should take into account both the generality of key processes such as modeling and agency, while also considering the potentially diverse ways these are expressed in specific cultural contexts. Similarly, program evaluation can examine the extent to which, say, efficacy has increased, while taking into account that the specific obstacles to high efficacy may be contextual and culturally bound.

Modification of Consummatory Lifestyles

Environmental devastation is affected not only by population size, but also by the level of consumption and by the damage to the ecosystem caused by the technologies used to supply the consumable products (Ehrlich, Ehrlich, & Daily, 1995). There are limits to the earth's carrying capacity. The global ecosystem cannot sustain burgeoning populations and high consumption of finite natural resources. The growing consumption needed to feed the global economy is exacting mounting environmental costs. The sociocognitive model lends itself readily to other types of lifestyle changes, such as environmental conservation and consummatory practices to promote environmental sustainability. For example, through an Indian serial drama that centered on preservation of the environment, villagers were motivated to take collective action to improve sanitation, reduce potential health hazards, adopt fuel conservation practices to reduce pollution, and launch a tree-planting campaign (Papa et al., 2000). They persuaded other villages to institute similar environmental practices.

Most people are probably unaware of how their purchases affect the environment. If they are to make decisions supportive of sustained development, they need to be informed of the ecological costs of their consummatory practices and to be enabled and motivated to turn enlightened concern into constructive courses of action. This change is best achieved through multiple modes of communication (Singhal & Rogers, 1999). Many lifelong consummatory habits are formed during childhood years. It is easier to prevent wasteful practices than to try to change them after they have become deeply entrenched as part of a lifestyle.

To address the environmental problems created by overconsumption, PCI produced a video focusing on the buying habits of teenagers, *The Cost of Cool,* for distribution to schools (Population Communications International, 2000). The video tracks the ecological costs of the manufacture of everyday items such as T-shirts and sneakers. Providing teenagers with sound information helps them make informed choices in their buying habits. As one viewer put it, "I'll never look at a T-shirt in the same way." Popular entertainment formats, such as music concerts, recordings, and videos, provide another vehicle for reaching mass youth populations. The impact of these complementary approaches requires systematic evaluation. The increasing magnitude of the environmental problem calls for multifaceted efforts to alter behavioral practices that devastate the ecological supports of life, as well as for evaluation strategies that track the contribution of the various components of the intervention.

Global problems instill a sense of paralysis in people that there is little they can do to reduce such problems. But global effects are the cumulative products of local actions. Encouragement to "Think globally, act locally" is an effort to restore in people a sense of efficacy that they can make a difference. The macrosocial approach implemented through the mass media can dramatize how consumption has countless environmental consequences. Knowledge alone, of course, is not enough. To enable and motivate viewers to effect large-scale changes, plotlines should show models struggling to preserve a healthy environment and promote policies supporting environmentally sustainable production and marketing of products.

Concluding Remarks

The field of psychology does not profit as it should from its theoretical advances because, for the most part, it lacks creative translational and social diffusion models. These are the vital, but weakest, links in the field of social change. Much attention is devoted to the development and predictive validity of our theories, but less to their social utility. Theories are predictive and operative tools. In the final analysis, the evaluation of a science of personal and social change will rest heavily on its social utility.

The present chapter provides a brief review of the basic principles of social cognitive theory and their applications at the individual and macrosocial levels to promote key changes that significantly improve the quality of peoples' lives. Health status plays an especially critical role because it can affect one's entire lifestyle. The quality of life that people lead can be seriously compromised by disease and chronic disability. Many of the losses in health functioning are irretrievable, which further adds to its consequential impact. We have the means to promote health and reduce the risk of disease. But vast populations lack access to such services. The health applications reviewed in this chapter describe the initial steps toward the development of models that hold promise of providing universal access to health promotive services for advancing the health of populations worldwide.

The applications at the macrosocial level address some of today's most pressing global problems. Dramatic serials are used as an extraordinarily effective vehicle for reaching vast numbers of people over a prolonged period on matters of vital concern to them. Viewers get deeply involved in the lives of the dramatized models and are inspired by them to take steps that can improve their lives. Radio versions of the serial dramas can reach vast rural populations. The global applications of this sociocognitive model are improving the quality of people's lives in diverse cultures and across diverse spheres of functioning. Some of the changes can contribute to the amelioration of the rapidly deteriorating ecological systems that have enormous consequences not only for the rest of one's life but for that of future generations.

Continued evaluation of these and other applications of social cognitive theory is essential to verifying their effectiveness, assessing the extent to which translation into interventions is culturally appropriate, and generating additional knowledge that can improve future applications.

ACKNOWLEDGMENTS

Some sections of this chapter include revised, updated, and expanded material from Bandura (1997, 2002b).

REFERENCES

Bandura, A. (1962). Social learning through imitation. In M. R. Jones (Ed.), *Nebraska Symposium on Motivation* (pp. 211–274). Lincoln: University of Nebraska Press.

Bandura, A. (1986). *Social foundations of thought and action: A social cognitive theory.* Englewood Cliffs, NJ: Prentice-Hall.

Bandura, A. (1991). Self-regulation of motivation through anticipatory and self-reactive mechanisms. In R. A. Dienstbier (Ed.), *Perspectives on motivation: Nebraska symposium on motivation* (Vol. 38, pp. 69–164). Lincoln: University of Nebraska Press.

Bandura, A. (1997). *Self-efficacy: The exercise of control.* New York: Freeman.

Bandura, A. (2000a). Health promotion from the perspective of social cognitive theory. In P. Norman, C. Abraham, & M. Conner (Eds.), *Understanding and changing health behaviour: From health beliefs to self-regulation* (pp. 239–339). Amsterdam: Harwood Academic.

Bandura, A. (2000b). Psychological aspects of prognostic judgments. In R. W. Evans, D. Baskin, & F. M. Yatsu (Eds.), *Prognosis of neurological disorders* (2nd ed., pp. 11–27). New York: Oxford University Press.

Bandura, A. (2001a). Social cognitive theory: An agentic perspective. *Annual review of psychology* (Vol. 52, pp. 1–26). Palo Alto, CA: Annual Reviews.

Bandura, A. (2001b). Social cognitive theory of mass communications. In J. Bryant & D. Zillman (Eds.), *Media effects: Advances in theory and research* (2nd ed., pp. 121–153). Mahwah, NJ: Erlbaum.

Bandura, A. (2002a). Social cognitive theory in cultural context. *Journal of Applied Psychology: An International Review, 51,* 269–290.

Bandura, A. (2002b). Environmental sustainability by sociocognitive deceleration of population growth. In P. Schmuck & W. Schultz (Eds.), *The psychology of sustainable development* (pp. 209–238). Dordrecht, the Netherlands: Kluwer.

Bandura, A. (2004). Health promotion by social cognitive means. *Health Education and Behavior, 31,* 143–164.

Bandura A. (2005). The evolution of social cognitive theory. In K. G. Smith & M. A. Hitt (Eds.), *Great minds in management* (pp. 9–35). Oxford, UK: Oxford University Press.

Bandura, A. (2006a). Toward a psychology of human agency. *Perspectives on Psychological Science, 1,* 164–180.

Bandura, A. (2006b). On integrating social cognitive and social diffusion theories. In A. Singhal & J. Dearing (Eds.), *Communication of innovations: A journey with Ev Rogers* (pp. 111–135). Beverly Hills, CA: Sage.

Bandura, A., & Walters, R. H. (1963). *Social learning and personality development.* New York: Holt, Rinehart & Winston.

Brown, S. J., Lieberman, D. A., Gemeny, B. A., Fan, Y. C., Wilson, D. M., & Pasta, D. J. (1997). Educational video game for juvenile diabetes care: Results of a controlled trial. *Medical Informatics, 22,* 77–89.

Brown, W. J., & Cody, M. J. (1991). Effects of a prosocial television soap opera in promoting women's status. *Human Communication Research, 18,* 114–142.

Chen, H-t. (2005). *Practical program evaluation: Assessing and improving planning, implementation, and effectiveness.* Thousand Oaks, CA: Sage.

Clark, M., Ghandour, G., Miller, N. H., Taylor, C. B., Bandura, A., & DeBusk, R. F. (1997). Development and evaluation of a computer-based system of dietary management of hyperlipidemia. *Journal of the American Dietetic Association, 97,* 146–150.

Clark, N., Gong, M., Kaciroti, N., Yu, J., Wu, G., Zeng, Z., et al. (2005). A trial of asthmas self-management in Beijing schools. *Chronic Illness, 1,* 31–38.

Cleland, J., Bernstein, S., Ezeh, A., Faundes, A., Glasierand, A., & Innis, J. (2006). Family planning: The unfinished agenda. *Lancet, 368,* 1810–1827.

DeBusk, R. F., Miller, N. H., Superko, H. R., Dennis, C. A., Thomas, R. J., Lew, H. T., et al. (1994). A case-management system for coronary risk factor modification. *Annals of Internal Medicine, 120,* 721–729.

Dongbo, F., McGowan, P., Yi-e, S., Lizhen, Z., Huiqin, Y., Jianguo, M., et al. (2003). Implementation and quantitative evaluation of chronic disease self-management programme in Shanghai, China: Randomized controlled trial, *Bulletin of the World Health Organization, 81,* 174–182.

Ehrlich, P. R., Ehrlich, A. H., & Daily, G. C. (1995). *The stork and the plow: The equity answer to the human dilemma.* New York: Putnam.

Fries, J. F., & Crapo, L. M. (1981). *Vitality and aging: Implications of the rectangular curve.* San Francisco: Freeman.

Fuchs, V. (1974). *Who shall live? Health economics and social choice.* New York: Basic Books.

Haskell, W. L., Alderman, E. L., Fair, J. M., Maron, D. J., Mackey, S. F., Superko, H. R., et al. (1994). Effects of intensive multiple risk factor reduction on coronary atherosclerosis and clinical cardiac events in men and women with coronary artery disease. *Circulation, 89,* 975–990.

Holman, H., & Lorig, K. (1992). Perceived self-efficacy in self-management of chronic disease. In R. Schwarzer (Ed.), *Self-efficacy: Thought control of action* (pp. 305–323). Washington, DC: Hemisphere.

Hyman D. J., Maibach E. W., Flora J. A., & Fortmann, S. P. (1992). Cholesterol treatment practices of primary care physicians. *Public Health Reports, 107,* 441–448.

Lieberman, D. A. (2001). Management of chronic pediatric diseases with interactive health games: Theory and research findings. *Journal of Ambulatory Care Management, 24,* 26–38.

Lieberman, D. A., & Brown, S. J. (1995). Designing interactive video games for children's health education. In K. Morgan, R. M. Satava, H. B. Sieburg, R. Mattheus, & J. P. Christensen (Eds.), *Interactive technology and the new paradigm for healthcare* (pp. 201–210). Amsterdam: IOS Press and Ohmsha.

Lorig, K., Chastain, R. L., Ung, E., Shoor, S., & Holman, H. (1989). Development and evaluation of a scale to measure perceived self-efficacy in people with arthritis. *Arthritis and Rheumatism, 32,* 37–44.

Lorig, K., Ritter, P., Dost, A., Plant, K., Laurent, D., & McNeil, I. (2008). The expert patients programme online, a 1-year study of an Internet-based self-management programme for people with long-term conditions. *Chronic Illness, 4,* 247–256.

Lorig, K., Ritter, P., Laurent, D., & Plant, K. (2006). Internet-based disease self-management: A randomized trial, *Medical Care, 44,* 964–971.

Lorig, K., Ritter, P., Laurent, D., & Plant, K. (2008). The Internet-based arthritis self-management program: A one-year randomized trial for patients with arthritis or fibromyalgia. *Arthritis and Rheumatism (Arthritis Care and Research), 59,* 1009–1017.

Lorig, K., Seleznick, M., Lubeck, D., Ung, E., Chastain, R. L., & Holman, H. R. (1989). The beneficial outcomes of the arthritis self-management course are not adequately explained by behavior change. *Arthritis and Rheumatism, 32,* 91–95.

Lorig, K., Sobel, D. S., Stewart, A. L., Brown, B. W., Bandura, A., Ritter, P., et al. (1999). Evidence suggesting that a chronic disease self-management program can improve health status while reducing hospitalization: A randomized trial. *Medical Care, 37,* 5–14.

Lorig, K. R., González, V., & Ritter, P. L. (1999). Community-based Spanish language arthritis education program: A randomized trial. *Medical Care, 37,* 957–963.

Lorig, K. R., & Holman, H. R. (2003). Self-management education: History, definition, outcomes, and mechanisms. *Annals of Behavioral Medicine, 26,* 1–7.

Lorig, K. R., Hurwicz, M., Sobel, D., & Hobbs, M. (2006). A national dissemination of an evidenced based self-management program: A translation study. *Patient Education and Counseling, 59,* 69–79.

Lorig, K. R., Ritter, P. L., & González, V. (2003). Hispanic chronic disease self-management: A randomized community-based outcome tiral. *Nursing Research, 52,* 361–369.

Lorig, K. R., Ritter, P. L., & Jacquez, A. (2005). Outcomes of border health Spanish/English chronic disease self-management programs. *Diabetes Educator, 31,* 401–409.

McKusick, L., Coates, T. J., Morin, S. F., Pollack, L., & Hoff, C. (1990). Longitudinal predictors of reductions in unprotected anal intercourse among gay men in San Francisco: The AIDS behavioral research project. *American Public Health, 80,* 978–983.

Muñoz, R., Lenert, L., Delucchi, K., Pérez-Stable, E., Stoddard, J., Pérez, J., et al. (2006). Toward evidence-based Internet interventions: A Spanish/English web site for international smoking cessation trials. *Nicotine and Tobacco Research, 8,* 77–87.

Nordin, I. (1999). The limits of medical practice. *Theoretical Medicine and Bioethics, 20,* 105–123.

O'Leary, A., Shoor, S., Lorig, K., & Holman, H. R. (1988). A cognitive-behavioral treatment for rheumatoid arthritis. *Health Psychology, 7,* 527–544.

Papa, M. J., Singhal, A., Law, S., Pant, S., Sood, S., Rogers, E. M., et al. (2000), Entertainment-education and social change: An analysis of parasocial interaction, social learning, collective efficacy, and paradoxical communication. *Journal of Communication, 50,* 31–55.

Poindexter, D. O. (2004). A history of entertainment-education, 1958–2000: The origins of entertainment-education. In A. Singhal, M. J. Cody, E. M., Rogers, & M. Sabido (Eds.), *Entertainment-education and social change: History, research, and practice* (pp. 21–31). Mahwah, NJ: Erlbaum.

Population Communications International. (2000). *Fifteenth anniversary.* New York: Author.

Reid, C. M., Murphy, B., Murphy, M., Maher, T., Ruth, D., & Jennings, G. (1994). Prescribing medication versus promoting behavioural change: A trial of the use of lifestyle management to replace drug treatment of hypertension in general practice. *Behaviour Change, 11,* 77–185.

Rogers, E. M., & Kincaid, D. L. (1981). *Communication networks: Toward a new paradigm for research.* New York: Free Press.

Rogers, E. M., Vaughan, P. W., Swalehe, R. M. A., Rao, N., Svenkerud, P., & Sood, S. (1999). Effects of an entertainment-education radio soap opera on family planning behavior in Tanzania. *Studies in Family Planning, 30,* 1193–1211.

Rosenthal, T. L., & Zimmerman, B. J. (1978). Social learning and cognition. New York: Academic Press.

Rudd, P. (1997). Compliance with antihypertensive therapy: Raising the bar of expectations. *American Journal of Managed Care, 4,* 957–966.

Rudd, P., Miller, N., Kaufman, J., Kraemer, H., Bandura, A., Greenwald, G., et al. (2004). Nurse management for hypertension: A systems approach. *American Journal of Hypertension, 17,* 921–927.

Ryerson, W. N. (1994). Population communications international: Its role in family planning soap operas. *Population and Environment: A Journal of Interdisciplinary Studies, 15*, 255–264.

Ryerson, W. N. (1999). *Population media center.* Shelburne, VT.

Ryerson, W. N. (2006). *Reduction of support for genital mutilation in Sudan.* Raw data.

Sabido, M. (1981). *Towards the social use of soap operas.* Mexico City, Mexico: Institute for Communication Research.

Sabido, M. (2002). *El tono* (The Tone). Mexico City: Universidad Nacional Autonoma de Mexico.

Singhal, A., Cody, M. J., Rogers, E. M., & Sabido, M. (Eds.). (2004). *Entertainment-education and social chante: History, research, and practice.* Mahwah, NJ: Erlbaum.

Singhal, A., & Rogers. E. M. (1999). *Entertainment-education: A communication strategy for social change.* Mahwah, NJ: Erlbaum.

Taylor, C., Bryson, S., Luce, K., Cunning, D., Celio, A., Abascal, L., et al. (2006). Prevention of eating disorders in at-risk college-age women. *Archives of General Psychiatry, 63*, 831–888.

Taylor, C., Winzelberg, A., & Celio, A. (2001). Use of interactive media to prevent eating disorders. In R. Striegel-Moor & L. Smolak (Eds.), *Eating disorders: New direction for research and practices* (pp. 255–270). Washington, DC: American Psychological Association.

Vaughan, P. W. (2003). *The onset of fertility transition in Tanzania during the 1990's: The role of two entertainment-education radio dramas.* Unpublished manuscript, Minneapolis, MN.

Vaughan, P. W., Rogers, E. M., Singhal, A., & Swalehe, R. M. A. (2000). Entertainment-education and HIV/AIDS prevention: A field experiment in Tanzania. *Journal of Health Communication, 5*, 81–100.

West, J. A., Bandura, A., Clark, E., Miller, N. H., Ahn, D., Greenwald, G., et al. (1999). *Self-efficacy predicts adherence to dietary sodium limitation in patients with heart failure.* Manuscript, Stanford University.

Westoff, C. F., & Rodriguez, G. (1995). The mass media and family planning in Kenya. *International Family Planning Perspectives, 21*, 26–31.

Whelton, P. K., Appel, L. J., Espeland, M. A., Applegate, W. B., Ettinger, W. H., Kostis, J. B., et al. (1998). Sodium reduction and weight loss in the treatment of hypertension in older persons. *Journal of American Medical Association, 279*, 839–846.

EDITORS' CONCLUDING COMMENTS
TO CHAPTER 2

Bandura provided a considerable amount of information about social cognitive theory and several examples from actual interventions. To help ensure that you understand the ways social cognitive theory applies to program design and evaluation, we invite you to take one of the interventions that Bandura discusses and draw out the elements of social cognitive theory on which the intervention relies. Then, based on that model, think about the various factors an evaluator might want to measure in a comprehensive, theory-driven evaluation based on Bandura's theory of change.

Bandura's comments about the need for a translational model foreshadow future chapters. In particular, Bickman and Reimer suggest that multiple theories will often need to be linked together to move from a general social psychological theory to an effective application. Before returning to this notion, we turn to another chapter that lays out a relatively general theory of change from social psychology. Like Bandura's social cognitive theory, it holds promise for application in a wide scope of programs.

EDITORS' INTRODUCTORY COMMENTS
TO CHAPTER 3

One of the ways that social psychology and program evaluation intersect is when social psychology's general theories of social behavior and behavior change are applied to programs and their evaluation. Human behavior is at the core of many major social problems, such as climate change and health crises including HIV/AIDS, obesity, coronary disease, and diabetes. Theories of behavior change offer the promise of helping to inform program development, implementation, formative improvement of programs in operation, and bottom-line summative evaluation of the merit and worth of programs. In the next chapter, social psychologist Icek Ajzen discusses the contribution of one general theory from social psychology, the theory of planned behavior (TPB), to the design and evaluation of behavioral interventions.

As Ajzen states, the theory of planned behavior posits that individual behavior generally results from three factors, the person's (1) attitude toward the behavior in question, (2) perceptions of social pressures for or against the behavior (social norms), and (3) perceptions that he or she is able to perform the behavior (perceived behavioral control). According to the theory of planned behavior, these three factors combine to predict the person's behavioral intentions, that is, the person's plans to engage in the behavior in question. Behavioral intentions, in conjunction with perceived control, are expected to translate into behavior. As Ajzen summarizes, the theory has been successful in explaining a range of behaviors, a form of success that increases confidence that TPB can be a useful guide to program design and evaluation.

Ajzen goes into detail on the way that TPB is typically tested, including how one can measure the various constructs (or conceptual variables) in the theory. As explained in the chapter, these procedures from social psychological research can provide an important guide for program development. For example, the preliminary or pilot research that goes into creating a standard TPB questionnaire can point to the specific beliefs that a program or other intervention can target to try to bring about change in the behavior of interest. The chapter offers several suggestions for program design and development. Given how often evaluators come across ineffective programs, guidance for the development of better programs is potentially quite important.

Ajzen also points out how TPB can be used in evaluation. His suggestions correspond to those made by advocates of theory-based evaluation, but refer specifically to the application of TPB. Among the benefits of TPB that Ajzen notes, consistent with the theory-driven evaluation approach discussed in subsequent chapters, is that when a program doesn't work, the theory and its methods can help identify why a program doesn't work.

CHAPTER 3

Behavioral Interventions
Design and Evaluation
Guided by the Theory of Planned Behavior

Icek Ajzen

Whether our goal is preventing disease or protecting the environment, discouraging drug abuse, or reducing intergroup conflict, modifying people's behavior is at the core of many efforts to improve the human condition. Intervention programs take many different shapes, from individual counseling to public service announcements, from small-group encounters to national campaigns. Some efforts represent long-term commitments, while others arise in response to immediate needs and are guided by little more than the practitioner's intuition. Social psychology can play an important part in these endeavors by providing suitable conceptual frameworks and methodological tools to help in the design and evaluation of behavioral interventions. Practitioners have long recognized the importance of theory as a basis for targeting an intervention and interpreting its effects (Bickman, 1987; Rossi, Lipsey, & Freeman, 2004; Weiss, 1972). In the spirit of Kurt Lewin's maxim that "there is nothing more practical than a good theory" (Lewin, 1952, p. 169), I propose the theory of planned behavior (Ajzen, 1988, 1991) as a potentially useful framework for the design and evaluation of behavioral interventions. Over the past 20 years, this theory has stimulated a wealth of research in various applied domains (Armitage & Conner, 2001), and it is being used increasingly in the context of behavioral interventions (Hardeman et al., 2002). In the first part of this chapter I describe the theory of planned behavior and the research it has generated, with particular emphasis on associated methods and procedures crucial to action research. This discussion is followed in the second part by a consideration of the theory's implications for behavioral interventions.

The Theory of Planned Behavior

First described in 1985 (Ajzen, 1985), the theory of planned behavior (TPB) is today one of the most popular social psychological models for the prediction of behavior. It has its roots in Ajzen and Fishbein's (1980) theory of reasoned action, which was developed in response to observed lack of correspondence between general dispositions, such as racial or religious attitudes, and actual behavior. Instead of dealing with broad attitudes of this kind, the TPB focuses on the behavior itself, and it goes beyond attitudes to consider such other influences on behavior as social norms and self-efficacy beliefs (for a recent overview of the theory, see Ajzen, 2005).

Briefly, according to the theory of planned behavior, human action is influenced by three major factors: a favorable or unfavorable evaluation of the behavior (attitude toward the behavior); perceived social pressure to perform or not perform the behavior (subjective norm); and perceived capability to perform the behavior (self-efficacy [Bandura, 1997]), or perceived behavioral control. In combination, attitude toward the behavior, subjective norm, and perception of behavioral control lead to the formation of a behavioral intention. As a general rule, the more favorable the attitude and subjective norm, and the greater the perceived behavioral control, the stronger should be the person's intention to perform the behavior in question. The relative importance of the three predictors as determinants of intentions can vary from behavior to behavior and from population to population. Finally, given a sufficient degree of control over the behavior, people are expected to carry out their intentions when the opportunity arises. Unfortunately, although we may be able to measure some aspects of actual control, in most instances we lack sufficient information about all the relevant factors that may facilitate or impede performance of the behavior. However, to the extent that people are realistic in their judgments, a measure of perceived behavioral control can serve as a proxy for actual control and contribute to prediction of the behavior in question. A schematic representation of the theory is shown in Figure 3.1. The solid arrow pointing from actual control to the intention–behavior link indicates that volitional control is expected to moderate the intention–behavior relation such that the effect of intention on behavior is stronger when actual control is high rather than low. That perceived behavioral control, when veridical, can serve as a proxy for actual control and be used to improve prediction of behavior is shown by the dotted arrows in Figure 3.1 that connect actual control to perceived control and perceived control to the intention–behavior link.[1]

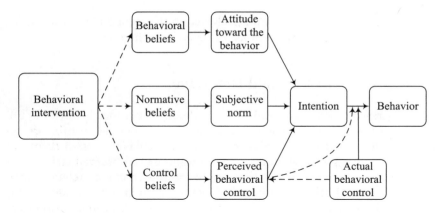

FIGURE 3.1. Expected effects of a behavioral intervention in the theory of planned behavior.

The Cognitive Foundation of Behavior

The TPB assumes that human social behavior is reasoned or planned in the sense that people take account of a behavior's likely consequences (behavioral beliefs), the normative expectations of important referents (normative beliefs), and factors that may facilitate or impede performance of the behavior (control beliefs). Although the behavioral, normative, and control beliefs people hold may sometimes be inaccurate, unfounded, or biased, their attitudes, subjective norms, and perceptions of behavioral control are thought to follow spontaneously and reasonably from these beliefs, produce a corresponding behavioral intention, and ultimately result in behavior that is consistent with the overall tenor of the beliefs.

Behavioral Beliefs and Attitudes

In the TPB, attitude toward a behavior is assumed to be a function of beliefs about the behavior's likely consequences (behavioral beliefs), together with the valence (positive or negative) attached to those consequences. A behavioral belief is a person's estimation of the likelihood (subjective probability) that performing a particular behavior will lead to a certain outcome. In their aggregate, behavioral beliefs produce a positive or negative overall attitude toward the behavior. Specifically, the positive or negative valence of each outcome contributes to the overall attitude in direct proportion to the subjective probability that the behavior will produce the outcome in question. For instance, a person might believe that it is unlikely (subjective probability) that regular exercise (the behavior) will improve physical fitness (a positive outcome). This same individual may also believe it is extremely likely that regular exercise will increase overall fatigue (a negative outcome). Here, the presumed likelihood of experiencing negative consequences from exercise outweighs the presumed likelihood of positive consequences. Under an expectancy-value model of attitude (Feather, 1982; Fishbein, 1963), this individual should hold a slightly negative attitude toward regular exercise.

People can form and hold many different beliefs about any given behavior, but only a relatively small number—perhaps 5 to 10—are readily accessible in memory. It is these accessible or salient beliefs that are assumed to be the prevailing determinants of the attitude. It follows that if we want to understand why people hold favorable or unfavorable attitudes toward a given behavior, and how their attitudes might be changed, we have to examine their salient behavioral beliefs. As we shall see, these beliefs are elicited in preliminary research with a representative sample of the research population.

Normative Beliefs and Subjective Norms

In an analogous fashion, salient normative beliefs constitute the basis for perceived social pressure, or subjective norms. A normative belief is a person's estimation of the likelihood (subjective probability) that a given referent individual or group (e.g., friends, family, one's physician or supervisor) would approve or disapprove of performing the behavior under investigation. The strength of the subjective norm is determined by the person's motivation to comply with the referent individual or group. For instance, an individual might believe that it is extremely likely that his family would approve of him engaging in regular physical exercise but only somewhat likely that his friends would approve of the same behavior. If the motivation to comply with friends is high, relative to the motivation to comply with family, this individual should only feel a moderate amount of social pressure (subjective norm) to engage in regular exercise.

Control Beliefs and Perceived Behavioral Control

Just as attitudes are based on salient behavioral beliefs and subjective norms on salient normative beliefs, so is perceived behavioral control based on salient control beliefs. These beliefs are concerned with the presence of factors that can facilitate or inhibit performance of the behavior. Control factors include required skills and abilities, availability or lack of time and money, cooperation by other people, and so forth.

A control belief is defined as a person's estimation of the likelihood (subjective probability) that a given facilitating or inhibiting factor will be present. For instance, I might believe that it is extremely unlikely that I will have enough time to exercise over the lunch hour. At the same time, I might be extremely confident that I have the requisite skills to exercise. Each control belief contributes to perceived behavioral control, or a sense of self-efficacy, in direct proportion to the factor's perceived power to facilitate or impede performance of the behavior. For instance, despite a high expectation of my ability to exercise, time pressures at work may exert more power to impede my exercise behavior, in effect, reducing perceived control over my exercise behavior.

Constructing a Standard TPB Questionnaire

A complete theory of planned behavior questionnaire includes measures of behavioral, normative, and control beliefs; measures of attitude toward the behavior, subjective norm, and perceived behavioral control; as well as measures of intention and, often, current or past behavior. The actual behavior to be predicted is assessed at a later point in time.

The Principle of Compatibility

Defining the Behavior

The first and in some ways most important preparation for constructing a standard TPB questionnaire is the identification of the behavior of interest. Any behavior can be defined in terms of four elements: the action, the target at which the action is directed, the context in which it is performed, and its time of occurrence (Ajzen & Fishbein, 1977). Consider the case of "using ecstasy at least once a week in the company of friends during the next 12 months." Defining this behavior's elements is somewhat arbitrary. The target element is the drug ecstasy. Using (i.e., taking the drug) is clearly part of the action element, but we could also include "at least once a week" in this element. Alternatively, once a week might be considered part of the time element, which would consist of "at least once a week during the next 12 months." Finally, "in the company of friends" defines the context element.

Compatibility

No matter how the elements of the behavior are defined, it is important to observe the principle of compatibility (Ajzen, 1988; Ajzen & Fishbein, 1980), which requires that all other constructs (attitude, subjective norm, perceived behavioral control, and intention) be defined in terms of exactly the same elements. Thus, the attitude compatible with this behavior is the attitude toward using ecstasy at least once a week in the company of friends during the next 12 months, the subjective norm is the perceived social pressure to do so, perceived behavior control refers to control over performing the defined behavior, and the intention to be assessed is the intention to perform this very behavior.

Specificity and Generality

The behavior in the above example is quite specific and would usually be of little interest. It is possible to increase the generality of one or more of its elements by means of aggregation or generalization. In fact, the time element "in the next 12 months" is already defined at a more general level than, say, "next Tuesday at 5:00 P.M." Similarly, in many cases we may not be particularly interested in a specific context. Thus, we may want to predict and understand use of ecstasy, regardless of the context (alone at home, in a bar with strangers, in the company of friends) in which it occurs. We can generalize the context element by recording how often the behavior is performed in all relevant contexts. The behavior would then be defined more simply as "using ecstasy at least once a week in the next 12 months."

A comparable argument can be made with respect to the target element. We may be concerned about use of illicit drugs in general, rather than use of ecstasy alone, in which case we would have to generalize across use of such different drugs as ecstasy, marijuana, cocaine, heroin, LSD, and so forth. The behavior of interest is then defined as "using illicit drugs at least once a week in the next 12 months."

Qualitative Preliminary Research

In the context of the TPB, substantive information about the considerations that guide people's behavior is obtained by examining the behavioral, normative, and control beliefs that are salient in the research population. These beliefs will often differ not only from one behavior to another but also from one population to another and even among subgroups in the same population. Moreover, salient beliefs will tend to change over time as people are exposed to new information. An accurate portrait of prevailing salient beliefs can therefore only be obtained by eliciting these beliefs from a representative sample of the research population. In the formative phase of the research, participants are given a few minutes to list the advantages and the disadvantages of performing the defined behavior (behavioral beliefs), the individuals or groups who approve and those who disapprove of the behavior (normative beliefs), and the factors that can facilitate or impede behavioral performance (control beliefs). In most applications, a given individual's own salient beliefs are of little interest. Instead, the beliefs listed by all participants in the pilot phase are content-analyzed, and the most frequently mentioned beliefs of each type are used to construct modal sets, that is, sets that represent the salient behavioral, normative, and control beliefs prevalent in the research population.

Quantification of TPB Constructs

The questionnaire used in the main part of the research quantifies the various TPB constructs. One purpose of the questionnaire is to assess salient beliefs. Two properties are assessed with respect to each behavioral beliefs: the strength of the belief that performing the behavior will produce a certain outcome and the positive/negative valence of that outcome. Suppose that one of the salient behavioral beliefs about using illicit drugs is that they help me unwind after a long day at work. As a measure of belief strength, participants are asked, typically on 7-point rating scales, how much they agree or disagree that using illicit drugs helps them to unwind after a long day at work or how likely or unlikely they judge this to be the case. To assess the valence of the outcome, they are asked to rate "unwinding after a long day at work" on a 7-point evaluative scale, such as a good–bad scale.

In a similar fashion, pairs of items assess normative and control beliefs. If friends were found to be one of the salient referents for the behavior of using illicit drugs, participants would be asked to rate how much their friends approve or disapprove of their performing this behavior (normative belief strength) and how motivated they are to comply with their friends.[2] Finally, suppose that one of the salient control factors identified in the pilot study was being offered drugs by friends. With respect to this factor, participants would be asked to rate the likelihood that they will be offered drugs by friends (in the next 12 months—control belief strength) and to what extent being offered drugs by friends would make it easier or more difficult for them to use illicit drugs (power of control factor).

In addition to assessing salient beliefs, the standard TPB questionnaire also secures measures of attitude, subjective norm, perceived behavioral control, and intention. It is common practice to use relatively simple, direct questions to assess these constructs. Attitudinal items are evaluative in nature, and bipolar adjective scales, such as good–bad, pleasant–unpleasant, and desirable–undesirable, are typically employed to assess attitudes toward the behavior—in our example, attitudes toward using illicit drugs in the next 12 months. Subjective norm items assess the extent to which important others would approve or disapprove of the behavior. Examples are, "Most people who are important to me think I should—I should not use illicit drugs in the next 12 months" and "It is expected of me that I not use illicit drugs in the next 12 months (likely–unlikely). To assess perceived control over performance of the behavior, we can formulate such items as, "It is up to me whether I use illicit drugs in the next 12 months" (agree–disagree) and "If I want to, I can abstain from using illicit drugs in the next 12 months" (likely–unlikely). Finally, a measure of intention is obtained with the aid of such direct questions as "I intend to use illicit drugs in the next 12 months" (disagree–agree) and "I have no plans of using illicit drugs in the next 12 months" (definitely false–definitely true).

Even though items of this kind appear to have face validity, development of the direct measures must observe accepted psychometric principles. This can be assured in the context of the preliminary research. Specifically, sets of items—perhaps as many as 8 or 10—are formulated for each construct, and the criterion of internal consistency (e.g., item-total correlations) is used to select items that best represent the intended constructs and that clearly discriminate among them.

As noted earlier, the standard TPB questionnaire will usually also include measures of current behavior. Participants can be asked whether they are currently using illicit drugs (frequently–sometimes–rarely–never), and how often they have used illicit drugs in the past, say in the past 12 months. As we shall see later in this chapter, these measures can be used to explore differences between users and nonusers of illicit drugs in terms of their beliefs, attitudes, subjective norms, perceptions of control, and behavioral intentions. For purposes of prediction, a measure of behavior is obtained later, as defined by the behavior's time element. In our example, we would reinterview participants one year after administration of the questionnaire to assess their drug use during the preceding 12 months.

Understanding Prevailing Behavior Patterns

Once constructed in accordance with the principles described above, the TPB questionnaire can be administered to a representative sample of the research population. Before we proceed to look for substantive explanations of the behavior, however, we must validate the theory's applicability to the current context. Hierarchical regression and structural equation techniques are typically used for this purpose. A measure of (current or later) behavior is predicted from intentions and perceived behavioral control; and intentions are in turn predicted from attitudes, subjective norms, and perceptions of control. These analyses provide information about the amount of variance in intentions and behavior that is explained by the theory's predictors. In addition, correlations are computed between belief aggregates and the corresponding measures of attitude, subjective norm, and perceived behavioral control. These correlations tell us how well the salient behavioral, normative, and control beliefs identified in the pilot study can account for the constructs they are assumed to explain.[3]

Empirical Support for the TPB

A large number of studies have applied the theory of planned behavior to examine the psychological antecedents of actions in various domains. It is beyond the scope of the present chapter to review this body of research (for summaries and meta-analyses, see Ajzen, 1991; Albarracin, Johnson,

Fishbein, & Muellerleile, 2001; Armitage & Conner, 2001; Downs & Hausenblas, 2005; Godin & Kok, 1996; Hagger, Chatzisarantis, & Biddle, 2002). Suffice it to note that, generally speaking, the theory has been well supported. Thus, with regard to the prediction of behavior, many studies have substantiated the predictive validity of behavioral intentions. Reviewing different meta-analyses covering diverse behavioral domains, Sheeran (2002) reported a mean correlation of .53 between intention and behavior. Also, it has been found that the addition of perceived behavioral control can improve prediction of behavior considerably, especially when performance of the behavior is difficult (Madden, Ellen, & Ajzen, 1992). For example, in a general sample of smokers, a measure of perceived behavioral control accounted for an additional 12% of the variance in smoking behavior over and above intentions; among postnatal women, the increase in explained behavioral variance due to perceived behavioral control was 34% (Godin, Valois, Lepage, & Desharnais, 1992).

Meta-analyses of the empirical literature have also provided evidence showing that intentions can be predicted with considerable accuracy from measures of attitudes toward the behavior, subjective norms, and perceived behavioral control or self-efficacy (Albarracin et al., 2001; Armitage & Conner, 2001; Hagger et al., 2002; Sheeran & Taylor, 1999). For a wide range of behaviors, attitudes are found to correlate well with intentions; across the different meta-analyses, the mean correlations ranged from .45 to .60. For the prediction of intentions from subjective norms, these correlations ranged from .34 to .42, and for the prediction of intention from perceived behavioral control, the range was .35 to .46. The multiple correlations for the prediction of intentions were found to range from .63 to .71.

Finally, the meta-analysis performed by Armitage and Conner (2001) also provided evidence for the proposition that attitudes, subjective norms, and perceptions of control can be predicted from corresponding sets of beliefs. The mean correlation between the expectancy-value index of behavioral beliefs and a direct measure of attitude toward the behavior was .50, and the same mean correlation was obtained between the normative belief index and subjective norm; the control belief index showed a mean correlation of .52 with perceived behavioral control.

Comparing Subgroups to Explain Intentions and Behavior

After establishing the overall fit of the model to our data, we turn to a detailed examination of behavioral, normative, and control beliefs in an effort to obtain substantive information about the behavior's determinants. By comparing subgroups of participants who are currently performing and not performing the behavior, or those who intend to perform it in the future with those who don't, we can gain insight into the considerations that guide people's actions. Research by Conner, Sherlock, and Orbell (1998) provides an example in the domain of illicit drug use. In the second of their two studies, members of a nightclub completed a theory of planned behavior questionnaire with respect to using ecstasy in the next two months. The sample was divided into those who held positive or neutral intentions to use ecstasy in the next two months (neutral or above neutral on the intention scale) and those who held negative intentions. The two groups were then compared in terms of their behavioral, normative, and control beliefs.[4] These comparisons revealed significant differences between participants with positive and negative intentions on almost all behavioral beliefs. For example, compared with the negative intention group, participants who held positive intentions judged it more likely that using ecstasy in the next two months would give them a sense of well-being, would be exciting, and would make them sociable; and as less likely that it would bring on mood swings, lead to physical side effects, or lead to the use of other drugs. There were, however, no significant differences in the judged likelihood that ecstasy use would produce a feeling of lethargy or that it would lead to more frequent use of the drug.

The influence of normative beliefs on intentions was also in evidence. In general, important others (close friends, partner, parents, other club members, and other ecstasy users) were believed to disapprove of ecstasy use. However, the subgroup of participants who intended to use ecstasy in the next two months saw their close friends and partners as disapproving less than did the participants who did not intend to use the drug. The differences with respect to other club members, other ecstasy users, and parents were not statistically significant; these referents were seen to be about equally disapproving of the behavior.

Finally, there were also significant differences in control beliefs. For example, people who intended to use ecstasy in the next two months were less likely to believe that they would have to pay a high price for the drug, and more likely to believe that they would be offered ecstasy and be with friends who use the drug.

Background Factors

According to the TPB, then, the major predictors of intentions and behavior follow reasonably from—and can be understood in terms of—behavioral, normative, and control beliefs. This approach, however, does not address the origins of these beliefs. Clearly, a multitude of variables could potentially influence the beliefs people hold: age, gender, ethnicity, socioeconomic status, education, nationality, religious affiliation, personality, general attitudes and values, intelligence, past experiences, exposure to new information, and so forth. The theory recognizes the potential importance of such factors, but they are considered background variables that can influence behavior indirectly by affecting behavioral, normative, and control beliefs. However, whether a particular background factor does indeed have an impact on beliefs is an empirical question. Furthermore, given the large number of potentially relevant background factors, it is difficult to know which should be considered without a content-specific theory to guide selection in the behavioral domain of interest. Content theories of this kind are not part of the TPB but can complement it by identifying relevant background factors and thereby extending our understanding of a behavior's determinants (see Petraitis, Flay, & Miller, 1995). With the aid of the theory of planned behavior we can not only examine whether a given background factor is related to the behavior of interest but also explain such an effect by tracing it to differences in behavior-relevant beliefs.

To give just one example, consider a study on outdoor recreational activities, including hunting (Hrubes, Ajzen, & Daigle, 2001). Participants in this study were hunters and nonhunting outdoor recreationists who completed a TPB questionnaire with respect to hunting. The questionnaire also assessed frequency of hunting during the preceding year, which served as the behavioral criterion. Regression of hunting frequency on intentions and perceived behavioral control resulted in a highly significant multiple correlation of .62; the multiple correlation for prediction of hunting intentions from attitudes toward hunting, subjective norms, and perceptions of control was .93.

The study also examined education as a potentially important background factor. Participants reported level of education ranging from failure to graduate from high school to postgraduate education. Level of education was found to have a correlation of –.52 with hunting intentions and –.35 with past hunting frequency, both highly significant. As educational level increased, intentions to go hunting and actual hunting behavior declined. Examination of salient behavioral, normative, and control beliefs helped to explain these effects. There were very few significant differences due to level of education in evaluations of outcomes associated with hunting, but there were large differences in perceptions that hunting would produce these outcomes. Among other disparities in behavioral beliefs, the more highly educated were less likely to expect that hunting enables them to view scenery and enjoy nature, to create or maintain significant relationships with family and friends, to relax and relieve stress, or to feel a sense of competence. With respect to normative support, the more educated participants were significantly less likely to believe that their friends or their families would encourage them to go hunting. Finally, control beliefs also revealed significant differences due to education, with the more highly educated likely to indicate that they were too busy to go hunting, that they lacked the requisite knowledge and skills, and that it would take great effort for them to go hunting.

The mediating function of beliefs was revealed by hierarchical regression analyses in which either hunting intentions or hunting frequency was regressed on level of education while controlling for the summed indices of behavioral, normative, and control beliefs. In the prediction of intentions, level of education barely raised the multiple correlation, from .885 to .893, and although this increase was statistically significant due to the large sample size ($N = 370$), the increase in explained variance was only 1%. When the criterion was hunting behavior, the multiple correlation based on the three belief indices was .54, and this correlation increased to .55 with the addition of educational level, accounting for less than 1% additional variance, an increase that was not statistically significant.

In short, although the TPB does not tell us whether a given background factor should or should not influence a given behavior, once an influential factor has been identified, the theory allows us to examine the reasons for its effect. Specifically, the theory postulates that background factors exert their influence on intentions and behavior indirectly by affecting the beliefs that provide the basis for the formation of intentions and thus for performance of behavior. It is not unreasonable to expect, for example, that the social background and life experiences of individuals with a relatively high level of education will lead them to form very different behavioral, normative, and control beliefs about hunting than one would find among individuals with lower levels of education. These differences in beliefs will produce differences in attitudes toward hunting, in subjective norms with respect to hunting, as well as in perceptions of behavioral control. These differences will then also be reflected in hunting intentions and actual hunting behavior.

Behavioral Interventions

The discussion up to this point suggests that, to be effective, behavioral interventions must change the behavioral, normative, and control beliefs that, according to the theory of planned behavior, guide performance of behavior. A behavioral intervention is in many ways similar to a background factor, as can be seen in Figure 3.1. Individuals subjected to an intervention are exposed to new information or experiences that may well change some of their behavior-relevant beliefs and, as a result, affect their intentions and behavior. However, the effectiveness of an intervention is not guaranteed. If it is found to influence behavior, its effects should be traceable to changes in beliefs. If the intervention fails to produce the desired behavioral change, then the theory of planned behavior can, as we shall see, help to identify the reasons for the failure.

Targeting an Intervention

Prior to designing a behavioral intervention, it is necessary to conduct preliminary research in which a standard TPB questionnaire is administered to a representative sample of the population under consideration. Because beliefs and, therefore, attitudes, subjective norms, and perceptions of control, can vary from population to population, and in the same population over time, we cannot rely for this information on research conducted in other populations or in the more distant past. By measuring the various components of the TPB, we can gain insight into the attitudinal, normative, and control factors that determine intentions and behavior. The most detailed, substantive information is provided by examining the specific behavioral, normative, and control beliefs that discriminate between individuals inclined and disinclined to perform the behavior of interest. By conducting regression or structural equation analyses of the data obtained in the pilot work, we also obtain information about the relative contributions of attitudes, subjective norms, and perceptions of behavioral control to the prediction of intentions; and about the relative contributions of intentions and perceptions of control to the prediction of behavior. All of this information can help guide development of an intervention strategy.

Mean Levels of Predictor Variables

When selecting targets for the behavioral intervention, that is, which beliefs we will try to change, one obvious consideration is whether there is much room for change in the designated target. Consider, for example, an intervention designed to reduce consumption of high-fat food among women over 40. If the preliminary research shows that, on average, women in this age group believe strongly that reducing consumption of high-fat food will result in loss of body fat, an intervention designed to strengthen this belief is unlikely to influence attitudes or behavior. The preliminary research may, however, also reveal a relatively low subjective probability associated with the belief that reducing the consumption of high-fat foods will lower the risk of developing diabetes. Because there is sufficient room for change, and virtually all women will value the outcome (lowering the risk of diabetes) positively, an intervention designed to strengthen this behavioral belief is likely to be more effective.

Relative Weights of Predictor Variables

If the preliminary research shows that there is room for change in at least some of the behavioral, normative, and control beliefs, additional considerations are the relative contributions of attitudes, subjective norms, and perceptions of control in the prediction of intentions and behavior. Generally speaking, the greater the relative weight of a given component, the more likely it is that changing that component will influence intentions and behavior (Ajzen, 1971; Trafimow & Fishbein, 1994a, 1994b). Consider, for example, a case in which attitudes toward the behavior explain a great deal of variance in intentions, subjective norms and perceptions of behavioral control contribute relatively little, and intentions account for most of the variance in behavior. It would seem reasonable to direct the intervention at behavioral beliefs in an attempt to make attitudes toward the behavior more favorable, thus affecting intentions and behavior.

This is not the only possible approach, however, and it may not even be the most effective approach. Estimates of the relative weights of attitudes, subjective norms, and perceptions of behavioral control are provided by standardized regression coefficients or by path coefficients. These weights are usually interpreted as corresponding to the relative importance of the predictors. Unfortunately, regression or path coefficients are affected by factors that may have little to do with the relative importance of the different predictors. Importantly, they are influenced by the degree of variance in the items used to assess the predictors. To return to the above example, imagine that a large proportion of women in the research population has low perceived control over reducing their consumption of high-fat foods. Because of the low variability in responses, this factor would not correlate well with intentions or behavior and would thus receive a low regression or path coefficient. Nevertheless, an intervention that succeeded in raising the level of perceived behavioral control among an appreciable proportion of women might well be effective. Moreover, following the intervention, there may be much more variability in perceived behavioral control, and we may now see a strong coefficient for this factor in the prediction of intentions and behavior.

In short, there are important differences between understanding the factors that control current behavior and how changes in these factors will impact later intentions and actions. A high regression coefficient suggests that the predictor in question is an important determinant of current intentions, and research suggests that targeting this predictor will tend to have a relatively strong impact on intentions. The implication of a weak regression or path coefficient, however, is less clear. It may correctly indicate that the predictor in question is not an important factor for the behavior and population under consideration. In that case, even if it were changed, it would have little impact on behavior. However, the regression coefficient for a given predictor may be low for other reasons, and, to the extent that there is room for change, it is possible that raising or lowering the average level of the predictor will have a significant impact on intentions and actions.

Targeting Belief Strength versus Scale Value

We saw that behavioral beliefs associate a behavior with certain outcomes, and they determine the attitude toward the behavior in line with the subjective values of these outcomes. The stronger the belief (i.e., the greater the perceived probability that the behavior will produce a given outcome) and the more favorable or unfavorable the outcome (its scale value), the stronger is the impact of the belief on the attitude. Similarly, subjective norms are determined by beliefs that specific referent individuals or groups approve of the behavior (belief strength) and motivation to comply with those referents (scale value). And perceived behavioral control is a function of the perceived probability that certain control factors are present (belief strength) and the power of these factors to facilitate or inhibit performance of the behavior (scale value).

To change attitude, subjective norm, or perceived behavioral control, it is possible to attack either the strength of some of the relevant beliefs, or to attack their scale values. Imagine, for example, that among the accessible behavioral beliefs about performing breast self-examinations (BSE) identified in pilot work is the belief that this procedure can lead to discovery of lumps that turn out to be benign, and that this possibility is valued negatively. In an intervention designed to promote BSE, we could try to persuade women either that this outcome is much less likely than they anticipate (change belief strength) or that discovery of benign lumps is not undesirable, perhaps because it is possible to get a quick check in the doctor's office. It is an empirical question which of these two approaches will work better. In any event, it is important to realize that changing one or two beliefs may not be sufficient to produce a change in attitude. In fact, a change in one belief may be offset by unanticipated changes in other beliefs (see Fishbein & Ajzen, 1981). Thus, women who are persuaded that discovering benign lumps is actually desirable (because the diagnosis can be quickly confirmed by a visit to the doctor's office) may also come to believe that having regular check-ups is more effective than performing self-examinations. Only when the balance of beliefs in the total aggregate shifts in the desired direction can we expect a change in attitude toward the behavior. Similar considerations apply to normative beliefs and motivation to comply, and to control beliefs and perceived power.

Attacking Existing Beliefs versus Introducing New Beliefs

It is often easier to produce change by introducing information designed to lead to the formation of new beliefs than it is to change existing beliefs. Elicitation of beliefs in the pilot study identifies not only beliefs that are salient in the population of interest, but also many beliefs that are not readily accessible, that is, beliefs mentioned by only a small proportion of respondents. For example, one or two participants in the pilot study may mention that performing breast self-examination produces a feeling of competence. Because most women do not associate this outcome with the behavior, it could be made a target of the intervention. To the extent that women come to believe it, their attitudes toward breast self-examination may become more favorable.

Accuracy of Beliefs

Beliefs represent the information people have about a behavior: its likely consequences, the normative expectations of others, and the likely impediments to its performance. Behavioral interventions provide information that changes some of these beliefs or that leads to the formation of new beliefs. It is important that the information provided be as accurate as possible. The ethical reasons for this requirement are obvious, but there are more practical reasons as well. We may be able to change attitudes, subjective norms, or perceptions of behavioral control by providing powerful but inaccurate information relevant to these factors. In the short term, this may actually be quite effective in that we may see attempts at behavioral expressions of the changes produced by the intervention. In the long run, however, people will realize that the promised consequences do not materialize, that important referents do not really expect them to perform the behavior, or that they do not, after all, have the required skills and resources to perform it. As a result, intentions and behavior will often revert to what they were prior to the intervention. Only when the new beliefs accurately reflect reality can we expect that the effect of the intervention will persist over time.

Deliberation versus Implementation

Stage models of behavior change have become increasingly popular over the past decade, especially in the domain of health psychology (Weinstein, Rothman, & Sutton, 1998). Generally speaking, these models postulate that behavior change involves movement through a sequence of discrete, qualitatively different phases. Distinctly different strategies are assumed to be required to promote change at different stages in the sequence. Many variants of stage models have been proposed, but by far the most popular is the transtheoretical model (Prochaska & DiClemente, 1983). In its most recent formulation, six stages of change are delineated: precontemplation, contemplation, preparation, action, maintenance, and termination (Prochaska & Norcross, 2002).

The theory of planned behavior is not inconsistent with a stage perspective, but it focuses on a single distinction between contemplation or deliberation on one hand and action on the other. This view parallels Gollwitzer's (Gollwitzer, 1999; Gollwitzer, Heckhausen, & Sellers, 1990) distinction between deliberative and implemental mindsets (see also Heckhausen, 1991). The deliberative phase is motivational in character. At this stage, people contemplate performance of a behavior and arrive at an intention to perform (or not to perform) the behavior in question. The TPB specifies the personal (attitude), social (subjective norm), and environmental or internal (perceived control) factors that guide this process. Once an intention to perform a behavior has been formed, individuals enter the implementation phase, which involves translating the intention into action.

It follows from this analysis that a behavioral intervention must accomplish two major objectives: it must motivate individuals to perform the behavior and, once this has been accomplished, it must ensure that the behavior will be carried out. Different strategies will usually be required to attain these objectives. Interventions based on the TPB target behavioral, normative, and / or control beliefs in an effort to produce positive intentions among participants who, prior to the intervention, either did not contemplate performing the behavior or were disinclined to do so. In the implementation stage, the theory focuses on control issues, dealing with internal and external factors that can facilitate or inhibit performance of the intended behavior.

The analysis also suggests that an intervention may fail to change behavior for two reasons. First, it may not effect the desired changes in behavioral, normative, and control beliefs; or obtained changes in the targeted beliefs may be offset by countervailing changes in other beliefs. As a result, attitudes, subjective norms, and perceptions of control will remain unchanged, and there will be no change in intentions. Second, if intentions have changed as expected, personal or environmental factors may prevent people from carrying out their newly formed intentions. Below we briefly consider strategies of intervention designed to produce changes in intentions and strategies that can help people translate those intentions into action.

Intervention Strategies

We have seen that the theory of planned behavior and its accompanying methodology can provide information about a behavior's determinants as well as general guidelines for behavior change strategies. It does not tell us, however, how to design a behavior change intervention. The theory is silent as to how beliefs are to be changed or how we can increase the likelihood that a newly formed intention will be carried out. However, social psychology offers a variety of possible approaches to behavior change that can be brought to bear on this issue.

Changing Beliefs

A number of available change strategies can influence the way people view performance of a behavior. These strategies range from one-on-one encounters, as in the case of a counseling or therapy session, through group discussions and workshops, to mass media campaigns, such as public service announcements. It is beyond the scope of this chapter to review these different approaches. Two examples will serve to illustrate use of different methods designed to motivate performance of a behavior in the context of the TPB.

Brubaker and Fowler (1990) reported the results of an intervention to encourage men to perform testicular self-examinations (TSEs) in order to enhance the chances of early detection of testicular cancer. In addition to testing the effectiveness of the intervention, this study also provided information about changes in some of the underlying determinants of the behavior. Male college students were exposed to a tape-recorded message based on the TPB that was designed to challenge unfavorable beliefs about the consequences of performing TSE. Participants in a second condition of the experiment were exposed to a message of equal length that provided general information about testicular cancer, and participants in a control condition received no message at all. All participants then completed a TPB questionnaire and, four weeks later, reported whether they had performed TSE in the interim.

The results of the study showed the effectiveness of the theory-based intervention. In the no-message control group, about 19% of the participants reported having performed TSE at the end of the 4-week period. This compares with about 44% in the general information group and fully 71% in the theory-based message condition. A structural equation analysis showed that exposure to the messages influenced beliefs with respect to performing TSE; that these changes in beliefs affected attitudes toward the behavior, subjective norms, and perceptions of behavioral control; and that changes in these three factors raised intentions to perform TSE, which, in turn, led to the observed increase in reported testicular self-examination.

Or, to take another example, consider a community-based intervention designed to increase condom use to prevent AIDS and other sexually transmitted diseases (Fishbein et al., 1997). The materials used in this intervention were role model stories designed to influence attitudes, subjective norms, or perceived behavioral control. Volunteers from the community distributed newsletters that contained the intervention materials. The stories had been related by members of the community who described how they had changed their beliefs or behaviors regarding condom use. Preliminary research was conducted to elicit accessible behavioral, normative, and control beliefs; to classify the population along a stage of change continuum; and to identify the accessible beliefs that discriminated between people at different stages. Because each community newsletter contained two or three role model stories, it was possible to target different stories to subpopulations at different stages of change. Clearly, the intervention used a mixture of techniques: It relied on the TPB to identify the critical beliefs to be changed, it borrowed from the transtheoretical model to segment the target population into different stages, and it drew from social cognitive theory (Bandura, 1986) for the use of role modeling. The intervention was found to be quite effective, producing changes in behavioral, normative, and control beliefs, and these changes were found to be reflected in intended and actual condom use.

Interventions based on the theory of planned behavior have used a variety of other methods as well. They have attempted to change intentions and behavior by enrolling individuals in an intensive 2-week workshop designed to change job-search strategies (Van Ryn & Vinokur, 1992), by introducing a prepaid bus ticket to encourage bus use (Bamberg, Ajzen, & Schmidt, 2003), by means of a short lecture delivered by a dental health educator to persuade mothers to limit their babies' sugar intake (Beale & Manstead, 1991), by placing a poster in student dormitories to encourage testicular self-examination (Brubaker & Wickersham, 1990), and by a variety of other intervention methods (see Hardeman et al., 2002 for a review). All of these strategies rest on the assumption that changes in behavioral, normative, and control beliefs are a prerequisite for changes in intentions and behavior. Dual-mode theories of persuasion, such as the elaboration likelihood model (Petty & Cacioppo, 1986) and the heuristic-systematic model (Chaiken, 1980), have shown that lasting belief change depends to an important degree on the mental engagement of the audience, in the sense that those exposed to an intervention need to process the information it contains in a systematic fashion, elaborating on its implications for them. This is often a difficult condition to meet in real-life settings, perhaps being one of the reasons for many an intervention's failure. If participants are unmotivated or unable to process the contents of an intervention carefully, the intervention is unlikely to be effective.

Closing the Intention–Behavior Gap

It is a common observation that people do not always act on their stated intentions. Empirical research on this problem can be traced to LaPiere's (1934) classic study on racial prejudice. A Chinese couple stopped at over 250 restaurants, coffee shops, hotels, motels, and inns while touring the United States and was admitted and received service without hesitation in 95% of the instances; yet in response to a letter of inquiry, 92% of the establishments replied that they would not accept members of the Chinese race. Subsequent investigations have produced similar findings. For example, among female college students who indicated intentions to release their photos with an African American male for a variety of purposes, approximately 40% failed to follow through (Linn, 1965), and in the health domain, between 26 and 57% of respondents failed to carry out their intentions to use condoms, to undergo a cancer screening, or to exercise (Sheeran, 2002).

Clearly, merely inducing favorable intentions may not be enough to produce a change in the target behavior. In these instances, two interventions may be required, one to produce the desired intention and another, very different intervention to facilitate performance of the intended behavior. When asked to explain why they failed to act on their intentions, people often mention that they simply forgot or that it slipped their minds (Orbell, Hodgkins, & Sheeran, 1997; Sheeran & Orbell, 1999). When this is the major problem, a very effective means for closing the intention–behavior gap is to prompt people to form an implementation intention (Gollwitzer, 1999). Simply asking people when, where, and how they will carry out their intentions greatly increases the likelihood that they will do so (Armitage, 2004; Sheeran & Orbell, 1999, 2000; Verplanken & Faes, 1999).

An example of this approach in the context of the theory of planned behavior is provided by a study of breast self-examination among female students and administrative staff (Orbell et al., 1997). Following administration of a TPB questionnaire, a subgroup of women in the intervention condition was asked to write down where and when they would perform breast self-examinations, that is, to formulate implementation intentions. This intervention was found to be highly effective. At the end of a 1-month follow-up, 64% of women who had established implementation intentions reported that they had performed self-examinations as opposed to only 14% in the no-intervention control group. All women in the implementation intention group who had indicated clear intentions to perform the examination reported actually doing so, whereas in the control group, of the women who intended to perform the examination, only 53% actually did.

If forgetting is indeed the main reason for failure to carry out intentions in a particular context, we could also try timely reminders as a possible intervention strategy. However, it should be clear that implementation intentions or reminders will be effective only to the extent that the individuals targeted by the intervention have the intention to perform the behavior in question. If they do not intend to perform the behavior, it makes little sense to ask them to plan how, where, and when they will implement their intentions or to remind them to perform the behavior.

Moreover, forgetting is not the only reason for people's failure to implement their intentions. Lack of adequate control over the behavior can make it difficult or impossible to perform an intended behavior. Internal factors, such as lack of sufficient willpower and perseverance or lack of requisite skills and resources, as well as external factors, such as a failure to obtain needed cooperation by another person, can interfere with planned behavior (see Ajzen, 1985 for a discussion). Various techniques have been developed to increase behavioral control, although these techniques have apparently not been used in a TPB context. Some methods focus on imbuing individuals with a sense of self-efficacy or perceptions of behavioral control. These methods can thus influence behavioral intentions, that is, the motivation to engage in the behavior, but they may also provide valuable information about actual behavioral performance. Among these methods are observational learning and modeling techniques (e.g., Bandura, Blanchard, & Ritter, 1969) and mental simulation (Taylor & Pham, 1996, 1998). Other methods are more clearly designed to provide individuals with the tools and other resources needed to overcome potential hurdles and gain actual control over behavioral performance. Successive approximation (Preston, Umbricht, Wong, & Epstein, 2001) and simulation of the desired behavior (Glang, Noell, Ary, & Swartz, 2005) are techniques that may be able to accomplish these goals.

Evaluating Effectiveness of Behavioral Interventions

It should be clear by now that the theory of planned behavior can serve not only to gain an understanding of a behavior's determinants and design an intervention guided by that understanding, but that it can also be used as a conceptual framework for evaluating the effectiveness of the interventions. Application of the TPB to impact assessment has the potential to provide two important kinds of information about the intervention. When the intervention is found to be effective in producing behavior change, the theory permits us to trace the intervention's impact by way of the behavior's psychological antecedents. This opens the way to making improvements in the design and delivery of the intervention and thus enhance its future effectiveness. When the intervention fails to produce changes in behavior, we can use information provided by the theory to identify the reasons for the failure. With this information in hand, we can redesign the intervention to overcome its deficiencies.

It is beyond the score of this chapter to discuss methods of evaluation research (for a recent overview, see Rossi et al., 2004). Ideally, an experimental or quasi-experimental design is employed in which an intervention group is compared with a suitable control group that is not exposed to the intervention of interest. A TPB questionnaire is administered in both groups, and behavior is assessed after the intervention. The information thus obtained allows us to examine the influence of the intervention on behavioral, normative, and control beliefs; to trace changes in these beliefs to changes in attitudes, subjective norms, and perceived behavioral control; and to trace changes in these factors to changes in intentions and, ultimately, to changes in behavior (see Figure 3.1).

Three critical questions must be addressed in this context. First, do the data support the theory's internal structure? That is, do they support the postulated links from beliefs through attitudes, subjective norms, and perceived control to intentions? We have seen that there is considerable evidence to show that, when validly assessed, the postulated relations are strong and significant.

The second question concerns the extent to which a change in behavioral intentions produces a change in actual behavior. We saw that this is by no means assured as people may simply forget to perform the intended behavior or may encounter unanticipated difficulties that prevent them for carrying out their intentions. A recent meta-analysis (Webb & Sheeran, 2006) tried to provide an empirical answer. The investigators identified 47 data sets from studies in which participants were assigned at random into intervention and nonintervention conditions, intentions were assessed, and differences in subsequent behavior were reported. Meta-analysis of the data showed that the interventions produced medium to large changes in intentions (sample-weighted average effect size $d = 0.66$) and that these effects on intentions led to small to medium-sized changes in behavior ($d = 0.36$). A mediational analysis showed that the effects of interventions on behavior were mediated by their effects on intentions. Controlling for changes in intentions significantly attenuated the effects of interventions on behavior, although the effects remained statistically significant. Moderator analyses performed by the investigators suggest that this residual impact of the intervention on behavior over and above changes in intentions may be due to issues of control. Rated actual control as well as perceived behavioral control moderated the effects of changes in intentions on changes in behavior. Changes in intentions had larger effects on behavior when participants were rated as having a high rather than low degree of control over the behavior. The same was true when participants' own perceptions of control over behavioral performance was high rather than low. In short, it appears that behavioral interventions can be quite effective in changing intentions and that these changes are generally translated into behavior especially when individuals have control over behavioral performance.

Finally, to discover the pathways by which an intervention had its impact, or the reasons for its failure, it is important to examine the targeted behavioral, normative, and / or control beliefs as well as other salient beliefs that were not explicitly attacked. An intervention may turn out to be ineffective because it failed to produce changes in the targeted beliefs. However, even when the targeted beliefs are changed in the desired direction, the intervention may still be ineffective if other beliefs changed in a countervailing manner, producing no net change in the overall belief composite. Thus, we may be able to change beliefs regarding some of the behavior's likely consequences, but other behavioral beliefs may change as well, leaving the overall belief index unmodified. As a result, we would not observe changes in attitudes toward the behavior. The same considerations apply to changes in normative and control beliefs. Similarly, a change in, say, the attitudinal component may be offset by a countervailing change in perceived behavioral control, leading to no change in intentions. To the best of my knowledge, behavioral interventions conducted in the framework of the TPB have not as yet undertaken such detailed analyses of changes in the underlying determinants of intentions and actions. Analyses of this kind can be of considerable value for evaluating an intervention's effectiveness, examining the processes activated by the intervention, and designing more effective interventions for future use.

Summary and Conclusions

In this chapter, I have tried to show that the theory of planned behavior is a useful conceptual framework for understanding the antecedents of behavior in different domains, to design interventions, and to evaluate an intervention's effectiveness. According to the theory, behavior follows reasonably from the information or beliefs people have about the behavior's likely consequences, about the normative expectations of important others, and about the required resources and possible barriers to behavioral performance. By targeting beliefs in these categories, a behavioral intervention can influence attitudes toward the behavior, perceived social pressure or subjective norms, as well as self-efficacy expectations or perceptions of behavioral control. Changes in these factors can produce changes in intentions, which are likely to be carried out to the extent that people have volitional control over the behavior. Various strategies can be used to produce changes in intentions or to enable performance of existing intentions. The theory of planned behavior can be a useful tool for tracing the effects of an intervention, determining reasons for an intervention's failure, and designing more effective intervention strategies.

NOTES

1. Although, conceptually, perceived control is expected to *moderate* the intention–behavior relation, in practice most investigators have looked at the additive effects of intention and perceptions of control. The reason for this practice is that empirically, even when an interaction is present in the data, statistical regression analyses often reveal only main effects. To obtain a statistically significant interaction requires that intention and perceived control scores cover the full range of the measurement scale. For most behaviors, however, a majority of respondents fall on one or the other side of these continua.

2. In addition, it is often also useful to measure descriptive normative beliefs by asking participants whether their friends use illicit drugs.

3. The different parts of the TPB can be evaluated simultaneously by means of path or structural equation analyses.

4. Only differences in belief strength were reported. It is not clear whether there were significant differences in outcome evaluations, motivations to comply with referents, or the perceived power of control factors.

RECOMMENDED READINGS

Ajzen, I. (2005). *Attitudes, personality, and behavior* (2nd ed.). Maidenhead, UK: Open University Press.

Fazio, R. H. (1990). Multiple processes by which attitudes guide behavior: The MODE model as an integrative framework. In M. P. Zanna (Ed.), *Advances in experimental social psychology* (Vol. 23, pp. 75–109). San Diego, CA: Academic Press.

Rossi, P. H., Lipsey, M. W., & Freeman, H. E. (2004). *Evaluation: A systematic approach* (7th ed.). Thousand Oaks, CA: Sage.

REFERENCES

Ajzen, I. (1971). Attitudinal vs. normative messages: An investigation of the differential effects of persuasive communications on behavior. *Sociometry, 34,* 263–280.

Ajzen, I. (1985). From intentions to actions: A theory of planned behavior. In J. Kuhl & J. Beckman (Eds.), *Action-control: From cognition to behavior* (pp. 11–39). Heidelberg, Germany: Springer.

Ajzen, I. (1988). *Attitudes, personality, and behavior.* Chicago: Dorsey Press.

Ajzen, I. (1991). The theory of planned behavior. *Organizational Behavior and Human Decision Processes, 50,* 179–211.

Ajzen, I. (2005). *Attitudes, personality, and behavior* (2nd ed.). Maidenhead, UK: Open University Press.

Ajzen, I., & Fishbein, M. (1977). Attitude-behavior relations: A theoretical analysis and review of empirical research. *Psychological Bulletin, 84,* 888–918.

Ajzen, I., & Fishbein, M. (1980). *Understanding attitudes and predicting social behavior.* Englewood-Cliffs, NJ: Prentice-Hall.

Albarracin, D., Johnson, B. T., Fishbein, M., & Muellerleile, P. A. (2001). Theories of reasoned action and planned behavior as models of condom use: A meta-analysis. *Psychological Bulletin, 127,* 142–161.

Armitage, C. J. (2004). Evidence that implementation intentions reduce dietary fat intake: A randomized trial. *Health Psychology, 23,* 319–323.

Armitage, C. J., & Conner, M. (2001). Efficacy of the theory of planned behavior: A meta-analytic review. *British Journal of Social Psychology, 40,* 471–499.

Bamberg, S., Ajzen, I., & Schmidt, P. (2003). Choice of travel mode in the theory of planned behavior: The roles of past behavior, habit, and reasoned action. *Basic and Applied Social Psychology, 25,* 175–188.

Bandura, A. (1986). *Social foundations of thought and action: A social cognitive theory.* Englewood Cliffs, NJ: Prentice-Hall.

Bandura, A. (1997). *Self-efficacy: The exercise of control.* New York: Freeman.

Bandura, A., Blanchard, E. B., & Ritter, B. (1969). Relative efficacy of desensitization and modeling approaches for inducing behavioral, affective, and attitudinal changes. *Journal of Personality and Social Psychology, 13,* 173–199.

Beale, D. A., & Manstead, A. S. R. (1991). Predicting mothers' intentions to limit frequency of infants' sugar intake: Testing the theory of planned behavior. *Journal of Applied Social Psychology, 21,* 409–431.

Bickman, B. (Ed.). (1987). *Using program theory in evaluation.* San Francisco: Jossey-Bass.

Brubaker, R. G., & Fowler, C. (1990). Encouraging college males to perform testicular self-examination: Evaluation of a persuasive message based on the revised theory of reasoned action. *Journal of Applied Social Psychology, 20,* 1411–1422.

Brubaker, R. G., & Wickersham, D. (1990). Encouraging the practice of testicular self-examination: A field application of the theory of reasoned action. *Health Psychology, 9,* 154–163.

Chaiken, S. (1980). Heuristic versus systematic information processing and the use of source versus message cues in persuasion. *Journal of Personality and Social Psychology, 39,* 752–766.

Conner, M., Sherlock, K., & Orbell, S. (1998). Psychosocial determinants of ecstasy use in young people in the UK. *British Journal of Health Psychology, 3,* 295–317.

Downs, D. S., & Hausenblas, H. A. (2005). The theories of reasoned action and planned behavior applied to exercise: A meta-analytic update. *Journal of Physical Activity and Health, 2,* 76–97.

Feather, N. T. (Ed.). (1982). *Expectations and actions: Expectancy-value models in psychology.* Hillsdale, NJ: Erlbaum.

Fishbein, M. (1963). An investigation of the relationships between beliefs about an object and the attitude toward that object. *Human Relations, 16,* 233–240.

Fishbein, M., & Ajzen, I. (1981). Acceptance, yielding, and impact: Cognitive processes in persuasion. In R. E. Petty, T. M. Ostrom & T. C. Brock (Eds.), *Cognitive responses in persuasion* (pp. 339–359). Hillsdale, NJ: Erlbaum.

Fishbein, M., Guenther-Grey, C., Johnson, W., Wolitski, R. J., McAlister, A., Rietmeijer, C. A., et al. (1997). Using a theory-based community intervention to reduce AIDS risk behaviors: The CDC's AIDS community demonstration projects. In M. E. Goldberg, M. Fishbein, & S. Middlestadt (Eds.), *Social marketing: Theoretical and practical perspectives* (pp. 123–146). Mahwah, NJ: Erlbaum.

Glang, A., Noell, J., Ary, D., & Swartz, L. (2005). Using interactive multimedia to teach pedestrian safety: An exploratory study. *American Journal of Health Behavior, 29,* 435–442.

Godin, G., & Kok, G. (1996). The theory of planned behavior: A review of its applications to health-related behaviors. *American Journal of Health Promotion, 11,* 87–98.

Godin, G., Valois, P., Lepage, L., & Desharnais, R. (1992). Predictors of smoking behaviour: An application of Ajzen's theory of planned behaviour. *British Journal of Addiction, 87,* 1335–1343.

Gollwitzer, P. M. (1999). Implementation intentions: Strong effects of simple plans. *American Psychologist, 54,* 493–503.

Gollwitzer, P. M., & Bayer, U. (1999). Deliberative versus implemental mindsets in the control of action. In S. Chaiken & Y. Trope (Eds.), *Dual-process theories in social psychology* (pp. 403–422). New York: Guilford Press.

Gollwitzer, P. M., Heckhausen, H., & Steller, B. (1990). Deliberative and implemental mind-sets: Cognitive tuning toward congruous thoughts and information. *Journal of Personality and Social Psychology, 59*, 1119–1127.

Hagger, M. S., Chatzisarantis, N. L. D., & Biddle, S. J. H. (2002). A meta-analytic review of the theories of reasoned action and planned behavior in physical activity: Predictive validity and the contribution of additional variables. *Journal of Sport and Exercise Psychology, 24*, 3–32.

Hardeman, W., Johnston, M., Johnston, D. W., Bonetti, D., Wareham, N. J., & Kinmonth, A. L. (2002). Application of the theory of planned behaviour in behaviour change interventions: A systematic review. *Psychology and Health, 17*, 123–158.

Heckhausen, H. (1991). *Motivation and action.* New York: Springer-Verlag.

Hrubes, D., Ajzen, I., & Daigle, J. (2001). Predicting hunting intentions and behavior: An application of the theory of planned behavior. *Leisure Sciences, 23*, 165–178.

LaPiere, R. T. (1934). Attitudes vs. actions. *Social Forces, 13*, 230–237.

Lewin, K. (1952). *Field theory in social science: Selected theoretical papers by Kurt Lewin.* London: Tavistock.

Linn, L. S. (1965). Verbal attitudes and overt behavior: A study of racial discrimination. *Social Forces, 43*, 353–364.

Madden, T. J., Ellen, P. S., & Ajzen, I. (1992). A comparison of the theory of planned behavior and the theory of reasoned action. *Personality and Social Psychology Bulletin, 18*, 3–9.

Orbell, S., Hodgkins, S., & Sheeran, P. (1997). Implementation intentions and the theory of planned behavior. *Personality and Social Psychology Bulletin, 23*, 945–954.

Petraitis, J., Flay, B. R., & Miller, T. Q. (1995). Reviewing theories of adolescent substance use: Organizing pieces in the puzzle. *Psychological Bulletin, 117*, 67–86.

Petty, R. E., & Cacioppo, J. T. (1986). The elaboration likelihood model of persuasion. In L. Berkowitz (Ed.), *Advances in experimental social psychology* (Vol. 19, pp. 123–205). New York: Academic Press.

Preston, K. L., Umbricht, A., Wong, C. J., & Epstein, D. H. (2001). Shaping cocaine abstinence by successive approximation. *Journal of Consulting and Clinical Psychology, 69*, 643–654.

Prochaska, J. O., & DiClemente, C. C. (1983). Stages and processes of self-change of smoking: Toward an integrative model of change. *Journal of Consulting and Clinical Psychology, 51*, 390–395.

Prochaska, J. O., & Norcross, J. C. (2002). Stages of change. In J. C. Norcross (Ed.), *Psychotherapy relationships that work: Therapist contributions and responsiveness to patients* (pp. 303–313). Oxford, UK: Oxford University Press.

Rossi, P. H., Lipsey, M. W., & Freeman, H. E. (2004). *Evaluation: A systematic approach* (7th ed.). Thousand Oaks, CA: Sage.

Sheeran, P. (2002). Intention–behavior relations: A conceptual and empirical review. In W. Stroebe & M. Hewstone (Eds.), *European review of social psychology* (Vol. 12, pp. 1–36). Chichester, England: Wiley.

Sheeran, P., & Orbell, S. (1999). Implementation intentions and repeated behaviour: Augmenting the predictive validity of the theory of planned behaviour. *European Journal of Social Psychology, 29*, 349–369.

Sheeran, P., & Orbell, S. (2000). Using implementation intentions to increase attendance for cervical cancer screening. *Health Psychology, 19*, 283–289.

Sheeran, P., & Taylor, S. (1999). Predicting intentions to use condoms: A meta-analysis and comparison of the theories of reasoned action and planned behavior. *Journal of Applied Social Psychology, 29*, 1624–1675.

Taylor, S. E., & Pham, L. B. (1996). Mental simulation, motivation, and action. In P. M. Gollwitzer & J. A. Bargh (Eds.), *The psychology of action: Linking cognition and motivation to behavior* (pp. 219–235). New York: Guilford Press.

Taylor, S. E., & Pham, L. B. (1998). The effect of mental simulation on goal-directed performance. *Imagination, Cognition and Personality, 18*, 253–268.

Trafimow, D., & Fishbein, M. (1994a). The importance of risk in determining the extent to which attitudes affect intentions to wear seat belts. *Journal of Applied Social Psychology, 24*, 1–11.

Trafimow, D., & Fishbein, M. (1994b). The moderating effect of behavior type on the subjective norm-behavior relationship. *Journal of Social Psychology, 134*, 755–763.

Van Ryn, M., & Vinokur, A. D. (1992). How did it work? An examination of the mechanisms through which an intervention for the unemployed promoted job-search behavior. *American Journal of Community Psychology, 20*, 577–597.

Verplanken, B., & Faes, S. (1999). Good intentions, bad habits, and effects of forming implementation intentions on healthy eating. *European Journal of Social Psychology, 29*, 591–604.

Webb, T. L., & Sheeran, P. (2006). Does changing behavioral intentions engender behavior change? A meta-analysis of the experimental evidence. *Psychological Bulletin, 132*, 249–268.

Weinstein, N. D., Rothman, A. J., & Sutton, S. R. (1998). Stage theories of health behavior: Conceptual and methodological issues. *Health Psychology, 17*, 290–299.

Weiss, C. H. (1972). *Evaluation research: Methods of assessing program effectiveness.* Englewood Cliffs, NJ: Prentice Hall.

EDITORS' CONCLUDING COMMENTS
TO CHAPTER 3

In an early section of the chapter, Ajzen describes the process for constructing a questionnaire based on the theory of planned behavior. In the context of program planning and evaluation, a questionnaire like this can serve several functions. Most obviously, the questionnaire that results can be used in a theory-driven evaluation (see Chapter 5), guiding the construction of a program theory. Consider the question: How else can program designers and evaluators use this questionnaire development process? One potentially important answer is that this process could be very useful early in a program's development, or during program redesign, to point out factors the program might target, such as subjective norms. The contribution of TPB to program design is further illuminated by Ajzen's later section on "targeting an intervention."

In the section on "background factors," Ajzen explains how a range of background variables, such as demographic and personality variables, might be relevant because they affect the key theoretical variables of attitudes, subjective norms, and perceived control. Why is this useful, relative to other less theoretically based approaches to evaluation? The answer, we believe, is that TPB provides a concise way of accounting for a wide range of individual difference and contextual variables. And it allows the evaluator to explain theoretically *why* these contextual and individual difference variables matter.

A fundamental question for program sponsors and evaluators involves the issue of generalizability. That is, will a program that is effective in one setting, with one set of clients, also be effective in another location with different types of clients? We invite you to consider, drawing on Ajzen's chapter, including the section on "targeting an intervention," how the theory of planned behavior might help evaluators think about generalizability.

EDITORS' INTRODUCTORY COMMENTS
TO CHAPTER 4

In the next chapter, like the previous two, Riemer and Bickman use program theory as a way of linking social psychology and evaluation. Unlike the two preceding chapters, however, Riemer and Bickman do not emphasize a single theory. Instead, they highlight the process of borrowing from multiple theories and bodies of research, mostly from social psychology (but also from related areas such as industrial-organizational and clinical psychology). They use the concept of "theory knitting" to describe the process of integrating concepts from multiple theories, as well as pragmatic considerations, to develop a program theory that matches the complexities of the social problem being addressed.

In addition, drawing on Chen (1990, 2005), Riemer and Bickman distinguish between the *change model* and the *action model* associated with a social program. In short, the change model refers to the relevant causal processes that are expected to underlie the program's effects. The action model, on the other hand, refers to the more tangible, specific things to be done to set in motion the underlying processes. Using language familiar to many researchers, the change model includes the relevant constructs, including mediators, while the action model emphasizes operationalizations. The chapter illustrates the use of existing social psychological theory and research to develop the change model. For the action model, the authors appear to draw as much on pragmatic considerations and experience as on existing research and theory. In a way, by separating out the action model the chapter reminds us that, although social psychological theories can be a great aid for those who are developing and evaluating programs, the theories will not by themselves provide the answer to every evaluation challenge.

The social problem that Riemer and Bickman address is: How can one improve the services provided by community-based mental health service agencies in order to improve the outcomes of children who suffer from mental health problems? In terms of content areas, this involves the intersection of social psychology with clinical and counseling psychology, and the authors draw on important concepts from each of these areas, as well as work from industrial/organizational psychology on how people respond to feedback. When theory knitting, one may have to pull together several different theoretical threads.

The chapter includes one other unique feature. One of the authors, Len Bickman, describes his own professional voyage. Len started as a young, talented social psychologist, but then more or less left the field and moved into program evaluation. More recently, he has created a kind of integration between the two, drawing heavily upon social psychology to do theory knitting to create and evaluate an empirically based program. One hope that led to the development of this book is that, by examining various linkages between social psychology and evaluation, future young and promising social psychologists can, if they wish, find an integration between the two—without having to take as long and circuitous a voyage as Bickman has had.

CHAPTER 4

Using Program Theory to Link Social Psychology and Program Evaluation

Manuel Riemer
Leonard Bickman

Imagine a social service agency intended to improve children's mental health outcomes. Also imagine a staff member who provides services to children and who continues, unaware, to use practices that were ineffective for previous young clients. In this chapter we describe how basic social psychological research and theories and program evaluation can be linked using program theory, and we illustrate this linkage using a program that addresses the problems that can arise when service deliverers do not have feedback about their work. We begin by using Bickman's experiences as a social psychologist turned program evaluator to discuss the current lack of a strong link between these two fields. Then, we provide a concrete example of a program theory that draws heavily from basic social psychological theories. We present both the change model and the action model for this program, called Contextualized Feedback System (CFS™), which is intended to improve the effectiveness of mental health services. We demonstrate how the rationale for each program component is derived from the change model, and we discuss the ongoing evaluation of this program, funded by the National Institute of Mental Health (NIMH), at a large mental health service provider.

A Personal Voyage from Social Psychology, to Evaluation, and Back to Social Psychological Theory

Although this chapter has two authors, the current section is based on the experiences of one, Leonard Bickman, and so is written in the first person singular (for more details, see Bickman, 2006). I (Bickman) was originally attracted to social psychology because I saw the potential it had to deal with applied problems. However, almost all the studies published when I was a young professor were laboratory studies that used college students as subjects. Nevertheless, I was optimistic that over time social psychology would obtain a balance between applied field research and the more theory-oriented laboratory studies. I could not have been more wrong in those expectations. Helmreich (1975) charted the proportion of laboratory experiments in the *Journal of Personality and Social Psychology* and noted an increase from 56% in 1961 to 84% in 1974. Rodrigues and Levine (1999) report a continued decrease in the use of longitudinal and field studies between 1986 and 1996. From my perspective, social psychology was regressing rather than making progress in dealing with real-world problems, at least in terms of the use of field methods that I believe are important for research on real-world problems.

Any efforts in the last 10 years to broaden social psychology also seem to me to have fallen short. I did a small survey of the articles published in the first two issues of 2006 in two of the elite journals in social psychology, *Journal of Experimental Social Psychology* (JESP) and *Journal of Personality and Social Psychology* (JPSP). JPSP published 20 studies, 17 with students and only three studies with nonstudents as subjects. JESP was even narrower, with 22 studies, 21 of which had student participants and one an Internet experiment with nonstudents. Moreover, very few collected data on actual behavior in the laboratory but instead used written questionnaires. It appears that modern social psychology has become even more removed from the real world, at least in terms of the methods and settings represented in its top journals.

It is easier, less expensive, more controllable, and quicker to hand out questionnaires than to conduct a field or laboratory experiment. However, I do not believe my colleagues are avoiding hard work. It is more likely that they simply do not think it is necessary to test their theories, often social cognitive theories, in ways other than having college students complete questionnaires or other measures in the lab. Another factor may be the chilling effect of Institutional Review Boards (IRBs). Many social psychological experiments, both field and laboratory, involve some degree of deception. Researchers may be reluctant to conduct such studies because of the perceived low probability of approval from an IRB. Social psychologists may also believe that it is more difficult to study meditational processes, a key concern in much of contemporary social psychology, in field settings.

Regardless of the cause, the shortage of real-world studies in social psychology led me to transition in other directions. However, the change from social psychologist to evaluator did not happen suddenly. While I eschewed the laboratory and still chose to use the real world as my stage, I did not deal directly with real problems. My first program of research on bystander intervention involved staging shopliftings in supermarkets to see how people responded. But I did not take the additional step of attempting to use our findings to design and evaluate programs to encourage bystander intervention.

A significant shift of my research to program evaluation occurred in 1976, when the Westinghouse Electric Company asked me to develop the Westinghouse Evaluation Institute while I continued to work part time at Loyola University. I directed several diverse program evaluations including those examining captioning for the deaf, crime prevention through environmental design, health education, nutritional programs for the elderly and a larger project on shoplifting and employee theft. After five years I moved to Vanderbilt University to direct the Kennedy Center's Program Evaluation Laboratory. Social psychology played a small role in my life after coming to Vanderbilt. There was a small graduate program in social psychology that lasted only a few years due in part to faculty attrition. My identity was that of an applied social researcher, methodologist, editor, and program evaluator. I had little use for social psychology.

As the typical evaluator I had no role in the problem definition and the design or implementation of the intervention. However, the developers of most of these interventions seemed unaware that they made critical assumptions that had little or no empirical or theoretical support. Many of the programs were developed out of "notions" of the problems and solutions or from an ideological belief system. I believed that a major reason these programs were so often found to be ineffective was that they lacked a sound conceptual underpinning.

Partially in response to this state of affairs, in 1987 I edited and contributed to a volume of *New Directions in Program Evaluation* on a topic that I called program theory. I argued that if we wanted to produce generalizable findings, then we needed to test the theory underlying the program, considering the program as just one instance of the theory. Accompanying the concept of theory was the related idea of logic models. These models conceptualized programs as having components that were linked in some presumably logical fashion, with linkages across components typically labeled as input, process, outputs, and proximal and distal outcomes. Many program theories are simply logic models. That is, they are internally consistent (logical) and describe the assumptions that the program appears to be making. However, it is rare for a model to be based on either social or behavioral science theory or research. And in my experience and that of many other evaluators, program models that lack a basis in sound research or theory are usually associated with programs that are ineffective.

Thus, the circle brings me back to social psychology as a source for program theory. In the next section, my co-author and I describe how we developed a program theory based on social psychological research. We show how the more than 50 years of social psychological research can be used to develop the intervention and guide our measurement. We used the model to plan an intervention to improve the outcomes of mental health treatment by providing feedback to the clinician on the client's progress.

Basic Psychological Research and the Real World

In understanding how the link between social psychology and program evaluation can be made via program theory, it is helpful to draw on Chen's (1990, 2005) conceptualization. He sees program theory "as a configuration of the prescriptive and descriptive assumptions held by stakeholders and thus underlying the programs stakeholders create" (Chen, 2005, p. 16). Descriptive assumptions concern the causal process underlying the program's effectiveness, that is, how the program is supposed to work in addressing its targeted social problem. Chen refers to this as the *change model*. Prescriptive assumptions, on the other hand, "prescribe those components and activities that the program designers see as necessary to a program's success" (p. 17). He called this part of the program theory the *action model*. The action model helps determine the program activities that are necessary to ensure that the processes described in the change model can occur.

As this description suggests, the link between social psychology and program evaluation is greatest for the change model. Chen (2005) referred to this kind of linkage as involving *"scientific theory-based programs."* As our example demonstrates, social cognitive psychology has much to offer in developing applied theories of behavior change. These well-established scientific theories have the potential to reduce the trial-and-error search for determinants of program outcomes. Social programs and its recipients are not the only ones to profit from this link, however. The use of social psychological theories in this context moves them beyond the laboratory and puts them to the test in real-world applications, which can further their validity and generalizability.

Linking these two worlds is not without challenges. Basic social psychological theories often describe a very narrow aspect of human behavior, tested under artificial conditions with a limited group of subjects (e.g., college students). This is due to the aforementioned desire to have tight control over the experimental conditions. Social programs, on the other hand, often deal with very complex problems that are affected by many different things and are targeted at populations that most often are quite different from the white middle-class college students typically studied in laboratory experiments. Tight control in basic social psychology research not only extends to reducing the influence of extraneous variables, but also results in a clearer operationalization of the independent and dependent variables. However, this conceptual advantage is obtained by increasing the threats to construct and external validity. Moreover, because in the real world most events are determined by multiple causes, it is unlikely that one can simply and directly apply a single social psychology theory in the development of a change model. Given that basic theorists are primarily interested in testing their theories, rather than solving a social problem, it is unlikely that multiple causes are considered in testing the theory.

What is needed, then, is a process that translates several basic theories and combines them into one coherent applied model of change. What we will present here is the result of a process that can be considered *theory knitting*. This was described by Kalmar and Sternberg (1988) as an approach to "integrate the best aspects of a set of given theories with one's own ideas regarding the domain under investigation" (p. 153). We believe that the creative integration of multiple basic theories is a promising approach to coping with real-world complexities. If theory knitting can be accomplished successfully, then basic psychological research will become more useful for practitioners who need solutions for real-world problems. In laying out the change and action model, we also illustrate the process we went through in theory knitting.

The Change Model

The change model of a program theory typically describes the program's goals and desired outcomes, as well as the determining factors (i.e., the intervention as well as the mediating and moderating variables). Thus, in describing the example of our program theory we begin by describing the goals of the program. Then, we describe step by step how the change model was created using different psychological theories. This will be followed by a description of how the change model was used to determine the program components and activities, that is, to develop the action model.

First, let us discuss the program goal. Our ultimate *goal* in developing this program is to improve the lives of children who suffer from mental health problems and their families by making the community-based mental health services they receive more effective. Thus, if our program is successful, the clinical outcomes of those children receiving services from agencies that used our program will be better than those of children served by comparable agencies. In reviewing the problems and successes of previous attempts to improve the outcomes of youth mental health services, we determined that the leverage point with the highest chance for change is likely to be at the clinician level (Bickman & Riemer, 2002). Clinicians in the fields have very diverse backgrounds with different levels of training and experience and with different approaches to treatment, and they work in diverse settings of service provisions (e.g., home-based vs. clinic). Thus, it was necessary to find an intervention that would fit with this diverse group and settings. Focusing on those treatment factors that are considered essential for *any* type of successful treatment was a logical choice. These so-called common factors include the therapeutic working relationship, treatment motivation, and clients' treatment expectancies (Karver, Handelsman, Fields, & Bickman, 2005). Thus, our *objective* was to develop a behavior change intervention for clinicians that will help them to become more effective in influencing these common factors, especially the therapeutic relationship. The intervention was designed to target those aspects of the common factors over which the clinician has control. Importantly, while the focus in our current application is on mental health clinicians and common factors, the theory that we developed (Riemer, Rosof-Williams, & Bickman, 2005; Sapyta, Riemer, & Bickman, 2005) is also applicable to other professions and goals. For example, we are conducting a four-year research project applying the theory to improving the leadership of school principals.

Knitting the Theory

With the goals and objectives in place, we began our search for potentially effective strategies for behavior change. The selection of the intervention was influenced by Leonard Bickman's writing and research on quality improvement (Bickman et al., 1995; Bickman & Salzer, 1997; Bickman & Peterson, 1990; Peterson & Bickman, 1992). A key component of quality improvement is the use of feedback. Although the concept of using feedback to improve services is not new (e.g., Shewhart, 1939), it had not been systematically applied to mental health services. In 1996 Bickman started working on a grant application to the NIMH to support research on using feedback in mental health. The first proposal on feedback was submitted in January 1997. It took several attempts to secure funding until the current feedback grant was funded in 2004. Persistence is important.

Later we came across Michael Lambert's work (e.g., Lambert, Hansen, & Finch, 2001). He successfully implemented a feedback intervention for clinicians of adult clients. More generally, the use of feedback interventions for changing behavior is supported by the work of Kluger and DeNisi (1996, 1998). They defined *feedback interventions* as "actions taken by an external agent to provide information regarding some aspect of one's task performance" (Kluger & DeNisi, 1996, p. 255). This definition differentiates feedback interventions from feedback that occurs without the intervention of external agents, such as internal feedback or feedback from the task itself.

In a meta-analysis, Kluger and DeNisi found an overall effect size of .41, across several fields, for feedback interventions. However, they also found that in one-third of the studies, feedback *decreased* performance. Rose and Church (1998) also found heterogeneous effects in their meta-analysis of educational feedback interventions. Thus, while feedback interventions was a promising approach, the factors leading to the desired behavior change needed to be more clearly delineated to increase the chances of success. There are several basic theories that provide some insight and on which we drew for our theory knitting.

Feedback and Change

What is the mechanism by which feedback motivates people to change their behavior? In addressing this question, existing theory and research suggested that we should consider the *sign of the feedback*, that is, whether the feedback is positive or negative.

Positive Feedback

Positive feedback is important for fostering one's self-efficacy by providing a feeling of enactive mastery (Bandura, 1977, 1982). In addition, positive feedback motivates people differently based on their orientation toward achievement (Higgins, 1997, 1998). In the case of people who are prone to fulfilling certain expectations or standards in order to avoid negative consequences, they will be less likely to increase effort after positive feedback. In contrast, those who are motivated to overachieve will redouble their efforts. Thus, positive feedback leads either to increased effort or to reduced or constant effort, depending on the person's motivational orientation. While it is important to consider these effects of positive feedback, we were mainly interested in the processes centered on negative feedback. This is based on our interest in changing behavior for those cases where service recipients are not making the expected progress, but the clinician appears not to be responding or even aware of this lack of progress.

Negative Feedback

What is the mechanism by which negative feedback causes people to change their behavior? The literature on self-regulation and control theories provides some insight. For these theories (Carver & Scheier, 1981; Miller, Galanter, & Pribram, 1960; Powers, 1973), behavior change is the result of a regulatory process that motivates an individual to readjust behavior if a discrepancy is observed between information about one's behavior and a behavioral standard (i.e., goal). Considered from this perspective, negative feedback works by making the discrepancy between the behavior and the goal salient. The question remains, however, as to what exactly it is that motivates persons to act if they become aware of this type of discrepancy. Thus, there is a need for more theory knitting.

The application of *cognitive dissonance* theory offers a useful approach for explaining the underlying cognitive-affective process. This theory posits that dissonance is aroused when individuals are confronted with information inconsistent with an important belief they hold (Harmon-Jones & Mills, 1999). Aronson's (1999a, 1999b) insight into what he labels as hypocrisy—that is, the situation in which people do not practice what they preach—is especially relevant. Aronson contends that dissonance is created when the self-concept, which usually does not include behaving in a hypocritical manner, is in conflict with behavior. This applies to failing to behave in a positive manner, such as conserving water (Dickerson, Thibodeau, Aronson, & Miller, 1992). Applying this to mental health professionals, one could expect that dissonance is generated when clinicians believe that they are using appropriate and effective treatment for their clients but feedback indicates that is not the case.

Festinger (1957) hypothesized that dissonant cognitions such as these induce a psychologically uncomfortable state of arousal that motivates persons to reduce the dissonance. In general terms, dissonance can be reduced by "removing dissonant cognitions, adding new consonant cognitions, reducing the importance of dissonant cognitions, or increasing the importance of consonant cognitions" (Harmon-Jones & Mills, 1999, p. 4). Thus, removing dissonant cognitions by changing behavior in a way that is more consistent with the goal is only one of several ways that dissonance could be reduced. This may explain some of the heterogeneity in the feedback effects demonstrated in meta-analyses (Kluger & DeNisi, 1996). We will explore this idea later in this chapter. First, we look more closely at those factors leading to the dissonance arousal.

Factors Leading to Dissonance

Drawing on several literatures (again, theory knitting), we concluded that there are two primary factors aspects that need to come together for dissonance to occur in the clinicians whose behaviors we hope to affect: (1) there needs to be a goal that is important to the clinician, and (2) there needs to be reliable and trusted information that the goal is not met. The first falls under the heading of goal commitment, while the second is the function of the feedback intervention.

Goal Commitment

According to Locke and Latham (2002), "the goal-performance relation-ship is strongest when people are committed to their goals" (p. 707). *Goal commitment* is defined as "the determination to try for a goal and the per-sistence in pursuing it over time" (Hollenbeck, Williams, & Klein, 1989, p. 18). But where does goal commitment come from?

The direct antecedents of goal commitment are goal attractiveness and goal expectancy (Hollenbeck & Klein, 1987; Hollenbeck et al., 1989). We define *goal attractiveness* as the subjective valence a certain goal has for the individual. The magnitude of a goal's attractiveness will depend on several higher-level goals to which it is related (instrumentality), as well as the attractiveness of these respective goals (Austin & Vancouver, 1996). Having good clinical outcomes, for example, can be attractive because this demonstrates one's effectiveness in helping the client and because it helps in obtaining the supervisor's praise, both of which are typically important to a professional. However, we must admit that assuming that one is effective and not exposing this belief to a test may be a more attractive alternative.

Goal expectancy can be defined as the anticipatory judgment about whether or not the goal can be accomplished within a certain time frame. Hollenbeck and Klein's (1987) model suggests that this judgment is influ-enced by situational factors, such as competing goals and supervisor sup-portiveness, as well as personal factors, such as ability and self-efficacy. This corresponds to Bandura's position that the overall expectation to accomplish a goal depends on an *outcome judgment* (involving situational factors) as well as on a *self-efficacy* judgment (Bandura, 1982, 1997). Ford (1992) described these two factors as context beliefs and capability beliefs. Situational or contextual factors can be perceived as facilitators or as bar-riers for accomplishing a goal. Facilitating factors, such as support of par-ents in establishing a good therapeutic relationship with an adolescent, can often be decisive in determining whether a therapist actually commits to a certain goal. Competing goals can reduce the level of commitment. Com-pleting lengthy paperwork in order to receive reimbursement, for example, can interfere with the amount of quality time that a clinician spends with a client in therapy or in learning about new therapies or guidelines. While in experimental settings these competing goals are either artificially elimi-nated or are less salient, they are critical in the context of real-world profes-sional behavior.

Among the personal factors, self-efficacy has been the one factor most consistently found to influence goal commitment and performance (Bandura, 1982; Gist & Mitchel, 1992; Lent, Brown, & Larkin, 1987; Locke, Frederick, Lee, & Bobko, 1984; Mone & Baker, 1992; Stajkovic & Luthans, 1998). Self-efficacy refers to self-beliefs concerning the ability to successfully perform a given task or behavior (Bandura, 1977). In a meta-

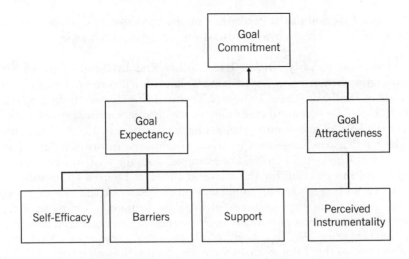

FIGURE 4.1. Goals.

analysis of 114 studies on the relationship of self-efficacy and work-related performance, Stajkovic and Luthans (1998) found a significant correlation (specifically, a weighted average correlation of $G(r_+)$) of .38 between these two constructs.

In summary, then, goal commitment is influenced by the goal's attractiveness as well as the goal expectation of the individual. The goal expectation itself is determined by situational factors such as organizational support and barriers as well as self-efficacy beliefs. Figure 4.1 provides an overview of these relationships. Consistent with the idea of theory knitting, this figure draws on several literatures from social psychology and related disciplines.

Feedback Intervention

ATTENTION TO THE FEEDBACK

As noted earlier, a precondition for dissonance to occur is the awareness that the behavior is inconsistent with an important goal. Feedback that is provided in the context of a feedback intervention must compete with feedback from other relevant sources in the individual's environment. The clinician must perceive this feedback as important and, thus, attend to it. Clearly we needed to understand the conditions under which the information provided by the external agent receives the attention of the individual and becomes an important factor in evaluating her own behavior. Taylor and Fiske (1978) explain that attention is "drawn to particular features of the environment either as a function of qualities intrinsic to those features

... or as a function of the perceiver's own disposition and temporary need states" (p. 281). The following discussion addresses both aspects.

Perceived Validity/Utility. Ilgen, Fisher, and Taylor offer probably the most comprehensive account of factors that influence the individual's processing of feedback (Ilgen, Fisher, & Taylor, 1979; Taylor, Fisher, & Ilgen, 1984). First, the perceived credibility of the feedback source strongly influences the level of attention to the feedback (Ilgen et al., 1979). The content of the feedback message also matters, notably the informational value of the content (Ilgen et al., 1979). For example, does the feedback contain new and useful information for the recipient that can be used to improve performance with regard to an important goal? Feedback can simply provide information about the outcomes of one's performance, or it can include corrective suggestions of how the performance can be enhanced to improve the outcomes (e.g., Wilson, Boni, & Hogg, 1997). Nyquist's (2003) meta-analysis shows that in most cases formative feedback is superior to feedback that provides only knowledge of results. Feedback can vary in several other ways as well. It can be: neutral or contain an evaluative judgment (Brockner & Higgins, 2001; Kluger & DeNisi, 1998; Shao, 1996); individualized or normative (i.e., one's performance is compared with others' outcomes) (e.g., Schultz, 1998; Smither, Wohlers, & London, 1995); immediate or delayed (Gibson, 2000); and delivered verbally, in writing, or in graphic form by a computer (Morris & Ellis, 1997). Finally, it can differ in its complexity.

As this quick review of feedback suggests, existing theory can be used as a diagnostic and planning tool to pinpoint factors that might increase attention to and the validity of the feedback, before providing the feedback intervention. Thus, in designing a feedback intervention, program developers should determine whether it is necessary first to enhance the *perceived validity and utility of the feedback*. Because large differences may exist among groups and settings in what is perceived as credible, we believe it is necessary to assess the credibility of the feedback source as well as preferences for feedback content and format before implementing a feedback intervention. Thus, we are arguing for a kind of formative evaluation to take place during program development. However, as a practical matter respondents may find it difficult to evaluate the feedback until they have had sufficient experience with it. Moreover, as researchers implementing a feedback intervention we are severely constrained by the claims that can be made about the usefulness of particular feedback. In the real world of commerce, unless your product is governed by the Food and Drug Administration (FDA), there are few limits on efficacy claims other than outright criminal fraud. Thus, feedback pioneers face an uphill battle until there is research to support validity claims. In our case all we could point to is the general research on feedback and a study using college students. Moreover achieving scientific credibility is not an assurance that the practitioner world will find the research findings as convincing evidence of effectiveness.

Accountability. London, Smither, and Adsit (1997) argue that if there is no *accountability* for using feedback, it will have little impact. Most recently, however, they also stressed the importance of self-determination in employees' self-development (London & Smither, 1999). If a professional perceives the external pressure as strongly interfering with her self-determination, it can easily provoke defensive strategies that are counterproductive. Therefore, interventions that are based on accountability and external pressure should be used with great sensitivity. Again the research paradigm produces a paradoxical situation. In a current project being directed by Bickman, feedback from teachers is being provided to over 70 school principals. However, in order to obtain principal volunteers, the researchers had to promise them that project personnel would never reveal their feedback to anyone else, thus eliminating any motivation associated with accountability.

Availability of Other Feedback Cues. Unlike the laboratory, the real world is rife with cues about the professional's performance. The potential power of the feedback intervention depends, in part, on the number and importance of these competing feedback cues.

Feedback Propensity. Herold and his colleagues stressed the importance of studying individual differences in the generation and processing of performance feedback (Herold & Fedor, 1998; Herold, Parsons, & Rensvold, 1996). In their empirical work, they found three factors reflecting individuals' feedback propensities (Herold et al., 1996). External feedback propensity describes individuals who generally like to seek out and receive external feedback. In contrast, individuals who have a high level of internal feedback propensity like and prefer self-generated feedback (e.g., evaluations based on their own personal observations). Internal feedback ability emerged as a third factor, reflecting the individual's perception of her ability to accurately generate reliable feedback without relying on external sources. These personal characteristics of individuals clearly influence the level of attention they will pay to external feedback.

To summarize, the major factors that influence the level of attention to the external feedback are the availability and validity of other feedback cues, the general perceived validity and utility of the external feedback, the degree of accountability, and the individuals' feedback propensity (see Figure 4.2 for an overview). Paying attention to the feedback is a necessary but not sufficient condition for feedback interventions to be effective. The feedback recipient also needs to accept the feedback as accurate.

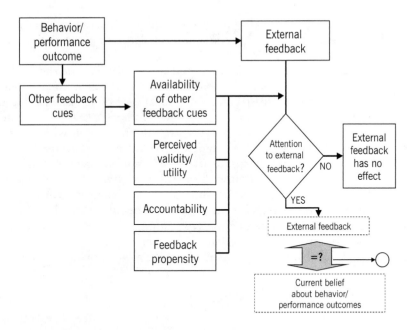

FIGURE 4.2. Major components of the attention to feedback process.

ACCEPTANCE OF THE FEEDBACK

As described earlier, the motivational force of dissonance arousal arises when a discrepancy is perceived between a self-standard (goal) and a behavior inconsistent with this standard. External feedback can serve as a source that determines and changes an individual's belief about her behavior. However, it is not certain that such belief reconfiguration will occur. When the feedback is negative, professionals may reject it rather than change their belief. This can be explained in terms of the belief–disconfirmation paradigm of cognitive dissonance (Festinger, Riecken, & Schachter, 1956; Harmon-Jones, 1999) and theories about self-serving bias (Blanton, Pelham, DeHart, & Carvallo, 2001; Sherman & Cohen, 2002). Cognitive dissonance theory posits that dissonance is aroused when individuals are confronted with information inconsistent with an important belief they hold (Harmon-Jones & Mills, 1999). However, professionals have two ways to reduce dissonance in this case. They can reject the external feedback as inaccurate, or they can change their belief about the outcomes of their behavior.

According to dissonance theory, the cognition with the lowest resistance to change is the one that most likely will be altered. A cognition's resistance to change is a function of several factors. One is its responsiveness to reality (Festinger, 1957; Walster, Berscheid, & Barclay, 1967). Is the external feedback or the prior belief about having good outcomes more likely to fail the reality test? For many individuals, their profession is an important part of their identity, such that professional failure would mean failure as a person. Indeed, to preserve their self-integrity, people tend to seek out and accept feedback information that is aligned with their positive self-image (Blanton et al., 2001; Sherman & Cohen, 2002). For instance, in a survey that asked 143 mental health counselors to grade their job performance on a scale from A+ to F, 66% rated themselves as A or better (Dew & Riemer, 2003)—a positive self-image that does not correspond with empirical evidence that treatment as usual is not as effective as one would hope (Bickman, 2002). In the face of overly positive self-evaluation of performance, external feedback that is negative will likely fail the reality test. If so, dissonance would be reduced by rejecting the external feedback rather than changing the professionals' current (positive) belief about their performance. Given this likelihood, additional efforts are needed to ensure that the external feedback is not perceived as a threat to the individual's personal integrity. Supervision plays an important role in this context. As shown later, the multiple threats of theory knitting will inform the action plan on this point.

A second factor that determines resistance to change of a cognitive element is its centrality and embeddedness in the overall cognitive structure (Festinger, 1957; Walster et al., 1967; Wicklund & Brehm, 1976). The more central or important a cognitive element is, the greater the probability that changing it would cause dissonance with other important cognitions and so the less willing the person will be to make that change. Overall performance is central for the professional's self-image. Therefore, accepting feedback that the outcome is below expectation is more likely to cause dissonance than rejecting that feedback. Given the likely resistance to negative feedback, to minimize its outright dismissal, (1) the feedback must be highly valued, (2) it should be personally important for the individual to rely on the external feedback, or (3) the individual should be held accountable for using the external feedback (accountability).

Professionals receive many varied sources of feedback about their performance. In this section, we showed that it is not enough to ensure a sufficient amount of attention to the feedback message. It is also crucial to mitigate the tendency of professionals simply to reject negative external feedback as inaccurate, given prior beliefs in the effectiveness of their current performance. External feedback must be accepted as accurate for it to cause the motivational dissonance arousal that result from a discrepancy between one's performance outcome and a self-standard. The processes described in this section are illustrated in Figure 4.3.

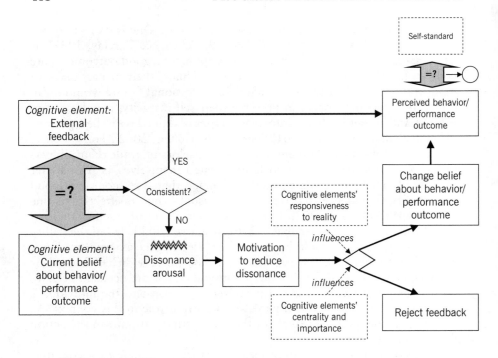

FIGURE 4.3. Major components of the acceptance of external feedback process in the CFIT.

From Dissonance to Behavior Change

As shown in Figure 4.3, for dissonance to be aroused first the feedback must be noticed. At this point, dissonance is avoided or reduced if the feedback is considered invalid and thus is rejected. If, however, the feedback is considered valid, then the professional is faced with another comparison, this one between the now validly perceived feedback and her self-standard. If these are inconsistent, then dissonance is aroused. Changing either the self-standard cognitive element or the cognitive element about the behavior can reduce this dissonance. Which choice is made depends on the causal attribution for the discrepancy and the resistance to change of the cognitive elements.

Causal Attributions

Weiner (1985) theorizes that the *causal attributions* people make as a consequence of success or failure can be described along three dimensions: locus of causality, stability, and controllability. Locus of causality refers to whether a person ascribes causes internally or externally. In 1971, Weiner and colleagues added the second dimension: stability (Weiner et al., 1971).

They reasoned that some causes fluctuate while others remain relatively stable. For example, inborn talent is a very stable cause while mood or effort is much more variable. Later, Weiner (1979) added the dimension of controllability by acknowledging that people can more reliably control some causes, such as effort, than they can control other causes, such as illness. McAuley, Duncan, and Russell (1992) further differentiated between causes that are controllable by others or by oneself. The location of a causal attribution along these causal dimensions critically influences the determination of the professional's dissonance reduction strategy and the behavioral consequences, as we will demonstrate in the following sections. The causal attribution process also determines how professionals will, in Aronson's terms, persuade themselves about the appropriate action in response to the feedback (Moore, 2000).

ALTERING THE COGNITIVE ELEMENT ABOUT GOAL STANDARD

Consider, for example, the stability dimension. If the cause is perceived as relatively stable, such as one's ability as a clinician (internal) or the child's family situation (external), then the expectation of better outcomes the next time will be relatively low (Weiner, 1985). If poor outcomes are attributed to stable and external factors, the consequence will be a lowering of outcomes expectancy. In contrast, a stable, internal attribution for poor outcomes will lead to decreased self-efficacy with regard to the specific goal (Bandura, 1982; Gist & Mitchel, 1992; Weiner, 1985). The consequence in both cases will be reduced goal commitment (Ilgen et al., 1979; Kluger & DeNisi, 1996). The third attributional dimension, controllability, influences whether the professional will change (or abandon) a higher order goal, such as being a good therapist, or instead will simply attend and commit to another more programmatic goal. If the perceived level of control is low in the face of poor outcomes, the professional might quit the job or, because that is often not a feasible option, may instead withdraw emotionally (Moore, 2000). Job burnout is often explained in terms of experiences of failure and a lack of perceived control (Maslach, Schaufeli, & Leiter, 2000). However, if poor outcomes have occurred but the perceived level of control is high, professionals may be motivated to change the problematic stable conditions, increasing the chance that future outcomes will be more consistent with expectations (Moore, 2000). As an example, consider a clinician who perceives that the negative feedback she received regarding a particular client was attributable to her lack of ability in building good working therapeutic relationships with clients. If she also believes that her lack of ability is not due to her lack of talent as a therapist, but rather to a deficiency of attainable skills, this internal but controllable causal attribution could result in increased commitment to other goals, such as committing to learning new therapeutic skills.

Thus, if the perceived level of control is high, then causal attributions of failure to stable and external conditions might result in an effort to change those conditions (Moore, 2000). The level of perceived control depends, in part, on the goal expectancy for each program goal. If, for example, the professional attends several training sessions to improve her abilities, but meets with little success, or she has no time for training because of competing demands, her expectation of effecting positive change will be low. This, in turn, will negatively affect her perception of level of control.

CHANGING THE BEHAVIORAL COGNITIVE ELEMENT

If the causal attribution is more variable than stable, then professionals are much more likely to change their behavioral cognitive element, and thus change their behavior, by increasing effort, shifting attention, or using a different treatment strategy. If, in addition, the causal attribution is external, the behavior will focus on changing those external conditions. In both cases, dissonance is reduced because of the anticipation that the behavioral change will add cognitions in the future that are consistent with the goal standard. However, behavioral change will not be required if the cause is perceived as being out of one's control—for example, if the therapist perceives the client's bad rating of therapeutic alliance was due to the client's mood that day and therefore unrelated to her behavior as a therapist. If external attributions are made, then simply decreasing the perceived importance of the behavioral outcomes (thus, negating the need for therapist behavior change) can reduce the dissonance.

RESISTANCE TO CHANGE

Two previously discussed factors help determine resistance to change in the face of negative feedback. The first is responsiveness to perceived reality. The more conclusive the information is about the actual cause (e.g., ability), the harder it will be to justify attributing the failure to a different cause (e.g., effort). However, the cause will be judged based not only on the current evidence, but also on previous experience and feedback (Bandura, 1982; Weiner, 1985; Weiner et al., 1971). If, for example, professionals consistently experience performance failure as internal, they will be more inclined to attribute the current cause in the same direction. Individual differences may matter, with people low in self-efficacy beliefs tending to attribute failure internally (Stajkovic & Sommer, 2000). Normative comparisons and one's implicit theories can also influence causal attribution (Hong, Chiu, Dweck, Lin, & Wan, 1999; Kelley & Michela, 1980; Weiner, 1985). For example, if it is commonly believed that a "difficult" child makes the development of therapeutic alliance a more Herculean task, then this factor is more likely to be considered the cause of failure.

The responsiveness of cognitions/beliefs to reality is not the only factor determining what type of causal attributions one makes. Sometimes, certain causal attributions have undesired consequences that make them less attractive. Consider, for example, attributing the cause to a stable internal factor such as ability. Often, such an attribution results in a necessary readjustment of a higher-level goal. This higher-level goal, in turn, could be linked to the self-concept. Thus, such an attribution would be unattractive because of the centrality and importance of the cognitive element within the overall cognitive structure. Indeed, many studies have shown that subjects tend to attribute failure to more variable causes such as effort, while they attribute success to stable factors such as ability (see Weiner, 1979, 1985). Sometimes, however, changing behavior (e.g., increasing effort) is seen as too challenging, perhaps due to a low sense of self-efficacy or too many competing demands (Bandura, 1982). In such a case, the professional would anticipate that the next outcome will be just as negative as the current one, causing new dissonance and possibly leading to resignation and symptoms of burnout. However, because people like to avoid dissonance (Festinger, 1957; Wicklund & Brehm, 1976), under these circumstances professionals may pay less attention to the external feedback in the future or reject it as inaccurate.

To summarize, if the performance outcome is inconsistent with the self-standard, it creates dissonance arousal and, in turn, motivation to reduce dissonance. Based on the judgment about the responsiveness to reality and the centrality and importance of each cognitive element, causal attributions are made and a corresponding action plan (cognitively, behaviorally, or both) is developed. One implication of the preceding discussion is that there are several ways that feedback about poor outcomes can be ignored or discounted or lead to attributions that will not facilitate improvements. Accordingly, the action plan will need to have features that will help channel feedback into the desired effects.

Putting It All Together

Figure 4.4 illustrates the complete change model, which we refer to as the contextualized feedback intervention theory (CFIT). The goal of the theory is to provide a basis for interventions designed to improve performance by changing the behavior of professionals. As shown on the left of the figure, two of the major determinants of human behavior are motivation and ability (Kanfer & Ackerman, 1989). According to Kluger and DeNisi (1996), feedback interventions are capable of affecting both motivation and ability. Other interventions, such as training, workshops, and coaching, may also be used to affect ability. Ideally these would be integrated into the feedback process as a formative component.

The application of this theory is based on the assumption that some aspect of job performance serves as the genesis for the feedback provided

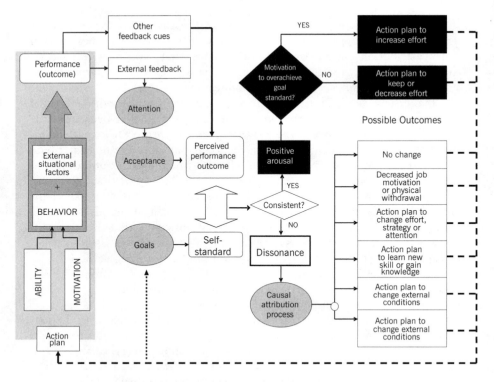

FIGURE 4.4. Overview of the complete change model.

to professionals. The belief–disconfirmation dissonance process that determines whether a person will initially reject the external feedback or include it in the self-evaluation judgment with other feedback cues is not displayed in detail in the model; neither is the causal attribution process demonstrated. The arrows connecting the dissonance process and the possible outcomes of this process to motivation, ability, and self-efficacy close the negative feedback loop described in self-regulation theories (see Carver & Scheier, 1981, 2000; Klein, 1989; Miller et al., 1960; Powers, 1973; Taylor et al., 1984).

Of course, the behavior of professionals is not the only factor determining the performance outcomes. Many situational factors external to professionals can strongly influence their success. For example, factors such as organizational climate can influence performance (Glisson & Hemmelgarn, 1998). We will not attempt to add this additional level of complexity to the model in this chapter, but we do recognize the importance of these situational factors and we are studying them as part of testing the validity of the CFIT. While the current model takes a more psychological than an organizational perspective, we assume that situational factors operate through the psychological mechanisms specified in the model (e.g., as perceived support and barriers).

It is important to note that, in order to describe and depict the processes in the model in a reasonable way, we had to simplify them. In reality, these processes will likely be less sequential and operate iteratively and parallel. Limited knowledge exists about how these processes unfold over a longer period of time because most studies are very time-limited. We hope to learn more about the time course of these processes in our ongoing evaluation.

The Action Model

In the previous section we described in detail our change model and how it was derived step by step from the research literature. In this section we describe how we used this change model to decide what program components are needed. That is, we will describe the action model we developed based on the change model. An overview of this action model is presented in Table 4.1. Based on the key elements in the change model, we divided it into four major sections: (1) goals, (2) external feedback, (3) causal attributions, and (4) ability. Next, we will present a short explanation for each program component section by section.

Goals

As suggested by the description of goals in the change model, we needed components that would ensure ongoing goal commitment to improving client outcomes. Thus, we looked for components that would increase (or sustain) the attractiveness of the goal, reduce barriers, provide support, and prevent a reduction in self-efficacy beliefs.

Initial CFIT User Training

We developed user training that is delivered using a train-the-trainer model so that training can be delivered locally and provided by locally trusted experts. The training includes elements that stress the importance of common factors (e.g., therapeutic alliance) in the success of clinical treatment. The training also demonstrates that by using feedback on common factors as well as available information on how to improve them (through online training modules and clinical supervisors), the clinicians will consider improvement to be a realistic and attainable goal.

TABLE 4.1. CFS™ Action Model

1. Goals		2. External feedback	
Program components	**Purpose**	**Program components**	**Purpose**
Initial CFS™ user training	Highlight the importance of the goal (goal attractiveness) and demonstrate feasibility of reaching it (goal expectations)	Sound and flexible measurement	Ensure perceived validity and utility of feedback and increase importance of feedback
Supervisor training (initial and ongoing)	Supervisor to provide support, reduce barriers, and prevent reduction in self-efficacy in cases of continuous negative feedback	Outcome as well as process information	Ensure perceived validity and utility of feedback
Short measures	Keep burden low (barriers)	Hierarchical structure of feedback	Ensure perceived utility of feedback
Timely feedback	Provide reliable information on progress towards the goal (can increase goal expectations)	Supervisor involvement	Ensure perceived validity and utility of feedback, increase importance of feedback, reduce threat of negative feedback, and provide accountability
Organizational consultation	Reduce barriers, ensure support, and ensuring that goal is an organizational value (goal attractiveness)	Implementation feedback	Provide accountability

3. Causal attributions		4. Ability	
Program components	**Purpose**	**Program components**	**Purpose**
Supervisor involvement	Direct clinicians to taking personal responsibility and changing behavior rather than dismissing the feedback or the goal	Online clinical training modules	Increase knowledge and skills
Online clinical training modules	Make changing behavior easier and consequently, make behavior change a more attractive attribution	Continuous feedback	Enable systematic learning from experience
Feedback on process	Direct clinicians to take personal responsibility and change behavior rather than blame others or the circumstances	Initial CFS™ user training and ongoing supervision	Increase knowledge and skills

Supervisor Training

Clinical supervisors are important sources for support and for the reduction (or increment) of barriers. Supervisors can also help clinicians to process the treatment session and the clinical feedback. In this role, they can prevent clinicians from reducing their self-efficacy beliefs if they are repeatedly receiving negative feedback. To foster this role and ensure the needed skills, clinical supervisors receive an intensive initial training as well as ongoing training through coaching calls. Supervisors can help reduce the likelihood that negative feedback will be rejected or attributed in ways that inhibit improved performance. Supervisor involvement, as noted later, is also critical for establishing accountability for clinical processes and outcomes, which are generally lacking in mental health service delivery.

Brief Measures

Completing clinical scales and similar paperwork can be a burden to clinicians and clients and as such become a real barrier to their utilization. We used sophisticated psychometric methods as well as creativity to reduce the clinical measures to the necessary minimum of items and develop a measurement schedule that allows completing a scheduled questionnaire set in only 5 to 8 minutes of a regular treatment session.

Timely Feedback

Often in clinical settings, feedback is provided after several months of treatment have passed or even after clients have been discharged. This makes it difficult, if not impossible, to use the information in making changes for the clients, especially given that clinical cases can differ significantly from each other. In our intervention, clinical information is collected weekly and is available to the clinicians as soon as the data have been entered via an online system that is integrated into other client management tasks. This makes the goal of actually affecting the current clinical process much more attainable.

Organizational Consultation

Depending on the organizational culture and climate, professional goals can be strongly influenced by organizational goals and values as well as those of your peers. In addition, the organizational structure can either facilitate or hinder the implementation of an intervention. For this reason, we developed an organizational consultation process that includes assessments of organizational commitment, culture, climate, leadership, and structure, as well as support calls where the results and potential problems are discussed. In addition, weekly phone meetings with the top change agents at the corporate level are conducted during the readiness, training, and initial implementation phases.

External Feedback

The factors we can directly affect that should lead clinicians to pay attention to the feedback and accept it are the perceived validity and utility of the feedback, how important the feedback information is to the clinician, whether the feedback poses a threat to the professional integrity of the clinicians, and whether they are held accountable.

Sound and Flexible Measurement

In developing the measurement battery that constitutes the foundation of the external feedback, we worked with a review panel of the service provider's clinical managers and clinicians in identifying the most important content areas. Based on this review we selected either existing scales or developed our own to cover these content areas. The scales were then evaluated in a large psychometric study. Problems were identified and corrected. The scales make up the core battery for the feedback intervention. However, because not all information needs can be anticipated or because they are too specific to be included in a core battery for all, we also developed flexibility in the online system that allows us to easily enter additional measures if needed. These can be selected and added to the measurement schedule by the clinicians on an as-need basis. With this combination of a sound core measurement battery, flexibility, and involvement of clinicians in the selection process of the measures, we intend to increase the perceived validity and utility of the feedback as well as make the feedback more important. Based on 2½ years of data collection we have revised them once more to not only make them briefer, without affecting their validity, but also to modify them so that they are more sensitive to change (Bickman, Athay, & Riemer, 2010).

Outcome as Well as Process Information

Many clinicians are known to be very process oriented. This is not surprising since they can influence the process directly, while there are many factors outside the clinician's control that affect clinical outcomes. Thus, feedback that is perceived as valid and useful by the clinicians ideally contains information about the treatment process. Our feedback intervention includes information about common factor processes such as therapeutic alliance, treatment motivation, perceived treatment impact, and caregiver involvement.

Hierarchical Structure of Feedback

Feedback is easiest to use when it is very simple, for example, a single number or a single symbol such as a green, yellow, or red button. However, there is nothing simple about the clinical treatment of youth with severe behavioral and emotional problems. Several factors of the treatment process interact and change over time in affecting clinical outcomes in complex ways. Thus, reducing this complexity to a single indicator does not seem to be the best choice. Instead, we chose to organize the feedback hierarchically. A few central indicators for major problems are selected and presented at the highest level. This allows a quick check when time is scarce or the client has been stable for a while. More detailed information is available that allows the clinicians to determine possible sources of problems and look at the interactions among several factors. This includes detailed trends, percentile rankings, alerts to extreme answers on specific items, and comparisons among different types of respondents (e.g., youth, caregiver, and clinician).

Supervisor Involvement

The original feedback is provided via an interactive online environment. While some people prefer receiving feedback this way, others prefer to receive feedback from a person they trust and respect. Providing the clinical supervisor with the same feedback information as the clinician and making the feedback reports a central part of supervision ensures that the feedback is delivered in both ways. The fact that the supervisor has access and pays attention to the feedback also can help increase the importance of that feedback and provide a certain level of accountability. Providing supervisors with training and ongoing coaching ensures that they fulfill their important role in a responsible and productive way.

Implementation Feedback

It is easy to dismiss an intervention if it is not implemented correctly. To help prevent this from happening, we provide weekly and quarterly implementation reports and work with the organizational leadership in providing local implementers with the needed support. This is an attempt to hold the clinicians accountable for the implementation of the intervention (i.e., completing weekly questionnaires with clients and their caregivers, review feedback reports, and complete training). If they are held accountable for the implementation, they are also signaled that the information they are collecting is considered to be important. However, this approach met with limited success since it is highly dependent on local leadership. Implementation fidelity and compliance was a major problem with about half of the feedback reports not even accessed. In our revision of the software and the training program we are considering alternative approaches to increase the degree and quality of implementation.

Causal Attributions

Based on the change model, it is important that the clinicians take some personal responsibility for negative feedback and belief that they can improve by changing their behavior. While these are internal cognitive-emotional processes, we believe that they can be influenced in several ways.

Supervisor Involvement

In reviewing the feedback reports as part of supervision, supervisors can discern when clinicians fail to take personal responsibility or feel they have no way of improving. Supervisors can process with the clinician what her responsibility has been and how she can better make a difference. Supervisors and clinicians can also discuss the accuracy of the feedback, the importance of the goal, and the steps clinicians can take toward having a more positive effect. Again, this requires a certain skill level from the supervisor, which in our intervention is enhanced through supervisor training and ongoing coaching. It also requires that local leadership make supervisor involvement a high priority.

Online Clinical Training Modules

The online clinical training modules provide the clinicians with information and tools that help them to determine the kind of changes that may be necessary to improve the treatment progress. This should reduce the resistance to making a causal attribution that includes personal responsibility by decreasing the fear of the consequences of doing so.

Feedback on Process

Information on clinical outcomes is often difficult to connect to the behavior of a clinician because it is too distal. Process information, on the other hand, is more proximal to the clinician's behavior. Consequently, including process information in the feedback helps the counselor to take personal responsibility and determine what she can do differently (e.g., pay more attention to the client's treatment motivation).

Ability

As can be seen in the change model in Figure 4.4, behavior is influenced by both motivation and ability. In the previous section we have shown how the different program components are thought to affect motivation to change behavior. In this section we will discuss how they affect the clinicians' ability as well.

Online Clinical Training Modules

As noted previously, the online training modules provide the clinicians with knowledge and skills that are directly relevant to the type of feedback they receive. The clinicians complete four training modules during the initial training phase of the project, but they can also return to the module at any time to use the tools and look up information. Supervisors are trained in supporting clinicians in integrating the knowledge from the module into the clinical practice.

Continuous Feedback

Trying to learn from experience without systematic feedback is like trying to hit a target while blindfolded. No amount of practice will improve your aim if there is little or no accurate feedback. Thus, providing systematic feedback, as we do in our intervention, enables the clinicians to learn more efficiently from their experience and increase their ability as mental health professionals.

Initial User Training and Ongoing Supervision

Through the initial user training as well as ongoing supervision by a trained clinical supervisor, clinicians are provided with information and ideas about how to best integrate the feedback information into their clinical practice and decision-making process.

Together, the different components in this section make up our program, which is called contextualized feedback systems (CFS™; Bickman, Riemer, Breda, & Kelley, 2006). It includes a comprehensive clinical measurement battery (Bickman, Riemer, Lambert et al., 2007), continuous timely online feedback on treatment progress and process, an intensive training model for clinicians as well as supervisors including online clinical training modules on common factors and coaching calls, implementation feedback and support, as well as organizational consulting. While the rationale for these different elements was derived from the change model, the selection and development of the actual CFS™ components was strongly influenced by our partner organization. This organization, Providence Service Corporation, Inc., is a major national provider of in-home counseling services for children and adolescents and is currently implementing CFS™ as their quality enhancement initiative. The Center for Evaluation and Program Improvement under the leadership of Leonard Bickman received a five-year R01 grant from NIMH to evaluate the effectiveness of CFS™ as implemented by Providence.

The Evaluation

We have completed data collection and are now starting data analysis, so the results of our experiment are not available at the time we are writing this chapter. The evaluation posed several challenges. First, it was difficult to meld our ambition of using a randomized experiment with the complexity of the model as well as the complexities of the real world outside of a research laboratory. We decided to use a mixed-method approach that allows us to test several key features of CFS™ as part of a randomized experiment as well as using qualitative approaches.

With the randomized experiment we will be testing two main hypotheses. First, does provision of frequent feedback improve the effectiveness of the services? The other key component being tested is the online clinical training modules on common factors, in particular training on therapeutic alliance. Only a randomly selected half of the clinicians has access to these modules.

The design of the study is a 2×2 factorial design, with feedback (weekly vs. 90 days) and online clinical training modules (access or no access) as the independent variables. There were 38 sites randomly assigned to the experimental conditions. Although site-level random assignment lowered the risk of potential contamination and disruption that could occur within a site, this large number of sites led us to our second major challenge.

Providence is an unusually large mental health service provider . It served 70,000 clients from 318 locations in 36 states, the District of Columbia, and Victoria, British Columbia, Canada as of March 31, 2008. But the organization is also very decentralized, and each location had to be recruited individually. Moreover, they had to volunteer to implement CFS™ as their quality enhancement initiative at their own expense. It was only with the patience and great enthusiasm of the corporate CFS™ leadership team that we were able to recruit a sufficient number of sites for the evaluation. The clear advantage of this approach is that CFS™ is being implemented not as a study, but rather as the company's own quality improvement initiative. Thus, if CFS™ is found to be effective, it is already fully functional as a commercial product in the real world. This has become a reality since the company has recently agreed to license CFS™ from Vanderbilt University for a 5-year period. Another challenge we faced is that the process of maintaining a complex administration schedule and providing fast feedback requires sophisticated computer programming. For this reason, another partner in the evaluation is a software development firm that specializes in client management software for mental health service providers. However, this organization was not up to the challenge, and so we have contracted with another software development firm to produce a new CFS™ that incorporates what we have learned over the last several years.

Yet another challenge is that we are both the program developer and the evaluator. We were able to use our knowledge about program theory, basic social science, and the importance of implementation fidelity in the development of the program. In addition, we are using the experience we are gaining during the evaluation and analysis to make important improvements to CFIT.

Summary

In this chapter, we have described how one of the authors left the field of social psychology only to return to it 30 years later. However, this homecoming did not mean joining what he and others see as a tendency for mainstream social psychologists to remain distant from the real world (Cook & Groom, 2004). Nor did we focus only on one theory, striving as social psychologists typically do to test the effects of a single causal construct that they developed. Rather, we weaved together several approaches that we thought would be helpful in the development and testing of an intervention. In part, this involved (1) searching for a practical and potentially powerful general intervention, the provision of feedback for our goal and objectives, and (2) drawing on various literatures to seek things that would enhance the effect of this intervention and minimize various risks to its effectiveness. Unlike much of mainstream social psychology, at least as represented in its premier journals, we concentrated on the utilization of multiple theories to help solve a social problem, in contrast to testing a particular theory.

We have introduced a complex program theory consisting of a science-based change model and an action model guided by the change model. In the process of developing this theory, we extracted what we believed were the best, most relevant, and, as much as possible, empirically grounded aspects of many established theories. Our goal was to meet the expressed need for applied theories that have their roots in basic science. We hope that future research will further establish the empirical validity of the theory as we have presented it here. Ultimately, however, the strength of the CFIT must be demonstrated in its practical application. We agree with Theil that "models are to be used, not believed" (1971).

ACKNOWLEDGMENT

This chapter was partially supported by National Institute of Mental Health Grant No. 5R01MH068589 to Leonard Bickman.

RECOMMENDED READINGS

Program Theory

Bickman, L. (2000). Summing up program theory. In P. Rogers, T. Hacsi, A. Petrosino, & T. Huebner (Eds.), *New directions for evaluation* (Vol. 87, pp. 103–112). San Francisco: Jossey-Bass.

Chen, H. (2005). *Practical program evaluation: Assessing and improving planning, implementation, and effectiveness.* Thousand Oaks, CA: Sage.

Donaldson, S. I. (2003). Theory-driven program evaluation in the new millennium. In S. I. Donaldson & M. Scriven (Eds.), *Evaluating social programs and problems: Visions for the New Millennium* (pp. 109–141). Mahwah, NJ: Erlbaum.

Turnbull, B. (2002). Program theory building: A strategy for deriving cumulative evaluation knowledge. *American Journal of Evaluation, 23*(3), 275–290.

Feedback

Bickman, L. (2008). A measurement feedback system (MFS) is necessary to improve mental health outcomes. *Journal of the American Association of Child and Adolescent Psychiatry, 47*(10), 1114–1119.

Ilgen, D. R., Fisher, C. D., & Taylor, M. S. (1979). Consequences of individual feedback on behavior in organizations. *Journal of Applied Psychology, 64*(4), 349–371.

Kelley, S. D., & Bickman, L. (2009). Beyond outcomes monitoring: Measurement feedback systems (MFS) in child and adolescent clinical practice. *Current Opinion in Psychiatry, 22*(4), 363–368.

Kelley, S. D., Bickman, L., & Norwood, E. (2009). Evidence-based treatments and common factors in youth psychotherapy. In B. Duncan, S. Miller, & B. Wampold (Eds.), *Heart and soul of change* (2nd ed.). Washington, DC: American Psychological Association.

Kluger, A. N., & DeNisi, A. (1996). *Effects of feedback intervention on performance: A historical review, a meta-analysis, and a preliminary feedback intervention theory.* Washington, DC: American Psychological Association.

Riemer, M., Rosof-Williams, J., & Bickman, L. (2005). Theories related to changing clinician practice. *Child and Adolescent Psychiatric Clinics of North America, 14*(2), 241–254.

Taylor, M. S., Fischer, C. D., & Ilgen, D. R. (1984). Individuals' reactions to performance feedback in organizations: A control theory perspective. *Research in Personnel and Human Resources Management, 2*, 81–124.

Relevant Scientific Theories

Aronson, E. (1999b). Dissonance, hypocrisy, and the self-concept. In M. E. Harmon-Jones & J. Mills (Eds.), *Cognitive dissonance—Progress on a pivotal theory in social psychology.* (pp. 103–126). Washington, DC: American Psychological Association.

Bandura, A. (1977). Self-efficacy: Toward a unifying theory of behavioral change. *Psychological Review, 84,* 191–215.

Carver, C. S., & Scheier, M. F. (1981). *Attention and self-regulation: A control-theory approach to human behavior.* New York: Springer-Verlag.

Festinger, L. (1957). *A theory of cognitive dissonance.* Evanston, IL: Row Peterson.

Harmon-Jones, E., & Mills, J. (1999). An introduction to cognitive dissonance theory and an overview of current perspectives on the theory. In M. E. Harmon-Jones & J. Mills, (Eds.), *Cognitive dissonance—Progress on a pivotal theory in social psychology* (pp. 3–21). Washington, DC: American Psychological Association.

Hollenbeck, J. R., & Klein, H. J. (1987). Goal commitment and the goal-setting process: Problems, prospects, and proposals for future research. *Journal of Applied Psychology, 72*(2), 212–220.

Locke, E. A., & Latham, G. P. (2002). Building a practically useful theory of goal setting and task motivation. *American Psychologist, 57*(9), 705–717.

Weiner, B. (1985). An attributional theory of achievement motivation and emotion. *Psychological Review, 92*(4), 548–573.

REFERENCES

Aronson, E. (1999a). The power of self-persuasion. *American Psychologist, 54,* 875–884.

Aronson, E. (1999b). Dissonance, hypocrisy, and the self-concept. In M. E. Harmon-Jones & J. Mills (Eds.), *Cognitive dissonance—Progress on a pivotal theory in social psychology* (pp. 103–126). Washington, DC: American Psychological Association.

Austin, J. T., & Vancouver, J. B. (1996). Goal constructs in psychology: Structure, process and content. *Psychological Bulletin, 120*(3), 338–375.

Bandura, A. (1977). Self-efficacy: Toward a unifying theory of behavioral change. *Psychological Review, 84,* 191–215.

Bandura, A. (1982). Self-efficacy mechanism in human agency. *American Psychologist, 37*(2), 122–147.

Bandura, A. (1997). *Self-efficacy: The exercise of control.* New York: W.H. Freeman & Co.

Bickman, L. (2002). The death of treatment as usual: An excellent first step on a long road. *Clinical Psychology: Science and Practice, 9*(2), 195–199.

Bickman, L., Athay, M. M., & Riemer, M. (2010). *Manual of the Peabody Treatment Progress Battery* (2nd ed.). Nashville, TN: Vanderbilt University.

Bickman, L., Guthrie, P., Foster, E. W., Lambert, E. W., Summerfelt, W. T., Breda, C., et al. (1995). *Evaluating managed mental health care: The Fort Bragg experiment*. New York: Plenum.

Bickman, L., & Peterson, K. A. (1990). Using program theory to describe and measure program quality. In L. Bickman (Ed.), *Advances in program theory, New directions for program evaluation*, No. 47 (pp. 61–72). San Francisco: Jossey-Bass.

Bickman, L., & Riemer, M. (2002). Reforming children's mental health services: Lessons from the past and suggestions for the future. Keynote Address, Quality Management and Outcome Monitoring, Concepts, tools and procedures for the optimization of psychotherapy, Center for Psychotherapy Research, Stuttgart Germany.

Bickman, L., Riemer, M., Breda, C., & Kelley, S. D. (2006). CFIT: A system to provide a continuous quality improvement infrastructure through organizational responsiveness, measurement, training, and feedback. *Report on Emotional and Behavioral Disorders in Youth, 4*, 88–87, 93–94.

Bickman, L., Riemer, M., Lambert, E. W., Kelley, S. D., Breda, C., Dew, S. E., et al. (Eds.). (2007). *Manual of the Peabody Treatment Progress Battery* [Electronic version]. Nashville, TN: Vanderbilt University.

Bickman, L., & Salzer, M. S. (Eds.). (1997). Measuring quality in mental health services [Special issue]. *Evaluation Review, 21*(3), 285–291.

Blanton, H., Pelham, B. W., DeHart, T., & Carvallo, M. (2001). Overconfidence as dissonance reduction. *Journal of Experimental Social Psychology, 37*(5), 373–385.

Brehm, J. W. (1956). Postdecision changes in the desirability of alternatives. *Journal of Abnormal and Social Psychology, 52*, 384–389.

Brockner, J., & Higgins, E. T. (2001). Regulatory focus theory: Implications for the study of emotions at work. *Organizational Behavior and Human Decision Process, 86*(1), 35–66.

Carver, C. S., & Scheier, M. F. (1981). *Attention and self-regulation: A control-theory approach to human behavior*. New York: Springer-Verlag.

Chen, H. (1990). Issues in constructing program theory. *New Directions for Program Evaluation, 47*, 7–18.

Chen, H. (2005). *Practical program evaluation: Assessing and improving planning, implementation, and effectiveness*. Thousand Oaks, CA: Sage.

Cook, T. D., & Groom, C. (2004). The methodological assumptions of social psychology. The mutual dependence of substantive theory and method choice. In C. Sansone, C. C. Morf, & A. T. Pantor (Eds.), *The Sage handbook of methods in social psychology* (pp. 19–44). Thousand Oaks, CA: Sage.

Dew, S., & Riemer, M. (2003). Why inaccurate self-evaluation of performance justifies feedback interventions. Paper presented at the 16th Annual Research Conference, A System of Care for Children's Mental Health. Tampa: University of South Florida.

Dickerson, C. A., Thibodeau, R., Aronson, E., & Miller, D. (1992). Using cognitive dissonance to encourage water conservation. *Journal of Applied Social Psychology, 22*(11), 841–854.

Festinger, L. (1957). *A theory of cognitive dissonance.* Evanston, IL: Row Peterson.

Festinger, L., Riecken, H. W., & Schachter, S. (1956). *When prophecy fails.* Minneapolis: University of Minnesota Press.

Ford, M. E. (1992). *Motivating humans.* Newbury Park, CA: Sage.

Gibson, F. P. (2000). Feedback delays: How can decision makers learn not to buy a new car every time the garage is empty? *Organizational Behavior and Human Decision Process, 83*(1), 141–166.

Gist, G. E., & Mitchel, T. R. (1992). Self-efficacy: A theoretical analysis of its determinants and malleability. *Academy of Management Review, 17*(2), 183–211.

Glisson, C., & Hemmelgarn, A. (1998). The effects of organizational climate and interorganizational coordination on the quality and outcomes of children's service systems. *Child Abuse and Neglect, 22*(5), 1–21.

Harmon-Jones, E. (1999). Toward an understanding of the motivation underlying dissonance effects: Is the production of aversive consequences necessary? In M. E. Harmon-Jones & J. Mills (Eds.), *Cognitive dissonance—Progress on a pivotal theory in social psychology* (pp. 71–99). Washington, DC: American Psychological Association.

Harmon-Jones, E., & Mills, J. (1999). An introduction to cognitive dissonance theory and an overview of current perspectives on the theory. In M. E. Harmon-Jones & J. Mills (Eds.), *Cognitive dissonance—Progress on a pivotal theory in social psychology* (pp. 3–21). Washington, DC: American Psychological Association.

Helmreich, R. (1975). Applied social psychology: The unfulfilled promise. *Personality and Social Psychology Bulletin, 1*(4), 548–560.

Herold, D. M., & Fedor, D. B. (1998). Individuals' interaction with their feedback environment: The role of domain-specific individual differences. *Research in Personnel and Human Resources Management, 16,* 215–254.

Herold, D. M., Parsons, C. K., & Rensvold, R. B. (1996). Individual differences in the generation and processing of performance feedback. *Educational and Psychological Measurement, 56*(1), 5–25.

Higgins, E. T. (1997). Beyond pleasure and pain. *American Psychologist, 52*(12), 1280–1300.

Higgins, E. T. (1998). Promotion and prevention: Regulatory focus as a motivational principle. In M. P. Zanna (Ed.), *Advances in experimental social psychology* (Vol. 30, pp. 1–46). New York: Academic Press.

Hollenbeck, J. R., & Klein, H. J. (1987). Goal commitment and the goal-setting process: Problems, prospects, and proposals for future research. *Journal of Applied Psychology, 72*(2), 212–220.

Hollenbeck, J. R., Williams, C. R., & Klein, H. J. (1989). An empirical examination of the antecedents of commitment to difficult goals. *Journal of Applied Psychology, 74*(1), 18–23.

Hong, Y. Y., Chiu, C. Y., Dweck, C. S., Lin, D., & Wan, W. (1999). Implicit theories, attributions, and coping: A meaning system approach. *Journal of Personality and Social Psychology, 77*(3), 588–599.

Ilgen, D. R., Fisher, C. D., & Taylor, M. S. (1979). Consequences of individual feedback on behavior in organizations. *Journal of Applied Psychology, 64*(4), 349–371.

Kalmar, D. A., & Sternberg, R. J. (1988). Theory knitting: An integrative approach to theory development. *Philosophical Psychology, 1*(2), 153–170.

Kanfer, R., & Ackerman, P. L. (1989). Motivation and cognitive abilities: An integrative/aptitude-treatment interaction approach to skill acquisition. *Journal of Applied Psychology, 74*(4), 657–690.

Karver, M. S., Handelsman, J. B., Fields, S., & Bickman, L. (2005). A theoretical model of common process factors in youth and family therapy. *Mental Health Services Research, 7*(1), 35–51.

Kelley, H. H., & Michela, J. L. (1980). Attribution theory and research. *Annual Review of Psychology, 31,* 457–501.

Klein, H. J. (1989). An integrated control theory model of work motivation. *Academy of Management Review, 14*(2), 150–172.

Klein, H. J., Wesson, M. J., Hollenbeck, J. R., Wright, P. M., & DeShon, R. P. (2001). The assessment of goal commitment: A measurement model meta-analysis. *Organizational Behavior and Human Decision Processes, 85*(1), 32–55.

Kluger, A. N., & DeNisi, A. (1996). *Effects of feedback intervention on performance: A historical review, a meta-analysis, and a preliminary feedback intervention theory.* Washington, DC: American Psychological Association.

Kluger, A. N., & DeNisi, A. (1998). Feedback interventions: Toward the understanding of a double-edged sword. *Current Directions in Psychological Science, 7*(3), 67–72.

Lambert, M. J., Hansen, N. B., & Finch, A. (2001). Patient-focused research: Using patient outcome data to enhance treatment effects. *Journal of Consulting and Clinical Psychology, 69*(2), 159–172.

Lent, R. W., Brown, S. D., & Larkin, K. C. (1987). Comparison of three theoretically derived variables in predicting career and academic behavior: Self-efficacy, interest congruence, and consequence thinking. *Journal of Counseling Psychology, 34*(3), 293–298.

Locke, E. A., Frederick, E., Lee, C., & Bobko, P. (1984). Effect of self-efficacy, goals, and task strategies on task performance. *Journal of Applied Psychology, 69*(2), 241–251.

Locke, E. A., & Latham, G. P. (2002). Building a practically useful theory of goal setting and task motivation. *American Psychologist, 57*(9), 705–717.

London, M., & Smither, J. W. (1999). Empowered self-development and continuous learning. *Human Resource Management, 38*(1), 3–15.

London, M., Smither, J. W., & Adsit, D. J. (1997). Accountability. *Group and Organization Management, 22*(2), 162–184.

Maslach, C., Schaufeli, W. B., & Leiter, M. P. (2000). Job burnout. *Annual Review of Psychology, 52,* 397–422.

McAuley, E., Duncan, T. E., & Russell, D. W. (1992). Measuring causal attributions: The revised Causal Dimension Scale (CDSII). *Journal of Social Psychology Bulletin, 81*(5), 566–573.

Miller, G. A., Galanter, E., & Pribram, K. H. (1960). *Plans and the structure of behavior.* New York: Henry Holt.

Mone, M. A., & Baker, D. D. (1992). Stage of task learning as a moderator of the goal-performance relationship. *Human Performance, 2*(2), 85–99.

Moore, J. E. (2000). Why is this happening? A causal attribution approach to work exhaustion. *Academy of Management Review, 25*(2), 335–349.

Morris, J., & Ellis, J. (1997). The effect of verbal and graphic feedback on the data-recording behavior of direct care trainers. *Behavioral Interventions, 12*(2), 77–104.

Nyquist, J. B. (2003). *The benefits of reconstructing feedback as a larger system of formative assessment: A meta-analysis.* Unpublished master's thesis, Vanderbilt University, Nashville, TN.

Peterson, K. A., & Bickman, L. (1992). Using program theory in quality assessments of children's mental health services. In H. Chen & P. H. Rossi (Eds.), *Using theory to improve program and policy evaluation* (pp. 165–176). Westport, CT: Greenwood.

Powers, W. T. (1973). Feedback: Beyond behaviorism. *Science, 179,* 351–356.

Riemer, M., Rosof-Williams, J., & Bickman, L. (2005). Theories related to changing clinician practice. *Child and Adolescent Psychiatric Clinics of North America, 14*(2), 241–254.

Rodrigues, A., & Levine, R. (Eds.). (1999). *Reflections on 100 years of experimental social psychology.* New York: Basic Books.

Rose, D. J., & Church, R. J. (1998). *Learning to teach: The acquisition and maintenance of teaching skills.* New York: Kluwer Academic/Plenum Publishers.

Sapyta, J., Riemer, M., & Bickman, L. (2005). Feedback to clinicians: Theory, research, and practice, *Journal of Clinical Psychology/In Session, 61*(2), 145–153.

Schultz, P. W. (1998). Changing behavior with normative feedback interventions: A field experiment on curbside recycling. *Basic and Applied Social Psychology, 2*(1), 25–36.

Shao, Y. (1996). Effects of feedback sign on task motivation and task performance: Mediators and moderators. *Psychology.* New Brunswick, NJ: Rutgers, The State University of New Jersey.

Sherman, D. K., & Cohen, G. L. (2002). Accepting threatening information: Self-affirmation and the reduction of defensive biases. *Current Directions in Psychological Science, 11*(4), 119–122.

Shewhart, W. (1939). *Statistical method from the viewpoint of quality control.* Washington, DC: U.S. Department of Agriculture.

Smither, J. W., Wohlers, A. J., & London, M. (1995). A field study of reactions to normative versus individualized upward feedback. *Group and Organization Management, 20*(1), 61–89.

Stajkovic, A. D., & Luthans, F. (1998). Self-efficacy and work related performance: A meta-analysis. *Psychological Bulletin, 124*(2), 240–261.

Stajkovic, A. D., & Sommer, S. M. (2000). Self-efficacy and causal attributions: Direct and reciprocal links. *Journal of Applied Social Psychology, 30*(4), 707–737.

Stone, J. (1999). What exactly have we done? The role of self-attribute accessibility in dissonance. In M. E. Harmon-Jones & J. Mills (Eds.), *Cognitive dissonance—Progress on a pivotal theory in social psychology* (pp. 149–173). Washington, DC: American Psychological Association.

Taylor, M. S., Fisher, C. D., & Ilgen, D. R. (1984). Individuals' reactions to performance feedback in organizations: A control theory perspective. *Research in Personnel and Human Resources Management, 2*, 81–124.

Taylor, S. E., & Fiske, S. T. (1978). Salience, attention and attribution: Top of the head phenomena. *Advances in Experimental Social Psychology, 11*, 249–288.

Theil, H. (1971). *Principles of econometrics.* New York: Wiley.

Walster, E., Berscheid, E., & Barclay, A. M. (1967). A determinant of preference among modes of dissonance reduction. *Journal of Personality and Social Psychology, 7*(2), 211–216.

Weiner, B. (1979). A theory of motivation for some classroom experiences. *Journal of Educational Psychology, 71*(1), 3–25.

Weiner, B. (1985). An attributional theory of achievement motivation and emotion. *Psychological Review, 92*(4), 548–573.

Weiner, B., Frieze, I., Kukla, A., Reed, L., Rest, S., & Rosenbaum, R. M. (1971). Perceiving the causes of success and failure. In D. K. E. Jones, H. Kelley, R. Nisbett, S. Valins, & B. Weiner (Eds.), *Attribution: Perceiving the causes of behavior* (pp. 95–120). Morristown, NJ: General Learning Press.

Wicklund, R. A., & Brehm, J. W. (1976). *Perspectives on cognitive dissonance.* Hillsdale, NJ: Erlbaum.

Wilson, C., Boni, N., & Hogg, A. (1997). The effectiveness of task classification, positive reinforcement and corrective feedback in changing courtesy among police staff. *Journal of Organizational Behavior Management, 17*(1), 65–99.

EDITORS' CONCLUDING COMMENTS TO CHAPTER 4

Riemer and Bickman focus on program development through most of their chapter. One of their key points involves drawing on multiple research areas and theories to try to knit together an intervention package that may be effective in the complexities of real-life contexts. We invite the reader to think about what if any theory knitting would be helpful for some of the other chapters in this volume that focus more on a single social psychological theory.

At the end of the chapter, Riemer and Bickman briefly discuss the ongoing evaluation of CFS™, the feedback program they developed. In describing the evaluation, the authors briefly present the evaluation design and the challenges they faced. Understandably, given that they only had a few pages for discussing the evaluation, the authors did not address a claim that many advocates of theory-driven evaluation, including Bickman, have made—that program theory can assist in evaluating the program. To take one important example, the program theory should help evaluators identify measures that correspond to the various steps in the theory. With measures of this kind, advocates of theory-driven evaluation argue that it can contribute both to program-improvement-oriented, formative evaluation and to more bottom-line, summative evaluation. We invite you to look back over the change model and action model for CFS™, and consider how the program theory could enhance program evaluation.

Riemer and Bickman also introduce the issue that they are both program developer and evaluator. They note that this could raise concerns about possible conflicts of interest. As developers of the program, might they, whether intentionally or unintentionally, shape the evaluation in ways that increase the odds the program will look successful? Because of this concern, some evaluation experts, such as Michael Scriven, argue strongly for an external evaluator, with no connection to the program, for serious summative evaluations. In contrast, in social psychology and many related areas, including clinical psychology, program developers or other advocates of a hypothesis commonly conduct tests of it. What are your thoughts about this discrepancy? In considering the discrepant positions, consider an important difference in practice between typical social psychology and typical evaluation, such as the likelihood of replication taking place before errors of inference have too great a cost.

EDITORS' INTRODUCTORY COMMENTS
TO CHAPTER 5

In the next chapter, Stewart Donaldson and Bill Crano address the intersection between theory-driven evaluation science and applied social psychology. Several theories of evaluation exist. These theories include prescriptions about such things as why evaluation should be done, what should count as credible evidence, how values should be infused into evaluation (and whose values), and what the evaluator should do to facilitate evaluation use. Theory-driven evaluation, sometimes known more specifically as program theory-driven evaluation, is one of these evaluation theories. It focuses on the construction or uncovering of a program theory—that is, on developing a model of why the program is supposed to work, including mediators. The theory-driven approach to evaluation typically leads to testing the program theory, as well as examining possible effects of the program, in the course of the evaluation.

Donaldson and Crano point to the existing overlap between theory-driven evaluation and applied social psychology. They also highlight the potential for an even stronger and happier marriage. As the chapter authors point out, the inclusion of social psychological concepts in program theories can have important benefits. For example, knowing why a program does or does not work—and not just whether it works—can increase the use of evaluation findings, as it apparently has in the case of DARE, a substance abuse prevention program the authors discuss. Several evaluations had shown DARE to be ineffective, or even to result in increased substance use. Following theory-driven findings that explained why DARE was not effective, the DARE program was revised with the financial support of a major foundation. Tests of program theory can provide the narrative, the explanation of why a program worked or didn't, and this can help persuade potential users of the evaluation of its accuracy.

To an extent, Donaldson and Crano also weave together highlights from previous chapters in this section.

CHAPTER 5

Theory-Driven Evaluation Science and Applied Social Psychology
Exploring the Intersection

Stewart I. Donaldson
William D. Crano

Throughout this volume the authors explore the vast intersection between evaluation and social psychology. In this chapter we narrow the focus somewhat. Our aim is to examine the intersection of a subarea within each field. We adopt this focus because the intersection in question is particularly well suited for advancing both evaluation and social psychology. To provide a context for our discussion, we begin with an overview of contemporary evaluation practice and evaluation theory. One particular evaluation theory, theory-driven evaluation science, will be described in some detail to provide readers with an understanding of its current position in evaluation theory and practice, as well as it aims and procedures. Next, an overview of applied social psychology is provided to show its relationship to the broader branch of psychology known as social psychology, as well as its goals and specific aims. Finally, the rich intersection between theory-driven evaluation science and applied social psychology is explored, illustrating how theory-driven evaluation science can be used to enrich applied social psychology and vice versa.

Contemporary Evaluation Practice

The profession of evaluation has grown rather dramatically since its early beginnings in the late 1960s. While there are many aspects to the field's development, several trends are worth noting here to provide a context for this chapter. First, Patton (2008) somewhat jokingly claimed that evaluation grew up "in the projects." That is, much of the early work in the profession of evaluation as we know it today was focused on project and program evaluation. However, since those early beginnings the evaluation profession has expanded its scope to include projects, programs, initiatives, interventions, policies, personnel, products, organizations, and technology, among other types of things that are evaluated. To reflect this dramatic expansion of activity, the largest professional evaluation association, the American Evaluation Association (AEA), which earlier had focused on program evaluation, has revised its mission as follows:

> The American Evaluation Association is an international professional association of evaluators devoted to the application and exploration of program evaluation, personnel evaluation, technology, and many other forms of evaluation. Evaluation involves assessing the strengths and weaknesses of programs, policies, personnel, products, and organizations to improve their effectiveness.

A second major trend affecting contemporary evaluation practice is the globalization of the profession and discipline of evaluation. The values of professionalism, accountability, and evidence-based practice have seemed to capture the fancy of governments, policy makers, and business and education leaders from a variety of sectors and industries across the globe (Donaldson, 2008). Considerable demand exists for evaluations that pursue credible evidence to determine "what works" and/or how to make an evaluand "work better." This demand is being experienced well beyond the more traditional settings such as Washington, D.C. and North America in general. One indicator of this trend is the expansion of professional societies where evaluators meet on a regular basis to discuss how best to practice evaluation, develop professional standards and guiding principles, participate in professional development, and keep abreast of the latest developments in the field. In 1980, there were 3 major evaluation professional societies, whereas today there are more 75. There is even a formal international evaluation association cooperation network, the International Organization for Cooperation in Evaluation, which was established to build evaluation capacity in most regions of the world (International Organization for Cooperation in Evaluation Website, 2009).

Another major trend that deserves attention is the multidisciplinary or transdisciplinary nature of the evaluation profession. First, professional evaluators come from a variety of disciplinary backgrounds, including areas such as social psychology, organizational behavior, public health, education, educational psychology, public policy, sociology, public administration, economics, and management. Evaluation is often used to examine the effectiveness of theories, principles, and interventions from these complementary disciplines. Further, many evaluations are enriched by having teams comprised of evaluators from multiple disciplines, sharing a variety of viewpoints. Evaluation has long been known as a multidisciplinary endeavor, and this characteristic is increasing.

A related but somewhat different notion is that evaluation can be conceptualized as a transdiscipline (Donaldson & Christie, 2006). Scriven (2003) provided the following vision for the future of evaluation science:

> I hope and expect that the essential nature of evaluation itself will crystallize in our minds into a clear and essentially universal recognition of it as a discipline, a discipline with a clear definition, subject matter, logical structure, and multiple fields of application. In particular, it will, I think, become recognized as one of the elite group of disciplines, which I call transdisciplines. These disciplines are notable because they supply essential tools for other disciplines, while retaining an autonomous structure and research effort of their own. (p. 19)

As one example of a transdiscipline, Scriven mentions statistics, which is recognized as a discipline of its own while providing key methods for many other disciplines. In this chapter, Scriven's notion of evaluation as transdiscipline will be explored in relation to applied social psychology in this chapter. The autonomous component of evaluation will be addressed in terms of a widely recognized evaluation theory, that is, theory-driven evaluation science (Donaldson, 2007). The potential contributions of theory-driven evaluation science to applied social psychology (and vice versa) will be explored to examine the intersection of these two fields and to suggest the value of expanding this rich intersecting domain. In the next section, we discuss the nature and importance of evaluation theory to contemporary evaluation practice, providing a context for our later discussion of this intersection.

Evaluation Theory

Evaluation theories are largely prescriptive. They "offer a set of rules, prescriptions, prohibitions, and guiding frameworks that specify what a good or proper evaluation is and how evaluation should be done" (Alkin, 2004). Thus, they are theories of evaluation practice that address such enduring themes as how to understand the nature of what we evaluate, how to assign value to programs and their performance, how to construct knowledge, and how to use the knowledge generated by evaluation (Donaldson & Lipsey, 2006; Shadish, Cook, & Leviton, 1991).

Shadish (1998) introduced his presidential address to the American Evaluation Association, entitled "Evaluation Theory Is Who We Are," with the following assertion:

> All evaluators should know evaluation theory because it is central to our professional identity. It is what we talk about more than anything else, it seems to give rise to our most trenchant debates, it gives us the language we use for talking to ourselves and others, and perhaps most important, it is what makes us different from other professions. Especially in the latter regards, it is in our own self-interest to be explicit about this message, and to make evaluation theory the very core of our identity. Every profession needs a unique knowledge base. For us, evaluation theory is that knowledge base. (p. 1)

Shadish also provided at least seven reasons why practicing evaluators should be thoughtful about evaluation theory:

- Evaluation theory provides a language that evaluators can use to talk with each other about evaluation.
- Evaluation theory encompasses many things in our field in which evaluators seem to care most deeply.
- Evaluation theory defines the themes of the majority of evaluation professional conferences.
- Evaluation theory provides evaluators with an identity that is different from the identity of other professionals.
- Evaluation theory provides the face that evaluators present to the outside world.
- Evaluation theory is the knowledge base that defines the profession.

These points suggest that evaluation theory has become a central and necessary thread in the social fabric of the evaluation profession. Evaluation theory can facilitate communication among evaluators practicing across the globe, help evaluation practitioners understand and share best practices, and provide the rationale for the various procedures evaluators recommend and use in practice (see Donaldson & Lipsey, 2006; Shadish, 1998).

There now exists a wide range of theories which suggest how best to practice contemporary evaluation science. Donaldson and Scriven (2003) illustrated these diverse perspectives on modern evaluation practice and discussed the relative advantages and disadvantages of integrating these evaluation theories versus embracing their differences. Others have also recently presented and analyzed the development of evaluation theories (e.g., Alkin, 2004; Stufflebeam, 2001). In one the most influential works on the foundations of evaluation and evaluation theory, Shadish, Cook, and Leviton (1991) concluded that theory-driven evaluation was one of the most advanced forms of evaluation theory, judging it more favorably than all of the other evaluation theories they examined. They characterized theory-driven evaluation as an ambitious attempt to bring coherence to a field in considerable turmoil and debate. Theory-driven evaluation was described as a comprehensive attempt to resolve dilemmas and incorporate the lessons from the applications of past theories to evaluation practice. Theory-driven evaluation incorporates the desirable features of past theories on how to practice evaluation without distorting or denying the validity of these previous positions. One purpose of this chapter is to illustrate how this highly evolved and widely used theory of evaluation practice can enhance, and be enhanced by, applied social psychology.

Theory-Driven Evaluation Science

Theory-driven evaluation science is an integrative theory of evaluation of practice that builds on lessons learned over the past four decades of evaluation practice. It is a contingency-based perspective, rejecting the notion that "one size fits all" in evaluation practice. It is also an evolving theory of practice that is designed to keep pace with, and adapt to, the changing landscape of evaluation. For example, theory-driven evaluation science is currently being adapted to the broad array and domains of evaluation practice (program, organizational, personnel, policy, etc.), as well as the expanding number of contexts such as those arising from the globalization of evaluation (Donaldson, in progress). For the purposes of this chapter, we are going to focus on one variant of this approach, program-theory driven evaluation science (Donaldson, 2007; Donaldson & Lipsey, 2006), which is particularly applicable to applied social psychology.

The confluence of evaluation theory, social science theory, and program theory constitutes this distinctive approach to evaluation broadly cast as "program theory-driven evaluation science" (Donaldson, 2007). Donaldson and Lipsey (2006) suggested that this integration of theory constitutes a (if not *the*) major way that evaluation contributes to social betterment by way of knowledge development. Donaldson (2007) provided the following definition:

> *Program theory-driven evaluation science* is the systematic use of substantive knowledge about the phenomena under investigation and scientific methods to improve, to produce knowledge and feedback about, and to determine the merit, worth, and significance of evaluands such as social, educational, health, community, and organizational programs.

The phrase *program theory-driven* (instead of theory-driven) is intended to clarify the meaning of the use of the word "theory" in this evaluation context. It specifies the type of theory (i.e., program theory in contrast to social psychological theory) that is expected to guide the evaluation questions and design. The phrase *evaluation science* is intended to underscore the use of rigorous scientific methods (i.e., qualitative, quantitative, and mixed methods) to answer key evaluation questions. Like all sciences, evaluation science involves a series of consensual, agreed-upon operations, based on logic, consensus, and data-correcting feedback (Crano & Brewer, 2002). The term *evaluation science* signals the emphasis placed on the guiding principle of *systematic inquiry* (American Evaluation Association, 2010) and the critical evaluation standard of *accuracy* (Yarbrough, Shulha, Hopson, & Caruthers, 2011).

We view *program theory-driven evaluation science* as essentially method neutral within the broad domain of social science methodology. Its focus on the development of program theory and evaluation questions frees evaluators from any initial presupposition that one methodology is of necessity advantaged over another. With its simple view that the choice of methods is contingent on the nature of the question to be answered and the form of an answer that will be useful, program theory-driven evaluation science reinforces the idea that neither quantitative, qualitative, nor mixed method designs are necessarily superior or applicable in every evaluation context (cf. Crano & Brewer, 2002; Donaldson, Christie, & Mark, 2008; Donaldson & Lipsey, 2006). Whether an evaluator uses case studies, observational methods, structured or unstructured interviews, online or telephone survey research, quasi-experimental or randomized experimental trials to answer the key evaluation questions is dependent on scientific judgment *and* discussions with relevant stakeholders about what constitutes credible evidence in the research context and what is feasible given practical and financial constraints (Donaldson, 2007).

In an effort to incorporate various lessons learned from the practice of theory-driven evaluation in recent years (e.g., Donaldson & Gooler, 2003) and to make this approach more accessible to evaluation practitioners, Donaldson (2007) presented a simple three-step model for understanding the basic activities of *program theory-driven evaluation science*:

1. Develop program theory.
2. Formulate and prioritize evaluation questions.
3. Answer evaluation questions.

Simply stated, evaluators work with stakeholders, first, to develop a common understanding of how a program is presumed to solve the social problem(s) of interest, second, to develop the implications and priorities for what aspects of program performance need to be examined, and, third, to design an evaluation that will provide valid information about those aspects.

Relevant social science theory and prior research (if available) are used to inform this process and to assess the plausibility of the relationships assumed between a program and its intended outcomes. Each program theory-driven evaluation also has the potential to contribute to an evolving understanding of the nature of the change processes that programs bring about, and how these processes can be optimized to produce social benefits. This orientation contrasts sharply with a history of evaluation practice replete with studies that reveal little about the mechanisms of change embodied in social programs, often referred to as "method-driven," "black box," or "input/output" evaluations. A program theory-driven approach focuses on which program components are most effective, the mediating causal processes through which they work, and the characteristics of the participants, service providers, settings, and the like that moderate the relationships between a program and its outcomes (Donaldson, 2007; Donaldson & Lipsey, 2006; Rossi, Lipsey, & Friedman, 2004; Weiss, 1998).

Applied Social Psychology

As introduced by Mark and colleagues in Chapter 1, social psychology is a branch of psychology concerned with the personality, attitudes, motivations, and behavior of the individual or group in the context of social interaction. The field emerged in the United States in the 1920s and boasts a much longer and larger tradition of empirically tested theoretical contributions than the field of evaluation (Prislin & Crano, in press). Topics include the influence of social cognition on behavior, the influence of social factors (such as peers) on a person's attitudes, beliefs, and behaviors, the functioning of small groups and large organizations, and the dynamics of face-to-face interactions (Smith & Mackie, 2007).

In his landmark text, *Applied Social Psychology*, Oskamp (1984) described "the crisis in social psychology," which included its growing lack of social relevance. Oskamp's text and many other writings to follow made the case for the value of applying social psychology to the important issues facing modern societies. These activities led to a renewed emphasis in social psychology now commonly known as applied social psychology. This new area focused on taking some aspect of the knowledge base of social psychology and applying it systematically for some social purpose. Applied social psychology had a powerful advocate in Donald Campbell, whose call for a more socially responsible psychology laid the scientific foundation for the evaluation profession, just as it helped pave the way for development of a more applied social psychology (Campbell, 1969).

As a result of a general movement in the field toward more serious concern for the potential contributions of research for the social good, a return to the mindset championed by Lewin (1966, 1997; Lewin & Gold, 1999; Lewin, Heider, & Heider, 1936) many years ago, applied social psychology came to be defined as the systematic application of social psychological constructs, principles, theories, intervention techniques, research methods, and research findings to the understanding and amelioration of social problems (Oskamp & Schultz, 1998).

Social psychology's reawakened appreciation of its obligations in the mid- to late 1960s was accompanied by a general social/political upheaval in the United States, and a more intense focus on building a more just and equitable society. Lyndon Johnson's Great Society programs challenged and changed the country in almost unimaginable ways. A list of its accomplishments and their continuing effects would take volumes, but just consider some of Johnson's programs, which affected all areas of society. The changes fostered by Johnson and the majority Democratic Congress included increased protections for civil rights, the war on poverty, Head Start, the Higher Education Act, the National Teacher Corps, Medicare and Medicaid, the National Endowment for the Humanities and PBS, and the construction of the Kennedy Center and the Hirshhorn Museum in Washington, D.C., among others.

Along with this massive federal intervention into the society came the need to evaluate its many outcomes. Arguably the most significant trigger of contemporary evaluation science was the need occasioned by Johnson's Great Society. Given the social nature of these programs, a marriage of applied social psychology with evaluation science was both inevitable and productive. Applied social psychologists now perform research and offer policy advice on real-world problems and social issues including drug abuse prevention, health promotion, environmental problems, legal issues, education questions, the mass media, and life in organizations, and their work is enlarged and influenced by evaluation science.

Oskamp and Schultz (1998) presented a useful discussion of the varied activities of applied social psychologists in evaluation contexts. In the latest edition of the classic text *Applied Social Psychology*, the authors explored the intersection of these complementary fields. Their observations provide examples of how social psychologists and evaluators have combined to examine the effectiveness of social psychological theories and principles in real-world settings. In doing so, they have shown how theory-driven evaluation is highly compatible with the goals and aspirations of applied social psychologists, and they discuss program theory-driven evaluations that have been used to test social psychological principles in the context of interventions to prevent the onset of adolescent substance abuse.

In the paragraphs that follow, we build on this work by illustrating some examples of social psychological examinations of ideas and theories of human behavior within the domain of theory-driven evaluation science. We also will discuss the potential of research methods developed by social psychologists to improve theory-driven evaluation science. This work will illustrate emerging opportunities for evaluation specialists and applied social psychologists to use theory-driven evaluation science to address pressing societal concerns.

A Sobering Example: D.A.R.E., an Idea That Deserved to Be Right but Wasn't

Adolescents' use of illicit drugs is a significant problem that has bedeviled parents, policy makers, community health operatives, and society in general for many years. Over the years, a multitude of programs have been adopted to stem the rising tide of this destructive behavior, and the Drug Abuse Resistance Education (D.A.R.E.) program is one of the most widespread (and expensive) of all school-based instruction-based drug prevention strategies. The program has been administered to more than 4.5 million school children, and has been adopted by more than 2,000 communities (Rogers, 1993).

DeJong's (1987) early evaluation of the D.A.R.E. program suggested some (limited) success, but his modestly sanguine results have not been replicated with any frequency. In a large-scale quasi-experimental investigation of more than 700 fifth-grade students, for example, Harmon (1993) found that the program did help children delay alcohol initiation. Further, it affected their attitudes toward drug-using peers and substance use. However, it did not reduce their use of tobacco or marijuana. Given that Harmon was forced to match schools (the actual unit of analysis) to determine program effects, even these semi-hopeful findings must be viewed with somewhat jaundiced eyes. A meta-analysis of a set of eight D.A.R.E studies failed to replicate Harmon's findings; it did suggest that the program had positive effects on knowledge of drugs, but it did not affect alcohol or marijuana use (perhaps surprisingly, the program did have a small effect on tobacco usage). Dukes, Stein, and Ullman (1996) conducted a 3-year longitudinal study of D.A.R.E.'s effects. Three years after D.A.R.E. training, the anti-drug attitudes, resistance, drug onset delay, attitudes toward police, and drug use of 497 sixth-grade students were contrasted with those of 352 students who had not been exposed to the program. The results were not encouraging. Three years after program implementation, measures comparing two groups of (now) ninth-grade youth were indistinguishable for all practical purposes. This program, which has been estimated to cost nearly $100 per child (Dukes et al.), had no discernible lasting effect on youth, with the possible exception that exposed youth held slightly stronger anti-drug attitudes—but these attitudes were not accompanied by attitude-consistent anti-drug behaviors.

The weight of the program evaluations suggests that D.A.R.E. did not work as hoped, but the results of the negative program evaluations do not indicate why this is so. A program theory-driven evaluation, however, could provide information about why D.A.R.E. was not effective. Such information could support a decision to jettison the approach or to refine its components so that it might provide the initially intended outcomes.

Research by Donaldson, Graham, and Hansen (1994) provided an indication of the utility of program theory-driven evaluation science in the context of the D.A.R.E. model. In their research, Donaldson et al. contrasted D.A.R.E.'s resistance training model with an approach based on normative education. Considerable research indicates that youth vastly overestimate the proportion of their friends and peers who engage in questionable activities (e.g., drug use) (Prinstein & Wang, 2005; Wolfson, 2000), and that these overestimates are further exaggerated when the adolescent responding also engages in the behavior (Crano, Gilbert, Alvaro, & Siegel, 2008). As might be expected from these results, Donaldson et al. (1994) found that normative training had a powerful effect on adolescents' estimates of the prevalence of substance use and on their judgments of the acceptability of such behaviors. These estimates and judgments, in turn, were related to actual tobacco, alcohol, and marijuana use one to two years after normative training.

These results are important for a number of reasons, one of which concerns program participants' perceptions of the frequency of behaviors that may be targeted in the prevention campaign. If adolescents infer that usage of a given substance is high (else why would so much attention be focused on the issue), the inflated estimate that might arise from such a conclusion may help contribute to the very problem the preventive program was designed to solve. This possibility, along with the negative detrimental effects of unsuccessful prevention efforts, to be discussed, must be included in considerations of the costs vs. potential benefits of all prosocial marketing campaigns.

Adolescents' refusal skills were enhanced after resistance training, but this enhancement did not seem to transfer to behavior. Thus, a central, axiomatic feature of the D.A.R.E. campaign appeared to be misdirected. These results emerged from theory-driven program evaluation, which expands the more typical evaluation model by imposing a consideration of the theoretical underpinnings of the phenomenon under study. The results of this study suggested strongly that a normative approach to understanding and attenuating adolescent illicit substance use was needed, and subsequent work revealed conditions under which "just say no" or resistance training alone was actually harmful, in that it promoted the onset of substance use (Donaldson, Graham, Piccinin, & Hansen, 1995). Later work by Blanton and colleagues has profited from these insights and has provided a fine-grained model of normative effects in illicit substance use that has proven successful in numerous empirical tests (e.g., see Blanton & Burkley, 2008). This epistemological progression exposes an important feature of program theory-driven evaluation science: its potential to foster theories whose initial development is grounded in empirical research. As will be shown, this method of theory development in applied social psychological contexts usually pays greater dividends than that which depends on logical deduction from abstract theoretical relations (Crano & Brewer, 2002).

Using Program Theory-Driven Evaluation Science to Advance Applied Social Psychology

One of the most natural intersections between evaluation and social psychology is the systematic examination of social psychology-based programs and interventions to improve some aspect of the human condition. Program theory-driven evaluation science can be used to examine these interventions across a wide range of settings and topic areas. For example, social psychological theory can be used to develop a program and its program theory specifying how the program is presumed to reach its desired outcomes. This program theory based on social psychological principles can be used to generate and prioritize a set of evaluation questions that might be pursued. This process also should explore and consider questions about the potential side effects or unintended consequences of the program. The feasibility and desirability of empirically testing these potential evaluation questions can be examined within implementation contexts.

For example, some programs based on social psychology are conducted in highly controlled environments and seek to answer questions about the program's efficacy. *Efficacy evaluations* are concerned with determining whether a program works under ideal conditions. Donaldson (2007) underscored the point that programs that are not found to be efficacious should not be turned loose on society. If positive effects are not observed under highly controlled, optimal conditions, the program should be abandoned or, if possible, revised before being implemented more widely in society. We will return to this recommendation in the context of the massive National Youth Anti-Drug Media Campaign (NYAMC), a multibillion dollar intervention that failed to deliver on its promise to reduce adolescent marijuana use in the United States. Unfortunately, in most circumstances, including the NYAMC, we do not have the luxury of designing and revising our programs by efficacy evaluations.

Much of evaluation practice is dominated by questions about program effectiveness, not efficacy. *Effectiveness evaluations* of programs being implemented for clients, service recipients, or consumers in "real-world" clinics, schools, health care systems, business organizations, not-for-profit community organizations, and the like often focus on questions related to the issue of whether or not the program makes a difference in society. Theory-driven evaluation science is one of a few evaluation approaches that works well across efficacy and effectiveness evaluations. It offers social psychologists a set of principles to help design, evaluate, and improve their attempts to apply social psychological theory and methods to ameliorate social problems. Ideally, programs would initially be based on social psychological tenets, and would subsequently take advantage of refinements from both theory-driven efficacy and effectiveness evaluations. These evaluations would provide empirical confirmation or disconfirmation of the theory or principles being examined, and maximize the beneficial effects of the program by helping to improve some aspect of the human condition. Expanding this intersection would likely increase applied social psychology's relevance and positive impact in real world settings.

Many social psychological theories can be used to guide programs and program theory-driven evaluations. In Chapter 2 (this volume), Bandura introduced social cognitive theory and illustrated how it has been used at the individual and macrosocial levels to promote key changes in health behavior and significantly improve the quality of people's lives across the world. Similarly, in Chapter 3, Ajzen illustrated how the theory of planned behavior, which has been supported by a substantial body of empirical research, can be useful for designing future interventions and evaluations aimed at addressing important health and social problems. Riemer and Bickman (Chapter 4, this volume) further provide concrete examples of how program theory and theory-driven evaluation can draw upon and rigorously test social psychological theories in "real-world" settings. Social psychological theories that hold up under rigorous theory-driven effectiveness evaluations become more credible and useful tools for preventing and solving a wide range of human problems.

In another line of recent applied social psychological research, Crano and his colleagues attempted to understand why the NYAMC appeared to have produced iatrogenic effects, whereby youth who witnessed more mass-mediated anti-drug ads became *more* likely to use marijuana than youth who were exposed less frequently to the ads. Unlike the evaluations of D.A.R.E., the fundamental assumption of the campaign—that the mass media could influence adolescents' attitudes—was not at issue. Considerable research in psychology and marketing shows that the media can be quite effective in altering people's beliefs and expectations. However, fundamental features of persuasive message design, features studied in the persuasion literature for the past half-century (e.g., Hovland, Janis, & Kelley, 1953) and carried forward into today's models of attitude change (e.g., see Petty & Cacioppo, 1986), appeared to have been misunderstood by the ad developers. Many of the NYAMC ads appeared bereft of any consideration of the features necessary to effect attitude change, much less stimulate behavior consistent with these attitudes. As such, the anti-drug messages that were used, and hence, the campaign itself, could not be expected to have had a positive effect, and it did not (Hornik, Jacobsohn, Orwin, Piesse, & Kalton, 2008).

The extensive longitudinal survey evaluation of participants, however, did provide useful information for understanding what went wrong. This evaluation, making use of a 4-year longitudinal panel survey of a nationally representative sample of adolescents and their parents, allowed us to extract useful information for future mass-mediated anti-drug campaigns. For example, Crano and colleagues found considerable variation in adolescent substance use status (Crano, Siegel, Alvaro, Lac, & Hemovich, 2008) and showed in a later study that these variations had a significant influence on the persuasiveness of different message factors (Crano, Siegel, Alvaro, & Patel, 2007). For example, middle school substance users were strongly resistant to messages that threatened physical harm. Conversely, vulnerable nonusers, who had yet to initiate usage but were considering doing so, were more sensitive to threats to social status. This was a reasonable result, as their motives for engaging in substance use were principally motivated by social concerns (Siegel, Alvaro, Patel, & Crano, 2009).

Contrary to much current practice, where message sources are designed to match the characteristics of their audience—young spokespersons speak to young audiences, old actors sell pills and life insurance to senior citizens—Crano et al. (2007) found that young adolescent inhalant users were susceptible to a message delivered by a medical doctor. However, when the same message was delivered by the same person, who was identified as (and appeared to be) a high school student, it failed to move users, but proved quite effective with the vulnerable subjects. This variation in susceptibility to messages as a function of source (peer vs. adult) and warning (physical vs. social harm) suggests that a campaign that does not tailor its messages to the particular susceptibilities of its audience is unlikely to succeed. Taking advantage of these evaluation results to develop theories of targeting and tailoring in communication is a direct result of a program theory-driven evaluation science orientation. Tailoring in the mass media admittedly is difficult; however, in schools, where considerable innovative instruction is delivered via computers, such a tack is feasible and recommended.

Another useful finding derived from the data of this apparent intervention failure suggests the potential harm of overwarning. Skenderian, Siegel, Crano, Alvaro, and Lac (2008), for example, examined changes in adolescents' expectancies regarding the deleterious effects of marijuana use and found they were significantly related to changes in respondents' later marijuana usage intentions. So, when adolescents' expectations that marijuana would cause them to lose their friends were disconfirmed through experience with marijuana, their subsequent intentions to use the drug increased significantly. This result points to the danger of promising outcomes that are unlikely to occur or that are easily or likely to be disconfirmed. The counter reaction in response to expectancy disconfirmations may be worse than if no expectations were induced in the first place.

This research, and recent theoretical developments on factors that enhance resistance to attitude change (e.g., Tormala, 2008), suggest that extreme caution must be exercised when developing social interventions. The usual fall-back that "anything's better than nothing" was rendered implausible by the results of the NYAMC. Given the iatrogenic results obtained, it is arguable that the campaign might have been better left on the cutting room floor. To be sure, much was learned in retrospect about what went wrong and what should have been done, but the price of this knowledge was high. Indeed, there remains a lingering regret that enough was known well in advance of the campaign to have created a truly effective intervention, if only sufficient time and thought had been invested in extrapolating treatment plans and variations from established theory. Obviously, an approach based on principles of program theory-driven evaluation science might have helped the program developers avoid the shortcomings that so readily revealed themselves when the intervention was brought to the field.

Taken together, these examples help illustrate the necessity and power of social psychological theory and principles to guide interventions, and even to learn from those interventions that have not delivered on their promise. They also demonstrate the potential of program theory-driven evaluation to sort out the effects of such intervention efforts and to improve both the program and social psychological theory.

Using Methods of Social Psychology to Improve Theory-Driven Evaluation Science

Another very important intersection of social psychology and evaluation is the sharing of methods and designs. Social psychologists have a stellar track record in improving how important constructs are measured in field settings (Crano, 2003), in providing rigorous designs that answer important research and evaluation questions, and in addressing the important validity issues that are key to producing credible and actionable evaluation evidence (Shadish, Cook, & Campbell, 2002). Of all of these tasks, one of the most fundamental certainly is the search for construct validity. Consideration of the work of one of the founding fathers of evaluation science, Donald Campbell, reveals an intense focus on this necessary feature of all work in our field. Do our measures provide a good match to the theoretical construct they are thought to measure? Do the instruments we design to indicate a construct relate to others with which they should, theoretically, and fail to do so with those they should not? It is not enough to implement programs that succeed. We must know how they succeed, and why. In their classic paper, Cronbach and Meehl (1955, pp. 299–300) observed that a construct was defined by the "network of associations ... in which it occurs," and, "unless the network makes contact with observations, and exhibits explicit, public steps of inference, construct validation cannot be claimed" (p. 291). In this sense, construct validity helps define the psychological reality of the ideas underlying our tests and measures, and allows us to gauge their worth in the scientific study of behavior.

To answer the how and the why of program success or failure requires moving beyond merely evaluating outcomes. It requires a sure grasp of the factors involved in a program's success or failure, as well as an understanding of how these factors interrelate. In short, understanding requires theory, and theory requires valid measurement of the constructs that define the theory. Theory-driven evaluation science combines the best of evaluation science with the insights of Cronbach, Meehl, Campbell, and other social psychologists. Theory-driven evaluation models formalize these requirements to arrive at this more complete knowledge of both outcome *and* process. The job is far from easy. It involves construct validation, theory, and a sure grasp of research and evaluation methods, so that these well-developed constructs and theories can be tested with certainty and fidelity.

Although this is a large order, there are many fine examples of this type of foundational work, developed to arrive at a better understanding of interventions we seek to employ and the behaviors we seek to influence. At perhaps the most abstract level of fundamental construct validation is the classic work of Campbell and Fiske (1959) on the multitrait–multimethod matrix (MTMM), a methodological *tour de force* that suggests a logical method of decomposing the relations among a set of different measures, each used to identify a set of different traits. The logic of the MTMM is that identical traits (even if measured by different instruments) ought to relate more strongly to one another than different traits measured by the identical instrument. Alas, although it contributes substantially to our methodological reveries, for practical purposes this model of understanding is unusable (Fiske & Campbell, 1992). The proper statistical analysis of the matrix remains unsettled after more than a half century (Campbell and Fiske suggested some logical "rules of thumb" to be used to evaluate validity in their approach), and there is little evidence that the analytic debate will be settled any time soon (Crano, 2000). Even so, and perhaps paradoxically, its potential to contribute to our understanding is difficult to overestimate. The MTMM of Campbell and Fiske (1959) focuses our attention on the basics of measurement; reminds us that our traits always contain traces of the ways in which they were measured; and emphasizes the critical significance of convergent and discriminant validity. Convergent validity extends Cronbach and Meehl's (1955) discussion of validation by demonstrating that our confidence in a construct is enhanced if it "converges" with other variables with which it is expected on the basis of theory to associate (convergent validity), and diverges from those with which it is expected to differ (discriminant validity). Having absorbed these lessons, and armed with a good theory, the theory-driven evaluation scientist is equipped to contribute both theoretically and substantively.

At a more concrete level, many innovations commonly used in social psychological research, though not restricted to this field, have nonetheless been used extensively in it. The use of somewhat exotic methods in social psychology probably is the result of the peculiar problems social psychologists encounter in their research. Let us return to the NYAMC to show how one such innovation was used. The politics of the NYAMC required that the program be put in the field with almost no lead time. President Clinton required almost immediate implementation, and this foreclosed the possibility of a pretest on adolescents' drug use. Also owing to political concerns, no control group was to be used—what president would want to go to a state and tell its governor that they would receive no intervention funding because his or her state was assigned to the no-treatment control condition?

How does one evaluate a program having no pretest and no control group? The options are few, but the evaluators decided on a novel and interesting approach: they would use a dose response approach, which required them to assess adolescents' exposure to the massive anti-drug campaign and relate exposure to substance use. Obviously, self-selection of this type renders the design quasi-experimental, but to try to offset the lack of randomized assignment to conditions, the evaluators made use of propensity scoring, a sophisticated matching approach. In their analysis, Hornik et al. (2003)

> controlled for parent characteristics and further controlled for any preexisting difference among exposure groups on school attendance, grade level, academic performance, participation in extra-curricular activities, plans for the future, family functioning, personal antisocial behavior, association with antisocial peers, use of marijuana by close friends, personal tobacco and/or alcohol use of a long-standing nature, and sensation-seeking tendencies. (p. xxxiii)

This approach promises a major improvement over the more standard single-variable matching that has caused so much trouble in the past (e.g., Campbell & Erlebacher, 1970). Its more widespread application in theory-driven evaluation science contexts might well help integrate this field of endeavor more closely with applied social psychology, and provide the means by which theories can be made to inform and enrich the evaluator's vision.

Under optimal conditions, the combined emphases of applied social psychology and theory-driven evaluation can result in a unique intersection of theory and practice, in which the theoretical concerns of the basic scientist are wed to the practical needs of the applied psychologist and program evaluator. This "best of all possible worlds" is certainly a world worth striving to attain, and theory-driven evaluation science provides the roadmap that may lead to it. All of this assumes an openness—which should be characteristic of all science—to the ideas of the other. Social psychologists must, as Campbell insisted, become more concerned with contributing to the general welfare, and evaluation science must become more intent on developing theories of the processes underlying the outcomes they seek to evaluate. The intersection of these interests is near. All that is necessary at this point is that each of these two important areas comes to a proper appreciation of the other.

Concluding Comment

Theory-driven evaluation science and applied social psychology have achieved much in their own right. However, in this chapter we have made the case that much more can be achieved if we increase the activity ongoing at the intersection of theory-driven evaluation science and applied social psychology. For example, we have shown that applied social psychologists can benefit greatly from using theory-driven evaluation science in their efforts to address important social issues. While career opportunities for social psychologists conducting evaluations will be explored later in this volume, it seems important to note here that theory-driven evaluation science holds great promise for enhancing the effectiveness and career success of applied social psychologists. We have also shown in this chapter that there is great potential for social psychological theories, principles, and methods to enhance the practice of program–theory-driven evaluation science. It is our hope that we will see much more activity at this intersection in the coming years, and perhaps more importantly, the potential of this intersection realized by more successful efforts preventing and ameliorating some of the most pressing social problems of our time.

REFERENCES

Ajzen, I., & Fishbein, M. (2005). The influence of attitudes on behavior. In D. Albarracín, B. T. Johnson, & M. P. Zanna (Eds.). *The handbook of attitudes.* New York: Routledge.

Albarracín, D., Johnson, B. T., & Zanna, M. P. (Eds.). (2005). *The handbook of attitudes.* New York: Routledge.

Alkin, M. C. (Ed.). (2004). *Evaluation roots.* Thousand Oaks, CA: Sage.

American Evaluation Association. (2010). *Guiding principles for evaluators.* Retrieved December 13, 2010, from *www.eva.org.*

Blanton, H., & Burkley, M. (2008). Deviance regulation theory: Applications to adolescent social influence. In M. J. Prinstein & K. A. Dodge (Eds.), *Under-*

standing peer influence in children and adolescents (pp. 94–121). New York: Guilford Press.

Campbell, D. T. (1969). Reforms as experiments. *American Psychologist, 24*, 409–429.

Campbell, D. T., & Erlebacher, A. (1970). How regression in quasi-experimental evaluation can mistakenly make compensatory education look harmful. In J. Hellmuth (Ed.), *The disadvantaged child: Vol. 2. Compensatory education: A national debate* (pp. 185–225). New York: Brunner-Mazel.

Campbell, D. T., & Fiske, D. W. (1959). Convergent and discriminant validation by the multitrait-multimethod matrix. *Psychological Bulletin, 56*, 81–105.

Crano, W. D. (2000). The multitrait-multimethod matrix as synopsis and recapitulation of Campbell's views on the proper conduct of scientific inquiry. In L. Bickman (Ed.), *Research design: Donald Campbell's legacy* (pp. 37–61). Thousand Oaks, CA: Sage.

Crano, W. D. (2003). Theory-driven evaluation and construct validity. In S. Donaldson & M. Scriven (Eds.), *Evaluating social programs and problems: Visions for the new millennium* (pp. 145–157). Mahwah, NJ: Erlbaum.

Crano, W. D. (in press). Experiments as reforms: Persuasion in the nation's service. In J. P. Forgas, J. Cooper, & W. D. Crano (Eds.), *The psychology of attitude and attitude change*. New York: Psychology Press.

Crano, W. D., & Brewer, M. B. (2002). *Principles and methods of social research*. Mahwah, NJ: Erlbaum.

Crano, W. D., Gilbert, C., Alvaro, E. M., & Siegel, J. T. (2008). Enhancing prediction of inhalant abuse risk in samples of early adolescents: A secondary analysis. *Addictive Behaviors, 33*, 895–905.

Crano, W. D., Siegel, J., Alvaro, E. M., & Patel, N. M. (2007). Overcoming adolescents' resistance to anti-inhalant messages. *Psychology of Addictive Behaviors, 21*, 516–524.

Crano, W. D., Siegel, J. T., Alvaro, E. M., Lac, A., & Hemovich, V. (2008). The at-risk adolescent marijuana nonuser: Expanding the standard distinction. *Prevention Science, 9*, 129–137.

Cronbach, L. J., & Meehl, P. E. (1955). Construct validity in psychological tests. *Psychological Bulletin, 52*, 281–302.

DeJong, W. (1987). A short-term evaluation of project DARE (Drug Abuse Resistance Education): Preliminary indications of effectiveness. *Journal of Drug Education, 17*(4), 279–294.

Donaldson, S. I. (2007). *Program theory-driven evaluation science: Strategies and applications*. Mahwah, NJ: Erlbaum.

Donaldson, S. I. (2008). In search of the blueprint for an evidence-based global society. In S. I. Donaldson, C. A. Christie, & M. M. Mark (Eds.), *What counts as credible evidence in applied research and evaluation practice?* Newbury Park, CA: Sage.

Donaldson, S. I., & Christie, C. A. (2006). Emerging career opportunities in the transdiscipline of evaluation science. In S. I. Donaldson, D. E. Berger, & K. Pezdek (Eds.), *Applied psychology: New frontiers and rewarding careers*. Mahwah, NJ: Erlbaum.

Donaldson, S. I., Christie, C. A., & Mark, M. M. (2008). *What counts as credible evidence in applied research and evaluation practice?* Newbury Park, CA: Sage.

Donaldson, S. I., & Gooler, L. E. (2003). Theory-driven evaluation in action: Lessons from a $20 million statewide work and health initiative. *Evaluation and Program Planning, 26,* 355–366.

Donaldson, S. I., Graham, J. W., & Hansen, W. B. (1994). Testing the generalizability of intervening mechanism theories: Understanding the effects of adolescent drug use prevention interventions. *Journal of Behavioral Medicine, 17,* 196–216.

Donaldson, S. I., Graham, J. W., Piccinin, A. M., & Hansen, W. B. (1995). Resistance-skills training and onset of alcohol use: Evidence for beneficial and potentially harmful effects in public schools and in private Catholic schools. *Health Psychology, 14,* 291–300.

Donaldson, S. I., & Lipsey, M. W. (2006). Roles for theory in contemporary evaluation practice: Developing practical knowledge. In I. Shaw, J. C. Greene, & M. M. Mark (Eds.), *The handbook of evaluation: Policies, programs, and practices* (pp. 56–75). London: Sage.

Donaldson, S. I., & Scriven, M. (2003). *Evaluation social programs and problems: Visions for the new millennium.* Mahwah, NJ: Erlbaum.

Dukes, R. L., Stein, J. A., & Ullman, J. B. (1996). Long-term impact of Drug Abuse Resistance Education (D.A.R.E). *Evaluation Review, 21*(4), 483–500.

Fiske, D. W., & Campbell, D. T. (1992). Citations do not solve problems. *Psychological Bulletin, 112*(3), 393–395.

Harmon, M. A. (1993). Reducing the risk of drug involvement among early adolescents: An evaluation of Drug Abuse Resistance Education (DARE). *Evaluation Review, 17*(2), 221–239.

Hornik, R., Jacobsohn, L., Orwin, R., Piesse, A., & Kalton, G. (2008). Effects of the National Anti-drug Media Campaign on youths. *American Journal of Public Health, 98,* 2229–2236.

Hornik, R., Maklan, D., Cadell, D., Barmada, C. H., Jacobsohn, L., Henderson, V. R., et al. (2003). Evaluation of the National Youth Anti-Drug Media Campaign. Retrieved December 15, 2009, *www.drugabuse.gov/PDF/DESPR/1203report.pdf.*

Hovland, C. I., Janis, I. L., & Kelley, H. H. (1953). *Communication and persuasion: Psychological studies of opinion change.* New Haven, CT: Yale University Press.

International Organization for Cooperation in Evaluation Website. (2009). *ioce.net.*

Lewin, K. (1966). *Principles of topological psychology* (trans. Fritz Heider & Grace M. Heider). Oxford, UK: McGraw-Hill.

Lewin, K. (1997). *Resolving social conflicts and field theory in social science.* Washington, DC: American Psychological Association.

Lewin, K., & Gold, M. (1999). *The complete social scientist: A Kurt Lewin reader.* Washington, DC: American Psychological Association.

Lewin, K., Heider, F., & Heider, G. (1936). *Principles of topological psychology.* New York: McGraw-Hill.

Oskamp, S. (1984). *Applied social psychology.* Englewood Cliffs, NJ: Prentice-Hall.

Oskamp, S., & Schultz, P. W. (1998). *Applied social psychology* (2nd ed.). Upper Saddle River, NJ: Prentice Hall.

Patton, M. Q. (2008). *Utilization-focused evaluation: The new century text* (4th ed.). Thousand Oaks, CA: Sage.

Petty, R. E., & Cacioppo, J. T. (1986). *Communication and persuasion: Central and peripheral routes to attitude change.* New York: Springer-Verlag.

Prinstein, M. J., & Wang, S. S. (2005). False consensus and adolescent peer contagion: Examining discrepancies between perceptions and actual reported levels of friends' deviant and health risk behaviors, *Journal of Abnormal Child Psychology, 33,* 293–306.

Prislin, R., & Crano, W. D. (in press). History of social influence research. In A. Kruglanski & W. Stroebe (Eds.), *History of social psychology.* New York: Psychology Press.

Rogers, E. M. (1993). Diffusion and re-invention of Project D.A.R.E. In T. E. Backer & E. M. Rogers (Eds.), *Organizational aspects of health communication campaigns: What works?* (pp. 139–162). Thousand Oaks, CA: Sage.

Rossi, P. H., Lipsey, M. W., & Friedman, H. E. (2004). *Evaluation: A systematic approach* (7th ed.). Thousand Oaks, CA: Sage.

Scriven, M. (2003). Evaluation in the new millennium: The transdisciplinary vision. In S. I. Donaldson & M. Scriven (Eds.), *Evaluating social programs and problems: Visions for the new millennium* (pp. 19–42). Mahwah, NJ: Erlbaum.

Shadish, W. R. (1998). Evaluation theory is who we are. *American Journal of Evaluation, 19*(1), 1–19.

Shadish, W. R., Cook, T. D., & Campbell, D. T. (2002). *Experimental and quasi-experimental designs for generalized causal inference.* Boston, MA: Houghton Mifflin.

Shadish, W. R., Cook, T. D., & Leviton, L. C. (1991). *Foundations of program evaluation: Theories of practice.* Newbury Park, CA: Sage.

Siegel, J. T., Alvaro, E. A., Patel, N., & Crano, W. D. (2009). " ... You would probably want to do it. Cause that's what made them popular": Exploring perceptions of inhalant utility among young adolescent non-users and occasional users. *Substance Use and Misuse, 44,* 597–615.

Skenderian, J. J., Siegel, J. T., Crano, W. D., Alvaro, E. E., & Lac, A. (2008). Expectancy change and adolescents' intentions to use marijuana. *Psychology of Addictive Behaviors, 22*(4), 563–569.

Smith, E. R., & Mackie, D. M. (2007). *Social psychology* (3rd ed.). New York: Psychology Press.

Smith, E. R., & Mackie, D. M (2007). *Social psychology* (3rd ed.). Philadelphia: Psychology Press.

Stufflebeam, D. L. (Ed.). (2001). Evaluation models. *New Directions for Evaluation, 89,* 7–98.

Tormala, Z. L. (2008). A new framework for resistance to persuasion: The resistance appraisals hypothesis. In W. D. Crano & R. Prislin (Eds.), *Attitudes and attitude change* (pp. 213–234). New York: Psychology Press.

Weiss, C. H. (1998). *Evaluation: Methods for studying programs and policies* (2nd ed.). Upper Saddle River, NJ: Prentice Hall.

Wolfson, S. (2000). Students' estimates of the prevalence of drug use: Evidence for a false consensus effect. *Psychology of Addictive Behaviors, 14,* 295–298.

Yarbrough, D. B., Shulha, L. M., Hopson, R. K., & Caruthers, F. A. (2011). *The program evaluation standards: A guide for evaluators and evaluation users* (3rd ed.). Newbury Park, CA: Sage.

EDITORS' CONCLUDING COMMENTS
TO CHAPTER 5

In addition to discussing the general linkage between program theory-driven evaluation science and applied social psychology, Donaldson and Crano pointed to the need for strong "construct validity" in such work. The term *construct validity* has a long history in the literature on tests and measurement. Drawing on that literature, Cook and Campbell (1979) applied the term in the context of experiments and quasi-experiments, which are often conducted to evaluate the effectiveness of programs and policies. Cook and Campbell described construct validity as the accuracy of inferences about abstract constructs based on specific research procedures. They applied it to both potential cause and effect variables. For example, if a DARE evaluator draws conclusions about the effect of "resistance skills prevention programs" on "substance use," construct validity asks whether these are valid labels for the treatment and outcome variables, respectively. Donaldson and Crano point out that construct validity concerns also apply to the other key variables in a program theory.

Donaldson and Crano note that social psychologists typically bring skills that can lead to increased construct validity in evaluation. This can be expanded to a more general point: Various content areas in social psychology can be applied to enhance the theory and practice of evaluation. We turn to several examples in the next section of this book.

PART III

Implications of Social Psychological Theory and Research for Meeting the Challenges of Evaluation Practice

EDITORS' INTRODUCTORY COMMENTS
TO CHAPTER 6

In the next chapter, Larry Sanna and his colleagues examine the implications for program evaluation of an interesting area of research and theory in social psychology, judgment biases. As illustrated in the chapter (and as detailed more fully in the reviews that Sanna et al. cite), the social psychological literature on biases demonstrates a wide array of potential shortcomings in everyday human judgments. Indeed, one way to justify the practice of systematic evaluation is by pointing out the many biases that frequently affect informal judgments about the merit and worth of a program.

Because most evaluation takes place over time, Sanna and his colleagues chose to focus on a set of "temporal biases." As the name suggests, these biases affect judgments that involve time. For example, the planning bias refers to a tendency to underestimate how long tasks will take to complete. For each of the several temporal biases reviewed in the chapter, the authors describe ways that the bias might affect programs and program evaluation. To take but one example, the planning fallacy can easily result in overly optimistic timelines for successful program implementation. Failure to account for this bias could lead to premature summative evaluation of a program that is more suited to continued formative evaluation.

In addition to describing and illustrating the implications of temporal biases for evaluation, the chapter authors discuss "debiasing." This refers to procedures that can help reduce or avoid the bias. Throughout the chapter, the authors draw on interesting evaluation experiences as well as on the literature in social psychology. Unlike the chapters in the previous section of the book, Sanna and his colleagues are not drawing on general social psychological theories of behavior and behavior change that can be the foundation of a program theory and of a theory-driven evaluation. Instead, like other chapters in this section, this chapter draws on social psychological research and theory that point to how evaluation practice can be improved, in this case by avoiding the potentially pernicious effects of temporal biases.

CHAPTER 6

Planning the Future and Assessing the Past
Temporal Biases and Debiasing in Program Evaluation

Lawrence J. Sanna
A. T. Panter
Taya R. Cohen
Lindsay A. Kennedy

All men are liable to error; and most men are, in many points,
by passion or temptation to it.
—JOHN LOCKE (1689/1979)[1]

The primary goals of program evaluation are to provide accurate information from which to plan effective strategies, improve existing programs, and demonstrate results of resource investments (for reviews see Rossi, Freeman, & Lipsey, 1999; Scriven, 1998; Shadish, Cook, & Leviton, 1991; Worthen, Sanders, & Fitzpatrick, 1996). However, people are imperfect decision makers. That people are "liable to error," in the sage words of philosopher John Locke, is vividly illustrated by decades of social psychological research uncovering an ever-growing number of biases that influence the accuracy of judgments under a variety of circumstances (for reviews see Gilovich, Griffin, & Kahneman, 2002; Kahneman, Slovic, & Tversky, 1982; Kerr, MacCoun, & Kramer, 1996; Pohl, 2005). In this chapter we suggest not only that knowledge of judgmental biases may aid program evaluators (and planners) in reaching more accurate and valid conclusions, but also that examining the biases in a program evaluation context may help social psychologists further understand how these biases operate in real-life settings.

Consider a five-year, multimillion dollar, multisite evaluation of U.S. health care programs, which we describe later in more detail. Despite the fact that many programs represented by the Steering Committee were not yet fully functional and staffed, that the research design was being subjected to hot debate, and that the measurement instruments were still under development, program planners nonetheless predicted an overly optimistic project completion time of five years. Program evaluators were ready to begin assessment at the start of the fourth year, but many components of the program were not yet even operational. Being overly optimistic in predicting task completion, a bias known as *planning fallacy* (Buehler, Griffin, & Ross, 1994) may affect judgments in many contexts. If the program timetable is overly optimistic, and if the evaluation plan ignores this possibility, one consequence is that premature summative evaluation is likely to occur. Under such circumstances, a potentially worthwhile but not yet successfully implemented program could be deemed ineffective.

Our chapter is organized as follows. We first describe a subset of biases that are particularly applicable to program evaluation: *temporal biases*, those biases involving judgments over time (for a review see Sanna & Chang, 2006). Although many biases could be relevant, we focus on temporal biases because program evaluation most often involves events that transpire over time (Rossi et al., 1999; Scriven, 1998; Shadish et al., 1991; Worthen et al., 1996). We describe some primary causes and consequences of four temporal biases that influence people's estimates of future task completion, confidence in strategies, emotional reactions, and outcome assessments while discussing implications for program evaluation. We end by providing a summary using an integrative model (Sanna & Schwarz, 2007; Schwarz, Sanna, Skurnik, & Yoon, 2007) of biasing and debiasing that was developed in other contexts but that may also help to explain biases in program evaluation. *Debiasing*, or techniques devised to lessen biases (Sanna, 2007), further suggest what might be done about biases. Our approach allows for connections between social psychological research on judgmental biases and program evaluation and also suggests some future directions.

Temporal Biases and Program Evaluation

The relevance of temporal biases to program evaluation can be illustrated by referring to the framework outlined by the Centers for Disease Control and Prevention (CDC, 1999), which has been adopted in several domains. Within this framework, program evaluators are instructed to progress though the following six steps that take place over time: (1) *engage stakeholders* (foster input, participation, and power-sharing among invested persons); (2) *describe the program* (scrutinize program features and intended functions); (3) *plan the evaluation design* (outline strategies and steps to be taken); (4) *gather credible evidence* (compile trustworthy and relevant data to be used to answer questions); (5) *justify conclusions* (provide pertinent analysis, interpretation, and recommendations); and (6) *ensure use and share lessons* (translate findings into informed decision making and appropriate action) (CDC, 1999). Temporal biases can be relevant to program planners and decision makers at many of these stages. The CDC framework is depicted in Figure 6.1, along with an indication of when the four temporal biases are most likely to occur. Likewise, an increased awareness of these biases can have consequences for program evaluators wanting to reach and convey more accurate and valid conclusions.

Planning Fallacy: Predicting You Will Finish Sooner

Planning fallacy, as mentioned previously, is a bias in estimating how long it will take to complete tasks. People are notoriously overly optimistic when predicting task completion times, believing they will finish tasks sooner than they actually do (Buehler et al., 1994; Kahneman & Tversky, 1979). This temporal bias is poignantly illustrated by large-scale planning debacles (for reviews see Flyvberg, Holme, & Soren, 2002; Hall, 1980; Schnaars, 1989). For example, the Sydney Opera House in 1957 was originally esti-

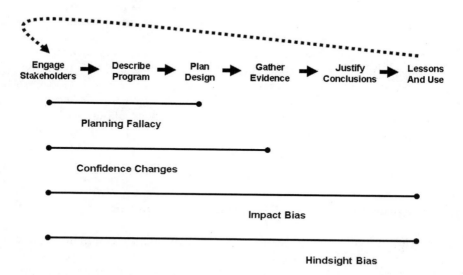

FIGURE 6.1. Temporal biases as related to program evaluation. The biases are depicted at points where they are most likely to occur, but because of the feedback loop (dashed line) it is possible that biases may also be relevant at other time points. The program evaluation process is adapted from the CDC (1999).

mated to be completed in 1963, but a scaled-down version actually opened in 1973—a decade late. The Eurofighter aircraft, conceived jointly by Britain, Germany, Italy, and Spain, was originally planned to be operational in 1997, but the first aircraft were not delivered until 2003. Boston's Central Artery/Tunnel project was estimated to be completed in 1999, but it is currently (2010) undergoing final repairs.

This bias is also found on a variety of personal activities, including completing household chores, holiday shopping, and laboratory tasks (Buehler et al., 1994; Kahneman & Tversky, 1979; Newby-Clark, Ross, Buehler, Koehler, & Griffin, 2000; Taylor, Pham, Rivkin, & Armor, 1998) for individuals and groups (Sanna, Parks, Chang, & Carter, 2005). For example, Buehler et al. (1994) asked students to predict when they would submit a completed thesis, and Sanna et al. (2005) asked groups to predict when they would complete a furniture fabrication task. In each case, individuals and groups predicted they would be finished much sooner than they actually did. Many academicians may have had similar experiences, taking home briefcases full of work on Friday only to have them return on Monday unopened, or underestimating chapter completion time when the plan seemed so easily doable when the contract was signed several years earlier—and our apologies to the current editors!

Examples and Implications for Program Evaluation

We suggest that planning fallacy occurs similarly when programs are planned and implemented. As we described previously, this can have negative consequences for program evaluation when projects take longer than expected and a premature summative evaluation occurs, resulting in the conclusion that a potentially worthwhile program is deemed ineffective simply because overly optimistic planners did not give it enough time. Similarly, the program evaluator who is ignorant of planning fallacy might fail to consider doing formative evaluation when it could be quite useful, because the evaluator falsely assumes that the program is mature and well implemented. In addition, understanding of the planning fallacy might prevent evaluators from reaching overly harsh, negative conclusions when they find a program does not meet the schedule specified in the original plan for program development and implementation.

Planning fallacy may also come into play when planning the evaluation process itself, particularly during the initial three stages of program evaluation (i.e., engaging stakeholders through planning the evaluation design, as depicted in Figure 6.1), and therefore program evaluators, stakeholders, and other invested parties ought to be wary of overly optimistic forecasts. An evaluator's overly optimistic forecast about an evaluation's completion time can result from a failure to recognize the multitude of factors that must be in place for an evaluation to be conducted and completed in a timely (predicted) manner. Thus, just as an awareness of planning fallacy can help an evaluator to avoid premature conclusions when seen from the perspective of program planners, an awareness of planning fallacy might also help evaluators to avoid being overly optimistic in their own estimates of evaluation completion.

For example, during the Steering Committee meeting for the evaluation of U.S. health care programs that we mentioned previously, which included program directors and local evaluators, each stakeholder expressed fears, concerns, hopes, and dreams about what they wanted to accomplish for their program with their grant and through the national evaluation. They discussed the questions they hoped to answer, the data they would collect, the information they would need to support their program for future rounds of funding, their ideas for a wide-reaching dissemination plan, and all of the papers they would write. The national evaluator had to grapple with the fact that some of the many programs were not yet fully functional and staffed, the research design was in progress and subject to heated debate (ongoing for the first 3 years of the grant), the measurement instruments were under development, and the existing program staff—and some program directors—had to be first convinced to collect data and then trained to do so. To ensure that project findings were "ready" for inclusion in submitted applications for supplemental funding beyond the fifth year, data would have to be collected over time, submitted to the national evaluator, cleaned, and fully analyzed by the fourth project year.

Given all of the complexities involved in most evaluation projects, as in this example, attempting to predict when one will be finished can be an especially daunting task. As we described, this is true not only for the program planners when implementing programs but also for the program evaluators when deciding on how to implement the evaluation. An evaluation of a comprehensive and multifaceted project over a 5-year period can be a very short time, even for what may appear at the outset to be simple program evaluations, and there are virtually innumerable ways to underestimate the number of subtasks to be completed, the goodwill of stakeholders, and the length of time and amount of effort it takes to engage all stakeholders for the evaluation design to be planned and the data collection process to begin.

What Can Be Done about Planning Fallacy?

The flip-side to judgment and decision-making biases is the question of whether anything can be done to eliminate, or at least lessen, the biases: That is, can judgmental biases be debiased? As we mentioned earlier in this chapter, debiasing refers to techniques, methods, and interventions designed to eliminate or lessen potential errors, distortions, or other mistakes in people's thinking, judgment, or decision making (Sanna, 2007). There are several possible causes of planning fallacy, which program evaluators would do well to keep in mind. Planning fallacy "involves a process of mental simulation that focuses on future planning but neglects past experience" (Buehler, Griffin, & MacDonald, 1997, p. 239). In short, when considering the future, people tend to focus on only possible success while neglecting the possible relevance of past failures to meet goals in similar situations. For example, Newby-Clark et al. (2000) demonstrated that when people think about future task completion times they focus mainly on elaborate scenarios that would lead to success rather than also considering scenarios that might lead to failure. The main problem with this, of course, is that when making any type of future prediction the possibility of things going wrong is at least conceivable (i.e., before one even starts).

One recommendation that follows directly from this analysis is for program evaluators to more strongly consider all of the potential obstacles that could happen along the way that might result in the program taking longer than planners had expected. Similarly, they could consider these same things when planning their own evaluations. Overly optimistic task completion times could occur, for example, because evaluators do not fully account for the fact that committees are not yet fully functional and staffed, the research design is still in progress and under debate, the measurement instruments are still under development, or a variety of any number of other exigencies that may occur along the way to impede progress. Inaccurately estimating task completion may be costly not only in terms of time but also, among other things, in terms of money, effort, and organizational esteem. One way that program evaluators might counteract some of these tendencies is by using evaluability assessments (Wholey, 1989), whereby the feasibility of an evaluation is periodically checked against predicted goal progress. The evaluation plan can then be revised in light of the evaluability assessment.

Planning fallacy can be exacerbated by several other factors that are likely to be in place during the course of program evaluation. First, not only do people primarily consider scenarios leading to early task completion when looking to the future, but if they do happen to think about poor outcomes they discount them by either convincing themselves that they are irrelevant or externalizing the causes of those poor outcomes (e.g., blaming temporary situational factors as responsible for tasks taking longer than predicted; see Buehler et al., 1994). Second, incentives for speedy task completion (monetary or otherwise) can further increase the planning fallacy (Buehler et al., 1997). These incentives may, for example, be put in place by overly ambitious organizations wanting quick evidence of a program's effectiveness. Although these incentives may lead to overly optimistic predictions, program evaluators should be made acutely aware of research indicating that optimistic predictions are not necessarily translated into earlier task completion (Buehler et al., 1997), which if not accounted for could possibly lead to great disappointment or disengagement with the evaluation process.

Confidence Changes: Becoming Uncertain about Your Strategy

People become less confident in possible success when events draw near than they are at a more distant time; this bias is known as *confidence changes*. This temporal bias is commonly illustrated by research on test-taking. Several studies have demonstrated that students become significantly less confident in their eventual success as the time to take an exam approaches than they are at a more distant time (Nisan, 1972; Sanna, 1999; Shepperd, Ouellette, & Fernandez, 1996). For example, Gilovich, Kerr, and Medvec (1993) found that participants who thought they would take a test immediately were less confident than those who thought they would take a test in 4 weeks. Decreasing confidence at the "moment of truth" is something most people experience to varying degrees. The prospective spouse who was supremely confident in choice of partner at engagement may experience "cold feet" on wedding day, or the student who was so sure when choosing a university later becomes not so sure at enrollment time.

Changes in confidence are not limited to academic settings. Job-seekers are more muted in their first salary estimates when asked just before entering the market than they are years in advance (despite the fact that average-salary trends increase over time), and patients are less confident in results when they are about to receive feedback from medical tests than they are immediately after the test is taken (despite the fact that the test itself has not changed in the intervening time). These are just a few examples (for a review see Carroll, Sweeny, & Shepperd, 2006). Changes in confidence are pervasive and may simply be one natural outgrowth of anticipating future events. From a program evaluation perspective, it is thus important to recognize that people's confidence in what they are about to do generally tends to decrease over time, potentially leading to uncertainty about previously chosen strategies.

Examples and Implications for Program Evaluation

We suggest that in a program evaluation context confidence changes may be particularly likely as evaluators move through the stages of engaging stakeholders to gathering credible evidence (see Figure 6.1). During the program evaluation process, program planners and stakeholders may be over-confident in the eventual success of how the evaluation and data gathering strategies will unfold when viewed from a more distant time. However, they may become more calibrated with the actual likelihood of success and failure as the evaluation's end is salient and near, perhaps even becoming underconfident. Program evaluators, stakeholders, and other invested parties need to recognize that these changes may occur: They may be extremely confident in their chosen strategies at the start of the evaluation but less so as data collection is about to begin. However, this decrease in confidence would not necessarily indicate that the program should be abandoned.

In fact, the most likely practical problem here may be that shifts in confidence will occur among various stakeholder groups, such as program staff, at different stages in the evaluation process. For example, drops in confidence may be most likely when the data collection is salient and when the evaluative conclusions are close at hand. In short, stakeholders may experience a type of evaluation anxiety (Donaldson, Gooler, & Scriven, 2002) as conclusions get near and the evaluation draws to a close, making them less confident in their previously chosen plan of action. This process might in turn lead stakeholders to shift from behaving cooperatively to behaving noncooperatively (e.g., refusal to cooperate with data collection) or even worse (e.g., various forms of sabotage). Recognizing that people's confidence may decrease over time, on the part of stakeholders and for the evaluators themselves, may help program evaluators avoid prematurely abandoning a strategy that will ultimately prove to be successful. In a sense, confidence changes share certain similarities with planning fallacy. With planning fallacy, people are overly optimistic at a distance in their anticipated task completion, while with confidence changes people are similarly overly confident at a distance in their eventual success than they are more proximally.

For example, in an evaluation of academic leadership programs in higher education, the initial optimism and confidence expressed in the grant proposal was subsequently dampened as barriers emerged during the evaluation process. These barriers included engaging a series of faculty governance groups in conversations about the upcoming evaluation, balancing directive guidance from the involved board requesting the evaluation, obtaining an accurate history of the early program years, ensuring sufficient numbers of participant interviews in a short time period, and preparing materials and articles for dissemination as the board looked on. Confidence shifts—from high confidence to a more muted level of confidence—in the possibility that a professional, high-quality evaluation could take place occurred during this time period.

What Can Be Done about Confidence Changes?

There are several causes of changes in confidence. People's anxiety, worry, or general arousal level may increase as the time of an event draws near (Shepperd, Grace, Cole, & Klein, 2005), and these increases in anxiety may be associated with thinking about better possibilities (e.g., "we could do better"; see Sanna, 1999, and Sanna & Meier, 2000). This perspective can cause people to lose confidence in whatever it is that they are about to undertake. As in many other areas, program evaluators, stakeholders, and other invested parties should keep in mind that anxiety increases may be only a natural response as one is about to do something, and possible ways of dealing with this evaluation anxiety (Donaldson et al., 2002) such as by reassuring stakeholders might be effectively implemented to keep confidence at a consistently high level.

Changes in confidence occur in part because people view the possibility of success as more likely than failure at a distant time but view the possibility of success and failure more equally at a near time (for a review see Carroll et al., 2006). In a program evaluation context this can be a double-edged sword, leading to either negative or positive consequences, depending on the circumstances. On the one hand, not recognizing that one may naturally experience increased anxiety as the time approaches to implement data collection may lead evaluators to prematurely abandon what it is they are doing. A change in strategy when one has in fact identified the correct strategy all along can have obviously detrimental effects.

On the other hand, a proper and thorough assessment of why one is experiencing confidence drops can also lead to a revision of strategies in a positive direction. For example, if one is feeling less confident because of the realization that various barriers are actually in place, or because one has actually failed to adequately prepare, then this can lead to a more constructive set of thoughtful evaluation activities, including increased consideration of methods, strategies, data analysis approaches, and effective modes of dissemination and presentation. In short, changes in confidence will no doubt occur during the course of an evaluation. It is up to the persons involved in the evaluation process to properly interpret its meaning and the appropriate course of action to be taken when continuing on to the later stages in the evaluation.

Impact Bias: Thinking You Will Be Happier (Sadder) about Results

There is little question that people do things in order to try to achieve happiness, but they may be very poor at anticipating exactly how they will feel after actually experiencing the events they anticipated (for a review see Gilbert, 2006). *Impact bias* refers to the fact that people predict that their emotional reactions to events will be more intense—have more impact—than actually turns out to be the case. Overpredicting future emotional impact is one of the most prevalent biases in affective forecasting (for a review see Wilson & Gilbert, 2003). For example, voters and students thought they would be happier or sadder after their preferred candidates or teams won or lost, respectively. Yet no differences in actual happiness (sadness) were observed between the supporters of winners and losers when asked afterwards (Wilson, Wheatley, Meyers, Gilbert, & Axom, 2000; see also Loewenstein & Schkade, 1999).

People do feel good when good things happen and bad when bad things happen, but the fact that actually experienced events do not have their anticipated affective impact may have important implications for program evaluation by influencing people's satisfaction with the program evaluation process and outcomes. We suggest that impact bias may be especially likely as one moves from engaging stakeholders to ensuring use and sharing lessons learned (see Figure 6.1). For example, program evaluators and other involved parties would likely anticipate high satisfaction, or they would not have begun the particular evaluation in that way. However, impact bias would result in actual experienced satisfaction being more muted. That is, even when the process turns out exactly as planned, people likely will not experience the same level of satisfaction as they anticipated when the process began.

Examples and Implications for Program Evaluation

Impact bias can matter because it suggests that people's expectations about outcomes in a program evaluation context may need to be effectively managed. More generally, impact bias may lead people to more extreme expectations, which could complicate the evaluation process. For example, if stakeholders have excessively positive anticipations, they might think that the evaluation may save them in some sense, in which case the evaluator may have to develop a more realistic timeline (Sridharan, Campbell, & Zinzow, 2006) or otherwise describe in greater detail what would be more reasonable expectations. Overly positive anticipated emotional states may be most likely on the part of those stakeholders who have a vested interest in obtaining a favorable evaluation. This may be especially true if those stakeholders were influential in seeing that the evaluation was conducted in the first place.

For example, stakeholders may be motivated to have the evaluation to turn out well for a variety of reasons, including personal program history and investment, interest in ensuring program sustainability, or local political forces. In the previously mentioned evaluation of academic leadership programs, many stakeholders were invested in the conduct of the evaluation by an external evaluator and anticipated relatively extreme and positive emotional reactions to what they thought ultimately would be the evaluation's findings. However, in the end, when the evaluator presented the balanced case of the program—in its historical context with detailed qualitative and quantitative interview data and summaries about the positive and negative program aspects—the stakeholders' initial extremely positive emotional views about what the findings would be very much muted, though still positive. If, for example, stakeholder groups are not as satisfied as they anticipated, they may be less likely to commission further evaluations even when the lessons learned may be greatly beneficial.

The opposite can also be true. In fact, experiences in program evaluation contexts suggest that people may be more likely to expect (or at least fear) that the evaluator will play the role of executioner rather than savior. That is, frequently different stakeholder groups exist, not all of whom commissioned the evaluation. Indeed, as an example, staff members sometimes believe (occasionally with justification) that the evaluation is being conducted to provide a rationale for discontinuing the program. Again, one job of the program evaluation process would be to manage reasonable expectations. Impact bias suggests that things are rarely as bad as one anticipates. Program evaluators can thus reassure their constituents by taking solace in the fact that poor outcomes are rarely experienced to be as bad as one expects (Gilbert et al., 1998), and that even negative outcomes are instructive in suggesting ways to improve the future.

What Can Be Done about Impact Bias?

One of the main causes of impact bias is that people tend to focus mainly on affective reactions to the anticipated event itself, without taking into account affective reactions to other events and occurrences that will also be happening at the time that the event is actually experienced (a phenomenon known as focalism—Wilson et al., 2000; or focusing illusion—Schkade & Kahneman, 1998). The stakeholders (and other invested parties) in the evaluation of the aforementioned academic leadership programs likely were envisioning at the outset of the evaluation only what it would feel like after the evaluation was successfully completed. However, once the evaluation was actually finished and findings were presented with a more detailed summary of the positives and negatives of the program, the extremely positive affect that was initially anticipated was notably more muted. More reasonable expectations for program planners and evaluation outcomes thus need to be managed.

Impact bias can also occur because people simply misconstrue what it will be like after the event really happens. In order words, evaluators, stakeholders, and other invested parties may have poorly construed notions about what the results of an evaluation will turn out to be, or what they may reveal. Perhaps the best thing to do in these cases is to attempt to find other circumstances in which similar procedures were used, or in which similar programs have been evaluated, and ask the people involved what their experiences were like—if you can do this while they are currently experiencing the outcomes, then this might be even better (Gilbert, 2006). It is possible that this may help to more accurately calibrate people's anticipated and actual emotional responses. In short, however, it may simply be that people's experienced affective reactions may never be quite what they anticipated, and thus program evaluators should attempt to account for this when discussing what to expect.

Hindsight Bias: Believing You Knew It All Along

Once event outcomes are known, people believe they "knew all along" what would happen even though pre-event predictions indicate otherwise; this is known as *hindsight bias* (Fischhoff, 1975). Hindsight bias has been documented in varied domains, including medical diagnoses, legal decisions, election results, athletic outcomes, and organizational responses (for reviews see Christensen-Szalanski & Willham, 1991; Guilbault, Bryant, Posavac, & Brockway, 2004; Hawkins & Hastie, 1990). For example, Arkes, Faust, Guilmette, and Hart (1988) asked groups of physicians to estimate the likelihood of particular medical diagnoses. Some physicians were simply asked to provide diagnoses after reading patients' case histories. Other physicians provided diagnoses after reading the same case histories but also included a description of the actual diagnoses. Physicians said they knew the diagnoses all along under conditions in which the diagnoses were provided to them than when they were not provided.

Hindsight bias can be seen at both personal and public levels. For example, students who come to view exam failures as inevitable may not take steps to improve, or security officials who, after the fact, view terrorist attacks as foreseeable may spend more time blaming than furthering future defense (Sanna & Schwarz, 2006). In each case, event outcomes are judged to be more likely once outcomes are known than when outcome information is unknown; one implication for program evaluation is that program evaluators and other involved parties may be unable to learn effectively from past experiences (Fischhoff, 1982). We suggest that hindsight bias may be most likely as one moves from engaging stakeholders to ensuring use and sharing lessons learned (i.e., pre-outcome to post-outcome; see Figure 6.1).

Examples and Implications for Program Evaluation

Hindsight bias can matter to programs, as well as to the program evaluation process, for several reasons. First, as mentioned previously, the conventional consideration is that hindsight bias can be problematic because people fail to learn—they already believe they knew what would happen, so why change? For example, a company that was repeatedly hired to conduct "independent" evaluations of government contracts focused on substance abuse bypassed several steps involving the engagement of stakeholders and began employing the same methods, the same approaches, and the same dissemination plans. There may be many reasons why a string of evaluations using the same methods and procedures may be commissioned. However, in this case, a nonvarying approach failed to account for the fact the circumstances were changing and were not identical across evaluations. However, the program evaluators came to believe after the first few evaluations that outcomes were obvious, and they continued using the same inflexible approaches even when these approaches were now inadequate and in fact no longer applied.

Second, in a program evaluation context, there may be another and perhaps even more relevant concern: People may fail to see the value of the whole evaluation process, which may then reduce the likelihood of interest in participating in and funding future evaluations. After all, for example, if a foundation staff member believes that evaluators never tell her anything she didn't already know, then why would she want to have the foundation continue to pay for more evaluations? Perhaps evaluators can attempt to avoid the hindsight-bias-based "so what" response by moving beyond a simple reporting of results, such as by making varied recommendations about program modifications or other changes that might follow from the results or by testing mediators in a theory-driven evaluation. This richer set of recommendations and conclusions might perhaps produce less susceptibility to hindsight bias.

What Can Be Done about Hindsight Bias?

Hindsight bias may in fact lead to circumventing the first major principle of systematic inquiry of the American Evaluation Association's (AEA) Guiding Principles for Evaluators (AEA, 2004), and thus evaluators need ways to avoid it. This principle states that evaluators should: (1) ensure the accuracy and credibility of the information they collect by using appropriate methods; (2) work with the client around issues related to formulating the research questions and potentially useful approaches for collecting data to address these questions; and (3) communicate their methodology clearly, accurately, and in ways that are comprehensible to their diverse audiences (AEA, 2004; Principle 1). The perception that one knew all along what the outcomes would be can affect each of these component principles.

One of the most frequently recommended strategies for counteracting hindsight bias is to generate alternative outcomes in an attempt "to convince oneself that it might have turned out otherwise" (Fischhoff, 1982, p. 343). The assumption is that, if many alternative outcomes were possible in foresight, having people (re)consider alternative possibilities after outcomes are already known may help to restore a foresight perspective, debiasing the bias—although as we shall see, this by itself may not always be effective (Sanna, Schwarz, & Stocker, 2002). Hindsight bias can also be decreased (as well as increased) by various self-serving motives. For example, people may be more likely to experience hindsight bias after success than failures, as such a pattern may allow them to take credit for their success but deny blame for their failures (Louie, Curren, & Harich, 2000; Mark & Mellor, 1991). Thus, people involved in the evaluation process should account for the possibility that these various motives may exist.

Other strategies might also help lessen hindsight bias. For example, similar to generating contrary thoughts, a suggestion from the literature on program theory proposes that in addition to developing the program theory that can guide an evaluation, the evaluator should also try to identify the "anti-theory" that represents how the program could go wrong, most importantly based on the concerns of program critics (Carvalho & White, 2004). From this perspective, this strategy could be viewed as a systematic evaluation debiasing procedure that requires generation of hypotheses contrary to the biases that we describe in this chapter. Other practical procedures may also be used to try to debias hindsight bias. In particular, for example, stakeholders might be asked to write down their predictions for the evaluation findings in advance (Patton, 1997) to try to counter hindsight bias. Once they are written down and referred to later, any deviations from predictions are unlikely to be viewed as having been known all along.

Summary

We suggested in this chapter that as movement is made from the process of engaging stakeholders through ensuring use and sharing lessons learned (and then back again), several temporal biases may influence judgments and decisions made within a program evaluation context. The temporal biases depicted in Figure 6.1 can be relevant to program planners and decision makers at many of these stages. Likewise, an increased awareness of biases can have consequences for program evaluators (and planners) wanting to reach and convey more accurate and valid conclusions. We focused on the four temporal biases of planning fallacy, confidence changes, impact bias, and hindsight bias. Our emphasis on these biases comes from the fact that program evaluation most often involves events that take place over time (Rossi et al., 1999; Scriven, 1998; Shadish et al., 1991; Worthen et al., 1996). For each bias, we described some primary causes and consequences while discussing implications for program evaluation. In this final section, we summarize findings while referring to an integrative model of biasing and debiasing (see Figure 6.2; for a more detailed discussion of the model see Sanna & Schwarz, 2007; Schwarz et al., 2007), and we suggest some further implications for program evaluation.

Further Implications for Program Evaluation

Throughout this chapter, we described the causes and consequences of biases, some implications of the biases for program evaluation, and what might be done to lessen (debias) the biases. Several of the biases may have common underlying factors, as illustrated by an integrative model (see Figure 6.2; Sanna & Schwarz, 2007; Schwarz et al., 2007). Although the

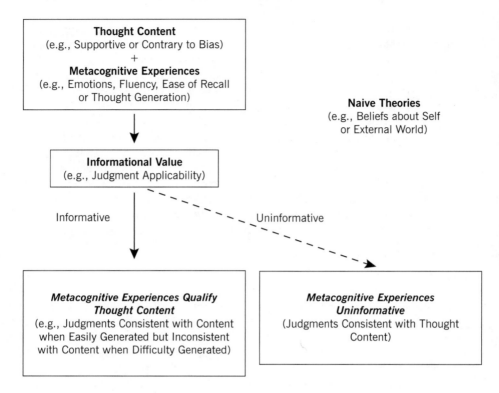

FIGURE 6.2. Metacognitive model of judgmental biases and debiasing. Solid arrows indicate the default path (i.e., metacognitive experiences are informative and qualify judgments); the dashed arrow indicates the path where metacognitive experiences are rendered uninformative to the judgment at hand. Based on Sanna and Schwarz (2007) and Schwarz, Sanna, Skurnik, and Yoon (2007).

model was developed in other contexts, we suggest that it might also be usefully applied to program evaluation. *Thought content*, what people are thinking about, is important to each of the biases. Thoughts supportive of biases produce them, whereas thoughts contrary to biases may counteract them. For example, as we described, planning fallacy results from thinking about successful task completion and ignoring relevant past failures (Buehler et al., 1994; Sanna et al., 2005), but considering possible impediments to task completion, and not discounting the relevance of past failures, may help eliminate it. Hindsight bias results from thinking about outcomes after they are already known (Hawkins & Hastie, 1990; Sanna et al., 2002), but considering alternatives that were once possible in foresight may help eliminate it.

The effects of thought content, however, are modified by *metacognitive experiences*, subjective experiences such as the ease or difficulty of thought generation or recall. For example, in a study of hindsight bias, Sanna, Schwarz, and Small (2002) had people read about a battle in the British-Gurkha war (from Fischhoff, 1975) in which they were told the British won. Participants were asked to list 2 or 10 reasons favoring either a British or Gurkha victory. If only thought content mattered, a British victory should seem more likely the more pro-British thoughts people generated and less likely the more pro-Gurkha thoughts they generated. But the exact opposite occurred: Listing 10 thoughts about a British victory (known outcome) decreased hindsight bias; listing 10 thoughts about a Gurkha victory (alternative outcome) increased it. This result cannot be explained by thought content alone. The known outcome was seen as unlikely when it was difficult to think of reasons for a British victory—if there were many reasons for a British victory, it would not be so hard to think of 10. Conversely, people inferred that alternative outcomes were unlikely when it was difficult to think of reasons for a Gurkha victory. Planning fallacy, confidence changes, and impact bias are also subject to the same interplay between thought content and metacognitive experiences (Sanna & Schwarz, 2004).

Similar metacognitive experiences are likely to be relevant in a typical program evaluation context. For example, consider the position of program advocates, who are already deeply invested in the program (and who may have used a good deal of personal effort or political capital to get the program in place) and who have strong a priori beliefs that the program will be effective. These advocating constituents may have a lot of trouble generating even a few counterarguments or alternative possibilities. They would also likely experience various motivational processes (Louie et al., 2000; Mark & Mellor, 1991) that could increase biases, such as hindsight bias (e.g., "If I knew all along the program would be ineffective, then why would I have given it the best years of my life?"). Conversely, for those who start as skeptics of the program, the opposite may be true. These skeptical constituents may be less able to think of even a few reasons to support the program. In short, whether there are program advocates or skeptics, evaluators may need to work hard at letting all constituents recognize and consider various sides to the issues.

From a theoretical perspective, biases and debiasing also depend on people's *naive theories*, beliefs about how one's thought processes and the external world operate, and the *informational value* of thoughts, or perceived applicability to the judgment at hand (Figure 6.2). For example, findings regarding experienced ease or difficulty in thought generation are consistent with the naive theory underlying the availability heuristic (Tversky & Kahneman, 1973); people judge frequency, probability, and typicality on the basis of the ease with which examples are brought to mind. Thoughts coming to mind easily make the target judgment appear likely; thoughts coming to mind with difficulty make the target judgment appear unlikely. Exactly how these theoretical processes play out in a program evaluation context is an intriguing area for future research. For example, perhaps stressful environments that make thought generation difficult could render metacognitive experiences uninformative (e.g., "It is so stressful; of course I cannot think well"). People will then fall back on thought content.

From a practical perspective, successful debiasing also requires at least four things (Wilson & Brekke, 1994). People must: (1) be aware of the potential bias; (2) be motivated to correct the bias; (3) recognize the direction and magnitude of the bias; and (4) be able to adequately control or adjust for the bias. Together, these four requirements may not always be easily achievable, but important advances in theory and research continue to point to ways of ultimately reaching that objective. Awareness of a bias can be a first step to reducing it. In fact, it is part of our motivation for writing this chapter, and we hope readers may begin to benefit from knowing at least a little more about biases. For example, as we described previously, awareness of the planning fallacy might help keep the evaluator from prematurely conducting a summative evaluation of a program that is nowhere near fully operational. Similarly, prior personal experience may also help to lessen biases, as might formal training (Lehman & Nisbett, 1990). For example, an evaluator planning her 20th evaluation, with experience in the previous evaluations showing that evaluations often take longer than expected and that programs commonly take longer to implement, may be less susceptible to planning fallacy.

Coda

We suggested in this chapter not only that greater knowledge of judgmental biases and their underlying processes may aid program evaluators (and planners) in reaching more accurate and valid conclusions, but also that examining the biases within a program evaluation context may provide a particularly informative real-life context for social psychologists to study and more fully understand how these biases operate. We emphasized temporal biases because they may be of particular relevance, as the program evaluation process takes place over time. But it is likely that other judgmental biases are also relevant to program evaluation (for reviews of the general bias literature see Gilovich et al., 2002; Kahneman et al., 1982; Kerr et al., 1996; Pohl, 2005). To our knowledge, there is little research directly connecting judgmental biases with program evaluation. Thus, in keeping with the theme of this book, we hope that our chapter helps to stimulate more integrative thinking in this regard. In the words of John Locke with which we began this chapter, although people "are, in many points, by passion or temptation" to biases, our hope is that we have also begun to suggest ways to help lessen bias.

ACKNOWLEDGMENTS

We thank the editors of this volume for their constructive and detailed suggestions, and the Better Decision Making (*BetterDecisionMaking.org*) laboratory group members at the University of North Carolina at Chapel Hill for their comments regarding this chapter.

RECOMMENDED READINGS

Gilovich, T., Griffin, D., & Kahneman, D. (2002). *Heuristics and biases: The psychology of intuitive judgment.* New York: Cambridge University Press.

Maruyama, G. (2004). Program evaluation, action research, and social psychology: A powerful blend for addressing applied problems. In C. Sansone, C. C. Morf, & A. T. Panter (Eds.), *Handbook of methods in social psychology* (pp. 429–442). Thousand Oaks, CA: Sage.

Sanna, L. J., & Chang, E. C. (Eds.). (2006). *Judgments over time: The interplay of thoughts, feelings, and behaviors.* New York: Oxford University Press.

Schwarz, N., Sanna, L. J., Skurnik, I., & Yoon, C. (2007). Metacognitive experiences and the intricacies of setting people straight: Implications for debiasing and public information campaigns. *Advances in Experimental Social Psychology, 39,* 127–161.

REFERENCES

Arkes, H. R., Faust, D., Guilmette, T. J., & Hart, K. (1988). Eliminating the hindsight bias. *Journal of Applied Psychology, 66,* 252–254.

Buehler, R., Griffin, D., & MacDonald, H. (1997). The role of motivated reasoning in optimistic time predictions. *Personality and Social Psychology Bulletin, 23,* 238–247.

Buehler, R., Griffin, D., & Ross, M. (1994). Exploring the "planning fallacy": Why people underestimate their task completion times. *Journal of Personality and Social Psychology, 67,* 366–381.

Carroll, P., Sweeny, K., & Shepperd, J. A. (2006). Forsaking optimism. *Review of General Psychology, 10,* 56–73.

Carvalho, S., & White, H. (2004). Theory-based evaluation: The case of social funds. *American Journal of Evaluation, 25,* 141–160.

Centers for Disease Control and Prevention. (1999, September 17). Framework for program evaluation in public health. *Recommendations and Reports, 48,* 1–40. Available at *www.cdc.gov/mmwr/preview/mmwrhtml/rr481a1.html.*

Christensen-Szalanski, J. J. J., & Willham, C. F. (1991). The hindsight bias: A meta-analysis. *Organizational Behavior and Human Decision Processes, 48,* 147–168.

Donaldson, S. I., Gooler, L. E., & Scriven, M. (2002). Strategies for managing evaluation anxiety: Toward a psychology of program evaluation. *American Journal of Evaluation, 23*, 261–273.

Fischhoff, B. (1975). Hindsight ≠ foresight: The effect of outcome knowledge on judgment under uncertainty. *Journal of Experimental Psychology: Human Perception and Performance, 1*, 288–299.

Fischhoff, B. (1982). Debiasing. In D. Kahneman, P. Slovic, & A. Tversky (Eds.), *Judgment under uncertainty: Heuristics and biases* (pp. 422– 444). New York: Cambridge University Press.

Flyvberg, B., Holme, M. S., & Soren, B. (2002). Underestimating costs in public works projects: Error or lie? *Journal of the American Planning Association, 68*, 279–295.

Gilbert, D. T. (2006). *Stumbling upon happiness.* New York: Knopf.

Gilovich, T., Griffin, D., & Kahneman, D. (2002). *Heuristics and biases: The psychology of intuitive judgment.* New York: Cambridge University Press.

Gilovich, T., Kerr, M., & Medvec, V. H. (1993). Effect of temporal perspective on subjective confidence. *Journal of Personality and Social Psychology, 64*, 552–560.

Guilbault, R. L., Bryant, F. B., Posavac, E. J., & Brockway, J. H. (2004). A meta-analysis of research on hindsight bias. *Basic and Applied Social Psychology, 26*, 103–117.

Hall, P. (1980). *Great planning disasters.* London: Weidenfeld & Nicolson.

Hawkins, S. A., & Hastie, R. (1990). Hindsight: Biased judgments of past events after the outcomes are known. *Psychological Bulletin, 107*, 311–327.

Kahneman, D., Slovic, P., & Tversky, A. (1982). (Eds.). *Judgment under uncertainty: Heuristics and biases.* New York: Cambridge University Press.

Kahneman, D., & Tversky, A. (1979). Intuitive prediction: Biases and corrective procedures. *Management Science, 12*, 313–327.

Kerr, N. L., MacCoun, R. J., & Kramer, G. P. (1996). Bias in judgment: Comparing groups and individuals. *Psychological Review, 103*, 687–719.

Lehman, D. R., & Nisbett, R. E. (1990). A longitudinal study of the effects of undergraduate education on reasoning. *Developmental Psychology, 26*, 952–960.

Locke, J. (1979). *An essay concerning human understanding (Claredon edition of the works of John Locke*; bk. 4, ch. 20, sect. 17, P. H. Nidditch, Ed.). New York: Oxford University Press. (Original work published 1689)

Loewenstein, G. F., & Schkade, D. (1999). Wouldn't it be nice? Predicting future feelings. In D. Kahneman, E. Diener, & N. Schwarz (Eds.), *Well-being: The foundations of hedonic psychology* (pp. 85–105). New York: Russell Sage Foundation.

Louie, T. A., Curren, M. T., & Harich, K. R. (2000). "I knew we would win": Hindsight bias for favorable and unfavorable team decision outcomes. *Journal of Applied Psychology, 85*, 264–272.

Mark, M. M., & Mellor, S. (1991). Effect of self-relevance of an event on hindsight bias: The foreseeability of a layoff. *Journal of Applied Psychology, 76*, 569–577.

Newby-Clark, I. R., Ross, M., Buehler, R., Koehler, D. J., & Griffin, D. (2000). People focus on optimistic scenarios and disregard pessimistic scenarios while predicting task completion times. *Journal of Experimental Psychology: Applied, 6,* 171–182.

Nisan, M. (1972). Dimension of time in relation to choice behavior and achievement orientation. *Journal of Personality and Social Psychology, 21,* 175–182.

Patton, M. Q. (1997). *Utilization-focused evaluation: The new century text.* Thousand Oaks, CA: Sage.

Pohl, R. F. (2005). *Cognitive illusions: A handbook on fallacies and biases in thinking, judgment and memory.* New York: Routledge.

Rossi, P. H., Freeman, H. E., & Lipsey, M. W. (1999). *Evaluation: A systematic approach* (6th ed.). Thousand Oaks, CA: Sage.

Sanna, L. J. (1999). Mental simulations, affect, and subjective confidence: Timing is everything. *Psychological Science, 10,* 339–345.

Sanna, L. J. (2007). Debiasing. In R. F. Baumeister & K. D. Vohs (Eds.), *Encyclopedia of social psychology* (Vol. 1, pp. 218–220). Thousand Oaks, CA: Sage.

Sanna, L. J., & Chang, E. C. (Eds.). (2006). *Judgments over time: The interplay of thoughts, feelings, and behaviors.* New York: Oxford University Press.

Sanna, L. J., & Meier, S. (2000). Looking for clouds in a silver lining: Self-esteem, mental simulations, and temporal confidence changes. *Journal of Research in Personality, 34,* 236–251.

Sanna, L. J., Parks, C. D., Chang, E. C., & Carter, S. E. (2005). The hourglass is half full or half empty: Temporal framing and the group planning fallacy. *Group Dynamics, 9,* 173–188.

Sanna, L. J., & Schwarz, N. (2004). Integrating temporal biases: The interplay of focal thoughts and accessibility experiences. *Psychological Science, 15,* 474–481.

Sanna, L. J., & Schwarz, N. (2006). Metacognitive experiences and human judgment: The case of hindsight bias and its debiasing. *Current Directions in Psychological Science, 15,* 172–176.

Sanna, L. J., & Schwarz, N. (2007). Metacognitive experiences and hindsight bias: It's not just the thought (content) that counts! *Social Cognition, 25,* 185–202.

Sanna, L. J., Schwarz, N., & Small, E. M. (2002). Accessibility experiences and the hindsight bias: I knew it all along versus it could never have happened. *Memory and Cognition, 30,* 1288–1296.

Sanna, L. J., Schwarz, N., & Stocker, S. L. (2002). When debiasing backfires: Accessible content and accessibility experiences in debiasing hindsight. *Journal of Experimental Psychology: Learning, Memory, and Cognition, 28,* 497–502.

Schkade, D. A., & Kahneman, D. (1998). Would you be happy if you lived in California? A focusing illusion in judgments of well-being. *Psychological Science, 9,* 340–346.

Schnaars, S. P. (1989). *Megamistakes: Forecasting and the myth of rapid technological change.* New York: Free Press.

Schwarz, N., Sanna, L. J., Skurnik, I., & Yoon, C. (2007). Metacognitive experiences and the intricacies of setting people straight: Implications for debiasing and public information campaigns. *Advances in Experimental Social Psychology, 39,* 127–161.

Scriven, M. (1998). Minimalist theory of evaluation: The least theory that practice requires. *American Journal of Evaluation, 19,* 57–70.

Shadish, W. R., Cook, T. D., & Leviton, L. C. (1991). *Foundations of program evaluation: Theories of practice.* Newbury Park, CA: Sage.

Shepperd, J. A., Grace, J., Cole, L. J., & Klein, C. (2005). Anxiety and outcome predictions. *Personality and Social Psychology Bulletin, 31,* 267–275.

Shepperd, J. A., Ouellette, J. A., & Fernandez, J. K. (1996). Abandoning unrealistic optimism: Performance estimates and the temporal proximity of self-relevant feedback. *Journal of Personality and Social Psychology, 70,* 844–855.

Sridharan, S., Campbell, B., & Zinzow, H. (2006). Developing a stakeholder-driven anticipated timeline of impact for evaluation of social programs. *American Journal of Evaluation, 27,* 148–162.

Taylor, S. E., Pham, L. B., Rivkin, I. D., & Armor, D. A. (1998). Harnessing the imagination: Mental simulation, self-regulation, and coping. *American Psychologist, 53,* 429–439.

Tversky, A., & Kahneman, D. (1973). Availability: A heuristic for judging frequency and probability. *Cognitive Psychology, 5,* 207–232.

Wholey, J. S. (1989). Introduction: How evaluation can improve agency and program performance. In J. S. Wholey & K. E. Newcomer (Eds.), *Improving government performance: Evaluation strategies for strengthening public agencies and programs* (pp. 1–11). San Francisco: Jossey-Bass.

Wilson, T. D., & Brekke, N. (1994). Mental contamination and mental correction: Unwanted influences on judgments and evaluations. *Psychological Bulletin, 116,* 117–142.

Wilson, T. D., & Gilbert, D. T. (2003). Affective forecasting. *Advances in Experimental Social Psychology, 35,* 345–411.

Wilson, T. D., Wheatley, T., Meyers, J. M., Gilbert, D. T., & Axom, D. (2000). Focalism: A source of durability bias in affective forecasting. *Journal of Personality and Social Psychology, 78,* 821–836.

Worthen, B. R., Sanders, J. R., & Fitzpatrick, J. L. (1996). *Program evaluation: Alternative approaches and practical guidelines* (2nd ed.). New York: Longman.

EDITORS' CONCLUDING COMMENTS TO CHAPTER 6

The primary focus of the previous chapter, of course, was to consider how the interesting social psychological phenomenon of temporal biases plays out in evaluation practice, as well as how evaluators can use an understanding of temporal biases to avoid their possible negative effects. We invite the reader to expand on the chapter by thinking about three questions.

First, how could social psychologists take advantage of evaluation as a testbed for further real-world study of temporal biases? For example, are there studies of debiasing that can be carried out in an evaluation context, adding to the external validity of this literature? Second, are there other judgment biases that operate in evaluation contexts, and, if so how, and what can be done for debiasing? After reading the chapter by Sanna and colleagues, it might be an interesting exercise for readers to review the literature on other judgment biases and consider how they apply in evaluation. And, third, what implications does all this have for the training and professional development of evaluators?

EDITORS' INTRODUCTORY COMMENTS TO CHAPTER 7

It is hard to overstate the importance of interpersonal and group processes in evaluation settings. In many evaluation contexts, stakeholders—members of groups that, as the term suggests, have a stake in the program being evaluated—are called on to accomplish such tasks as deciding on appropriate evaluation questions, interpreting evaluation findings, and planning organizational responses to evaluation results. With some evaluation approaches, generally called participatory evaluation approaches, stakeholders are responsible for conducting many if not all aspects of the evaluation itself. Stakeholders often participate in groups, such as a focus group to discuss priorities for the evaluation questions. Basic research in social psychology can offer evaluation a great deal in terms of improved understanding of interpersonal and group processes.

In the next chapter, Tindale and Posavac focus on three broad areas of group research that may benefit program evaluators who work with groups of stakeholders. These are group polarization, shared information and cognitions, and trust and motivation in groups. Tindale and Posavac describe each of these and how they can operate in a program evaluation context. They also review the literature on how each can be addressed and present implications for evaluation. Like the previous chapter, and unlike the chapters of Part I, the focus is not on a major theory of change that can guide theory-driven evaluation. Rather, the focus is on aspects of social psychological research and theory that can help guide evaluation practice, by providing evaluators with concepts and approaches to use in meeting challenges that arise in practice.

Perhaps most notably, Tindale and Posavac argue against a one-size-fits-all approach to working with stakeholder groups. They note that the challenges for group processes differ depending on the specific circumstances. In addition to discussing group polarization, shared information and cognitions, and trust and motivation in groups, Tindale and Posavac close the chapter with suggestions about a general model or way of thinking that can aid evaluators in deciding how best to approach the group processes and interpersonal relations involved in specific situations.

CHAPTER 7

The Social Psychology of Stakeholder Processes

Group Processes and Interpersonal Relations

R. Scott Tindale
Emil J. Posavac

Approximately 15 years ago, we were involved in a training needs assessment for a large, national social service organization (Posavac et al., 1996). The organization wanted to assess the viability of selecting at least some of their entry-level management staff from the ranks of the nonexempt employees (i.e., workers paid by the hour with little if any managerial or supervisory obligations, such as a swimming teacher). One aspect of the evaluation involved a survey of entry- and middle-level managers to ascertain the knowledge, skills, abilities, attitudes, and values they felt were necessary for successful job performance in their various positions. (By way of background, entry-level managers at different branches of the organization often fulfilled different functions depending on the size and location of the branch—small branches may only have an overall "athletics director" where larger locations may have a director for each type of sport, e.g., "swimming director" in charge of all swimming teachers, pool scheduling, etc.) After interviewing a few branch CEOs and reviewing the management assessment literature, we put together a rather lengthy survey and wanted to pilot test it with two groups of managers—one entry-level and one middle-level or above. Both groups were scheduled on a Saturday, with the entry-level manager group in the morning and the middle-level managers in the afternoon. Both groups were of comparable size and composition (in terms of gender, ethnicity, etc.), and all of the members came from the general metro area where the main headquarters for the organization was located.

The main purpose of the meetings was to assess whether the survey questions were understandable, whether the response scales made sense and were easy to use, and whether other aspects of the jobs or the organization in general should be included in some way in the survey. The morning session involved the entry-level managers. Although the atmosphere was pleasant enough initially, within minutes of the start of the actual discussion the participants took on a rather adversarial role toward the evaluation team, with the general animosity gradually increasing throughout the entire meeting. The session participants complained about item wordings and section headings and often commented that they could have written a much better survey on their own. Each attempt on our part to explain what we intended or to get more specific suggestions on how to better label sections and write items seemed to lead to greater animosity. By the end, it was clear they liked neither our survey nor us very much and felt the entire exercise had been a waste of their time.

Over lunch we attempted to diagnose what had gone wrong, but we did not have time to make any major changes before the afternoon session. So we proceeded in much the same way that afternoon. We were surprised and elated when the afternoon sessions went smoothly. The entire session remained pleasant. Participants in this session helped us to reword some problem items on a few of the scales. They also gave us some excellent suggestions for additional skills and values to be included. In other words, while the morning session could not have gone worse, the afternoon session could not have gone better. How could two seemingly similar groups react so differently to basically the same situation and process? One of the issues we will attempt to address in this chapter is how perceptions of a task influence both group processes and outcomes. In general, we hope to show that although group and interpersonal processes can be very beneficial to the overall evaluation process, this is not necessarily so. Indeed, group and interpersonal processes can, under some circumstances, be a major hindrance to a successful evaluation.

Each section of the chapter focuses on a different aspect of group and interpersonal processes, first outlining the basic findings from the social psychology literature and then discussing their potential relevance to program evaluation processes and outcomes. Finally, we will discuss some potential prescriptions for how best to take advantage of the natural group processes for maximizing the utility of stakeholder participation in the evaluation process.

Group Polarization

Theory and Research

One of the most well-established findings in the social psychological literature on groups is group polarization (Kameda, Tindale, & Davis, 2003;
Myers & Lamm, 1976). Originally discovered by Stoner (1961), group
polarization occurs when group member preferences, following group
interaction, shift to a position more extreme on the preference dimension as
compared to the positions they held prior to group discussion. Usually this
shift goes in the direction most members were leaning toward initially. The
effects of polarization also show up in the group's collective or consensus
judgments if there is one. That is, the group will reach consensus on a position more extreme than the average of the individual member's preferences
prior to the group interaction. For example, if members of an investment
club are discussing a range of investment options ranging from conservative
to risky and if most of the members favor options on the risky side, then
after discussion most of the members will favor options that are even riskier
than those they chose originally. If the group must reach consensus on a
single option, the option they choose collectively will be riskier than the
average preference prior to their discussion. Group polarization has been
demonstrated in mock jury decision making (Kameda, 1991; Tindale &
Davis, 1983), reward allocation decisions (Tindale & Davis, 1985), group
attitude judgments (Moscovici & Zavalloni, 1969), and hiring/promotion
decisions (Tindale, 1989).

A number of social psychological processes are (or can be) involved
in group polarization. First, simple majority processes have been shown to
lead to polarization (Kameda et al., 2003; Stasser, Kerr, & Davis, 1989).
Members' preferences tend to move toward the preference supported by the
largest faction within the group. If, on average, members are leaning in a
particular direction (i.e., toward one pole or the other on the dimension of
interest), then a simple majority/plurality process will lead to the group's
response being more extreme than the average individual response prior
to group discussion (Stasser et al., 1989). However, even when no consensus is required, positions with greater support at the beginning of discussion also provide for an "information" advantage. Assuming most group
members have based their preference to some degree on the information
available to them, positions with greater support will also be supported
during discussion with a greater number of positive arguments. Vinokur
and Burnstein (1974) showed that preference and information distributions
in groups tended to correspond and that simply exchanging information
among group members could lead to polarization.

Other social processes can also lead to polarization. Probably the
most heavily researched social process associated with group polarization

is social comparison (Festinger, 1954; Sanders & Baron, 1977). Festinger argued that one of the main ways in which people decide what opinions and preferences are correct or appropriate is by comparing their current positions to those of similar others. Myers (1982) and Sanders and Baron (1977) have shown that simply finding out that other group members are more extreme in the currently favored direction can lead members to shift their positions in the same direction, even when no additional information is exchanged. More recent research has also shown that comparison processes can be particularly strong when members identify strongly with the group (Hogg, 2001; Mackie, 1986). For many groups, the most typical member (prototype) is one who is most extreme on an important dimension for the group or most different from some well-defined outgroup (Hogg, 2001). Members who identify strongly with the group try to be more like the prototype and can change to more extreme positions when they realize the central members of the group hold more extreme positions. Thus, both informational and normative social influence, group identification, and basic group consensus processes can all lead to group polarization.

Implications for Program Evaluation

Although group polarization is often seen as a problem or weakness of group decision making, in most cases it is probably a strength (Kameda et al., 2003). First, majorities are often right, and recent work has shown that majority decision processes are as accurate, or more so, than other more computationally costly mechanisms (e.g., averaging, assessing member expertise, etc.; see Hastie & Kameda, 2005; Sorkin, West, & Robinson, 1998). Thus, group polarization tends to move groups in the "correct" or better direction. Second, group members tend to be more committed to projects and positions about which they feel strongly (Eagly & Chaiken, 1993). Because group polarization typically moves members to more extreme positions, it is likely that members will be more committed to positions and solutions coming out of the group discussion and will be more likely to put effort into implementing those solutions.

However, group polarization could also work against the goals of the stakeholders who have commissioned the evaluation. There are many stakeholder groups to consider (see Posavac & Carey, 2007). Sometimes evaluators have assumed that all groups share the goals of those who fund the program to be evaluated or who manage the organization of which the program is a part. Our situation involved at least three stakeholder groups: (1) the central administration of the national organization, (2) senior and middle-level managers of local branches of the organization, and (3) entry-level managers in local branches. An overriding goal of the national organization was to assure the continued success of the organization. A critical objective of senior and middle-level managers was to expand the shrinking pool of people eligible to fill entry-level positions. Although entry-level managers valued these objectives, their most immediate concern was to be assured of their own competence and their position within the organization. Thus, managers at the middle level and above valued the project, but entry-level managers could have felt threatened. Meeting with entry-level managers in a group setting led to their becoming more polarized against the needs assessment than they initially were as individuals. Thus, having some idea as to how supportive stakeholders are toward the basic purposes of evaluation projects would be good information to have before bringing stakeholders together for group discussions. Such discussions will be beneficial to the degree that group members are supportive of the process and share the same goals as the evaluators and those commissioning the evaluators. If support is lacking and goals are not shared, group discussions could inhibit the evaluation process.

Shared Information and Cognitions

Theory and Research

Recent ideas on the social psychology of groups have conceptualized many types of groups as information-processing systems (Hinsz, Tindale, & Vollrath, 1997). Two key aspects of information processing in groups involve (1) the degree to which information is shared already among the group members and (2) the processes involved in locating and communicating information that is not shared among the members. Much of the research in the area has flowed from the groundbreaking work by Stasser and his colleagues (Stasser & Stewart, 1992; Stasser & Titus, 1985, 1987), using the "hidden profile" paradigm. Stasser and Titus (1985) had four-person groups choose the best of three candidates for student council president. The entire set of relevant information tended to favor a particular candidate, but Stasser et al. distributed the information in such a way that no one group member had all of the relevant information. In addition, the information about the candidates that was shared by the group members tended to favor a less optimal candidate. Even though the group as a whole had at its disposal the information needed to reach an optimal solution, they spent most of their discussion time exchanging information that every member already had and, thus, often chose the less desirable candidate. This basic finding has now been replicated in dozens of studies using a variety of different tasks and types of groups (Gigone & Hastie, 1996; Greitemeyer, & Schulz-Hardt, 2003; Larson, Foster-Fishman, & Keys, 1994).

Research has demonstrated the role of a number of processes underlying the basic phenomena (Kerr & Tindale, 2004). First, information held by multiple members has a much higher probability of being brought up during group discussion than information held by a single member (Stasser,

1992). Larson et al. (1994) have also shown that shared information is more likely than unshared information to be repeated during discussion. Second, especially in hidden profile situations, premature closure may play a role (Karau & Kelly, 1992; Kruglanski & Webster, 1996). The need to reach consensus in situations where most of the members already share the same preference may lead to reduced information exchange and early consensus. Third, there is evidence that people prefer to both receive and present shared information (Wittenbuam, Hubbel, & Zuckerman, 1999). People are perceived as more competent, knowledgeable, and credible when they share information that others already know. Finally, recent research has shown that initial member preferences formed from shared information tend to be difficult to change, even if new information becomes available (Brodbeck, Kerschreiter, Mojzisch, Frey, & Schulz-Hardt, 2002).

A fair amount of research has also focused on how to increase the amount of unshared information that is discussed (Stasser & Birchmeier, 2003). One of the most useful interventions is to keep groups discussing the particular issue longer. Larson et al. (1994) found that shared information has a definite advantage early on, but once much of the shared information has been discussed, any new information brought up is likely to be unshared. Thus, encouraging thorough discussion and preventing premature closure help to ensure that uniquely held information will be presented to the other group members. Unshared information is also more likely to be discussed if its implications are counter to those of the shared information and if most of the information is held by a single group member (Brauer, Judd, & Jacquelin, 2001; Stewart & Stasser, 1998). This ensures that at least one member has a different initial preference and tends to lead to a more thorough discussion. Allowing group members to use memory aids or keep the initial information at their disposal can also help more unique information to be shared during discussion (Sawyer, 1997; Tindale, Sheffey, Scott, & Stasser, 1993). In addition, there is some evidence that training group members (or leaders) to explore more information can also be helpful (Larson et al., 1994; Wittenbaum, 1998). Finally, studies have shown that giving groups an accuracy goal or norm (Postmes, Spear, & Cihangir, 2001), or telling group members there is a correct solution to the problem (Stasser & Stewart, 1992), increases information sharing and group performance.

One of the most effective techniques for improving storage and recall of information in groups is through *transactive memory systems* (Wegner, 1997). A transactive memory system uses group members as memory storage units and includes a metacognitive framework for understanding which members have which information. If each member tried to store all relevant information for the group, the group's overall memory capabilities would be little better than those of any given individual. However, if different members of the group are responsible for different pieces or types of information, the collective memory capacity of the group is considerably larger than the capacity of a single individual member's memory. This increased capacity cannot be utilized effectively without everyone knowing which members know what. A fair number of studies on memory-related tasks have shown that groups with a well-formed transactive memory system can outperform groups without such a system (Hollingshead, 1998; Moreland, 1999; Wegner, Erber, & Raymond, 1991).

Other types of shared cognitive structures have also been found to influence group processes and outcomes (Tindale, Kameda, & Hinsz, 2003). Recent research has found that, if group members all share a particular representation or model of the task/situation, then behaviors and outcomes consistent with that representation become more prevalent (Tindale, Smith, Thomas, Filkins, & Sheffey, 1996). Such shared task representations help to explain why groups are superior problem solvers, relative to individuals (Laughlin, 1980; Laughlin & Ellis, 1986). When group members all share the appropriate background knowledge or conceptual system associated with a particular problem, a single member with a correct solution can often easily demonstrate its correctness to the other members, leading to it being the group's collective choice. Unfortunately, similar processes seem to occur when group members share an inappropriate representation of the task. Tindale et al. (1996) have shown that groups perform more poorly than individuals when the members share a task representation that is intuitively plausible, but normatively or logically incorrect. In general, information and alternatives consistent with the shared representation are more influential in the group, regardless of whether they are accurate representations of reality.

Implications for Program Evaluation

One of the key roles of stakeholder groups in evaluation is to provide relevant information to the evaluation team (Edwards & Newman, 1982; Posavac & Carey, 2007). Accuracy and completeness are both worthy goals for stakeholder involvement. However, given the research on information sharing in groups, different elicitation techniques would be necessary to meet both of these goals. Assuming for the moment that members of stakeholder groups have an accurate representation of their organization or program, eliciting information from them as a group will probably ensure that the most accurate and central information is obtained. Information that is shared by many members is probably more valid than information held by a single individual member (Kameda & Tindale, 2006). In addition, information being brought up in the presence of other members can be validated by consensus and corrected if minor inaccuracies exist (Vollrath, Sheppard, Hinsz, & Davis, 1989).

If completeness is the main goal, however, then getting information from each individual member separately will probably be more useful. Unshared or unique information is much less likely than shared information to be brought up during group discussion (Stasser & Titus, 1985). In addition, even if groups are asked to be complete, each group member can only speak while others are not speaking (Diehl & Stroebe, 1987). Such blocking effects reduce the amount of information generated in a group setting. Even though groups will generate more information than any single individual, the total amount of information generated will be less than would be obtained by interviewing each individual separately and then combined across the interviews. One can also ascertain the "sharedness" of the information with this second approach by simply noting the amount of redundancy. However, the individual generation approach often will be far more time consuming. Thus, which goal—accuracy or completeness—is more central to the goals of the evaluation should guide how groups are used to generate information.

Given that groups often develop transactive memory systems, whether formally or informally, simply asking members to specify who should be contacted for which type of information will also aid in obtaining information accurately and efficiently. Understanding where different types of expertise are located in the group will help to ensure that the evaluators get the information they need from the appropriate source. Also, if only certain types of information are necessary for the evaluation, understanding the transactive memory system will help avoid redundancies and inefficiencies.

Stakeholder groups naturally play a useful and necessary role in program evaluation. However, evaluators should also be sure to look for situations where stakeholders may share misconceptions about the issues associated with the evaluation. One common misconception is that evaluation is always and solely about success or failure of the program (Posavac & Carey, 2007). In our experience, few stakeholders seem to think about evaluation as leading to program refinement. Bringing people together who share this misconception can amplify defensiveness. More generally, evaluators should examine whether there are misconceptions about the program. For example, Posavac and Hartung (1977) discovered that the staff of a counseling center thought of themselves as providing depth psychotherapy delivered to long-term clients. A simple summary of the center's files showed that the modal client had come to six sessions. Such misconceptions might well be rare because stakeholders will usually have both accurate and insightful information about their particular program or organization. However, when using groups to generate information or to reach consensus on relevant issues, shared misconceptions can lead groups to emphasize information and objectives that are not accurate representations of the problems or issues involved. Bringing the individual stakeholders together as a group will not correct the misconceptions; rather, it may reinforce them. Tindale et al. (1998) have found that group members are often more confident in their erroneous conclusions after discussing them in the group. Consensus is typically an indicator of validity, but not always.

Motivation and Trust in Groups

Theory and Research

Although stakeholder groups can provide much needed information to an evaluation project, they also must at some point pay attention to the feedback derived from the project, accept the implications of the feedback, and then carry out the proposed changes or interventions (Posavac & Carey, 2007). In order for the stakeholders to "buy into" the process and the potential changes stemming from it, the stakeholders must trust the evaluators and be motivated to cooperate with and follow through on their recommendations. In other words, stakeholders must be motivated to change.

Trust has been identified as a key element to both group cooperation and performance (Burt, 1999; Kramer, 2001). Putting effort into a group task often requires trust that others will also exert such efforts so that the group will be successful (Kerr, 1983). Work on conflict resolution and negotiation has shown that trust and a willingness to exchange information can help negotiators find common ground and opportunities for added value beyond simple compromise (Thompson, 2001). Many standard conflict resolution techniques (tit-for-tat, G.R.I.T., etc.) require initial steps of cooperation and concession making in order to foster trust by the opposing party. Kramer (2001) has found that multiple instances of trust-developing behaviors are particularly important in noisy environments where actions do not always correspond to intended outcomes. Thus, if the findings of an evaluation are to be used, the first thing evaluators must do is to gain the trust of the stakeholders with whom they will interact and those who are to implement the changes suggested by the evaluation.

Assuming trust has been established, the degree to which stakeholders will cooperate with and follow through on the evaluator's recommendations will depend on how motivated they are to do so. A number of group-level processes can affect group member motivations. Probably the most heavily researched of these processes are social facilitation and social loafing (Latané, Williams, & Harkins, 1979; Zajonc, 1965). Social facilitation involves the increased effort that people put into an individual-level performance task when they perform in the presence of other people (Baron, 1986). Although there are many aspects to the increase in level of motivation, much of it seems to derive from a greater focus of attention due to distraction and potential evaluation (Muller & Butera, 2007). This increased effort tends to lead to performance increments when people are working on well-learned tasks, but results in performance decrements when people are working on difficult or newly learned tasks (Zajonc, 1965).

Probably the more worrisome process for most group settings is social loafing (Latané et al., 1979). Since the early work of Steiner (1972), it has been well documented that groups rarely perform up to their full potential. Early theorists assumed that the major aspects of process losses in groups were due to coordination issues. However, Latané et al. performed a series of now classic experiments in which they could estimate the size of expected coordination losses. They compared individuals either clapping or shouting as loud as they could alone or in groups of various sizes and recorded the total amount of sound generated. The potential group performance in such situations is simply the sum of the amounts of sound generated by each of the individuals alone. However, they also calculated the amount of sound degradation expected in each group size if one were to assume that the group members clapped or shouted at random starting times, which would indicate the expected degree of sound loss due to lack of coordination. The Latané study found that coordination losses accounted for less than half of the actual performance losses in groups. This implied that individuals were clapping and shouting less loudly when they performed these behaviors in a group as opposed to when they performed them alone. Latané et al. coined the term *social loafing* to describe the motivation loss portion of the process losses they observed. This effect has now been replicated hundreds of times with a variety of different physical and cognitive tasks (Karau & Williams, 1993).

Although prevalent in many group situations, social loafing is most likely to occur under a specific set of circumstances (Karau & Williams, 1993). First, performance must be perceived by the group members as a group-level phenomenon. As mentioned earlier, in individual performance settings, the presence of other people tends to increase performance for simple tasks. Second, it must be difficult for individual group members to perceive their own contribution to the group. Harkins, White, and Utman (2000) have shown that if either external- or self-evaluation of members' performances is allowed in situations in which acceptable performance is definable, loafing effects are reduced or eliminated. Social loafing has also been shown to be more prevalent in situations where individual group members remain relatively anonymous in terms of their contribution to the group. Harkins and Syzmanski (1988) have shown that setting goals and allowing group members to monitor their individual performance relative to those goals eliminates loafing, even if the goals are virtually unattainable.

Another issue that affects motivation in groups is diffusion of responsibility (Latané & Darley, 1970). Although similar in some respects to social loafing, this issue tends to occur in nonperformance group situations as well. In essence, when group members feel it is the group's responsibility to perform some behavior or operation, as the size of the group increases, each member feels somewhat less responsible for carrying out the specific behavior. Diffusion of responsibility is particularly likely to occur in situations where role definitions within the group are vague or the group is taking on new responsibilities without assigning those responsibilities to specific group members. A good way to alleviate such concerns is by providing clear role and duty assignments within a group so that responsibility is defined well and cannot be diffused.

A number of studies have also found situations where being in a group can actually increase motivation. First, Williams and Karau (1991) showed that if a member perceives him/herself to be the only group member capable of performing a task important to the group (and to that member), that member will work extra hard to perform well. Williams and Karau referred to this as the "social compensation" effect. More recently, Kerr (2001; see also Messe, Hertel, Kerr, Lount, & Park, 2002) described a series of studies that attempt to understand the Koehler Effect (Koehler, 1926). Koehler found that dyad rowing teams could occasionally perform better as a team than the sum of their individual rowing abilities would predict. Kerr (2001) has ascertained that such effects are most likely to occur when the two team members are moderately different in terms of ability. In such situations, the less able member tends to increase his or her effort so as to not detract from the performance of the more able member. Such effects seem to occur mainly for what Steiner (1972) termed *conjunctive tasks*—tasks in which the group can perform no better than their least able member.

Both motivation gains and losses in groups can be explained (at least in part) by simple expectancy-value models of motivation (Karau & Williams, 1993; Shepperd, 1993; Vroom, 1969). Such models assume that people will exert effort on a task to the degree that performance on the task leads to valuable outcomes and their effort leads to the desired level of performance. In situations where group members perceive their efforts as identifiable and instrumental to group performance or attaining some group goal, then group members remain motivated in group settings. If they see their performance as crucial for group success, they work even harder than they might individually. However, if the outcomes are not seen as valuable or if it is difficult for group members to see how their performance actually affects the group's performance, they tend to work less hard in a group setting. Other factors, such as social comparison and self-presentation, can also come into play (Hertel, Kerr, Scheffler, Geister, & Messe, 2000; Stroebe, Diehl, & Abakoumkin, 1996). Nevertheless, much of the variance in these studies can be explained by the degree to which group members can clearly see the relation between their efforts, group performance, and the value associated with such performance.

Implications for Program Evaluation

Unless a summative evaluation simply leads to the cancellation of an ill-conceived program, a successful evaluation must have the support of the stakeholders involved, both during the evaluation and later as promising improvements are implemented (Posavac & Carey, 2007). The most important element in gaining such support is engendering trust. If the program managers and staff have instigated the evaluation process, gaining trust may be straightforward. Still, keeping all aspects of the evaluation transparent in terms of both what is planned and why such plans have been made remains important. When an evaluation is imposed by funding agents or by managers not immediately associated with the program, it is quite possible for evaluators to be seen as critics or enemies. Evaluators must avoid an "us–them" feeling between stakeholders and evaluators. Having the stakeholders perceive that they are part of the same team with the evaluators will go a long way in fostering trust (Gaertner, Dovidio, Anastasio, Backman, & Rust, 1993; Hogg & Abrams, 1988).

Probably the next most important aspect of achieving stakeholder support is to get them involved early and keep them involved throughout the process. Staff must also come to see how the developing evaluation can benefit them. In our needs assessment project, the entry-level managers might have been won over by our stressing the values and traditions of the organization. It might have been a challenge, but if we had been more sensitive to their concerns we might have been able to avoid or reduce the antagonism. Further, the project might have gotten started more smoothly if we had alerted the national personnel director to the danger associated with the group process. The personnel director had spoken glowingly of the organization and the spirit of the local managers to us. He might have been able to paint those values to entry-level managers in a way that increased their trust in us as well in helping them see how the project served values that local managers shared.

Sharing organization-relevant values might have increased both trust and the degree to which entry-level managers felt a sense of ownership of the project, leading them to feel that they had a part in the planning process (Greenberg & Colquitt, 2005). People are more likely to cooperate with and continue to support evaluation projects in which they feel positively involved (Posavac & Carey, 2007). The evaluators should also try to make it very clear what role the stakeholders play in the evaluation process and why that role is crucial to a successful evaluation. Both diffusion of responsibility and social loafing are reduced when individuals can see how their contribution affects the final outcome for the group. Clear role definitions and feelings of voice or ownership are probably most important during the implementation stage of the evaluation process. Often the evaluators are no longer around when changes need to be implemented. And change is always somewhat effortful. It is quite likely that many excellent suggestions for change were never implemented simply because no one felt that it was their responsibility to make them happen. Helping stakeholders to see how changes in their specific behaviors will help the organization to reach the goals outlined in the evaluation project will help to ensure that such changes are, in fact, enacted.

Concluding Remarks

Every evaluation situation is different and involves different groups of stakeholders. Thus, there is no single best way to bring all stakeholder groups into the evaluation process. What we have attempted to do here is to discuss some of the group-level processes (and individual-level processes that are affected by being in a group) in an attempt to outline how they might come into play during an evaluation. Probably the best advice we can provide is to think carefully about who the relevant stakeholders are, what role they could play in the evaluation, and how they might, as a group, react to the evaluation situation.

A useful template for thinking about such issues might be Vroom and Yetton's (1973) managerial decision-making model. Vroom and Yetton argue that when deciding what role subordinates should play in managerial decision making, there are two major criteria to consider: quality and acceptance. The model then poses a series of questions, the answers to which guide the manager in deciding what type and how much of a role the subordinates should play in the decision-making process. (See Vroom & Yetton, 1973, for a complete set of the questions and decision points.) Although not all aspects of the model would be equally relevant to evaluators, both quality and acceptance issues pertain and stakeholders play a role in both. For example, one of the questions posed by the model (adapted here for evaluation) is "Are the goals of each of the stakeholder groups the same as those of the evaluators and those who commissioned the evaluation?" If the answer to this question is "no," the model would argue against bringing the stakeholders together as a group and allowing their consensus to guide decisions. The types of decision processes discussed by the model range from completely autocratic, involving no input from the group, to completely participative, where the group discusses and reaches consensus on the particular decision issue. For some issues (e.g., what type of evaluation design to use or how to assess the validity of measures), the decisions should be left almost completely to the research design experts, namely, the evaluators. However, issues concerning the criteria of quality to use or the average abilities of clients to complete surveys or the likelihood of clients coming to an interview would be questions better addressed to the program-level stakeholders. Evaluators should make sure to address these issues up front rather than running into problems later in the processes.

Going back to our initial example, one thing we had not thought about before putting together our two focus groups was how the project (hiring entry-level managers from the ranks of nonexempt employees) might be perceived differently by the two groups. In retrospect, it makes sense that the group of entry-level managers might see the project more negatively than would managers at higher levels of the organization. Entry-level managers may have perceived the project as a threat to their jobs, or at least as somewhat insulting in that the project implied that their experience and training did not differentiate them to any great degree from the nonexempt employees. Thus, it was probably ill advised to bring members of this stakeholder group together in a focus group environment without getting them involved earlier and without making any attempt to influence their perceptions of the project. We hope that our chapter may help future evaluators to anticipate such problems and avoid similar negative experiences.

ACKNOWLEDGMENT

Preparation of this chapter was partially funded by the National Science Foundation, Grant BCS-0820344, to the first author.

REFERENCES

Baron, R. (1986). Distraction-Conflict theory: Progress and problems. In L. Berkowitz (Ed.) *Advances in experimental social psychology* (Vol. 19, pp. 1–40). New York: Academic Press.

Brauer, M., Judd, C. M., & Jacquelin, V. (2001). The communication of social stereotypes: The effects of group discussion and information distribution on stereotypic appraisals. *Journal of Personality and Social Psychology, 81,* 463–475.

Brodbeck, F. C., Kerschreiter, R., Mojzisch, A., Frey, D., & Schulz-Hardt, S. (2002). The dissemination of critical, unshared information in decisionmaking groups: The effects of prediscussion dissent. *European Journal of Social Psychology, 32,* 35–56.

Burt, R. S. (1999). Entrepreneurs, distrust, and third parties: A strategic look at the dark side of dense networks. In L. Thompson, J. M. Levine, & D. M. Messick (Eds.), *Shared cognitions in organizations: The management of knowledge* (pp. 213–244). Mahwah, NJ: Erlbaum.

Diehl, M., & Stroebe, W. (1987). Productivity loss in brainstorming groups: Toward the solution of a riddle. *Journal of Personality and Social Psychology, 53,* 497–509.

Eagly, A. H., & Chaiken, S. (1993). *The psychology of attitudes.* Fort Worth, TX: Harcourt Brace Jovanovich College Publishers.

Edwards, W., & Newman, J. R. (1982). *Multiattribute evaluation*. Beverly Hills, CA: Sage.

Festinger, L. (1954). A theory of social comparison processes. *Human Relations, 7*, 117–140.

Gaertner, S. L., Dovidio, J. F., Anastasio, P. A., Backman, B. A., & Rust, M. C. (1993). Reducing intergroup bias: The common ingroup identity model. *European Review of Social Psychology, 4*, 1–26.

Gigone, D., & Hastie, R. (1996). The impact of information on group judgment: A model and computer simulation. In E. Witte & J. H. Davis (Eds.), *Understanding group behavior: Consensual action by small groups* (Vol. 1, pp. 221–251). Mahwah, NJ: Erlbaum.

Greenberg, J., & Colquitt, J. A. (2005). *Handbook of organizational justice*. Mahwah, NJ: Erlbaum.

Greitemeyer, T., & Schulz-Hardt, S. (2003). Preference-consistent evaluation of information in the hidden profile paradigm: Beyond group-level explanations for the dominance of shared information in group decisions. *Journal or Personality and Social Psychology, 84*, 322–339.

Harkins, S. G., & Syzmanski, K. (1988). Social loafing and self-evaluation with an objective standard. *Journal of Experimental Social Psychology, 24*, 354–365.

Harkins, S. G., White, P., & Utman, C. (2000). The role of internal and external sources of evaluation in motivating task performance. *Personality and Social Psychology Bulletin, 26*, 100–117.

Hertel, G., Kerr, N. L., Scheffler, M., Geister, S., & Messe, L. A. (2000). Exploring the Koehler motivation gain effect: Impression management and spontaneous goal setting. *Zeitschrift fur Sozialpsycholoie, 31*, 204–220.

Hinsz, V. B., Tindale, R. S., & Vollrath, D. A. (1997). The emerging conception of groups as information processors. *Psychological Bulletin, 121*, 43–64.

Hogg, M. A. (2001). Social categorization, depersonalization, and group behavior. In M. A. Hogg & R. S. Tindale (Eds.), *Blackwell handbook of social psychology: Group processes* (pp. 56–85). Oxford, UK: Blackwell.

Hogg, M. A., & Abrams, D. (1988). *Social identifications: A social psychology of intergroup relations and group processes*. London: Routledge.

Hollingshead, A. B. (1998). Retrieval processes in transactive memory systems. *Journal of Personality and Social Psychology, 74*, 659–671.

Kameda, T. (1991). Procedural influence in small-group decision making: Deliberation style and assigned decision rule. *Journal of Personality and Social Psychology, 61*, 245–256.

Kameda, T., & Hastie, R. (2005). The robust beauty of the majority rule. *Psychological Review, 112*, 494–508.

Kameda, T., & Tindale, R. S. (2006). Groups as adaptive devices: Human docility and group aggregation mechanisms in evolutionary context. In M. Schaller, J. A. Simpson, & D. T. Kenrick (Eds.), *Evolution and social psychology* (pp. 317–342). New York: Psychology Press.

Kameda, T., Tindale, R. S., & Davis, J. H. (2003). Cognitions, preferences, and social sharedness: Past, present and future directions in group decision making. In S. L. Schneider & J. Shanteau (Eds.), *Emerging perspectives on judgment and decision research* (pp. 458–485). New York: Cambridge University Press.

Karau, S. J., & Kelly, J. R. (1992). The effects of time scarcity and time abundance on group performance quality and interaction process. *Journal of Experimental Social Psychology, 28*, 542–571.

Karau, S. J., & Williams, K. D. (1993). Social loafing: A meta-analytic review and theoretical integration. *Journal of Personality and Social Psychology, 65*, 681–706.

Kerr, N. L. (1983). Motivation losses in small groups: A social dilemma analysis. *Journal of Personality and Social Psychology, 45*, 819–828.

Kerr, N. L. (2001). Motivation gains in performance groups: Aspects and prospects. In J. Forgas, K. D. Williams, & L. Wheeler (Eds.), *The social mind: Cognitive and motivational aspects of interpersonal behavior* (pp. 350–370). New York: Cambridge University Press.

Kerr, N. L., & Tindale, R. S. (2004). Small group decision making and performance. *Annual Review of Psychology, 55*, 623–656.

Koehler, O. (1926). Physical performance in individual and group situations. *Industrielle Psycholtechnik, 3*, 274–282.

Kramer, R. M. (2001). Golden rules and leaden worlds: Exploring the limitations of Tit-for-Tat as a social decision rule. In J. Darley, D. M. Messick, & T. Tyler (Eds.), *Ethics and social influence* (pp. 177–199). Mahwah, NJ: Erlbaum.

Kruglanski, A. W., & Webster, D. M. (1996). Motivated closing of the mind: "Seizing" and "freezing." *Psychological Review, 103*, 263–283.

Larson, J. R., Jr., Foster-Fishman, P. G., & Keys, C. B. (1994). Discussion of shared and unshared information in decision-making groups. *Journal of Personality and Social Psychology, 67*, 446–461.

Latané, B., & Darley, J. M. (1970). *The unresponsive bystander: Why doesn't he help.* Englewood Cliffs, NJ: Prentice Hall.

Latané, B., Williams, K., & Harkins, S. (1979). Many hands make light the work: The causes and consequences of social loafing. *Journal of Personality and Social Psychology, 37*, 822–832.

Laughlin, P. R. (1980). Social combination processes of cooperative, problem-solving groups on verbal intellective tasks. In M. Fishbein (Ed.), *Progress in social psychology* (Vol. 1, pp. 127–155). Hillsdale, NJ: Erlbaum.

Laughlin, P. R., & Ellis, A. L. (1986). Demonstrability and social combination processes on mathematical intellective tasks. *Journal of Experimental Social Psychology, 22*, 177–189.

Mackie, D. M. (1986). Social identification effects in group polarization. *Journal of Personality and Social Psychology, 50*, 720–728.

Messe, L. A., Hertel, G., Kerr, N. L., Lount, R. B., & Park, E. S. (2002). Knowledge of partner's ability as a moderator of group motivation gains: An exploration of the Kohler Discrepancy Effect. *Journal of Personality and Social Psychology, 82*, 935–946.

Moreland, R. L. (1999). Transactive memory. In L. Thompson & J. Levine (Eds.), *Learning who knows what in work groups and organizations* (pp. 3–31). Mahwah, NJ: Erlbaum.

Moscovici, S., & Zavalloni, M. (1969). The group as a polarizer of attitudes. *Journal of Personality and Social Psychology, 12*, 125–135.

Muller, D., & Butera, F. (2007). The distracting effect of self-evaluation threat in coaction and social comparison. *Journal of Personality and Social Psychology, 93,* 194–211.

Myers, D. G. (1982). Polarizing effects of social interaction. In H. Brandstatter, J. H. Davis, & G. Stocker-Kreichgaurer (Eds.), *Group decision making* (pp. 125–162). London: Academic Press.

Myers, D. G., & Lamm, H. (1976). The group polarization phenomenon. *Psychological Bulletin, 83,* 602–627.

Posavac, E. J., & Carey, R. G. (2007). *Program evaluation: Methods and case studies* (7th ed.). Englewood Cliffs, NJ: Prentice Hall.

Posavac, E. J., Dew, D. E., Jr., Tindale, R. S., Dugoni, B. L., Sheffey, S., & Koch, M. S. (1996). High aspiration hourly workers as potential entry-level professional employees. *Journal of Career Development, 23,* 151–165.

Posavac, E. J., & Hartung, B. (1977). An investigation into the reasons people choose a pastoral counselor instead of another type of psychotherapist. *Journal of Pastoral Care, 31,* 23–31.

Postmes, T., Spears, R., & Cihangir, S. (2001). Quality of decision making and group norms. *Journal of Personality and Social Psychology, 80,* 918–930.

Sanders, G., & Baron, R. S. (1977). Is social comparison irrelevant for producing choice shifts? *Journal of Experimental Social Psychology, 13,* 303–314.

Sawyer, J. E. (1997). *Information sharing and integration in multifunctional decision-making groups.* Paper presented at the Society of Judgment and Decision Making Annual Meeting, Philadelphia, PA.

Shepperd, J. A. (1993). Productivity loss in performance groups: a motivation analysis. *Psychological Bulletin, 113,* 67–81.

Sorkin, R. D., West, R., & Robinson, D. E. (1998). Group performance depends on the majority rule. *Psychological Science, 9,* 456–463.

Stasser, G. (1992). Pooling of unshared information during group discussions. In S. Worchel, W. Wood, & J. A. Simpson (Eds.), *Group process and productivity* (pp. 48–67). Newbury Park, CA: Sage.

Stasser, G., & Birchmeier, Z. (2003). Group creativity and collective choice. In P. Paulus & B. Nijstad (Eds.), *Group creativity: Innovation through collaboration* (pp. 85–109). Oxford, UK: Oxford University Press.

Stasser, G., Kerr, N. L., & Davis, J. H. (1989). Influence processes and consensus models in decision-making groups. In P. Paulus (Ed.), *Psychology of group influence* (2nd ed., pp. 279–326). Hillsdale, NJ: Erlbaum.

Stasser, G., & Stewart, D. (1992). Discovery of hidden profiles by decision-making groups: Solving a problem versus making a judgment. *Journal of Personality and Social Psychology, 63,* 426–434.

Stasser, G., & Titus, W. (1985). Pooling of unshared information in group decision making: Biased information sampling during discussion. *Journal of Personality and Social Psychology, 48,* 1467–1478.

Stasser, G., & Titus, W. (1987). Effects of information load and percentage of shared information on the dissemination of unshared information during group discussion. *Journal of Personality and Social Psychology, 53,* 81–93.

Steiner, I. D. (1972). *Group processes and productivity.* New York: Academic Press.

Stewart, D. D., & Stasser, G. (1998). The sampling of critical, unshared information in decision-making groups: The role of an informed minority. *European Journal of Social Psychology, 28,* 95–113.

Stoner, J. A. F. (1961). *A comparison of individual and group decisions involving risk.* Unpublished Master's thesis, Massachusetts Institute of Technology.

Stroebe, W., Diehl, W., & Abakoumkin, G. (1996). Social compensation and the Kohler Effect: Toward a theoretical explanation of motivation gains in group productivity. In E. Witten & J. H. Davis (Eds.), *Understanding group behavior: Small group processes and interpersonal relations* (Vol. 2, pp. 37–65). Mahwah, NJ: Erlbaum.

Thompson, L. (2001). *The mind and heart of the negotiator* (2nd ed.). Upper Saddle River, NJ: Prentice-Hall.

Tindale, R. S. (1989). Group vs. individual information processing: The effects of outcome feedback on decision-making. *Organizational Behavior and Human Decision Processes, 44,* 454–473.

Tindale, R. S., Anderson, E. M., Smith, C. M., Steiner, L., & Filkins, J. (1998). *Further explorations of conjunction errors by individuals and groups.* Paper presented at the British Psychological Society Social Psychology Section Conference, Canterbury, UK.

Tindale, R. S., & Davis, J. H. (1983). Group decision making and jury verdicts. In H. H. Blumberg, A. P. Hare, V. Kent, & M. F. Davies (Eds.), *Small groups and social interaction* (Vol. 2, pp. 9–38). Chichester, UK: Wiley.

Tindale, R. S., & Davis, J. H. (1985). Individual and group reward allocation decisions in two situational contexts: The effects of relative need and performance. *Journal of Personality and Social Psychology, 48,* 1148–1161.

Tindale, R. S., Kameda, T., & Hinsz, V. B. (2003). Group decision making. In J. Cooper & M. Hogg (Eds.), *Sage handbook of social psychology* (pp. 381–403). London: Sage.

Tindale, R. S., Sheffey, S., Scott, L. A., & Stasser, G. (1993). *Procedural effects on information sharing in groups.* Paper presented at the 16th Nags Head Conference on Groups, Networks, and Organizations, Highland Beach, FL.

Tindale, R. S., Smith, C. M., Thomas, L. S., Filkins, J., & Sheffey, S. (1996). Shared representations and asymmetric social influence processes in small groups. In E. Witte & J. H. Davis (Eds.), *Understanding group behavior: Consensual action by small groups* (Vol. 1, pp. 81–103). Mahwah, NJ: Erlbaum.

Vinokur, A., & Burnstein, E. (1974). The effects of partially shared persuasive arguments on group induced shifts: A group problem solving approach. *Journal of Personality and Social Psychology, 29,* 305–315.

Vollrath, D. A., Sheppard, B. H., Hinsz, V. B., & Davis, J. H. (1989). Memory performance by decision-making groups and individuals. *Organizational Behavior and Human Decision Processes, 43,* 289–300.

Vroom, V. H. (1969). Industrial social psychology. In G. Lindzey & E. Aronson (Eds.), *Handbook of social psychology* (2nd ed., Vol. 5, pp. 196–286). Reading, MA: Addison-Wesley.

Vroom, V. H., & Yetton, P. W. (1973). *Leadership and decision making.* Pittsburgh, PA: University of Pittsburgh Press.

Wegner, D. M. (1987). Transactive memory: A contemporary analysis of the group mind. In B. Mullen & G. R. Goethals (Eds.), *Theories of group behavior* (pp. 185–208). New York: Springer-Verlag.

Wegner, D. M., Erber, R., & Raymond, P. (1991). Transactive memory in close relationships. *Journal of Personality and Social Psychology, 61,* 923–929.

Williams, K. D., & Karau, S. J. (1991). Social loafing and social compensation: The effects of expectations of coworker performance. *Journal of Personality and Social Psychology, 61,* 570–581.

Wittenbaum, G. M. (1998). Information sampling in decision-making groups: The impact of members' task-relevant status. *Small Group Research, 29,* 57–84.

Wittenbaum, G. M., Hubbell, A. P., & Zuckerman, C. (1999). Mutual enhancement: Toward an understanding of collective preference for shared information. *Journal of Personality and Social Psychology, 77,* 967–978.

Zajonc, R. (1965). Social facilitation. *Science, 149,* 269–274.

EDITORS' CONCLUDING COMMENTS
TO CHAPTER 7

Lessons from research on group and interpersonal processes may help illuminate various aspects of the interactions between evaluator and stakeholders. For instance, the decision to use individuals or groups of stakeholders to accomplish evaluation tasks should be based on a number of considerations discussed by Tindale and Posavac. These include (1) the extent of shared goals among group members, (2) whether accuracy or completeness are the primary goals for the task, (3) the extent to which group members share the same information about the problem to be addressed, and (4) whether there are misconceptions about the task that may be amplified in a group setting. Tindale and Posavac offer some relatively simple strategies evaluators might use to improve group functioning under certain conditions, such as providing an accuracy norm when group members share a significant amount of the information needed to solve a problem, and avoiding extensive group discussion when there is a risk that a misconception might be amplified.

There are, however, many aspects of the stakeholder interaction process that remain to be explored in the context of evaluation practice. For instance, some research on group polarization suggests that group discussion can lead to negative outcomes when group members do not share the same goals. This could lead one to avoid group discussion under these conditions. On the other hand, evaluation scholars such as House and Howe (1999) recommend group discussion among stakeholders with seemingly opposing goals. They maintain that dialogue and deliberation among stakeholders with seemingly opposing goals can help to uncover the "real interests" of those involved in the evaluation (House & Howe, 1999). Without further empirical research, it is difficult to say with any degree of certainty whether—or when—discussion among stakeholders with disparate views should be recommended or avoided.

Indeed, there has been relatively little empirical research on the operation of groups in actual evaluation settings. Research conducted outside of the laboratory setting, with real evaluation stakeholders, conducting meaningful tasks, may reveal unique relationships and/or boundary conditions previously not discovered in the lab. For example, some basic social psychology research seems to assume, at least implicitly, that the "group" is fairly homogeneous. But mixed allegiances are a reality when working with group of evaluation stakeholders. Issues of accountability to different constituencies and self-interest in group dynamics may begin to play a more central role in research on actual stakeholder group processes than it does in typical laboratory settings. Readers might also consider how variables such as the status and power of individual stakeholders are likely to impact participation in a group setting. The social psychology–evaluation intersection would no doubt benefit from broadening the scope of group research to take advantage of the complexities and realities that apply to actual evaluation, where the stakes, power differentials, group allegiances, and so on are likely to be stronger than can be achieved in a social psychology lab.

EDITORS' INTRODUCTORY COMMENTS
TO CHAPTER 8

Social psychologists who conduct applied research are motivated by the possibility that their work might make a positive difference in the world. Likewise, evaluators are motivated by the possibility that the evaluations they conduct can make a difference. For example, evaluation findings might point to improvements that can be made in a program or contribute to decisions that continue and expand effective programs. For evaluations to make a positive difference, however, they must be used.

Use is a long-standing concern in the evaluation literature. Early evaluators, in the heyday of the 1960s and 1970s, sometimes appeared simply to assume that evaluation findings would be used, at least if the methods were of sufficient quality. However, the many evaluation reports that ended up collecting dust on shelves led to something of a crisis in evaluation. Infrequent use also promoted systematic research on evaluation use. This research in turn led to distinctions such as that between "conceptual use," that is, an evaluation's effect on the way someone thinks, and "instrumental use," that is, an evaluation's effect on direct action, such as a program staff manager's modification of a program or a school principal's decision to adopt a new program.

In the next chapter, Monique Fleming discusses the application of a set of related areas of social psychology—attitudes, persuasion, and social influence—to evaluation use. Fleming first reviews alternative types of evaluation use. She also discusses key aspects of the literature on attitude change and persuasion. For example, she describes the two general routes to persuasion specified in prominent theories. In general terms, one of these routes involves change that arises from thoughtful consideration of information, while the other route involves change that stems from more superficial cues such as the expertise of the person making an argument.

Fleming considers possible pathways to evaluation use in light of key research and theory from social psychology. She summarizes suggestions about enhancing use that have been made in the evaluation literature, and she assesses the quality of these ideas in relation to lessons from the social psychological literature. She reviews important findings from the social psychological literature and explores their potential implications for evaluation use. In closing the chapter, Fleming describes the potential benefits of a closer intersection between social psychologists interested in persuasion and related processes, on the one hand, and evaluators concerned about evaluation use, on the other.

CHAPTER 8

Attitudes, Persuasion, and Social Influence
Applying Social Psychology to Increase Evaluation Use

Monique A. Fleming

Imagine that a university is considering implementing a policy requiring seniors to pass comprehensive exams in their major prior to graduation. Imagine further that an evaluation is available which shows the effects of implementing a similar exam policy at other schools. Will the evaluation be used in making the decision? The present chapter outlines how social psychological theory and research on attitudes, persuasion, and social influence can enhance our understanding of when evaluations will be used and why, by enhancing our understanding of the processes through which evaluations influence attitudes and behavior.

Use is widely considered the primary purpose for evaluation in theory, research, and practice (e.g., Henry & Mark, 2003; Kirkhart, 2000; Patton, 1978; Preskill & Caracelli, 1997). Several types of use have been proposed. *Instrumental use* involves the effects of an evaluation on decision making and actions, such as continuing, expanding, revising, or terminating a policy or program. In contrast, *conceptual use* involves, not direct action, but learning from an evaluation about a policy or program, such as why it works, how it can be implemented, or about its participants (see Leviton & Hughes, 1981, for a discussion of the origins of these and other types of use). If in the example of senior comprehensive exams, the evaluation of the exams policy at other schools led the university to adopt the exams policy, this would be a form of instrumental use, specifically, *diffusion*, in which an evaluation at one location leads to the adoption of a policy or program elsewhere.

The attention to attitudes, persuasion, and social influence in this chapter, as well as its attention to the processes that may mediate use, fits well with recent attempts in the evaluation literature to expand the focus from use to evaluation *influence* (Henry & Mark, 2003; Kirkhart, 2000; Mark & Henry, 2004). Mark and Henry (2004) point out that "the past literature has identified possible precursors of use (e.g., credibility of the evaluation, stakeholder involvement), as well as general forms of possible use (e.g., instrumental, conceptual), but for the most part has ignored the change processes through which evaluation influences attitudes, motivations, and action." (p. 45). They draw on influence theories and research in the social sciences, including social psychology, for insights into change processes that might plausibly mediate the effects of variables such as stakeholder involvement on use. Put simply, they ask what the intermediate steps may be through which evaluation findings and evaluation processes can lead ultimately to downstream evaluation use. Henry and Mark propose that evaluations can influence cognition and affect such as attitudes (conceptual use); motivation; and behavior (instrumental use), through a variety of general influence processes such as elaboration and use of heuristics (see Table 8.1). They suggest that contingencies will determine when a par-

TABLE 8.1. A Model of Alternative Mechanisms That May Mediate Evaluation Influence

Type of process/ outcome	Level of analysis		
	Individual	Interpersonal	Collective
General influence	**Elaboration** **Heuristics** Priming Skill acquisition	**Justification** **Persuasion** **Change agent** **Minority-opinion influence**	Ritualism **Legislative hearings** **Coalition formation** **Drafting legislation** Standard setting **Policy consideration**
Cognitive and affective	Salience **Opinion/attitude valence**	Local descriptive norms	Agenda setting **Policy-oriented learning**
Motivational	Personal goals and aspirations	Injunctive norms Social reward Exchange	Structural incentives Market forces
Behavioral	New skill performance **Individual change in practice**	**Collaborative change in practice**	**Program continuation cessation, or change** **Policy change** **Diffusion**

Note. From Mark and Henry (2004, p. 41). Copyright 2004 by Sage Publications, Ltd. Reprinted by permission. Bold added.

ticular influence process is likely to operate or not, and that if no initial influence process occurs, then other effects further down the causal chain, including use, also will not occur. Mark and Henry (2004) intend their framework to be a starting point, and they refer the reader to the respective social science literatures for more detail.

This chapter provides this additional detail for, and further elucidates, concepts relevant to attitudes, persuasion, and social influence. The hope is that this will facilitate more evaluation work that draws on the persuasion literature, with a further hope that such efforts will in turn contribute to the persuasion literature. Although it is broader in scope, the Mark and Henry framework provides a useful stepping-off point for considering the implications of the social psychological literature on attitudes, persuasion, and social influence for program and policy evaluation. Accordingly, Table 8.1 presents in bold those terms in Mark and Henry's (2004) framework that are relevant to attitudes, persuasion, and social influence. The persuasion literature has not generally focused on the effects of influence processes on motivation and has instead looked at motivation as a determinant of influence process. However, much of the persuasion literature supports the idea that information such as findings from an evaluation can influence attitudes and behavior through general influence processes such as elaboration and use of heuristics, and generally there is much conceptual overlap.

Attitudes, Persuasion, and Social Influence

In the program and policy literature, "evaluation" refers to systematic procedures for studying a program or policy, suggesting improvements, or providing an assessment of its merit and worth. The attitude literature also uses the term *evaluation*, but in a somewhat narrower sense referring to individuals. According to that literature, an *attitude* is a person's overall evaluation of an object (e.g., issues, ideas, programs, people) and refers to how good or bad, positively or negatively, or favorably or unfavorably, one views an object of judgment (e.g., "the policy of senior comprehensive exams"; see Eagly & Chaiken, 1993; Petty & Cacioppo, 1981). Thus, the term *attitude* corresponds to what Mark and Henry (2004) refer to as opinion/attitude valence (see Table 8.1, column 1, row 2). Changing attitudes (or beliefs) by presenting facts and information is referred to as *persuasion* or *attitude change* (Petty & Wegener, 1998). These more neutral terms are considered to encompass both education (i.e., learning)—in which information is presented relatively objectively—and propaganda—in which some information may be withheld so that one conclusion appears more reasonable than another (Petty & Cacioppo, 1981). The terms *persuasion* and *attitude change* also include cases in which the opinions of a group affects an individual's attitudes, a type of *social influence*. This type of social influence has primarily been studied by examining the effects of the opinions of ingroup versus outgroup sources on attitudes, along with minority-opinion versus majority-opinion influence (see Fleming, 2009; Fleming & Petty, 2000; Mackie & Queller, 2000; Prislin & Wood, 2005; van Knippenberg, 1999, 2000, for reviews).[1] Learning is considered an outcome of general influence processes, as in Mark and Henry's (2004) framework (policy-oriented learning; see Table 8.1, column 3, row 2). However, in the attitude literature, persuasion and minority-opinion influence are also typically considered outcomes of general influence processes, rather than general influence processes themselves. This is because more recent research suggests that interpersonal influence and other types of influence occur through the same processes. A possible implication is that, as evaluation theory and practice moves ahead in terms of looking at influence processes, even more detailed analyses than those suggested in Table 8.1 may be possible, and it will be important to examine which are more useful in guiding evaluation practice. The following sections provide one such possible detailed analysis in the realm of attitude change.

Thoughtful and Nonthoughtful Attitude Change Processes

Contemporary models of persuasion, the Elaboration Likelihood Model (ELM; Petty & Cacioppo, 1986a, 1986b) and the heuristic–systematic model (HSM; Chaiken, Lieberman, & Eagly, 1989), propose that attitude change can occur through one of two general types of processes. Most scholars of this literature agree that the empirical evidence seems to be explained best by these "dual-route" models, relative to single-route alternatives (e.g., Priester & Fleming, 1997; see Chen & Chaiken, 1999 and Petty & Wegener, 1998, 1999 for reviews; see Figure 8.1 for a schematic representation). From the dual-route models, it appears that one general way that attitudes can be changed is through a *thoughtful process* that involves elaboration. When elaboration occurs, individuals think carefully about issue-relevant information presented in a persuasive message, and they base their attitude on their idiosyncratic cognitive responses to the message (Figure 8.1, right). Alternatively, attitudes can be changed through relatively *nonthoughtful processes*. Often these processes depend on the presence of relatively simple "peripheral cues" in the persuasion context, such as the number of arguments listed (Petty & Cacioppo, 1984), simple associations (e.g., as in classical conditioning, Staats & Staats, 1958), or simple decision rules stored in memory (i.e., heuristics, such as message "length implies strength," Chaiken, 1987; Figure 8.1, left). Thus, like Mark and Henry, the persuasion literature views elaboration and the use of heuristics (see Table 8.1, column 1, row 1) to be general influence processes.

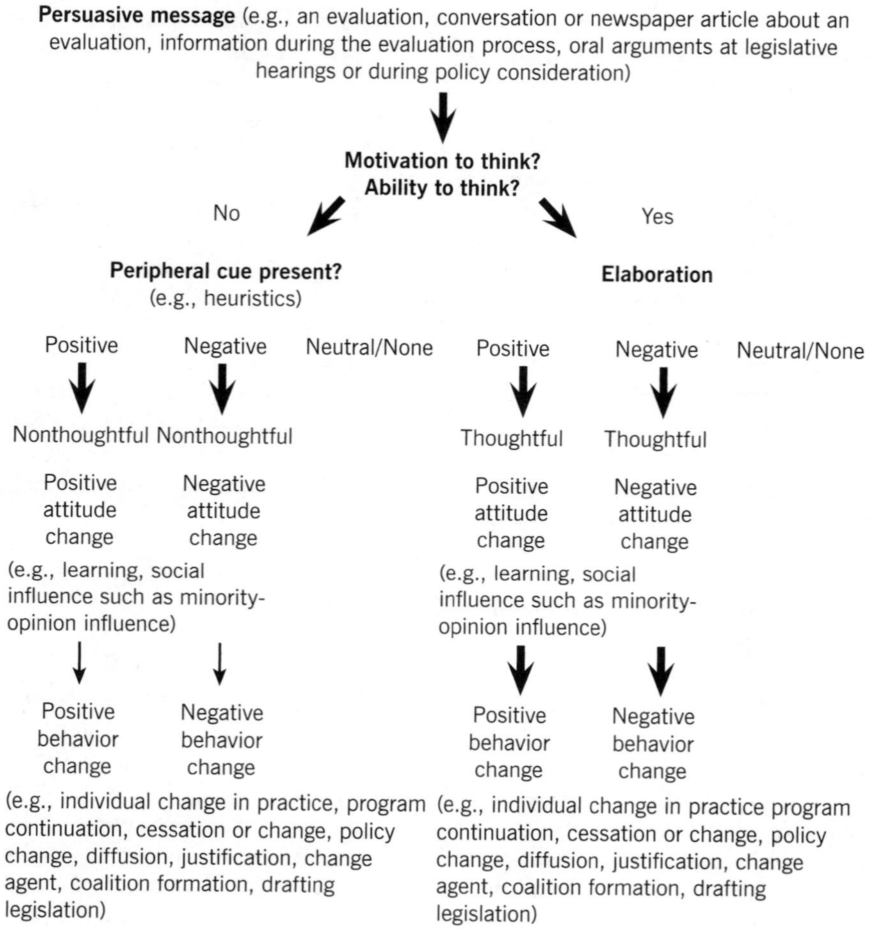

Persuasive message (e.g., an evaluation, conversation or newspaper article about an evaluation, information during the evaluation process, oral arguments at legislative hearings or during policy consideration)

↓

Motivation to think?
Ability to think?

No ↙   ↘ Yes

Peripheral cue present?   **Elaboration**
(e.g., heuristics)

Positive   Negative   Neutral/None   Positive   Negative   Neutral/None

↓   ↓   ↓   ↓

Nonthoughtful Nonthoughtful   Thoughtful   Thoughtful

Positive   Negative   Positive   Negative
attitude   attitude   attitude   attitude
change   change   change   change

(e.g., learning, social   (e.g., learning, social
influence such as minority-   influence such as minority-
opinion influence)   opinion influence)

↓   ↓   ↓   ↓

Positive   Negative   Positive   Negative
behavior   behavior   behavior   behavior
change   change   change   change

(e.g., individual change in practice, program   (e.g., individual change in practice program
continuation, cessation or change, policy   continuation, cessation or change, policy
change, diffusion, justification, change   change, diffusion, justification, change
agent, coalition formation, drafting   agent, coalition formation, drafting
legislation)   legislation)

FIGURE 8.1. A schematic of proposed mechanisms of evaluation influence from dual-route persuasion models.

The "persuasive message" is conceptualized broadly here, and as suggested by Mark and Henry (2004), an evaluation report, a conversation about an evaluation, a newspaper article about an evaluation, or information communicated during participation in the evaluation process itself, would all be considered persuasive messages (Figure 8.1, top). In addition, it seems plausible to suggest that testimony and oral arguments about an evaluation presented at legislative hearings and during policy consideration, included by Mark and Henry as general influence processes (see Table 8.1, column 3, row 1), could also be considered persuasive messages, which could lead to persuasion through either of these processes.

Determinants of Attitude Change Process

As recognized by Mark and Henry (2004), contingencies will determine when an attitude change process is likely to operate or not. Attitudes are more likely to be changed through a thoughtful than a nonthoughtful process to the extent that individuals are motivated and able to engage in elaboration of attitude-relevant information (see Figure 8.1, "row" 2; e.g., see Petty & Wegener, 1998, 1999; and Petty & Briñol, 2010, for recent reviews). When are attitudes more likely to be changed through a thoughtful than a nonthoughtful process because of *higher motivation* to elaborate? Thoughtful attitude change due to higher motivation is more likely to occur when: the message topic is personally relevant to recipients rather than personally irrelevant (Petty & Cacioppo, 1979); recipients believe they are solely responsible for message evaluation (Petty, Harkins, & Williams, 1980); they are individually accountable (Tetlock, 1983); they expect to discuss the issue with a partner (Chaiken, 1980); surprisingly, the majority opinion is counter to theirs or the minority opinion is the same as theirs (Baker & Petty, 1994; see also Petty, Fleming, Priester, & Harasty Feinstein, 2001); or they are higher in intrinsic enjoyment of elaboration and have chronic tendencies to thoughtfully elaborate persuasive information regardless of such factors as personal relevance (i.e., high Need for Cognition, Cacioppo & Petty, 1982). Similarly, attitudes are more likely to be changed through a thoughtful than a nonthoughtful process due to higher *ability to elaborate* when no distractions are present in the persuasion context (e.g., Petty, Wells, & Brock, 1976); ample time is provided to elaborate (e.g., Kruglanski & Freund, 1983); the message is repeated a moderate number of times (e.g., Cacioppo & Petty, 1979); the message is simple or easy to understand rather than complex or difficult to understand (e.g., Hafer, Reynolds, & Obertynski, 1996); recipients can pace themselves rather than when pacing of a message is external (e.g., the message is presented in print rather than by video or radio; see Chaiken & Eagly, 1976; Wright, 1981); or they have been educated with the prior knowledge necessary to comprehend message arguments (Wood, Rhodes, & Biek, 1995). To take but a few of the implications of these several research findings for program and policy evaluation, thoughtful processing is more likely for those stakeholders who are most invested in the evaluation or program and who have the background knowledge and time to make sense of the evaluation findings.

If individuals are not motivated or are not able to elaborate, then if persuasion occurs it is more likely to occur through a nonthoughtful process (see Figure 8.1, "row" 2, left). For example, message recipients can be more persuaded by ingroup than outgroup sources (e. g., messages that come from the same stakeholder group) through a nonthoughtful process of simply relying on the message source's position when the topic is irrelevant to the ingroup (and is of low personal relevance, Fleming, 2009), and thus motivation or ability to think is low (Mackie, Gastardo-Conaco, & Skelly, 1992; van Knippenberg, Lossie, & Wilke, 1994). Similarly, message recipients' mood can affect attitudes directly without affecting recipients' thoughts in response to a message, with positive mood leading to more positive attitudes than neutral mood, when motivation or ability to think is low (e.g., the topic is of low personal relevance or importance; Petty, Schumann, Richman, & Strathman, 1993). Other factors also contribute to persuasion via a nonthoughtful process (Petty & Cacioppo, 1986a; see Petty & Wegener, 1998, and Petty & Briñol, 2010, for reviews). Among those factors relevant to evaluation is perceived source expertise. When motivation or ability to think is low (e.g., the topic is of low personal relevance or importance), stakeholders who believe the evaluator is high in expertise may be persuaded in a nonthoughtful way (Chaiken & Maheswaran, 1994).[2]

Consequences Associated with Different Attitude Change Processes

The process through which attitudes are changed has been shown to have important consequences. Relative to attitudes that are changed through a relatively nonthoughtful process, attitudes changed through a thoughtful process are stronger in the sense that they are more likely to persist over time (e.g., Haugtvedt & Petty, 1992), and they are more likely to guide behavior (e.g., Cacioppo, Petty, Kao, & Rodriguez, 1986; Priester, Nayakankuppam, Fleming, & Godek, 2004; see Petty, Haugtvedt, & Smith, 1995, and Petty & Briñol, 2010, for reviews). In fact, Priester and colleagues (2004) found that at times attitudes changed through a nonthoughtful process may not guide behavior at all. Thus, the persuasion literature suggests an important possibility not discussed by Mark and Henry: that some general influence processes (thoughtful, e.g., elaboration) are more likely to result in attitudes that guide behavior than other influence processes (nonthoughtful, e.g., the use of heuristics).

Behavior is conceptualized broadly in the persuasion literature. "Behavior" in that literature would clearly include individual behaviors such as a change in practice by program practitioners (e.g., teachers begin to mix whole-language and phonics instruction after learning that combining the approaches is more effective than either one separately; see Patton, 1997, cited in Henry & Mark, 2003; see also Table 8.1, column 1, row 4). Although less frequently examined, the persuasion literature would also include as behavior the collaborative change in practice (see Table 8.1, column 2, row 4) and the collective decisions about program continuation, cessation, or change, policy change, and diffusion (see Table 8.1, column 3, row 4) that Mark and Henry (2004) incorporate. For example, Shestowsky, Wegener, and Fabrigar (1998) found that high Need for Cognition individuals exert more influence on group decisions than do low Need for Cognition individuals because they generate more, and more valid, arguments to support their views. This suggests that individuals who have formed their attitudes more thoughtfully in turn have more influence on such group actions. This finding is potentially quite important for thinking about the sequence of events that may be involved in moving toward ultimate evaluation use. Having an intended user interested in applying the evaluation findings (Patton, 1997) may not be enough; the intended user may need to have engaged in thoughtful processing of the evaluation findings. This observation links to four actions that Mark and Henry conceptualize as general influence processes (and that the persuasion literature would seem to include as behavior): including evaluation findings in an attempt to persuade others (i.e., justification); rising to action as a change agent focused on changing organizational policies; forming a coalition to change policy; and drafting legislation (see Table 8.1, columns 2 and 3, row 1). Each of these behaviors would be more likely (and more likely to be effective) to the extent that attitudes were changed through thoughtful elaboration of an evaluation rather than through a relatively nonthoughtful process. Thus, knowing the process through which evaluations have had their initial influence allows us to make predictions about the likelihood of other change processes being initiated and, more generally, of understanding when evaluations are likely to affect instrumental use as well as attitudes.

Increasing Evaluation Use by Increasing Elaboration

In sum, theory and research on attitudes, persuasion, and social influence suggests that if one wants an evaluation to influence behavior as well as attitudes with respect to a program or policy, then one wants to foster thoughtful (rather than nonthoughtful) attitude change. Thoughtful attitude change is *self*-persuasion: it involves recipients' own thoughts in response to information leading to attitude change. Consider a dean at the university in our example, who reads from the evaluation of the exam policy: "Students' grade point average increased by 31% at a University which had implemented the exams, but only by 8% at comparable schools which did not use the exam." Imagine that the dean had a number of positive thoughts in response, such as "Comprehensive exams seem to lead students to learn more," and consider that her attitude toward implementing an exams policy became more positive as a result of these thoughts. This would be an example of thoughtful attitude change. Alternatively, if the dean was in a positive mood while reading the evaluation because she was eating M&Ms, and her attitude toward implementing an exams policy became more positive as a result of her mood, this would be an example of nonthoughtful attitude change (Petty et al., 1993). Even if the revised attitudes were equally positive in both cases, the dean's behavior with regard to implementing senior comprehensive exams would be more likely to be affected as a result of the thoughtful attitude change than the nonthoughtful change. And this difference may greatly matter for subsequent change processes that might be triggered by the evaluation. Thus, for example, when her attitude toward implementing senior comprehensive exams was thoughtfully formed, the dean would be more likely to use evaluation findings in an attempt to persuade others to implement the exams (i.e., justification); rise to action as a change agent focused on changing the university's policy on senior comprehensive exams; form a coalition to change the university's policy on senior comprehensive exams; and draft new university policy. In addition, she would be more likely to exert influence on group decisions, and thus collective decisions about policy change (diffusion) would be more likely to be affected.

Evaluation theory and research has found or suggested that several factors increase evaluation use. The social psychological literature may help clarify why these factors are effective. It seems likely that the factors that are effective in facilitating use do so because they help stimulate attitude change that results from thoughtful elaboration of an evaluation's findings, and thus create attitude change that is more likely to guide subsequent behavior. In other words, persuasion processes (as demonstrated in the social psychological literature) may plausibly mediate previously observed effects of variables on evaluation use, as suggested by Henry and Mark (2003; Mark & Henry, 2004). An examination of two influential approaches to increasing use illustrates this idea.

Surveys of evaluators and practitioners reveal that the approach of Utilization-focused evaluation (Patton, 1978, 1986, 1997, 2003) has become central to the practice of most professional evaluators. For example, 71% of respondents agreed with the central premise of this approach, that "The evaluator's primary function is to maximize intended uses by intended users of evaluation data" (Cousins, Donohue, & Bloom, 1996, p. 215; see also Preskill & Caracelli, 1997). In this approach to increasing use, a subset of stakeholders—people who have a vested interest in an evaluation—who understand, value, and care about evaluation, and who actively seek information to make judgments and predict the outcomes of program activity, are identified as intended users. These intended users accept responsibility for applying evaluation findings and implementing recommendations (or otherwise using the findings as intended), and the evaluator attends to their interests. The evaluator collaborates with the intended users to help them determine what kind of evaluation they need, including choosing the most appropriate content, methods, timeline, theory, and uses for their situation. This is done through an extensive interactive process prior to conducting an evaluation, so that the evaluation examines program or policy outcomes that are of high interest and relevance to intended users, and uses methods that are seen as particularly valid and reliable by intended users. During this process, the evaluator helps nonscientists understand methodological issues so that they can judge for themselves the tradeoffs involved in choosing among the strengths and weaknesses of design options and methods alternatives. Once data have been collected and organized for analysis, intended users are actively and directly involved in interpreting findings, making judgments based on the data, and generating recommendations. Utilization-focused evaluation is premised on the idea that, by actively involving intended users, the evaluator is training users in use, preparing the groundwork for use, and reinforcing the intended utility of evaluation every step along the way. Research supports this approach and has found that the more that stakeholders have been actively involved with and interested in an evaluation—that is, the more the "personal factor" is present— the more likely they are to understand and feel ownership of the evaluation process and findings (or program), and to use evaluations (Patton, 1997; see Cousins, 2003, for a recent review).

From a persuasion perspective, several aspects of Utilization-focused evaluation seem likely to increase the ability to think about an evaluation. For example, educating intended users in methodology and how to interpret findings should arm them with the prior knowledge they need to comprehend message arguments. Likewise, by actively and directly involving intended users in interpreting findings, making judgments based on the data, and generating recommendations, the utilization-focused evaluator helps provide recipients with enough time to elaborate message arguments, reduces distractions in the persuasion context, offers message repetition, and allows stakeholders to pace themselves through message contents. Other aspects of Utilization-focused evaluation seem likely to increase motivation to think about an evaluation. For example, those chosen as intended users are people who understand, value, and care about evaluation, and who actively seek information to make judgments and predict the outcomes of program activity. Thus, the message recipients are already highly motivated to think about the evaluation, analogous to high Need for Cognition individuals in past social psychological research. And involving intended users in discussions to interpret findings, make judgments based on the data, and generate recommendations seems likely to result in recipients expecting to discuss the issue with others and to feel individually responsible for message evaluation because their contributions will be public. Thus, the Utilization-focused evaluation approach seems likely to foster thoughtful attitude change that in turn is likely to guide behavior. In this way, the social psychological literature may help explain why this evaluation approach appears to increase instrumental use. At the same time, the social psychological literature suggests that what is important may not be the Utilization-focused approach to evaluation per se. If another approach also were to succeed in creating the motivation and ability to process the evaluation thoughtfully, it should be equally likely to achieve instrumental use. In addition, greater attention to the literature on attitudes, persuasion, and social influence may help evaluators, whether Utilization-focused or not, interact with stakeholders in ways that increase evaluation use—including ways that involve communication with stakeholders.

Torres, Preskill, and Piontek (1996) make recommendations to evaluators about more effective ways to communicate and report evaluation findings. According to a survey of evaluators' experiences, it appears that certain reporting practices will increase use. Of the factors that Torres et al. note, some seem likely to increase stakeholders' ability to think. For example, the surveyed evaluators stated that clear language was key to successful communicating and reporting efforts. Clear language is likely to result in an evaluation report that is simple and easy to understand. Torres et al. cite a study (Lynch, 1986) showing that easy-to-read evaluation reports, as rated by an independent judge, increased instrumental use (program expansion): in submissions over a 4-year period, the U.S. Department of Education's Joint Dissemination Review Panel approved for national dissemination 86% of the educational programs with evaluation reports independently rated as "Good" (easy to read, understandable, well organized, and including sufficient information), 50% of the programs with reports rated "OK," and 17% of the programs with reports rated "Poor" (difficult to read, disorganized, omitting relevant information, and presenting irrelevant information). Clear writing in evaluation reports is likely to increase the ability of recipients to understand the evidence presented regarding the effectiveness of a program and its implications, leading to thoughtful attitude change and ultimately use.

Analogous to message repetition, Torres et al. recommend that the evaluators provide drafts of formal interim reports and final reports and that they use handouts during oral presentations of findings. Handouts can increase audience understanding by supplying them with something to refer to in the future and by offering a recap during the presentation should their attention lapse or should they miss the meaning of something the evaluator is saying. Torres and colleagues also recommend allocating time for clients and stakeholders to review the reports, and they found that evaluators include an abstract-like executive report at the front of each copy of the final report for up to 75% of the evaluations they do. High-quality executive summaries should make it more likely that even audience members who have limited time would have enough time to think about the evaluation. Similarly, Torres et al. recommend preparing evaluation reports using the quicker-to-read chart essay format, in which information is presented in two-page spreads with the right-hand page providing detailed narrative and the left-hand page bulleting the major points (Stallworth & Roberts-Gray, 1987). Each of these practices would be expected to increase ability to think about an evaluation's contents. Thus, Torres and colleagues' recommendations for communicating and reporting evaluation findings also seem likely to foster thoughtful attitude change that is likely to guide behavior, perhaps explaining why these techniques increase instrumental use. Attention to the social psychological literature might suggest other reporting techniques to facilitate thoughtful processing, such as the inclusion of thought-provoking questions or probes in reports and briefings (e.g., asking readers to consider how important it is if the introduction of comprehensive exams is associated with a small, say 4% increase in graduates' employment within 6 months; e.g., Petty, Cacioppo, & Heesacker, 1981).

Use of Argument Quality and Thought Listings in Uncovering Attitude Change Processes

In the social psychological literature, it is common to manipulate the quality of arguments contained in a persuasive message and to measure the thoughts that are generated during message exposure. These are two convergent methods of determining through which route, thoughtful or nonthoughtful, persuasion has taken place (see Petty & Cacioppo, 1986a). Individuals who engage in thoughtful elaboration are more persuaded and report more positive thoughts when a message contains strong as opposed to weak arguments. In contrast, for those who rely on less thoughtful, peripheral cues, argument strength has a smaller effect on attitudes and thoughts (Petty, Cacioppo, & Goldman, 1981). This is because the more one thinks about strong arguments, the better they seem, the more positive one's thoughts, and the more positive one's resulting attitude. In contrast, the more one thinks about weak arguments, the more specious they seem, the more negative one's thoughts, and the more negative one's resulting attitude. Thus, increased elaboration of a message can increase persuasion when the arguments presented are strong and can decrease persuasion when the arguments presented are weak (Petty & Cacioppo, 1979; Petty, Wells, & Brock, 1976). In either case (i.e., after exposure to strong or to weak arguments), the resulting attitudes are likely to guide behavior, because they were thoughtfully formed. Thus, the social psychological literature provides support for the view that methodological quality, or more generally perceived credibility of evaluation findings, can be important for evaluation use (Henry, 2008).

For persuasion studies, messages differing in argument quality are developed empirically. First the researcher generates intuitively plausible "strong" and "weak" arguments in favor of a position on a target issue (e.g., "in favor of implementing senior comprehensive exams"). These arguments are then pilot tested by giving them to members of the intended recipient population, who are told to think about each argument carefully and to rate how persuasive it is. Very persuasive arguments are included in the "strong" message, and very unpersuasive arguments are included in the "weak" message. In a second pilot testing, members of the intended recipient population are given one of these messages, and are told to think about and evaluate it carefully, and then to complete a thought listing measure in which they are instructed to record the thoughts elicited by the message (see Cacioppo & Petty, 1981, p. 318; Petty & Cacioppo, 1986a, p. 38, for instructions). These thoughts are then coded (by participants or independent coders blind to condition) as to whether they are favorable, unfavorable, or neutral toward the position advocated. A "strong" message contains arguments such that when participants are instructed to think about the message, the thoughts that they generate are predominantly favorable. A "weak" message contains arguments such that when participants are instructed to think about the message, the thoughts that they generate are predominantly unfavorable. Positive thoughtful attitude change (i.e., attitude change toward the advocated position) occurs in response to a strong message when the profile of issue-relevant thoughts elicited by the arguments is more favorable than the profile available prior to message exposure (Figure 8.1, near right). Negative thoughtful attitude change (i.e., boomerang in the direction opposite to the advocated position) occurs in response to a weak message when the profile of thoughts elicited by the arguments is less favorable than the profile available prior to message exposure (see Figure 8.1, middle right). No attitude change occurs when the profile of thoughts is not more positive or negative than the profile available prior to message exposure, or is neutral, as one could imagine would occur when arguments are irrelevant to the issue, or the evidence is ambiguous or based on poor methodology (see Figure 8.1, far right), unless message recipients assume these are the best arguments to be found and thus anticipate conflicting reactions and respond negatively (Priester, Petty, & Park, 2007). The plausibility and strength of particular arguments may vary widely across different populations and times, and thus messages are pretested and adapted as necessary for new recipients.

Recommendations included in an evaluation would be considered message positions. Weiss (1998) has suggested that ignoring a seriously flawed evaluation, as well as using well-conducted evaluations, should both be considered instances of *improved use*. When thoughtful attitude change is fostered, use is likely to be facilitated by the presence of strong arguments that are relevant to the issue and based on what message recipients perceive to be reliable methods, and that have implications (and thus lead to thoughts) that support the evaluation's recommendation. In contrast, consider the case in which recommendations are bolstered with weak arguments that are relevant to the issue and based on what message recipients perceive to be reliable methods, but that have implications (and thus lead to thoughts) that disagree with the evaluation's recommendation. In such a case, thoughtful processing is likely to lead to unintended use of the evaluation's findings—not to support or act upon the evaluation's recommendations, but rather to make the opposite decision. This could represent a novel example of Weiss's (1998) improved use: ignoring the *recommendation* due to flawed or poor reasoning, but relying on the implications of the findings themselves from a well-conducted evaluation.

Increasing Intended Use with Strong Arguments

In sum, theory and research on attitudes, persuasion, and social influence suggests that if an evaluator wants to increase intended instrumental use in which both an evaluation's findings and recommendations are used (e.g., Kirkhart, 2000; Patton, 1997), then he or she should foster thoughtful positive attitude change by ensuring that the evaluation contains strong arguments. Recall the evaluation of the comprehensive exams, and consider a situation in which the evaluation recommended implementing the exams and that the dean read, as before, the strong argument: "Students' grade point average increased by 31% at a University which had implemented the exams, but only by 8% at comparable schools which did not use the exam." If the dean had a positive thought in response (e.g., "Exams lead students to learn more") and changed her attitude toward implementing an exams policy to be more positive as a result of this thought, this would be an example of thoughtful *positive* attitude change. And this positive attitude is likely to lead her to act toward implementing senior comprehensive exams. Imagine, instead, that the evaluation of the exams in our example recommended implementing the exams but the dean read a weak argument: "Students' anxiety increased by 31% at a University which had implemented the exams, but only by 8% at comparable schools which did not use the exam." If the dean had a negative thought in response ("Exams needlessly stress students out and are a net negative") and became more negative in her attitude toward implementing an exams policy as a result, this would be an example of thoughtful *negative* attitude change, and this negative attitude is likely to lead her to act toward *preventing* implementation of senior comprehensive exams.

Many variables that evaluation theory and research suggest are effective in increasing use appear to do so at least in part by contributing to the creation of arguments that evaluation consumers would find strong and supportive of the recommendations. The predictable result, drawing on considerable social psychological theory and research, is thoughtful positive attitude change and intended use when the evaluation consumers think about and elaborate on the evaluation results and recommendations. Returning to our two examples, several aspects of Utilization-focused evaluation seem likely to result in the creation of arguments that the evaluation's recipients would find strong. For example, this approach to evaluation endorses attending to the interests of intended users, determining what kind of evaluation they need, identifying which outcomes are of high interest and relevance to intended users and which methods are seen as particularly valid and reliable by intended users, and involving intended users in interpreting findings, making judgments based on the data, and generating recommendations. All of these seem analogous to the pilot testing that social psychological researchers conduct, and seem likely to result in determining which arguments the intended users would find strong with regard to particular recommendations. Thus, the Utilization-focused evaluation approach may foster thoughtful positive attitude change that is likely to guide behavior and thus lead to intended instrumental use.

Similarly, some of the factors discussed by Torres and colleagues seem likely to lead to evaluation reports that contain arguments that will be perceived as strong by evaluation audiences. In Lynch's (1986) study, "Good" reports may have been more likely to be approved because they included sufficient information, and thus were perceived as containing stronger arguments, whereas the "Poor" reports omitted relevant information and presented irrelevant information. Evaluators that Torres and her colleagues surveyed said that the content of successful communicating and reporting efforts included providing specific recommendations. This could help recipients identify which message arguments they perceive as strong, because "strong" and "weak" arguments are defined relative to a particular message position. Past research has shown that message recipients often have difficulty drawing the correct conclusion or position on their own (McGuire, 1969), so explicit recommendations provide a framework that makes judging argument quality easier. Torres et al. also suggest that recommendations should easily follow from the evaluator's knowledge of the evaluation data; this should make it more likely that arguments will support the recommendation and thus will be perceived as strong. They further recommend that evaluators take their particular audience's perspective about what questions are important and what types of data are most credible in deciding what to emphasize in oral presentations and executive summaries, while keeping in mind that different users will want different information even for the same evaluation question. Such techniques should increase the likelihood that the evaluator creates strong arguments. Finally, Torres et al. suggest that the evaluator submit initial recommendations to stakeholders for review and discussion and, if the discussion leads away from recommendations that he or she feels the findings clearly suggest, then the evaluator should listen carefully to understand why stakeholders do not see a particular recommendation as valid. This corresponds to the idea of pilot testing the strength of arguments. In short, Torres and colleagues' recommendations for communicating and reporting evaluation findings may be valuable precisely because they tend to foster thoughtful positive attitude change that is likely to guide behavior and thus lead to intended instrumental use. Future work for evaluation practice might test additional procedures for creating strong messages (e.g., actual assessment, when interacting with stakeholders, of perceived argument strength). Of course, Weiss (1998) reminds us that evaluators should not attempt to make strong arguments when the evidence for intended use is weak.

Objective versus Biased Thinking

Notably, research in persuasion under the dual-route framework has found that elaboration can be objective or biased and that both lead to strong attitudes that are predictive of behavior. This finding is important given that a common concern in theories of evaluation use is that the individual's interpretations of evaluation findings may be colored in a biased manner to support a previously held viewpoint, leading to misuse that involves mischaracterization of the evaluation's findings (e.g., Sabatier & Jenkins-Smith, 1999). The Elaboration Likelihood Model holds that thinking will be objective when motivation to think is relatively objective—such as when no a priori judgment is preferred and a person's implicit or explicit goal is to seek the truth "wherever it might lead,"—and when ability to think is relatively objective—such as when knowledge and its retrieval are unbiased (Petty & Cacioppo, 1986b). Similarly, the Heuristic–Systematic Model suggests that thinking will be objective when individuals have an accuracy motive to seek the truth (unless there are biasing cognitive factors such as a biased store of knowledge). In contrast, the model suggests that thinking will be biased when individuals have a defensive motive to protect existing, self-definitional attitudes and beliefs, or an impression management motive to hold attitudes and beliefs that will satisfy current social goals (Chaiken, Giner-Sorolla, & Chen, 1996; Chen & Chaiken, 1999). For example, when message recipients do not have a previous commitment to a position, those who are accountable to or expect to discuss an issue with others with unknown views think objectively about a persuasive message (Chaiken, 1980; Petty et al., 1980; Tetlock, 1983). Conversely, the thoughts of recipients who are accountable to those with known views are biased in the direction of the known views (e.g., Chen, Shechter, & Chaiken, 1996; Higgins & McCann, 1984; Tetlock, 1983). When recipients have a previous commitment to a position, and motivation and ability to elaborate are high, thoughts are more likely to be biased in the direction of the initial attitude the stronger that initial attitude is (e.g., the more it has been formed through a relatively thoughtful process—Haugtvedt & Wegener, 1994; the more accessible it is—Houston & Fazio, 1989; see Petty & Krosnick, 1995 for a review of the effects of attitude strength on resistance to counterattack).

Argument quality constrains biased thinking. Biased thinking entails a bias in the valence of thoughts that come to message recipients' minds, such that they selectively search for and find the strengths in the arguments when they prefer to agree with the message, but search for and find the flaws in the arguments when they prefer to disagree with the message. By design, strong arguments facilitate positive thoughts and thus are easier to find strengths in and harder to find flaws in, whereas weak arguments facilitate negative thoughts and thus are easier to find flaws in and harder to find strengths in. Perhaps because of this, in general, biased thinking appears to be more likely when the message contains information that is ambiguous or mixed rather than clearly strong or weak (e.g., Chaiken & Maheswaran, 1994; see Petty & Wegener, 1998, and Petty & Briñol, 2010, for reviews). Here again, the social psychological literature provides support for the argument that methodological quality, or more generally perceived credibility, can be important for evaluation use (Henry, 2008).

Improving Use by Fostering Objective Rather Than Biased Elaboration

In sum, theory and research on attitudes, persuasion, and social influence suggest that if one wants an evaluation to foster attitude change through objective rather than biased thinking, one wants to set up conditions in which motivation to think is relatively objective and ability to think is relatively objective, and avoid conditions in which motivation or ability to think are biased. In addition, one wants to include strong arguments in evaluations and avoid having to include information that is ambiguous, for example, due to poor methodology. These findings on biased processing are potentially quite important in evaluation contexts. Stakeholders often have existing positions about the merit and worth of the program or policy being evaluated, which could result in a motive to process in a predetermined direction. In addition, the participants in evaluations are sometimes chosen explicitly to represent a particular stakeholder group, which could function like being accountable to a group with a known view and thus bias elaboration. Thus, some evaluation practices would seem likely to foster biased elaboration of evaluation findings. Fortunately, the literature suggests techniques that may reduce bias in the elaboration of evaluation findings, in addition to methodological quality.

Many current and advocated evaluation practices seem likely to lead to attitude change that results from objective rather than biased elaboration of evaluation findings. To return to our two examples, many of the motivation and ability variables identified in the Utilization-focused evaluation approach and in Torres and colleagues' research—education, time, reducing distractions, message repetition, recipient pacing, Need for Cognition, sole responsibility for message evaluation, and message simplicity—tend to affect thinking in a relatively objective manner. In addition, Torres, Preskill, and Piontek (1996) recommend positioning the evaluation within an organizational learning context, framing "positive" and "negative" findings as problem-solving feedback and a learning opportunity, rather than presenting pronouncements of the program's worth or indications of failure. This would seem to position program participants as problem solvers involved in implementing program improvements (rather than as possible culprits). It also carefully distinguishes personnel from program evaluation, so as to deemphasize findings' reflection on individuals' performance. Such suggestions to encourage a learning orientation amongst evaluation audiences seem likely to promote objective rather than biased elaboration of evaluation findings and thus lessen the likelihood of misuse.

In addition, the finding that being accountable to others with unknown views fosters objective thinking suggests possible practices for reducing biased thinking. Indeed, Campbell and Mark (2006) have manipulated the accountability audience for stakeholders participating in planning related to a hypothetical evaluation. They suggest that being accountable to a group with mixed views, or perhaps being asked to be responsible to an abstraction such as the common good, could be beneficial. Further, some procedures for evaluation practice might help both to reduce biased thinking and to balance any biased thinking that remains at the individual level. Evaluators such as House and Howe (1999) endorse the implementation of deliberative group processes with representatives from different stakeholders interacting. This would seem to reduce biased thinking because each stakeholder anticipates interacting with others with varying initial views. And the deliberative group process should further reduce the consequences of any individual-level biased processing that occurs.

Generally, it would seem that keeping evaluation audiences focused on the goal of the human betterment that a program or policy is designed to address, rather than on the success of a particular program or policy incarnation, may remind recipients that their ultimate goal is to learn which techniques best meet client needs or ameliorate a social problem. Such a perspective should promote objective thinking. And being mindful in policy arenas not to put decision makers in situations where they need to strongly prefer an a priori position to preserve their self-interest should decrease biased thinking. For example, L. Ross (personal communication, January 16, 1993), suggests that, in the United States, instead of electing politicians based on the particular policy solution they propose for ameliorating a societal issue—which sets up a scenario in which the politician prefers the policy's success rather than failure, because his political career depends on it—politicians should be elected based on the societal issues they commit to solving through trial and error. Ross argues that such a shift would reduce politicians' preference for evidence supporting the success of a particular program and instead encourage a learning orientation.

Remaining Questions and Methods for Future Research

As suggested throughout this chapter, a consideration of the persuasion literature in the context of evaluation use suggests a number of important hypotheses for both evaluation and persuasion theory and research. Many hypotheses regarding mediation were proposed in the previous three sections, such as the notion that educating intended users in methodology and in how to interpret findings leads to increased use because it increases their ability to think by providing them with the prior knowledge they need to comprehend message arguments. These hypotheses are fairly well grounded in existing persuasion research, but have not yet been tested in the program and policy evaluation contexts specifically.

Other variables have been found to increase evaluation use, but persuasion research has not yet examined their effects on persuasion processes. For example, evaluators surveyed by Torres et al. (1996) said that successful evaluation reports and briefings include tables and figures to increase understanding. This suggests that visuals (assuming they are simple and clear, and report findings perceived to be strong) may increase ability to think about a persuasive message, an interesting hypothesis for research. Torres and colleagues further suggest that using a variety of sentence lengths, print colors, heading styles, and the active voice compels people to read an evaluation, suggesting that these variables may increase motivation to think, a possibility that is also important to investigate. In addition, persuasion research could benefit from examining a wider range of behaviors potentially resulting from thoughtful attitude change, such as whether individuals who have formed their attitudes more thoughtfully in turn are more likely to engage in downstream behaviors to influence others, such as including evaluation findings in an attempt to persuade others (i.e., justification); rising to action as a change agent focused on changing organizational policies; forming a coalition to change policy; and drafting legislation.

In other cases, persuasion research has yielded findings that seem inconsistent with recommendations for best evaluation practice, and thus further research is needed to resolve the ambiguity. For example, persuasion research has found that persuasion is more likely to occur through a thoughtful than a nonthoughtful process when a message is written, rather than when it is presented by video or radio, because recipients can pace themselves (Chaiken & Eagly, 1976; Wright, 1981). This finding suggests that using written rather than video or radio presentation should increase use when the message contains strong arguments and is elaborated. In contrast, Torres et al. (1996, p. 158) recommend using oral or video rather than written presentation to increase use: "Written reports serve important archival purposes, including accountability needs, but they are quite impotent if change and improvement are the expectation. Well-informed talk is a more powerful means by which to report good and bad findings and actively engage stakeholders in the shared commitment to better programs (Mathison, 1994, p. 303)." Perhaps the discrepancy arises because, in many evaluation settings, reports may go unread, while in social psychological studies the experimental setting typically forces study participants to be exposed to the message, regardless of the medium. In any case, resolution of this and other inconsistencies between the two literatures could both improve the persuasion literature and provide better guidance for evaluation practice.

Social psychologists and evaluation theorists and researchers could readily conduct tests of such hypotheses generated by evaluation practice and findings by examining whether a variable of interest affects attitudes through a thoughtful or nonthoughtful process, and if thoughtful, through objective or biased thinking. One common method for doing so is to manipulate the variable of interest, while also independently manipulating argument quality, and then to measure attitudes and thought valence (see Petty & Cacioppo, 1986a, Ch. 2, for a description of general persuasion procedures). For example, to examine the hypothesis that educating intended users in methodology and how to interpret findings increases instrumental use because it increases users' ability to think, two levels of the variable of interest (e.g., high versus low education in methodology and how to interpret findings) and two levels of argument quality (strong versus weak), could be examined, with attitudes, thoughts, and instrumental use measured. Participants would be randomly assigned to one of the four conditions, in which they receive the appropriate persuasive message (high methods education/strong arguments; high methods education/weak arguments; low methods education/strong arguments; or low methods education/weak arguments). The extent of attitude change in one condition relative to another is typically measured by assessing attitudes after message exposure with semantic differentials anchored with evaluative adjectives (e.g., "senior comprehensive exams": good-bad, beneficial-harmful, wise-foolish, and favorable-unfavorable). Relative attitude change can also be measured by agreement with single-item evaluative statements (e.g., "To what extent do you agree with the proposal that college seniors should take a comprehensive exam before graduating?" (1) *do not agree at all*; to (11) *agree completely*; see Petty & Cacioppo, 1986a, Ch. 2, for a discussion of alternative attitude measures and experimental designs to assess absolute level of attitude change such as use of a pre-message exposure attitude measure and external control group). Thought valence is measured, as in pilot testing, by having message recipients list the thoughts they had while being exposed to the persuasive message. These thoughts are then coded by participants or trained judges as to whether they are favorable, unfavorable, or neutral toward the position advocated. Next, a thought positivity index is created, for example, by subtracting the number of negative thoughts from the number of positive thoughts (e.g., Fleming, Petty, & White, 2005; see Cacioppo & Petty, 1981, for evidence of the reliability and validity of the thought listing technique and alternative valence and nonvalence indices).

If the variable of interest affects the amount of objective thinking, then argument strength (strong vs. weak) will have a bigger effect on attitudes and thought positivity in the condition that elicits greater thinking (e.g., high methods education) than in the condition that elicits less thinking (e.g., low methods education). In the language of analysis of variance, there will be a two-way interaction between the variable of interest and argument quality. In addition, for the condition that elicits greater thinking, the effect of argument quality on attitudes may be mediated by thought valence (e.g., Petty, Fleming, & White, 1999). If instead the variable of interest biases elaboration, then a main effect of the variable on attitudes and thought valence should occur, and the variable's effect on attitudes should be mediated by thoughts (see also Petty & Cacioppo, 1986a, Ch. 2, for a discussion). If instead the variable of interest leads to nonthoughtful attitude change (i.e., serves as a peripheral cue), then its effect on attitudes should occur regardless of argument quality. That is, a main effect of the variable on attitudes should be found, unmoderated by argument quality. In addition, the variable should have a direct effect on attitudes, unmediated by recipients' thoughts.[3]

Summary

It has been said that "changing an individual's attitude from positive to negative or vice versa is one end-state that most evaluators would cite if asked to describe how an individual would be likely to 'use' an evaluation" (Henry & Mark, 2003, p. 300). Such attitude change corresponds to what the evaluation literature calls conceptual use. However, from the perspective that evaluation aspires to contribute to social betterment, interest in attitude change presumably exists because evaluators assume that the newly changed attitude will eventually affect behavior, that is, instrumental use, or other variables of interest. The contemporary persuasion literature suggests that behavior is more likely to be affected, and the attitude is more likely to be consequential, if the attitude change occurs through a thoughtful process than if it occurs through a nonthoughtful process. Thus, knowing the process through which an evaluation affects attitudes is likely to increase our understanding of when the evaluation will be used instrumentally (if thoughtful attitude change has occurred) or not (nonthoughtful attitude change or no attitude change has occurred). Understanding the process through which attitude change occurs is also likely to increase our understanding of when instrumental use will be intentional (positive attitude change has resulted from elaboration of strong arguments) or unintentional (negative attitude change has resulted from elaboration of weak arguments), and when appropriate use (attitude change has resulted from objective thinking) or misuse (attitude change has resulted from biased thinking) will occur.

In closing, efforts to better integrate persuasion research and evaluation could be profitable in several ways. The persuasion literature could benefit from hypotheses generated from evaluation practice, such as about the benefits of tables and graphs and about the possible dangers of written messages when people can self-select to be exposed to the message, and downstream attempts to persuade others. And both social psychology and evaluation might benefit from systematic research on the influence pathways that Mark and Henry (2004) suggest may operate in response to evaluation findings and processes (see Table 8.1 for the possible processes they suggest may combine in a multistep pathway). From the perspective of evaluation, such an integration may yield insight into the processes through which variables previously found to increase use have their effects, and also suggest new ways to increase evaluation influence.

As reviewed in this chapter, many of the current evaluation practices thought to increase use seem to include techniques that are likely to lead to attitude change that results from a thoughtful, objective consideration of an evaluation that contains strong arguments—precisely the kind of attitude change that is more likely to guide subsequent behavior. Thus, the social psychological literature on persuasion processes might provide a way of accounting for the success of evaluation practices that increase intended instrumental use. The persuasion perspective suggests that such approaches are sufficient to increase use—to the extent that they increase motivation and ability to think, increase the likelihood that findings included in an evaluation will be perceived as strong, and foster objective thinking—but are not necessary. Work on persuasion suggests other ways that use can be increased through thoughtful attitude change. For example, Patton (2003) argues from the Utilization-focused evaluation perspective that, "If decision makers have shown little interest in the study in its earlier stages, they are not likely to suddenly show an interest in using the findings at the end. They won't be sufficiently *prepared* for use" (p. 226, emphasis in original). But such a perspective cannot explain cases of use by recipients lacking initial interest in the study, such as occurs in diffusion. In diffusion, an evaluation leads to the adoption of a policy or program elsewhere, presumably in a context in which stakeholders may not have even known about the evaluation prior to its completion. In contrast, the persuasion perspective suggests that the attitudes of recipients who are not involved in conducting an evaluation can still be changed through a thoughtful process by the evaluation if they are motivated and able to elaborate its contents when they are exposed to it, which is likely to lead to use. As this example suggests, a persuasion perspective is likely to be useful for evaluation theory, research, and practice.

NOTES

1. The second type of social influence, in which others influence individuals' public behavior without influencing their private, internalized attitudes by inducing compliance, obedience, or conformity to norms, could increase use when attitude change is not possible. This second type of social influence is more likely the more the behavior of the target of influence is observable to others (i.e., the more proximal the source(s) of influence are, with sources who are physically nearer being more influential than sources who are physically distant), the more the target of influence cares about how others in the group will view them (i.e., the stronger the source(s) of influence, with sources of higher status, credibility, and power over the target's outcomes being more influential), and the greater the number and consensus of the source(s) of influence (with few or no others disobeying or behaving differently from the norm being more influential than many; Latané, 1981).

2. It is important to note that these variables—ingroup sources, mood, and source expertise—do not invariably lead to nonthoughtful attitude change, and have also been found to lead to thoughtful attitude change when motivation and ability to think are high (see Petty & Wegener, 1998, and Petty & Briñol, 2010, for reviews). For example, an ingroup source has been found to affect attitudes through a thoughtful process of increasing thinking about the persuasive message when the message topic is relevant to the ingroup, and thus motivation and ability to think are high (Mackie et al., 1990). These findings suggest that interpersonal influence and other types of influence occur through the same processes.

3. Other methods have also been used to determine the route, thoughtful or nonthoughtful, through which persuasion has taken place. For example, correlations between thought valence and post-message attitudes tend to be greater when elaboration is high (e.g., Chaiken, 1980; Petty & Cacioppo, 1979), and high message elaboration can produce longer reading or exposure times than more cursory analyses (e.g., Mackie & Worth, 1989; see Cacioppo & Petty, 1981; Petty & Cacioppo, 1986a, Ch. 2; Petty & Wegener, 1998, p. 328; Wegener, Downing, Krosnick, & Petty, 1995, for reviews and discussions of alternative methods). Mere number of thoughts has also been used as an indicator of extent of thinking, but thought valence is more commonly used for this purpose because people can still write down thoughts about the topic even if they paid no attention to the specific information presented. Indeed, persuasion studies have found that thought valence is more polarized in response to strong than weak arguments in high than low thought conditions (e.g., high versus low personal relevance of the message topic; e.g., Petty & Cacioppo, 1979), whereas people typically write down the same number of thoughts in high- versus low-thought conditions (see Petty & Cacioppo, 1986, Ch. 2, for a review and discussion of this issue).

RECOMMENDED READINGS

Chen, S., & Chaiken, S. (1999). The heuristic–systematic model in its broader context. In S. Chaiken & Y. Trope (Eds.), *Dual-process theories in social psychology* (pp. 73–96). New York: Guilford Press.

Eagly, A. H., & Chaiken, S. (1993). *The psychology of attitudes.* Fort Worth, TX: Harcourt, Brace, Jovanovich.

Fleming, M. A., & Petty, R. E. (2000). Identity and persuasion: An elaboration likelihood approach. In D. J. Terry & M. A. Hogg (Eds.), *Attitudes, behavior, and social context: The role of norms and group membership* (pp. 171–199). Mahwah, NJ: Erlbaum.

Mackie, D. M., & Queller, S. (2000). The impact of group membership on persuasion: Revisiting "Who says what to whom with what effect?" In D. J. Terry & M. A. Hogg (Eds.), *Attitudes, behavior, and social context: The role of norms and group membership* (pp. 171–199). Mahwah, NJ: Erlbaum.

Maio, G., & Haddock, G. (2009). *The psychology of attitudes and attitude change.* London, UK: Sage.

Petty, R. E., & Briñol, P. (2010). Attitude change. In R. F. Baumeister & E. J. Finkel (Eds.), *Advanced social psychology: The state of the science.* Oxford, UK: Oxford University Press.

Petty, R. E., & Cacioppo, J. T. (1986). *Communication and persuasion: Central and peripheral routes to attitude change.* New York: Springer-Verlag.

Petty, R. E., & Krosnick, J. A. (1995). *Attitude strength: Antecedents and consequences.* Mahwah, NJ: Erlbaum.

Petty, R. E., & Wegener, D. T. (1998). Attitude change: Multiple roles for persuasion variables. In D. T. Gilbert, S. T. Fiske, & G. Lindzey (Eds.), *The handbook of social psychology* (Vol. 1, pp. 323–390). Boston: McGraw-Hill.

Petty, R. E., & Wegener, D. T. (1999). The elaboration likelihood model: Current status and controversies. In S. Chaiken & Y. Trope (Eds.), *Dual-process theories in social psychology* (pp. 37–72). New York: Guilford Press.

Prislin, R., & Wood, W. (2005). Social influence in attitudes and attitude change. In D. Albarracín, B. T. Johnson, & M. P. Zanna (Eds.), *The handbook of attitudes* (pp. 671–706). Mahwah, NJ: Erlbaum.

van Knippenberg, D. (1999). Social identity and persuasion: Reconsidering the role of group membership. In D. Abrams & M. A. Hogg (Eds.), *Social identity and social cognition* (pp. 315–331). Oxford, UK: Blackwell.

REFERENCES

Baker, S. M., & Petty, R. E. (1994). Majority and minority influence: Source position imbalance as a determinant of message scrutiny. *Journal of Personality and Social Psychology, 67,* 5–19.

Baron, R. M., & Kenny, D. A. (1986). The moderator-mediator variable distinction in social psychological research: Conceptual, strategic, and statistical considerations. *Journal of Personality and Social Psychology, 51,* 1173–1182.

Briñol, P., & Petty, R. E. (2005). Individual differences in attitude change. In D. Albarracín, B. T. Johnson, & M. P. Zanna (Eds.), *The handbook of attitudes* (pp. 575–615). Mahwah, NJ: Erlbaum.

Cacioppo, J. T., & Petty, R. E. (1979). Effects of message repetition and position on cognitive responses, recall, and persuasion. *Journal of Personality and Social Psychology, 37,* 97–109.

Cacioppo, J. T., & Petty, R. E. (1981). Social psychological procedures for cognitive response assessment: The thought-listing technique. In T. Merluzzi, C. Glass, & M. Genest (Eds.), *Cognitive assessment* (pp. 309–342). New York: Guilford Press.

Cacioppo, J. T., & Petty, R. E. (1982). The need for cognition. *Journal of Personality and Social Psychology, 42,* 116–131.

Cacioppo, J. T., Petty, R. E., Kao, C. F., & Rodriguez, R. (1986). Central and peripheral routes to persuasion: An individual difference perspective. *Journal of Personality and Social Psychology, 51,* 1032–1043.

Campbell, B. C., & Mark, M. M. (2006). Toward more effective stakeholder dialogue: Applying theories of negotiation to policy and program evaluation. *Journal of Applied Social Psychology,* 2834–2863.

Chaiken, S. (1980). Heuristic versus systematic information processing in the use of source versus message cues in persuasion. *Journal of Personality and Social Psychology, 39,* 752–766.

Chaiken, S. (1987). The heuristic model of persuasion. In M. P. Zanna, J. M. Olson, & C. P. Herman (Eds.), *Social influence: The Ontario Symposium* (Vol. 5, pp. 3–39). Hillsdale, NJ: Erlbaum.

Chaiken, S., & Eagly, A. H. (1976). Communication modality as a determinant of message persuasiveness and message comprehensibility. *Journal of Personality and Social Psychology, 34,* 605–614.

Chaiken, S., Giner-Sorolla, R., & Chen, S. (1996). Beyond accuracy: Defense and impression motives in heuristic and systematic processing. In P. M. Gollwitzer & J. A. Bargh (Eds.), *The psychology of action: Linking cognition and motivation to behavior* (pp. 553–578). New York: Guilford Press.

Chaiken, S., Lieberman, A., & Eagly, A. H. (1989). Heuristic and systematic processing within and beyond the persuasion context. In J. S. Uleman & J. A. Bargh (Eds.), *Unintended thought* (pp. 212–252). New York: Guilford Press.

Chaiken, S., & Maheswaran, D. (1994). Heuristic processing can bias systematic processing: Effects of source credibility, argument ambiguity, and task importance on attitude judgment. *Journal of Personality and Social Psychology, 66,* 460–473.

Chen, S., & Chaiken, S. (1999). The Heuristic-Systematic Model in its broader context. In S. Chaiken & Y. Trope (Eds.), *Dual-process theories in social psychology* (pp. 73–96). New York: Guilford Press.

Chen, S., Shechter, D., & Chaiken, S. (1996). Getting at the truth or getting along: Accuracy- versus impression-motivated heuristic and systematic processing. *Journal of Personality and Social Psychology, 71,* 262–275.

Cohen, G. L. (2003). Party over policy: The dominating impact of group influence on political beliefs. *Journal of Personality and Social Psychology, 85,* 808–822.

Cousins, J. B. (2003). Utilization effects of participatory evaluation. In T. Kellaghan, D. L. Stufflebeam, & L. A. Wingate (Eds.), *International handbook of educational evaluation* (pp. 245–265). Boston: Kluwer.

Cousins, J. B., Donohue, J., & Bloom, G. (1996). Collaborative evaluation in North America: Evaluators' self-reported opinions, practices, and consequences. *Evaluation Practice, 17*(3), 207–226.

Eagly, A. H., & Chaiken, S. (1993). *The psychology of attitudes.* Fort Worth, TX: Harcourt, Brace, Jovanovich.

Fleming, M. A. (2009). Group-based brand relationships and persuasion: Multiple roles for identification and identification discrepancies. In D. J. MacInnis, C. W. Park, & J. R. Priester (Eds.), *Handbook of brand relationships* (pp. 151–169). New York: M. E. Sharpe.

Fleming, M. A., & Petty, R. E. (2000). Identity and persuasion: An elaboration likelihood approach. In D. J. Terry & M. A. Hogg (Eds.), *Attitudes, behavior, and social context: The role of norms and group membership* (pp. 171–199). Mahwah, New Jersey: Erlbaum.

Fleming, M. A., Petty, R. E., & White, P. H. (2005). Stigmatized targets and evaluation: Prejudice as a determinant of attribute scrutiny and polarization. *Personality and Social Psychology Bulletin, 31,* 496–507.

Hafer, C. L., Reynolds, K., & Obertynski, M. A. (1996). Message comprehensibility and persuasion: Effects of complex language in counter attitudinal appeals to laypeople. *Social Cognition, 14,* 317–337.

Haugtvedt, C. P., & Petty, R. E. (1992). Personality and persuasion: Need for cognition moderates the persistence and resistance of attitude changes. *Journal of Personality and Social Psychology, 63*(2), 308–319.

Haugtvedt, C. P., & Wegener, D. T. (1994). Message order effects in persuasion: An attitude strength perspective. *Journal of Consumer Research, 21*(1), 205–218.

Henry, G. T. (2008). When getting it right matters: The case for high quality policy and program impact. In S. Donaldson, T. C. Christie, & M. M. Mark (Eds.), *What counts as credible evidence in applied research and evaluation practice?* Newbury Park, CA: Sage.

Henry, G. T., & Mark, M. M. (2003). Beyond use: Understanding evaluation's influence on attitudes and actions. *American Journal of Evaluation, 24*(3), 293–314.

Higgins, E. T., & McCann, C. D. (1984). Social encoding and subsequent attitudes, impressions, and memory: "Content-driven" and motivational aspects of processing. *Journal of Personality and Social Psychology, 47,* 26–39.

House, E., & Howe, K. (1999). *Values in evaluation and social research.* Thousand Oaks, CA: Sage.

Houston, D. A., & Fazio, R. H. (1989). Biased processing as a function of attitude accessibility: Making objective judgments subjectively. *Social Cognition, 7,* 51–66.

Kirkhart, K. (2000). Reconceptualizing evaluation use: An integrated theory of influence. In V. Caracelli & H. Preskill (Eds.), *The expanding scope of evaluation use: New directions for evaluation* 88 (pp. 5–24). San Francisco: Jossey-Bass.

Krosnick, J. A., & Petty, R. E. (1995). Attitude strength: An overview. In R. E. Petty & J. A. Krosnick (Eds.), *Attitude strength: Antecedents and consequences* (pp. 1–24). Mahwah, NJ: Erlbaum.

Kruglanski, A. W., & Freund, T. (1983). The freezing and un-freezing of lay-inferences: Effects of impressional primacy, ethnic stereotyping, and numerical anchoring. *Journal of Experimental Social Psychology, 19,* 448–468.

Latané, B. (1981). The psychology of social impact. *American Psychologist, 36,* 343–356.

Leviton, L. C., & Hughes, E. F. X. (1981). Research on the utilization of evaluations: A review and synthesis. *Evaluation Review, 5*(4), 525–548.

Lynch, K. B. (1986). Style versus substance in evaluation reports. *Evaluation Practice, 7*(4), 75–76.

Mackie, D. M., Gastardo-Conaco, M. C., & Skelly, J. J. (1992). Knowledge of the advocated position and the processing of in-group and out-group persuasive messages. *Personality and Social Psychology Bulletin, 18,* 145–151.

Mackie, D. M., & Queller, S. (2000). The impact of group membership on persuasion: Revisiting "Who says what to whom with what effect?" In D. J. Terry & M. A. Hogg (Eds.), *Attitudes, behavior, and social context: The role of norms and group membership* (pp. 171–199). Mahwah, NJ: Erlbaum.

Mackie, D. M., & Worth, L. T. (1989). Processing deficits and the mediation of positive affect in persuasion. *Journal of Personality and Social Psychology, 59,* 5–16.

Mackie, D. M., Worth, L. T., & Asuncion, A. G. (1990). Processing of persuasive in-group messages. *Journal of Personality and Social Psychology, 58,* 812–822.

Mark, M. M., & Henry, G. T. (2004). The mechanisms and outcomes of evaluation influence. *Evaluation, 10,* 35–57.

Mathison, S. (1994). Rethinking the evaluator role: Partnerships between organizations and evaluators. *Evaluation and Program Planning, 17*(3), 299–304.

McGuire, M. J. (1969). The nature of attitudes and attitude change. In G. Lindzey & E. Aronson (Ed.), *Handbook of social psychology* (2nd ed., Vol. 3, pp. 136–314). Reading, MA: Addison-Wesley.

Patton, M. Q. (1978). *Utilization-focused evaluation.* Beverly Hills, CA: Sage.

Patton, M. Q. (1986). *Utilization-focused evaluation* (2nd ed.). Beverly Hills, CA: Sage.

Patton, M. Q. (1997). *Utilization-focused evaluation: A new century text* (3rd ed.). Thousand Oaks, CA: Sage.

Patton, M. Q. (2003). Utilization-focused evaluation. In T. Kellaghan, D. I. Stufflebeam, & L. A. Wingate (Eds.), *International handbook of educational evaluation* (pp. 223–244). Boston: Kluwer.

Petty, R. E., & Briñol, P. (2010). Attitude change. In R. F. Baumeister & J. Finkel (Eds.), *Advanced social psychology: The state of the science*. Oxford, UK: Oxford University Press.

Petty, R. E., & Cacioppo, J. T. (1979). Issue-involvement can increase or decrease persuasion by enhancing message-relevant cognitive responses. *Journal of Personality and Social Psychology, 37,* 1915–1926.

Petty, R. E., & Cacioppo, J. T. (1981). *Attitudes and persuasion: Classic and contemporary approaches*. Dubuque, IA: Wm. C. Brown.

Petty, R. E., & Cacioppo, J. T. (1984). The effects of involvement on responses to argument quantity and quality: Central and peripheral routes to persuasion. *Journal of Personality and Social Psychology, 46,* 69–81.

Petty, R. E., & Cacioppo, J. T. (1986a). *Communication and persuasion: Central and peripheral routes to attitude change*. New York: Springer-Verlag.

Petty, R. E., & Cacioppo, J. T. (1986b). The elaboration likelihood model of persuasion. In L. Berkowitz (Ed.), *Advances in experimental social psychology* (Vol. 19, pp. 123–205). New York: Academic Press.

Petty, R. E., Cacioppo, J. T., & Goldman, R. (1981). Personal involvement as a determinant of argument-based persuasion. *Journal of Personality and Social Psychology, 41,* 847–855.

Petty, R. E., Cacioppo, J. T., & Heesacker, M. (1981). Effects of rhetorical questions on persuasion: A cognitive response analysis. *Journal of Personality and Social Psychology, 40,* 432–440.

Petty, R. E., Fleming, M. A., Priester, J. R., & Harasty Feinstein, A. (2001). Individual- versus group-interest violation: Surprise as a determinant of argument scrutiny and persuasion. *Social Cognition, 19,* 418–442.

Petty, R. E., Fleming, M. A., & White, P. H. (1999). Stigmatized sources and persuasion: Prejudice as a determinant of argument scrutiny. *Journal of Personality and Social Psychology, 76,* 19–34.

Petty, R. E., Harkins, S. G., & Williams, K. D. (1980). The effects of group diffusion of cognitive effort on attitudes: An information processing view. *Journal of Personality and Social Psychology, 38,* 81–92.

Petty, R. E., Haugtvedt, C. P., & Smith, S. M. (1995). Elaboration as a determinant of attitude strength: Creating attitudes that are persistent, resistant, and predictive of behavior. In R. E. Petty & J. A. Krosnick (Eds.), *Attitude strength: Antecedents and consequences* (pp. 93–130). Mahwah, NJ: Erlbaum.

Petty, R. E., & Krosnick, J. A. (1995). *Attitude strength: Antecedents and consequences*. Mahwah, NJ: Erlbaum.

Petty, R. E., Schumann, D. W., Richman, S. A., & Strathman, A. J. (1993). Positive mood and persuasion: Different roles for affect under high- and low-elaboration conditions. *Journal of Personality and Social Psychology, 64,* 5–20.

Petty, R. E., & Wegener, D. T. (1998). Attitude change: Multiple roles for persuasion variables. In D. T. Gilbert, S. T. Fiske, & G. Lindzey (Eds.), *The handbook of social psychology* (Vol. 1, pp. 323–390). Boston: McGraw-Hill.

Petty, R. E., & Wegener, D. T. (1999). The elaboration likelihood model: Current status and controversies. In S. Chaiken & Y. Trope (Eds.), *Dual-process theories in social psychology* (pp. 37–72). New York: Guilford Press.

Petty, R. E., Wells, G. L., & Brock, T. C. (1976). Distraction can enhance or reduce yielding to propaganda. *Journal of Personality and Social Psychology, 34,* 874–884.

Preskill, H., & Caracelli, V. J. (1997). Current and developing conceptions of use: Evaluation use topical interest group survey results. *Evaluation Practice, 18*(3), 209–225.

Priester, J. R., & Fleming, M. A. (1997). Artifact or meaningful theoretical constructs?: Examining evidence for nonbelief- and belief-based attitude change processes. *Journal of Consumer Psychology, 6,* 67–76.

Priester, J. R., Nayakankuppam, D. J., Fleming, M. A., & Godek, J. (2004). The A^{2}SC^2 Model: The influence of attitudes and attitude strength on consideration and choice. *Journal of Consumer Research, 30,* 574–587.

Priester, J. R., Petty, R. E., & Park, K. (2007). Whence univalent ambivalence?: From the anticipation of conflicting reactions. *Journal of Consumer Research, 34,* 11–21.

Prislin, R., & Wood, W. (2005). Social influence in attitudes and attitude change. In D. Albarracín, B. T. Johnson, & M. P. Zanna (Eds.), *The handbook of attitudes* (pp. 671–706). Mahwah, NJ: Erlbaum.

Sabatier, P. A., & Jenkins-Smith, H. C. (1999). The advocacy coalition framework: An assessment. In P. A. Sabatier (Ed.), *Theories of the policy process* (pp. 117–166). Boulder, CO: Westview Press.

Shestowsky, D., Wegener, D. T., & Fabrigar, L. R. (1998). Need for cognition and interpersonal influence: Individual differences in impact on dyadic decisions. *Journal of Personality and Social Psychology, 74,* 1317–1328.

Staats, A. W., & Staats, C. K. (1958). Attitudes established by classical conditioning. *Journal of Abnormal and Social Psychology, 57,* 37–40.

Stallworth, Y., & Roberts-Gray, C. (1987). Reporting to the busy decision maker. *Evaluation Practice, 8*(2), 31–35.

Tetlock, P. E. (1983). Accountability and complexity of thought. *Journal of Personality and Social Psychology, 45,* 74–83.

Torres, R. T., Preskill, H. S., & Piontek, M. E. (1996). *Evaluation strategies for communicating and reporting: Enhancing learning in organizations.* Thousand Oaks, CA: Sage.

van Knippenberg, D. (1999). Social identity and persuasion: Reconsidering the role of group membership. In D. Abrams & M. A. Hogg (Eds.), *Social identity and social cognition* (pp. 315–331). Oxford, UK: Blackwell.

van Knippenberg, D. (2000). Group norms, prototypicality, and persuasion. In D. J. Terry & M. A. Hogg (Eds.), *Attitudes, behavior, and social context: The role of norms and group membership* (pp. 157–170). Mahwah, NJ: Erlbaum.

van Knippenberg, D., Lossie, N., & Wilke, H. (1994). In-group prototypicality and persuasion: Determinants of heuristic and systematic message processing. *British Journal of Social Psychology, 33,* 289–300.

Wegener, D. T., Downing, J., Krosnick, J. A., & Petty, R. E. (1995). Measures and manipulations of strength-related properties of attitudes: Current practice and future directions. In R. E. Petty & J. A. Krosnick (Eds.), *Attitude strength: Antecedents and consequences* (pp. 455–487). Mahwah, NJ: Erlbaum.

Weiss, C. H. (1998). Improving the use of evaluations: Whose job is it anyway? *Advances in Educational Productivity, 7,* 263–276.

Wood, W., Rhodes, N., & Biek, M. (1995). Working knowledge and attitude strength: An information processing analysis. In R. E. Petty & J. A. Krosnick (Eds.), *Attitude strength: Antecedents and consequences* (pp. 283–313). Mahwah, NJ: Erlbaum.

Wright, P. L. (1981). Cognitive responses to mass media advocacy. In R. E. Petty, T. M. Ostrom, & T. C. Brock (Eds.), *Cognitive responses in persuasion* (pp. 263–282). Hillsdale, NJ: Erlbaum.

EDITORS' CONCLUDING COMMENTS
TO CHAPTER 8

Fleming provides a thoughtful and interesting exploration of the intersection between classic areas of social psychology and a key practice challenge for evaluators, that is, how to increase the likelihood that their findings will be used. In reviewing this chapter, three different exercises might be—if you'll pardon the expression—of use. First, if you have had experience in evaluation, review what you did to facilitate use in light of the social psychological theory and research that Fleming reviews. Also, what does this theory and research suggest that you might have done differently? Second, the social psychological work that Fleming reviews suggests that different ways of facilitating use might be beneficial under different circumstances. Can you identify two different conditions for which the evaluator might benefit from different strategies for facilitating use? Third, echoing back to Bandura and other early chapters, might it be the case that an evaluator will need something of a "translational theory" to put some of the lessons from the social psychological literature on attitudes, persuasion and social influence into practice? For example, Fleming's review of the literature indicates that sometimes it will be beneficial to increase stakeholders' motivation to process and elaborate on evaluation findings. Consider how an evaluator might attempt to translate this into practice.

EDITORS' INTRODUCTORY COMMENTS
TO CHAPTER 9

When programs are put into place, a common general goal is to change some aspect of human behavior. Substance abuse prevention programs are intended to reduce the use and abuse of alcohol, marijuana, cocaine and other drugs. Most criminal justice programs are intended to reduce the commission of crime. A STEM (i.e., science, technology, engineering and mathematics) program may be implemented to try to increase students' entry into STEM majors and occupations. And so on.

But how can we tell whether behavior has changed? Sometimes it will be possible to observe behavior directly or from reliable records, as when we see which college major was selected by each student in a STEM program or a comparison group. In other cases, community-level data may suffice, as when we compare change in crime rates over time in a community with a new criminal justice program, compared to another community without the program. Often, however, evaluators attempt to assess behavior change by asking study participants about their behavior.

In the upcoming chapter, Norbert Schwarz and Daphna Oyserman examine the nature of self-reports of behavior from the perspective of a growing body of research from social and cognitive psychology on self-reports. As Schwarz and Oyserman explain, the processes that people go through to report on their own behavior are considerably more complex than might appear on first glance. Correspondingly, numerous factors can affect self-reports of behaviors.

The chapter's discussion of the steps a person takes in answering a behavioral question includes several do's and don'ts for evaluators (or others who employ self-reports of behavior). The chapter also examines specific methods for constructing behavioral measures, with both pitfalls and promise noted. Schwarz and Oyserman conclude with a list of recommendations for evaluators. As they note, while asking good questions about behavior does not involve a simple checklist or formula, research from social psychology can do much to inform this aspect of evaluation practice.

CHAPTER 9

Asking Questions about Behavior
Self-Reports in Evaluation Research

Norbert Schwarz
Daphna Oyserman

Most interventions aim at changing people's behaviors. Accordingly, most evaluation studies include attempts to assess problem behaviors and to monitor their change over time. The questions used are usually straightforward, like these apparently simple questions about alcohol consumption: "Have you ever drunk beer, wine, wine coolers, whiskey, gin, or other liquor?" and, "How many times have you had beer, wine, or other= liquor in the past month?" These questions were adapted from Park and colleagues (2000), but similar questions can be found in many prevention studies and government health surveys in which participants are asked to self-report on the frequency of their behaviors in a specified period of time.

In posing such questions, researchers hope that participants will (1) understand the question, (2) identify the behavior of interest, and (3) retrieve relevant instances of the behavior from memory. When the question inquires about the actual frequency of the behavior, researchers further hope that participants (4) correctly identify the relevant reference period (e.g., "last month"), (5) search this reference period to retrieve all relevant instances of the behavior, (6) correctly date the recalled instances to determine whether they fall within the reference period, and (7) correctly add up all instances of the behavior to arrive at a frequency report. Once participants determined the frequency of their behavior, they are (8) often required to map this frequency onto the response alternatives provided by the researcher. Finally, participants are expected to (9) candidly provide the result of their recall effort to the interviewer. Implicit in these—rarely articulated—hopes is the assumption that people *know* what they do and *can* accurately report on their behavior, although they may not always be willing to do so. From this perspective, the evaluator's key task is to ask clear questions about meaningful behaviors in a setting that allows for candid reports. Unfortunately, participants can rarely live up to these hopes.

This chapter illuminates why participants' can't deliver what researchers hope for and aims to help researchers to develop a more realistic approach. For this purpose, we introduce evaluation researchers to the cognitive and communicative processes underlying self-reports, drawing on extensive research at the interface of survey methodology and psychology (for comprehensive reviews see Sirken et al., 1999; Sudman, Bradburn, & Schwarz, 1996; Tourangeau, Rips, & Rasinski, 2000). Our discussion follows the key steps of the question-answering process and addresses (1) how respondents interpret the questions asked; (2) retrieve relevant information from memory; (3) draw inferences that allow them to move from the accessible information to a plausible answer; and (4) report the answer to the researcher. Throughout, our focus is on questions about behavior. For a discussion of questions about attitudes and evaluative judgments, including issues related to assessing program satisfaction, see Schwarz (2008) and Schwarz and Strack (1999). For a discussion of the implications of cultural differences on survey responses see Schwarz, Oyserman, and Peytcheva (2010).

Understanding the Question

As a first step, respondents need to understand the question to be able to provide a meaningful answer. Unfortunately, respondents' interpretation often fails to match what the researcher had in mind, even when the question is apparently simple and straightforward. For example, the expression "reading a magazine" has different meanings for different respondents, ranging from having seen it at the newsstand to having read it cover to cover (Belson, 1981). Hence, the question that a respondent answers may not be the question that the evaluator wanted to ask. Nor do the answers provided by different respondents necessarily pertain to the same behavior. To avoid such problems, textbooks urge researchers to avoid unfamiliar and ambiguous terms (see Bradburn, Sudman, & Wansink, 2004, for good advice). But ambiguities remain even when all terms are thoroughly familiar. When asked "What have you done today?" participants will understand the words, but they still need to determine what the researcher is interested in: Should they report, for example, that they took a shower or not? Merely understanding the words of a question, that is, its *literal meaning*, is not enough to answer it. Instead, an appropriate answer requires an understanding of the *pragmatic meaning* of the question: What does the questioner want to know?

To infer what the questioner wants to know, participants draw on the tacit assumptions that underlie the conduct of conversations in everyday life (for reviews, see Clark & Schober, 1992; Schwarz, 1996). These assumptions can be summarized in the form of several conversational maxims (Grice, 1975). A *maxim of relation* asks speakers to make their contribution relevant to the aims of the ongoing conversation. In daily life, we expect communicators to take contextual information into account and to draw on previous utterances in interpreting later ones. Yet, in standardized research situations this normal conversational behavior is undesired, and researchers expect respondents to interpret each question in isolation. This, however, is not what respondents do: They continue to interpret questions in context, and this gives rise to context effects in question interpretation. A *maxim of quantity* requests speakers to make their contribution as informative as is required, but not contribute more information than is required. This maxim invites respondents to provide information the questioner seems interested in, rather than other information that may come to mind or information that is inappropriate given the relationship between the two—or, what is colloquially termed "too much information." Moreover, it discourages the reiteration of information that has already been provided earlier, or that "goes without saying." A *maxim of manner* holds that a speaker's contribution should be clear rather than obscure, ambiguous, or wordy. Hence, research participants assume that the researcher "chose his wording so they can understand what he meant—and can do so quickly" (Clark & Schober, 1992, p. 27). Participants therefore believe that the most obvious meaning is likely to be the correct one—and if they cannot find an obvious meaning, they will look to the immediate context of the question to determine one. While all participants are likely to be subtly influenced by immediate context, context sensitivity is likely to be higher in societies that are higher in collective cultural values and in contexts that cue collective mindsets (for details, see Oyserman, Coon, & Kemmelmeier, 2002; Oyserman, & Lee, 2007, 2008; Schwarz et al., 2010).

Open versus Closed Question Formats

With these conversational maxims in mind, let us return to the question, "What have you done today?" Suppose that this question is part of an evaluation of a drop-in center for people with serious mental illness. The evaluator's goal is to assess whether the center helps structure participants' day and increases their performance of daily social and self-maintenance behaviors. To avoid cues that may increase socially desirable responding, the evaluator has deliberately chosen this open-ended global question. What kinds of information are program participants and control respondents likely to provide?

Most likely, program participants will be aware that daily self-maintenance behaviors are of interest in this context and will report on them. In contrast, a control group of nonparticipants is unlikely to infer that the researcher is interested in brushing teeth, showering, or other grooming that they may interpret either as "things that go without saying" or as "too much information," and may therefore not report on the occurrence of these behaviors. As a result of these differential assumptions about what constitutes an "informative" answer, even a low level of self-maintenance behaviors among program participants may match or exceed the reports obtained from the control group, erroneously suggesting that the drop-in center is highly successful in helping its clients to return to normal routines. Similarly, drop-in participants who, having been maintaining daily self-maintenance behaviors for a while may, find them less noteworthy than participants who just re-acquired these skills, raising additional comparison problems.

As an alternative approach, the evaluator may present a close-ended list of relevant behaviors. On the positive side, such a list would reduce the ambiguity of the open-ended question by indicating which behaviors are of interest, ensuring that control respondents report on behaviors that otherwise "go without saying." On the negative side, the list would also provide program participants with cues that may increase socially desirable responding. In addition, it may remind both groups of behaviors that may otherwise be forgotten. As a result of these influences, *any* behavior is more likely to be endorsed when it is presented as part of a close-ended question than when it needs to be volunteered in response to an open-ended question. At the same time, however, a close-ended list reduces the likelihood that respondents report activities that are *not* represented on the list, even if the list offers a generic "other" response. What's not on the list is apparently of little interest to the researcher, and hence not reported. Accordingly, open- and close-ended question formats reliably result in different reports (see Schwarz & Hippler, 1991, for a review). On balance, a close-ended format is usually preferable if a reasonably complete list can be generated, although the tradeoffs need to be considered in each specific case.

Frequency Scales

Suppose the evaluator of an anger management program asks participants how frequently they felt "really irritated" or "got into a fight" recently. To answer this question, respondents have to determine what the researcher means by "really irritated" and "got into a fight." Does irritation refer to major or to minor annoyances? Are fights physical or verbal? To identify the intended meaning, participants may consult the *response alternatives* provided to them. If the response alternatives present low-frequency categories, for example, ranging from "less than once a year" to "more than once a month," they convey the idea that the researcher has relatively rare events in mind. If so, respondents may conclude that the irritation question refers to major annoyances, which are relatively rare, and not to minor irritations, which are likely to be more frequent. Conversely, a scale that presents high-frequency response alternatives, such as "several times a day," may suggest that the researcher is mostly interested in minor irritations because major annoyances are unlikely to be so frequent (see Schwarz, Strack, Müller, & Chassein, 1988, for experimental support). Thus, identically worded questions can acquire different meanings when accompanied by different frequency alternatives, leading respondents to report on substantively different behaviors.

Because response scales carry meaning, evaluators need to consider the implications of the response scale for the behavior in question: Does the scale convey information that is likely to influence respondents' interpretation of the question in unintended ways? Note also that it is problematic to compare reports of the "same" behavior when these reports were provided along different response scales. Hence, comparisons across samples and sites cannot be made with confidence if the questions were not asked in identical ways—including the nature of the response scale and whether the response was open- or close-ended.

Reference Periods

Similar meaning shifts can arise from changes in the reference period. Suppose an evaluator asks participants, in an open-ended format, how often they felt depressed, angry, and so on during a specified time period. Respondents again need to infer what type of anger or other emotion the researcher has in mind. When an anger question pertains to "last year," they may conclude that the researcher is interested in major annoyances because minor annoyances would probably be forgotten over such a long time period. Conversely, when the "same" question pertains to "last week," respondents may infer that the researcher is interested in minor annoyances because major annoyances may not happen every week. Supporting these predictions, Winkielman, Knäuper, and Schwarz (1998) observed that changes in the reference period shifted respondents' question interpretation and the resulting behavioral reports. It is therefore important to choose a reference period that is consistent with the intended meaning and to test respondents' interpretation at the questionnaire development stage, using the cognitive interviewing techniques we address in the next section.

Question Context

Suppose an evaluator of a family-based intervention asks, "How often in the past year have you fought with your parents?" What is the evaluator asking about: physical fights, fights that result in punishments, squabbles over whose turn it is to do the dishes, "silent" disagreements? Respondents may turn to adjacent questions for relevant cues. When we asked teens how often they "fight" with their parents, we observed lower rates of "fighting" when this question followed questions about delinquency than when it preceded them (Oyserman, unpublished data). When queried, it turned out that teens understood the term *fight* to mean a physical altercation in which they hit their parents when the question was presented in the context of questions about stealing, gang fights, and so on, but not otherwise. To take what may be a more obvious example, a term like "drugs" may be interpreted as referring to different substances in the context of questions about one's health and medical regime than in the context of questions about delinquency.

Contextual influences of this type are limited to questions that are substantively related. However, whether questions are substantively related may not always be obvious at first glance. To identify such influences at the questionnaire development stage, it is useful to present the question with and without the context to different pilot test participants, asking them to paraphrase the question's meaning. In most cases, this is sufficient to identify systematic shifts in question meanings.

Safeguarding against Surprises

As the preceding examples illustrate, answering a question requires respondents to go beyond the literal meaning of the words to infer what the questioner wants to know. To do so, respondents turn to the context of the research conversation, much as they would be expected to in daily life (for a more detailed analysis see Schwarz, 1996). To safeguard against surprises at the question comprehension stage, we urge evaluators to look over their draft questionnaires and ask themselves: "What may my respondents conclude from the context of each question, the reference period, the response alternatives, and similar features? Is this what I want them to infer?" Next, evaluators may check each question for common problems; Lessler and Forsyth (1996) offer an extensive checklist for this purpose. Once corrections have been made based on such a review, respondents' interpretation of questions can be explored in relatively inexpensive pilot tests using a variety of cognitive interviewing procedures, which were designed to gain insight into respondents' thought processes (for reviews, see the contributions in Schwarz & Sudman, 1996, and Chapter 2 of Sudman et al., 1996).

Recalling Relevant Information

Once respondents understand what they are to report on, they need to retrieve relevant information from memory. In evaluation research, many questions about respondents' behavior are frequency questions, pertaining, for example, to how often they used a service or engaged in some risky behavior. Researchers typically hope that respondents will identify the behavior of interest, scan the reference period, retrieve all instances that match the target behavior, and finally count these instances to determine the overall frequency of the behavior. However, respondents are unlikely to follow such a "recall-and count" strategy, unless the events in question are highly memorable and their number is small (see Conrad & Brown, 1996, for a discussion). In fact, several factors render this strategy unsuitable for most of the behaviors of interest to evaluators.

First, memory decreases over time, even when the event is relatively important and distinctive. For example, Cannell, Fisher, and Bakker (1965) observed that only 3% of their respondents failed to report an episode of hospitalization when interviewed within 10 weeks of the event, yet a full 42% did so when interviewed one year after the event.

Second, when the question pertains to a frequent behavior, respondents are unlikely to have detailed representations of numerous individual episodes of a behavior stored in memory. Instead, the various instances of closely related behaviors blend into one global, knowledge-like representation that lacks specific time or location markers (e.g., Linton, 1982). This renders individual episodes of frequent behaviors indistinguishable and irretrievable.

Third, autobiographical knowledge is not organized by categories of behavior like "drinking alcohol" or the like. Instead, the structure of autobiographical memory can be thought of as a hierarchical network that includes *extended periods* (like "the years I lived in New York") at the highest level of the hierarchy. Nested within this high-order period are lower-level extended events pertaining to this time, like "my first job" or "the time I was married to Lucy." Further down the hierarchy are *summarized events*, which correspond to the knowledge-like representations of repeated behaviors noted above (e.g., "During that time, my spouse and I quarreled a lot"). *Specific events*, such as a particular instantiation of a disagreement, are represented at the lowest level of the hierarchy. To be represented at this level of specificity, however, the event has to be rather unique. As these examples illustrate, autobiographical memory is primarily organized by time ("the years in New York") and relatively global themes ("first job"; "first marriage") in a hierarchical network (see Belli, 1998, for a comprehensive review). This network "permits the retrieval of past events through multiple pathways that work top-down in the hierarchy, sequentially within life themes that unify extended events, and in parallel across life themes that involve contemporaneous and sequential events" (Belli, 1998, p. 383). Thus, thinking of the "years in New York" would lead to information about the first job and first marriage (top-down) and thinking about the first marriage may prompt memories of a later marriage (within theme). Any specific event that comes to mind along the way may prompt memories of other events. Such searches take considerable time, and their outcome is somewhat haphazard, depending on the entry point into the network at which the search started. Hence, using multiple entry points and forming connections across different periods and themes will improve recall.

Researchers have developed a number of strategies that attempt to attenuate these problems, ranging from encouraging respondents to take their time to breaking a complex recall task into several simpler ones. Each of these strategies comes with specific advantages and disadvantages that require informed tradeoffs (see Schwarz & Oyserman, 2001, for a review and discussion). One noteworthy strategy with many helpful features and few drawbacks is the use of event history calendars.

Event History Calendars

Event history calendars are designed to take advantage of the nested structure of autobiographical memory (Belli, 1998). In a typical study, respondents are presented with a grid. The rows of the grid pertain to different aspects of their lives (e.g., where they lived, who they lived with, which jobs they had), and the columns represent time (e.g., years or months). Respondents reconstruct periods of their lives by completing this grid, going back and forth as successful recall of one aspect of their lives brings to mind other aspects that pertain to other parts of the grid. This structure supports the flexible use of multiple retrieval strategies within the hierarchically nested structure discussed above. Moreover, respondents are encouraged to take as much time as they need to complete the recall task and are told that accuracy is of great importance. Such encouragement reliably increases recall quality (see Cannell, Miller, & Oksenberg, 1981). Finally, event history calendars explicitly encourage the correction of earlier answers as newly recalled information qualifies earlier responses. Such correction opportunities are usually missed under regular interview formats, where respondents can rarely return to earlier questions.

Initially developed to assess extended periods of life, event history calendars can be adapted to any time period. To help respondents recall their alcohol consumption during the last week, for example, respondents may be given a calendar grid that provides a column for each day of the week, cross-cut by rows that pertain to relevant contexts. For example, they may be asked to enter for each day of the week what they did, who they were with, if they ate out, and so on. Reconstructing the last week in this way provides a rich set of contextual cues, with entries in one row often prompting memories relevant to a different row. Based on this rich network of associations, individual episodes are more likely to be retrieved than under any other method and any given episode may prompt additional memories.

Although the usefulness of event history calendars has been primarily demonstrated for the long-term recall of major events (like employment histories, criminal histories, or illness histories), the method can be adapted to shorter time periods and the assessment of more mundane behaviors (see Belli, 1998, for a review). While costly in terms of interview time, we consider such adaptations to be among the most promising developments in the assessment of behavioral reports.

Safeguarding against Surprises

In our experience, many recall questions would never be asked if researchers first tried to answer them themselves. Answering the questions you intend to ask is therefore an important first step. If you find it difficult, despite all the motivation you bring to the task, your respondents will probably find it next to impossible. Nevertheless, they will play by the rules and provide an answer, inaccurate as it may be. It is therefore better to lower one's goals and design a more realistic, limited, and less demanding task than to pursue an ideal data set that exceeds respondents' abilities. To explore what respondents can and cannot report, evaluators can draw on cognitive interviewing techniques to identify likely recall and estimation problems in pilot tests (see Schwarz & Sudman, 1996). These techniques include, for example, a think aloud process in which participants are asked to say what they are thinking as they work on a question—what does each word mean, what comes to mind as they come up with an answer. More often than not, the experience will be sobering. No matter how much effort we put into question design, however, the best we can usually hope for is a reasonable estimate, unless the behavior is rare and of considerable importance to respondents. Next, we turn to respondents' estimation strategies.

Inference and Estimation

Given the difficulties associated with a recall-and-count strategy, it is not surprising that respondents usually resort to inference and estimation strategies to arrive at a plausible estimate (for reviews, see Conrad & Brown, 1996; Sudman et al., 1996, Ch. 9). We illustrate this with two particularly common strategies, which draw on subjective theories about the stability of one's behavior and on information provided by the questionnaire.

What My Behavior Must Have Been: Theory-Driven Inferences

To answer questions about past behaviors, respondents often use their current behavior as a benchmark and ask themselves if there is reason to believe that their past behavior was similar to, or different from, their present behavior. If they see no reason to assume their behavior has changed over time, they use their present behavior as an estimate of their past behavior. If they do believe their behavior has changed, they adjust the initial estimate to reflect the assumed change (see Ross, 1989, for a comprehensive review). The resulting reports of past behavior are correct to the extent that respondents' subjective theories of stability and change are correct. Unfortunately, this is rarely the case.

In many domains, people assume an unrealistically high degree of stability, resulting in underestimates of the degree of change that has occurred over time. Accordingly, retrospective estimates of income (Withey, 1954) and of tobacco, marijuana, and alcohol consumption (Collins, Graham, Hansen, & Johnson, 1985) were found to be heavily influenced by respondents' income or consumption habits at the time of interview. On the other hand, when respondents have reason to believe in change, they will detect change, even though none has occurred. For example, Ross and Conway (1986) had students participate in a study skills training that did not improve their skills on any objective measure (and was not expected to do so). Following the training, researchers asked participants to recall how skilled they were before the training. Applying a plausible theory of change, namely, that the training improved their skills, participants inferred that their prior skills must have been much worse than they were after training. Hence, they retrospectively reported having had poorer pretraining skills than they indicated before the training, apparently confirming the intervention's success. This result was obtained despite incentives to respondents to recall their earlier answers as accurately as possible. As Ross and Conway (1986) noted, you can always get what you want by revising what you had.

This possibility is particularly troublesome for evaluation research, given that most interventions are likely to evoke a subjective theory of change. As a result, respondents may reconstruct their earlier behaviors as having been more problematic than they were, apparently confirming the intervention's success—provided they believe the intervention was likely to help them (a belief that entails a subjective theory of change). Conversely, they may reconstruct their earlier behaviors as having been less problematic, and closer to their current behaviors, if they believe the intervention was unlikely to help them (a belief that entails a subjective theory of stability).

As this discussion indicates, asking program participants to report on how their behavior has changed over the course of the intervention, or what their behavior was prior to the intervention, is likely to result in theory-driven reconstructions. These reconstructions are useless as measures of objective change, although they may be of interest as measures of participants' subjective perceptions. To assess actual change, we need to rely on before-after or treatment-control comparisons—and if we have missed asking the right question before the intervention, little can be done after the fact to make up for the oversight.

Inferences Based on the Research Instrument: Frequency Scales

In many studies, researchers ask respondents to report the frequency of their behavior by checking the appropriate alternative from a list of quantitative response alternatives. For example, a question about the frequency of physical symptoms may present one of these response scales:

Low-Frequency Scale	High-Frequency Scale
( ) *never*	( ) *twice a month or less*
( ) *about once a year*	( ) *once a week*
( ) *about twice a year*	( ) *twice a week*
( ) *twice a month*	( ) *daily*
( ) *more than twice a month*	( ) *several times a day*

Consistent with the relevance maxim of conversation, participants assume that the researcher constructed a meaningful scale that is relevant to their task. Specifically, they assume that the values in the middle range of the scale correspond to the "average" or "usual" behavior and that the extremes of the scale correspond to the extremes of the distribution. As already seen in the section on question comprehension, the scale values are likely to influence respondents' interpretation of the question. In addition, they influence respondents' frequency estimates and related judgments.

Frequency Estimates

Respondents are likely to use the range and midpoint of the response alternatives as a frame of reference in estimating their own behavioral frequency. For example, they may infer that the midpoint represents the average or typical response and that the endpoints represent unusually high or low frequencies in the population. This means that responses are more likely to cluster at the mean if respondents assume that they are average. For example, when asked how much time they spent on homework using a close-ended scale, the average response of eighth graders in three inner-city schools did not differ from the midpoint of the scale, which represented 2 to 3 hours a week, but when the same children were asked the question without a scale, the average response was almost double, closer to 4 hours a week (Oyserman, 2009).

Moreover, in comparing responses to higher frequency and lower frequency scales, the above described estimation strategies result in higher frequency estimates along scales that present high- rather than low-frequency response alternatives. For example, Schwarz and Scheuring (1992) asked

60 patients of a German mental health clinic to report the frequency of 17 symptoms along one of the two scales shown above. Across 17 symptoms, 62% of the respondents reported average frequencies of more than twice a month when presented with the high-frequency scale, whereas only 39% did so when presented with the low-frequency scale. Overall, then, the two frequency scales resulted in a mean difference of 23 percentage points! The impact of response alternatives was strongest for the ill-defined symptom of "responsiveness to changes in the weather," where 75% of the patients reported a frequency of more than twice a month along the high-frequency scale, whereas only 21% did so along the low-frequency scale. Conversely, the influence of response alternatives was least pronounced for the better defined symptom "excessive perspiration," with 50% versus 42% of the respondents reporting a frequency of more than twice a month in the high- and low-frequency scale conditions, respectively.

This influence of frequency scales has been observed across a wide range of different behaviors, including health behaviors, sexual behaviors, and consumer behaviors (see Schwarz, 1999, for a review). As expected on theoretical grounds, the effect is more pronounced the more poorly the behavior is represented in memory, which forces respondents to rely on an estimation strategy. When the behavior is rare and important, and hence well represented in memory, the impact of response alternatives is small because no estimation is required. Finally, when a respondent engages in the behavior with high regularity (e.g., "every Sunday"), its frequency can easily be derived from this rate information, again attenuating the impact of frequency scales (Menon, Raghubir, & Schwarz, 1995).

Subsequent Judgments

In addition to affecting respondents' behavioral reports, response alternatives may also influence subsequent judgments. Given respondents' assumption that the scale reflects the distribution of the behavior, checking a value on the scale amounts to determining one's location in the distribution, which influences subsequent comparative judgments. Accordingly, the patients in Schwarz and Scheuring's (1992) study of physical symptoms reported higher health satisfaction when the high-frequency scale suggested that their own symptom frequency was below average, compared to when the low-frequency scale suggested their symptom frequency was above average. Note that this higher report of health satisfaction was obtained despite the fact that the former patients reported a higher symptom frequency in the first place, as seen above. Findings of this type show that respondents extract comparison information from their own placement on the scale and use this information in making subsequent comparative judgments.

Not all judgments, however, are comparative in nature. When asked how satisfied we are with our health, we may compare our own symptom frequency to that of others. Yet, when asked how much our symptoms bother us, we may not engage in a social comparison but may instead draw on the absolute frequency of our symptoms. In this case, we may infer that our symptoms bother us more when a high-frequency scale induced estimates of high symptom frequency. Accordingly, in another study, patients who reported their symptom frequency on one of the above scales reported that their symptoms bothered them more when they received a high- rather than a low-frequency scale (Schwarz, 1999). Thus, the same high-frequency scale elicited subsequent reports of higher health satisfaction (a comparative judgment) or of higher subjective suffering (a noncomparative judgment), depending on whether a comparative or a noncomparative judgment followed the symptom report.

Implications

Given the wide use of numeric response alternatives, it is worth highlighting the methodological implications of using this format. First, numeric response alternatives influence respondents' interpretation of what the question refers to, as seen in the section on question comprehension. Hence, the same question stem, in combination with different frequency alternatives, may result in the assessment of differentially extreme behaviors. Second, respondents' use of frequency scales as a frame of reference influences the obtained behavioral reports. This calls the interpretation of the absolute values into question and undermines the comparability of reports provided along different scales. Third, because all respondents draw on the same frame of reference, frequency scales tend to homogenize the obtained reports. This reduces the observed variance as well as the likelihood that extreme groups are accurately identified. Fourth, the impact of response alternatives is more pronounced to the extent respondents cannot recall relevant episodes from memory. Hence, reports of behaviors that are poorly represented in memory are more affected than reports of behaviors that are well represented (e.g., Menon et al., 1995). This may exaggerate or attenuate any actual differences in the relative frequency of the behaviors, depending on the specific frequency range of the scale. Fifth, for the same reason, respondents with poorer memory for the behavior under study are more likely to be influenced by response alternatives than are respondents with better memory. This can result in misleading conclusions about actual group differences (Schwarz, 2003). Sixth, the range of response alternatives may influence subsequent comparative and noncomparative judgments. Hence, respondents may arrive at evaluative judgments that are highly context dependent and may not reflect the assessments they would be likely to make in daily life. Finally there may be systematic cross-cultural differences in sensitivity to these effects and in the domains of sensitivity. This may produce particularly misleading effects in studies involving participants of differing sociocultural backgrounds (Schwarz et al., 2010; Uskul, Oyserman, & Schwarz, 2010).

To avoid these systematic influences of response alternatives, it is advisable to ask frequency questions in an open response format, such as, "How many times a week do you … ? ____ times a week." Note that such an open format needs to specify the relevant units of measurement to avoid answers such as "a few." While the answers will be error prone, due to the difficulty of accurate recall, they will at least not be systematically biased by the frequency scale chosen by the evaluator.

An Alternative?: Vague Quantifiers

Given the reviewed difficulties, researchers may be tempted to simplify the respondents' task by using *vague quantifiers*, such as "sometimes" or "frequently." If respondents can't provide the desired details anyway, perhaps such global reports provide a viable alternative route? Unfortunately, this is not the case (see Pepper, 1981, for an extensive review).

Vague quantifiers do not reflect the absolute frequency of a behavior. Rather, they reflect its frequency *relative* to the respondent's expectations. Hence, the same response (e.g., "sometimes") denotes different frequencies in different content domains and for different respondents. For example, "frequently" suffering from headaches reflects higher absolute frequencies than "frequently" suffering from heart attacks, which undermines comparisons across different behaviors. Similarly, suffering from headaches "occasionally" denotes a higher frequency for respondents with a medical history of migraine than those without, which undermines comparisons across respondents.

These and related ambiguities (Pepper, 1981) render vague quantifiers inadequate for the assessment of *objective* frequencies, despite the high popularity of their use. Instead, vague quantifiers provide an indirect assessment of the relationship between the frequency of a behavior and respondents' expectations. If the latter information is of interest, it can be assessed in more direct ways.

Safeguarding against Surprises

The undesirable influence of frequency scales is easily avoided by using an open-ended format, as discussed earlier. Respondents' reliance on subjective theories, on the other hand, presents a more complex problem. Most important in the context of evaluation research, the mere participation in any program is likely to evoke a subjective theory of change—or why else would one participate in it? This theory, in turn, may guide inferences that apparently confirm the expected changes (Ross, 1989). Worse, different groups—like voluntary and involuntary participants—may rely on different theories, resulting in differential reports that suggest differential effectiveness. Again, cognitive pilot tests can alert researchers to participants' inference strategies and provide an opportunity to explore participants' subjective theories.

Reporting the Answer: Confidentiality and Self-Presentation

Once respondents arrive at an answer in their own mind, they need to report it to the researcher. At this point, they may find it embarrassing to admit that they did not engage in a desirable behavior or did engage in an undesirable one, and they may "edit" their answers to ensure a more favorable self-presentation. Such deliberate misrepresentation of one's behavior is limited to highly threatening questions—that is, questions pertaining to highly desirable or undesirable behaviors (Bradburn et al., 2004; DeMaio, 1984). Importantly, what is considered desirable or undesirable may often depend on the specific nature of the social situation: While admitting that one has tried drugs may seem threatening to some teenagers when interviewed by an adult, admitting that one has never tried drugs may seem as threatening to some teens when interviewed by a peer. Moreover, respondents may be concerned that disclosing illegal behavior may have negative consequences.

Not surprisingly, socially desirable responding is more frequently observed in face-to-face interviews than in self-administered questionnaires, which provide a higher degree of confidentiality (e.g., Krysan, Schuman, Scott, & Beatty, 1994; Smith, 1979). Hence, it is important to guarantee the privacy and confidentiality of respondents' answers. Accordingly, settings in which other household members, or bystanders, can overhear the questions and answers are best avoided. If that is not feasible, the threatening question may be presented in writing and the respondent may return the answer in a sealed envelope, which has the additional advantage of maintaining the privacy of the response vis-à-vis the interviewer. Bradburn et al. (2004) provide detailed advice on the use of a wide range of question wording and confidentiality techniques, and we encourage readers to consult their suggestions.

Finally, a word of caution is appropriate. Many researchers attempt to preempt respondents' possible confidentiality concerns by presenting detailed privacy and confidentiality assurances at the beginning of the interview and in an introductory letter that invites participation in a study. In fact, this is often required by Institutional Review Boards. Unfortunately, this strategy is likely to backfire. Prior to the actual interview, respondents cannot evaluate how threatening the questions might be. Given the maxims of conversation, they will infer from the researchers' assurances that they are likely to face embarrassing questions about sensitive topics—or why else would the researchers feel a need to provide these assurances? Once respondents see the actual questions, they may find them less sensitive than the assurances suggested. But many respondents may never see the questions, having decided not to participate when they pondered their likely nature (see Singer, Hippler, & Schwarz, 1992). It is therefore preferable to introduce confidentiality assurances in low-key terms at the initial contact stage and to provide specific confidentiality information at the relevant point in the interview, thus giving respondents an opportunity to make a truly informed decision.

What to Do?

As this review indicates, self-reports of behavior and opinions can be profoundly influenced by the research instrument. Unfortunately, there are no silver bullets of questionnaire design that assure accurate answers. Instead, many design options come with their own specific tradeoffs, as we noted throughout this chapter. Hence, there is no alternative to thinking one's way through the specifics in each particular case. Despite these caveats, observation of a few simple points is likely to spare evaluators many headaches down the road:

First, answer every question yourself. If you find the task difficult, chances are that your respondents will find it nearly impossible.

Second, keep in mind that your questionnaire is not a neutral instrument that merely collects information from respondents. It is also a source of information that respondents use to make sense of the questions you ask (Schwarz, 1996). Hence, ask yourself what your respondents may infer from features of the questionnaire, including the response alternatives, the reference period, the content of related questions, the title of the questionnaire, and the sponsor of the study. Make sure that those features are consistent with the intended meaning of your questions.

Third, consult models of "good" questions. They can serve as useful starting points, but will usually require adjustment for the specific purpose at hand. We highly recommend Bradburn and colleagues' (2004) *Asking Questions* for this purpose.

Fourth, pilot test your questions with cognitive interviewing techniques that can alert you to the comprehension and recall problems that respondents encounter. Chapter 2 of Sudman et al.'s (1996) *Thinking about Answers* provides an introduction to these techniques, which can be employed with a small number of respondents from the target population. Pilot test your questions, adjust them—and test them again.

Fifth, familiarize yourself with the basic psychology of asking and answering behavioral questions, to which this review provided an introduction. More comprehensive treatments can be found in *Thinking about Answers* (Sudman et al., 1996) and *The Psychology of Survey Response* (Tourangeau et al., 2000). An understanding of the basic principles is essential for appropriate questions and informed tradeoffs.

Sixth, encourage your respondents to invest the effort needed for providing accurate answers. Something as simple as acknowledging that the task is difficult, and instructing them that accuracy is important and they should take all the time they need, can improve performance (see Cannell et al., 1981, for example, instructions).

Seventh, where feasible, capitalize on the hierarchically nested structure of autobiographical memory by providing a meaningful context for respondents' memory search. Consider Event History Calendars as a possible format (see Belli, 1998).

Finally, ensure through interviewer training that your interviewers understand the intended meaning of your questions. Allow your interviewers to clarify questions when needed (Schober & Conrad, 2002) and make such clarifications part of the interviewer training.

We realize that some of these recommendations require a considerable commitment of time in questionnaire development. Moreover, since answering questions well takes time, our recommendations also may require difficult choices as to what is really central to the evaluation (and so should be measured well) and what should not be attempted since it is unlikely that everything can be measured well. On the bright side, the time spent on good questionnaire design is a negligible cost in the overall budget of an evaluation study—and mistakes made at this stage cannot be corrected later on. The *GIGO* principle of "garbage in, garbage out" applies as much to evaluation research as to any other field. In the end, study results cannot be more meaningful than the raw data on which they are based. We therefore hope that the science underlying the collection of raw data will eventually figure as prominently in the training of evaluation researchers as in the training in the statistical techniques used to mine those data.

ACKNOWLEDGMENT

In preparing this chapter, we have drawn freely on Schwarz and Oyserman (2001); we thank the American Evaluation Association for permission to use this material.

REFERENCES

Belli, R. (1998). The structure of autobiographical memory and the event history calendar: Potential improvements in the quality of retrospective reports in surveys, *Memory*, 6, 383–406.

Belson, W. A. (1981). *The design and understanding of survey questions*. Aldershot, England: Gower.

Bradburn, N., Sudman, S., & Wansink, B. (2004). *Asking questions* (2nd ed.). San Francisco: Jossey-Bass.

Cannell, C. F., Fisher, G., & Bakker, T. (1965). Reporting on hospitalization in the Health Interview Survey. *Vital and Health Statistics* (PHS Publication No. 1000, Series 2, No. 6). Washington, DC: U.S. Government Printing Office.

Cannell, C. F., Miller, P. V., & Oksenberg, L. (1981). Research on interviewing techniques. In S. Leinhardt (Ed.), *Sociological methodology 1981* (pp. 389–437). San Francisco: Jossey-Bass.

Clark, H. H., & Schober, M. F. (1992). Asking questions and influencing answers. In J. M. Tanur (Ed.), *Questions about questions* (pp. 15–48). New York: Russell Sage.

Collins, L. M., Graham, J. W., Hansen, W. B., & Johnson, C. A. (1985). Agreement between retrospective accounts of substance use and earlier reported substance use. *Applied Psychological Measurement*, 9, 301–309.

Conrad, F. G., & Brown, N. R. (1996). Estimating frequency: A multiple strategy perspective. In D. Herrmann, M. Johnson, C. McEvoy, C. Hertzog, & P. Hertel (Eds.), *Basic and applied memory: Research on practical aspects of memory* (Vol. 2, pp. 167–178). Hillsdale, NJ: Erlbaum.

DeMaio, T. J. (1984). Social desirability and survey measurement: A review. In C. F. Turner & E. Martin (Eds.), *Surveying subjective phenomena* (Vol. 2, pp. 257–281). New York: Russell Sage.

Grice, H. P. (1975). Logic and conversation. In P. Cole & J. L. Morgan (Eds.), *Syntax and semantics, Vol. 3: Speech acts* (pp. 41–58). New York: Academic Press.

Krysan, M., Schuman, H., Scott, L. J., & Beatty, P. (1994). Response rates and response content in mail versus face-to-face surveys. *Public Opinion Quarterly*, 58, 381–399.

Lessler, J. T., & Forsyth, B. H. (1996). A coding system for appraising questionnaires. In N. Schwarz & S. Sudman (Eds.), *Answering questions: Methodology for determining cognitive and communicative processes in survey research* (pp. 259–292). San Francisco: Jossey-Bass.

Linton, M. (1982). Transformations of memory in everyday life. In U. Neisser (Ed.), *Memory observed: Remembering in natural contexts* (pp. 77–91). San Francisco: Freeman.

Menon, G., Raghubir, P., & Schwarz, N. (1995). Behavioral frequency judgments: An accessibility-diagnosticity framework. *Journal of Consumer Research*, 22, 212–228.

Oyserman, D. (2009). *Self-reports of homework*. Unpublished data, Institute for Social Research, Ann Arbor, MI.

Oyserman, D., Coon, H., & Kemmelmeier, M. (2002). Rethinking individualism and collectivism: Evaluation of theoretical assumptions and meta-analyses. *Psychological Bulletin, 128,* 3–73.

Oyserman, D., & Lee, S. S. W. (2007). Priming "culture": Culture as situated cognition. In S. Kitayama & D. Cohen (Eds.), *Handbook of cultural psychology* (pp. 255–279). New York: Guilford Press.

Oyserman, D., & Lee, S. W. (2008). Does culture influence what and how we think? Effects of priming individualism and collectivism. *Psychological Bulletin, 134,* 311–342.

Park, J., Kosterman, R., Hawkins, D., Haggerty, K., Duncan, T., Duncan, S., et al. (2000). Effects of the "Preparing for the Drug Free Years" curriculum on growth in alcohol use and risk for alcohol use in early adolescence. *Prevention Science, 1,* 337–352.

Pepper, S. C. (1981). Problems in the quantification of frequency expressions. In D. W. Fiske (Ed.), *Problems with language imprecision* (New Directions for Methodology of Social and Behavioral Science, Vol. 9). San Francisco: Jossey-Bass.

Ross, M. (1989). The relation of implicit theories to the construction of personal histories. *Psychological Review, 96,* 341–357.

Ross, M., & Conway, M. (1986). Remembering one's own past: The construction of personal histories. In R. M. Sorrentino & E. T. Higgins (Eds.), *Handbook of motivation and cognition* (pp. 122–144). New York: Guilford Press.

Schober, M. F., & Conrad, F. G. (2002). A collaborative view of standardized survey interviews. In D. Maynard, H. Houtkoop-Steenstra, N. C. Schaeffer, & J. van der Zouwen (Eds.), *Standardization and tacit knowledge: Interaction and practice in the survey interview* (pp. 67–94). New York: Wiley.

Schwarz, N. (1996). *Cognition and communication: Judgmental biases, research methods, and the logic of conversation.* Hillsdale, NJ: Erlbaum.

Schwarz, N. (1999). Frequency reports of physical symptoms and health behaviors: How the questionnaire determines the results. In D. C. Park, R. W. Morrell, & K. Shifren (Eds.), *Processing medical information in aging patients: Cognitive and human factors perspectives* (pp. 93–108). Mahwah, NJ: Erlbaum.

Schwarz, N. (2003). Self-reports in consumer research: The challenge of comparing cohorts and cultures. *Journal of Consumer Research, 29,* 588–594.

Schwarz, N. (2008). Attitude measurement. In W. Crano & R. Prislin (Eds.), *Attitudes and persuasion* (pp. 41–60). Philadelphia: Psychology Press.

Schwarz, N., & Hippler, H. J. (1991). Response alternatives: The impact of their choice and ordering. In P. Biemer, R. Groves, N. Mathiowetz, & S. Sudman (Eds.), *Measurement error in surveys* (pp. 41–56). Chichester, UK: Wiley.

Schwarz, N., & Oyserman, D. (2001). Asking questions about behavior: Cognition, communication, and questionnaire construction. *American Journal of Evaluation, 22,* 127–160.

Schwarz, N., Oyserman, D., & Peytcheva, E. (2010). Cognition, communication, and culture: Implications for the survey response process. In J. A. Harkness, M. Braun, B. Edwards, T. P. Johnson, L. Lyberg, P. Ph. Mohler, et al. (Eds.), *survey methods in multinational, multiregional and multicultural contexts* (pp. 177–190). New York: Wiley.

Schwarz, N., & Scheuring, B. (1992). Selbstberichtete Verhaltens- und Symptom-häufigkeiten. (Frequency-reports of psychosomatic symptoms.) *Zeitschrift für Klinische Psychologie, 22,* 197–208.

Schwarz, N., & Strack, F. (1999). Reports of subjective well-being: Judgmental processes and their methodological implications. In D. Kahneman, E. Diener, & N. Schwarz (Eds.), *Well-being: The foundations of hedonic psychology* (pp. 61–84). New York: Russell Sage.

Schwarz, N., Strack, F., Müller, G., & Chassein, B. (1988). The range of response alternatives may determine the meaning of the question: Further evidence on informative functions of response alternatives. *Social Cognition, 6,* 107–117.

Schwarz, N., & Sudman, S. (1996). *Answering questions: Methodology for determining cognitive and communicative processes in survey research.* San Francisco: Jossey-Bass.

Singer, E., Hippler, H. J., & Schwarz, N. (1992). Confidentiality assurances in surveys: Reassurance or threat? *International Journal of Public Opinion Research, 4,* 256–268.

Sirken, M., Hermann, D., Schechter, S., Schwarz, N., Tanur, J., & Tourangeau, R. (Eds.). (1999). *Cognition and survey research.* New York: Wiley.

Smith, T. W. (1979). Happiness. *Social Psychology Quarterly, 42,* 18–30.

Sudman, S., Bradburn, N. M., & Schwarz, N. (1996). *Thinking about answers: The application of cognitive processes to survey methodology.* San Francisco: Jossey-Bass.

Tourangeau, R., Rips, L. J., & Rasinski, K. (2000). *The psychology of survey response.* New York: Cambridge University Press.

Uskul, A. K., Oyserman, D., & Schwarz, N. (2010). Cultural emphasis on honor, modesty or self-enhancement: Implications for the survey response process. In J. A. Harkness, M. Braun, B. Edwards, T. P. Johnson, L. Lyberg, P. Ph. Mohler, et al. (Eds.), *Survey methods in multinational, multiregional and multicultural contexts* (pp. 191–202). New York: Wiley.

Winkielman, P., Knäuper, B., & Schwarz, N. (1998). Looking back at anger: Reference periods change the interpretation of (emotion) frequency questions. *Journal of Personality and Social Psychology, 75,* 719–728.

Withey, S. B. (1954). Reliability of recall of income. *Public Opinion Quarterly, 18,* 31–34.

EDITORS' CONCLUDING COMMENTS
TO CHAPTER 9

Schwarz and Oyserman's review of the social and cognitive psychology research on self-reports can be a great help for evaluators who need to ask questions about behavior. You might want to ask yourself about the conditions under which self-reports of behavior are likely to be among the key measures in an evaluation (and conversely, when other kinds of measures will predominate). Keep in mind the ethical, financial, time, and other resource constraints that might preclude using other kinds of measures.

If you want to go more deeply into Schwarz and Oyserman's presentation, the following exercise may be useful. Consider an evaluation that you know about, or find a brief report of an evaluation (a search with the terms evaluation and journal will quickly locate a number of journals through which you can look). Did the evaluation include self-reports about behavior? If so, as best as you can tell, did the evaluators follow the suggestions laid out by Schwarz and Oyserman? Could they have done better? If the evaluation did not include self-reports about evaluation, why not, do you think? What measures of this type might they add? And how would they construct such a measure, according to the lessons of the chapter?

Like the other chapters in this section, this one has examined how social psychology can help address challenges that evaluators face in practice. There are many possibilities other than those presented in this section, and we hope that some readers will be motivated to think about the application of other areas of social psychology to evaluation.

PART IV

Evaluation–Social Psychology Links in Important Areas of Practice

The Present and Promise of Evaluation Contributing to Social Psychology

EDITORS' INTRODUCTORY COMMENTS
TO CHAPTER 10

In the next chapter, Robert Cialdini and his colleagues, Noah Goldstein and Vladas Griskevicius, describe their studies of environmental interventions, including the lessons they see from this work for social psychologists. Environmentally oriented interventions, aimed largely at energy conservation, were an important focus in an earlier generation of applied social psychology. Today, interest in the environment—from policy makers, evaluators, social psychologists, and the general public—seems likely to grow as global climate change becomes more widely recognized as a key challenge. As the next chapter illustrates, social psychology can contribute to efforts to promote behavior that is environmentally sensitive. As the chapter also illustrates, evaluation should be an important component of initiatives that are designed to increase environmentally friendly behaviors. This chapter, like the others in this section of the book, focuses on particular content areas in which evaluation and social psychology can be mutually informing.

Cialdini and his coauthors identify two key lessons for social psychologists from their evaluations of environmental interventions. We discuss and expand on these two lessons in the notes after the chapter. Before you move on to the chapter, however, we'd like to highlight some of its lessons about evaluation and about the integration of evaluation and social psychology.

First, this chapter, like several previous ones, raises interesting points about the role of theory, whether explicit or implicit, in the design of interventions. As you will see, the first study described in the chapter tests a set of alternative theories that Cialdini and his colleagues inferred by looking at actual practice. Specifically, they observed ways that hotels ask guests to reuse towels. That Cialdini and colleagues identified implicit theories in this way is not surprising. As Donaldson and Crano (Chapter 5) point out, theory-driven evaluators often identify the implicit theory that guided the developers of an intervention. But as Donaldson and Crano also point out, and as several other chapters illustrate (e.g., Aizen, Bandura, Bickman), interventions can instead be driven by relevant social psychological theory. The research summarized in this chapter shows this potential source of intervention theory as well, with Cialdini and his colleagues drawing on past social psychological work on social norms. Their findings show that, at least in the case of these environmental interventions, change efforts guided by good social psychology theory and research can be more effective than those guided by the implicit or intuitive theories that people would otherwise use.

Cialdini's chapter illustrates a second point about evaluation, involving what kind of things can be evaluated. When people think about evaluation, they might be inclined to think about the evaluation of large, complex, multicomponent social and educational programs like Head Start, welfare reform, or Teach for America. This chapter shows that more defined *practices*, like a printed card about reusing towels, can also be evaluated. So too a public service announcement. For some social psychologists, evaluating a relatively simple practice may feel more comfortable than evaluating a complex, multicomponent program. This is because, as the studies in this chapter suggest, it may be easier to test a particular theoretical process when evaluating a single practice. In contrast, as Riemer and Bickman discuss in Chapter 4, other social psychologists may be attracted to the prospect of drawing on multiple theories to develop more complex interventions that may be more likely to change well-entrenched, problematic behaviors.

Expanding on the upcoming chapter, we suggest a third point about evaluation and its intersection with social psychology. We invite you, as you read the chapter, to think about how research like Cialdini et al.'s might fit in a longer sequence of evaluative studies. For example, an evaluator might want to follow up on Cialdini's towel use studies with an evaluation that examines additional outcome variables such as the hotel's actual water and detergent use. The evaluator could compare improvements in these outcomes, over time, in a set of hotels that implement the social psychology-driven intervention, compared to hotels that keep using their current towel use request. This could be done using what is called an interrupted time-series design. The evaluator might further draw on the results to estimate the environmental impact that would occur if all hotels implemented the new practice. Basic researchers often see randomized experiments as the ultimate, the endpoint, and a series of research. In evaluation, however, various sequences of studies may make sense, depending on the circumstances.

CHAPTER 10

What Social Psychologists Can Learn from Evaluations of Environmental Interventions

Robert B. Cialdini
Noah J. Goldstein
Vladas Griskevicius

A while ago, one of us led a research team seeking to examine the effectiveness of certain theoretically relevant request strategies. In addition, we sought to test the strategies in a naturally occurring setting involving meaningful commitments from targets of the requests. We hit upon blood donations as providing the kind of commitments and setting we desired. But arranging for the experimental tests necessitated the cooperation of the local blood services organization, from which we needed equipment, trained personnel, and records. This required that we convince the blood services people that the proposed collaboration would be worthwhile not just to us (for the purposes of testing our theories and building our vitae) but to their organization's vitality.

Although we thought that we had made a compelling case in these regards, employing in the process everything the social psychological literature told us about successful persuasion, the organization's chief administrator hung back from authorizing our project. It wasn't until a junior member of his staff quietly informed us of the reason for her boss's reluctance that we understood what we had left out of our persuasive approach. "None of you has given blood yet," she whispered during a break in one of our meetings. Mildly chastised but properly enlightened, we asked just before the meeting's close how we might contribute to the organization's important goals by donating a pint or two of blood ourselves. An opportunity was arranged, blood was drained, and full approval of our project followed within the week.

Because evaluation research often involves the delicate process of influencing various stakeholders to undertake investigations of relevant programs and—just as importantly—to employ the results of those investigations properly, it makes sense that evaluation researchers can profit from the lessons of well over a half-century of social psychological research into the processes of social influence and persuasion. See, for example, the treatment of certain of these issues by Tinsdale and Posavac (Chapter 4) and by Fleming (Chapter 5) of this volume.

As our blood donation experience demonstrates, however, at the same time and for some of the same reasons, it is also the case that social psychologists can profit from the lessons learned by evaluation researchers regarding how social influence and persuasion operate within the context of interventions. Over the past several years, we and our coworkers have been examining the effectiveness of various communication practices employed by organizations dedicated to enhancing pro-environmental action. Although not full, formal evaluations of the organizations' programs, the interventions often involved tests of existing practices against novel practices not currently employed by these organizations. In the process, we gained some valuable insights into the ways that persuasion and social influence work.

Lesson 1: People Underestimate the Power of Fundamental Social Influence

Scholars of various kinds, including some renowned social psychologists, have long documented the powerful influence that observed social behavior has on spurring subsequent similar behavior in the observers (e.g., Festinger, 1954; Le Bon, 1895/1960; MacKay, 1841/1932; Milgram, Bickman, & Berkowitz, 1969). For example, In the Milgram, Bickman, and Berkowitz (1969) study, New Yorkers were significantly more likely to stop and stare at an empty spot in the sky if others were doing so; and the more others who were looking up, the more passersby followed suit. What proved surprising to us and our coworkers, given the ubiquity and strength of the evidence, is how little note people take of this potent form of influence when, as tacticians, they decide how to influence the actions of others. As a consequence, they may fail to implement practices that can be highly productive. For example, much more than is currently the case, pro-environmental program developers would be well advised to focus their messages on evidence that many people *do* act to preserve the environment.

To investigate this idea, we examined resource conservation choices in hotel rooms, where guests often encounter a card asking them to reuse their towels. As anyone who travels frequently knows, this card may urge the action in various ways. Sometimes it requests compliance for the sake of the environment; sometimes it does so for the sake of future generations; and sometimes it exhorts guests to cooperate with the hotel in order to save resources. What the card *never* says, however, is that the majority of guests do reuse their towels when given the opportunity. We suspected that this omission was costing the hotels—and the environment—plenty. Here's how we tested our suspicion.

Evaluating the Effectiveness of Hotel Room Recycling Appeals

With the establishment of environmental programs by hotels, travelers are increasingly being encouraged to reuse their towels to help conserve environmental resources by saving energy and reducing the amount of detergent-related pollutants released into the environment. The favorable consequences of such pro-environmental action are considerable, as an average 150-room hotel would save 72,000 gallons of water and 39 barrels of oil, and would obviate the release of 480 gallons of detergent into the environment in the course of a year if most guests complied with the appeal. In almost all cases, the appeal comes in the form of a strategically placed card in the hotels' washrooms. This information is commonly accompanied by various environment-related pictures in the background, ranging from rainforests to rainbows to raindrops to reindeer. We have been recording the content of the cards employed by dozens of hotels over the past 5 years, finding in the process that the messages on those cards most frequently attempt to boost towel-recycling efforts by focusing guests on basic environmental protection. Specifically, guests are usually informed that reusing one's towels will conserve natural resources and help save the environment from further adulteration and depletion. Two other common but less pervasive types of messages are those appealing to guests' sense of social responsibility to future generations and those informing the guests of the substantial potential savings to the hotel, which implicitly might be interpreted as passing the savings onto its clientele in the long run.

In addition, another type of message that seems to be used with increasing frequency is based on the concept of cooperation through incentives. In such messages, guests are told that by reusing their towels they will become cooperating partners with the hotel in furthering its conservation efforts. To encourage cooperation in such cases, guests are sometimes told that if they reuse their towels, the hotel will donate some percentage of those savings to environmental causes. Considering the known motivational power of incentives, practitioners who employ this type of message presumably believe that it will yield an enhanced towel reuse rate relative to the standard environmental protection appeal.

We were interested in learning how well each of these signs motivates consumers to participate in such a program. To that end, we worked with the management at a local hotel to use four signs that we created our-selves (Goldstein, Cialdini, & Griskevicius, 2007, 2008). The four mes-sages were chosen to reflect the purest forms of the four most common types of appeals we had observed in our informal survey. All of the signs were identical in two respects. First, on the front, they informed guests that they could participate in the program by placing their used towels on the washroom towel rack or curtain rod. Second, on the back, they provided information regarding the extent to which the environment would benefit and energy would be conserved if most guests participated in the program. The cards differed, however, in the persuasive appeals designed to stimulate towel recycling. Each of the four signs communicated its message using a short headline in boldface and capital letters; additional text was located underneath that further explicated the appeal:

1. *Environmental protection* appeal: "HELP SAVE THE ENVIRON-MENT. You can show your respect for nature and help save the environment by reusing your towels during your stay."

2. *Social responsibility for future generations* appeal: "HELP SAVE RESOURCES FOR FUTURE GENERATIONS. Future genera-tions deserve our concern. Please do your part to protect the envi-ronment and conserve dwindling resources for future generations to enjoy. You can help preserve these precious resources for all of us by reusing your towels during your stay."

3. *Environmental cooperation* appeal: "PARTNER WITH US TO HELP SAVE THE ENVIRONMENT. In exchange for your par-ticipation in this program, we at the hotel will donate a percentage of the energy savings to a nonprofit environmental protection orga-nization. The environment deserves our combined efforts. You can join us by reusing your towels during your stay."

4. *Benefit to the hotel* appeal: "HELP THE HOTEL SAVE ENERGY. The hotel management is concerned about the rising expense to the hotel of energy, labor, and other resources. You can help the hotel save energy by reusing your towels during your stay."

The room attendants were trained to record whether guests partici-pated in the program. The data revealed that the environmental appeal, cooperation appeal, and social responsibility for future generations appeal elicited approximately the same degree of participation (an average of 30.2%), whereas the benefit to the hotel appeal was easily the least effec-tive in stimulating towel reuse (15.6%). Thus, we found, not surprisingly, that arguing for one's own interest was counterproductive. In addition, the statistically significant difference in participation rate between that appeal and the other three was encouraging in that it informed us that guests were indeed reading our signs.

Descriptive Norms

It is important to note, however, that there is another type of motivator that we have never observed being utilized in all of the appeals that we have surveyed—the descriptive norm. A descriptive norm refers to the action that is commonly performed in a given situation, and it motivates behavior by informing individuals of what is likely to be effective or adaptive conduct there (Cialdini, Reno, & Kallgren, 1990). Observing how others behave in a given situation supplies information about what kind of behavior is normal, which becomes an especially powerful guiding factor in novel or ambiguous situations (Festinger, 1954; Schultz, Nolen, Cialdini, Goldstein, & Griskevicius, 2007). A wide variety of research shows that the behavior of others in the social environment shapes individuals' interpretations of and responses to the situation (Milgram et al., 1969; Sherif, 1936). When individuals perceive sufficient social support for a particular behavior, they tend to follow the lead of others because this mental shortcut saves them time and cognitive effort while providing an outcome that has a high probability of being effective.

A great deal of social psychological research supports the supposition that descriptive norms should be more effective in eliciting participation in the towel reuse program than will standard appeals. For instance, in one study, residents of a Los Angeles suburb received information describing the regular curbside recycling behavior of many of their neighbors. This information produced an immediate increase in the amount of material recycled. In addition, when observed up to a month later, they were recycling more trash than ever. These improvements did not occur, however, among residents who received only a plea to recycle for the good of the environment (Schultz, 1999).

To investigate whether the efficacy of hotel signs might be improved through utilization of a descriptive norm-based appeal, in a follow-up study, we assessed the impact of a novel message. Based on information indicating that nearly three-quarters of guests in hotels that utilize such conservation programs do participate at least once during their stay, we created a sign stating, "JOIN YOUR FELLOW GUESTS IN HELPING TO SAVE THE ENVIRONMENT. Almost 75% of guests who are asked to participate in our new resource savings program do help by using their towels more than once. You can join your fellow guests in this program to help save the environment by reusing your towels during your stay."

We found the towel reuse rates were significantly higher in the descriptive norm condition (44.1%) than in the environmental protection condition (35.1%) and the environmental cooperation condition (30.7%). That is, simply informing guests that the majority of other guests at the hotel had participated in the program motivated guests to reuse their towels to a greater extent than purely appealing to their concern for the environment or offering them an incentive for environmental cooperation.[1]

In summary, of the various persuasive messages we tested, the one that was most effective was the descriptive norm message, which informed guests that the majority of prior guests at the hotel had in fact participated in the towel reuse program at least once during their stay; moreover, it was an appeal that we have never previously observed in the in-room messaging of any hotel. Apparently, this simple but effective type of appeal hasn't occurred in the persuasive efforts of hotel conservation program developers because they do not recognize that it will work as powerfully as it does.

Whose Descriptive Norms Do Individuals Follow?

To this point, we have described how individuals tend to adhere to the behavioral norms of others, but one central question remains to be addressed: Whose norms are individuals most likely to follow? A close examination of Leon Festinger's social comparison theory (1954) reveals that when making decisions under uncertainty, individuals tend to follow the norms of others who seem similar to them. That is, individuals look to others who not only share similar characteristics with them, but also who share (or have shared) the environment or circumstances in which the decision must be made.

Recall that the descriptive norm used in our second study informed guests that similar others—that is, the majority of other guests who had previously stayed at the hotel—had reused their towels at least once during their respective stays. We decided to take the perceived similarity one step further by conducting yet another hotel study in which some occupants saw an appeal communicating the descriptive norm specifically for the guests who had previously stayed in the occupants' rooms. Thus, in addition to the standard environmental appeal and the descriptive norm appeal used in the prior studies, participants in this condition of our third hotel-based study read: "In a study conducted in Fall 2003, 75% of the guests who stayed in this room participated in our new resource savings program by using their towels more than once. You can join your fellow guests in this program to help save the environment by reusing your towels during your stay."[2]

Consistent with our prior evidence, the descriptive norm condition using the hotel's previous guests as the reference group yielded a significantly higher towel reuse rate (44.0%) than did the standard environmental appeal (37.2%). More interesting, however, was the finding that the descriptive norm condition using the rooms' previous occupants as the standard of comparison produced an even higher towel reuse rate (49.3%) relative to the descriptive norm message that used the hotel's previous guests, in general, as the reference group. Although it is possible to argue that the difference between the rates of the two descriptive norm conditions is small (and only marginally significant), one would be hard pressed to find a manager who wouldn't take a chance on a nearly costless 10% increase in savings simply by changing the wording on a sign.

At first, it may seem counterintuitive that guests would be more likely to follow the norms of those who previously stayed in their specific room than those who stayed in others' rooms throughout the hotel. That is, from a purely logical standpoint, there is no rational reason to believe that the behaviors of those previously occupying one's room are any more valid than the behaviors of those previously occupying the room next door, for example. However, the social psychological literature points to some ways to better understand this puzzling state of affairs. First, sharing commonalities, even seemingly irrelevant ones, with another individual has been found in most cases to increase one's affinity toward that other person. For example, sharing the same birthday, fingerprint type, or physical space with another person has been found to induce surprisingly powerful feelings of affection between individuals (Burger, Messian, Patel, del Prado, & Anderson, 2004; Burger, Soroka, Gonzago, Murphy, & Somervell, 2001). Second, although the other descriptive normative messages also seemed to convey the normative behavior of those who were in the same environment (i.e., that particular hotel), the room-based descriptive normative messages conveyed the normative behavior of a group of individuals who had been in an even more proximal environment—literally the exact same environment (i.e., that specific room) in which those participants were staying. And it is generally most adaptive for one to follow the behavioral norms associated with the particular environment, situation, or circumstances that most closely match one's own environment, situation, or circumstances. Thus, individuals may develop this general tendency into a mental shortcut, which, like other mental shortcuts, can sometimes lead to judgments, decisions, and behaviors not entirely based on a logical analysis. The findings from this research suggest that communicators, policy makers, and managers implementing a descriptive normative component to their persuasive appeals or information campaigns should ensure that the norms of the reference group are as situationally similar to the intended audience's circumstances as possible.

Interim Conclusion

The hotel studies we conducted demonstrated that the normative messages, which were messages that we have never seen utilized by hotel chains, fared better at spurring participation in the hotels' environmental conservation programs than did the types of messages most commonly used by hotel chains—in particular, those that focus on environmental protection and those that focus on cooperation through incentives. In addition to validating the motivation power of norms in a real-world setting with participants who had no idea that they were under study, our comparative evaluation provided a lesson that social psychological research had not previously offered: Putative persuaders, in this instance hotel environmental program developers, frequently ignore or severely underestimate the persuasive impact that others' behavior can have on the choices of a target audience; as a consequence, they can engage in suboptimal influence attempts. This general lesson was supported in a second environmental intervention conducted, this time, at the Petrified Forest National Park in Arizona.

Testing the Effectiveness of Admonitions against Environmental Crime

When seeking to encourage prosocial conduct, not only may program developers err by failing to trumpet the desirable behavior of others, they may also make the flip-side mistake of publicizing the *undesirable* behavior of others and thereby normalizing such behavior. Take, for instance, the case of an antivandalism program in Arizona's Petrified Forest National Park, which is regularly in crisis because of the estimated theft of more than a ton of wood per month by visitors. As part of the program, new arrivals quickly learn of the past thievery from prominently placed signage: "Your heritage is being vandalized every day by theft losses of petrified wood of 14 tons a year, mostly a small piece at a time." Although it is understandable that park officials would want to instigate corrective action by describing the dismaying size of the problem, such a message ought to be far from optimal. Indeed, by normalizing the unwanted activity, the message stands a good chance of backfiring.

As a case in point, not long ago a graduate student of the first author visited the Petrified Forest National Park with his fiancée—a woman he described as the most honest person he'd ever known, someone who had never taken a paperclip or rubber band without returning it. They quickly encountered the park sign warning visitors against stealing petrified wood and decrying the 14 tons of pilfered wood each year. While still reading the sign, he was shocked to hear this otherwise wholly law-abiding woman whisper, "We'd better get ours now."

More generally, because they don't give sufficient weight to the power of descriptive normative information, social program developers have an understandable tendency to try to mobilize action against a problem by depicting it as regrettably frequent. This is certainly not unique to environmental programs: Information campaigns stress that alcohol and drug use is intolerably high, that adolescent suicide rates are alarming, and that rampant polluters are spoiling the environment. Although these claims may be both true and well intentioned, the campaigns' creators have missed something critically important: Within the statement "Look at all the people who are doing this *undesirable* thing" lurks the powerful and undercutting normative message "Look at all the people who *are* doing it." It is conceivable, then, that in trying to alert the public to the widespread nature of a problem, public service communicators can make it worse.

To explore this possibility as it applied to individuals' decisions to despoil the environment, the first author and his coworkers conducted an experimental test (described in Cialdini, 2003). At the Petrified Forest National Park, we alternated a pair of signs at the beginnings of three separate paths that wound through high-theft areas of the park. The first sign urged visitors not to take wood, and it depicted a scene showing three thieves in action, which we felt would have the effect of normalizing the undesirable conduct. Our other sign also urged visitors not to take wood, but it depicted a lone thief, which we hoped would have the effect of marginalizing the undesirable conduct. Visitors who passed the first type of sign became significantly more likely to steal than control participants who passed no sign at the beginnings of the paths (7.92% versus 2.96%), whereas those visitors who passed the second type of sign were least likely to steal (1.67%) Thus, because they underappreciate the power of descriptive normative information, program developers can engage in tactics that are counterproductive.

At the outset of this section, we chronicled the tendency of many communicators to try to reduce the incidence of a problem by describing it as regrettably frequent. We have argued that such a tendency is misguided because it presents audience members with a muddled normative picture, implying that the targeted activity is socially disapproved but widespread. However, there is another sense in which this tendency may be misguided. Often, the problem behavior is not widespread at all. It only comes to seem that way by virtue of a vivid and impassioned presentation of its unwelcome levels of occurrence and/or injurious consequences.

The study we conducted on the theft of petrified wood offers a good example. Our results, as well as other findings (Roggenbuck, Widner, & Stratton, 1997), indicate that very few visitors remove pieces of wood from the park when given the opportunity—fewer than 3%. Still, because the park receives approximately a million visitors per year, the number of thefts is objectively high and the consequences are dire for the park environment. Therefore, the park signage we initially observed was accurate in claiming, "Your heritage is being vandalized every day by theft losses of petrified wood of 14 tons a year, mostly a small piece at a time." Even so, by focusing visitors solely on the fact that thefts did occur with destructive regularity, well-intentioned park officials may have erred twice. Not only did they set the force of descriptive norms against park goals (by implying that thievery was pervasive), they missed the opportunity to harness the force of those same norms in behalf of park goals (by failing to label the thieves accurately as a tiny minority).

This particular method for "turning lemonade into lemons" is far from limited to pro-environmental endeavors. After a university-based eating disorder education program featuring the testimony of many young women describing their harmful eating behaviors, participants showed more disorder symptoms than before (Mann et al., 1997). After a suicide prevention program that informed New Jersey teenagers of the alarming number of adolescents who take their own lives, participants became more likely to see suicide as a potential solution to their own problems (Shaffer, Garland, Vieland, Underwood, & Busner, 1991). After exposure to an alcohol use deterrence program that included exercises in which participants role-played resisting their classmates' repeated urgings to drink, junior high school students came to believe that alcohol use was more common among their peers than they originally thought (Donaldson, Graham, Piccinin, & Hansen, 1995). This last study frames the relevant issues nicely. Well-meaning program designers turned something likely to have positive consequences (the true descriptive norm for drinking) into something likely to have negative consequences (an exaggerated descriptive norm for drinking) (Prentice & Miller, 1993). In fact, the opposite strategy seems warranted by our findings: Persuasive interventions should employ information and techniques that marginalize rather than normalize undesirable conduct.

In general, the results of the hotel and the Petrified Forest National Park studies demonstrated to us something we hadn't previously recognized, which we labeled Lesson 1. It was that, when deciding how to best persuade an audience in a particular situation, people frequently underestimate the power of information concerning how similar others have acted or are acting there. In addition, a second lesson emerged when we sought to have the findings of the Petrified Forest National Park study properly implemented by Park officials, who—to our bewilderment—decided not to implement those findings at all.

Lesson 2: Having Research Accepted by an Organization Often Requires That the *Researchers* First Be Accepted by the Organization

After we reported the outcomes of the theft study to Petrified Forest National Park administrators, they decided not to change the relevant aspects of their signage. Instead, they asked their Park Rangers to conduct an informal survey of visitors that inquired into the visitors' perceptions of the factors that would affect the looting of petrified wood. The administrators' ultimate decision not to implement our findings was based on evidence from those Park Ranger interviews with several visitors, who felt that information indicating that the theft problem at the park was sizable would not increase the likelihood of stealing wood but would decrease it. We were both puzzled and dismayed that park officials would weight visitors' informally recorded subjective responses more than our more rigorously obtained evidence in their signage decision. At first, we sought to understand that choice in terms of the regrettable lack of understanding of and confidence in soundly conducted social science research within the larger society (Cialdini, 1997, 2005). Upon further reflection, we recognized the likelihood of a second explanation as well: To park professionals we were outsiders—with no special commitment to or familiarity with Park affairs—presuming to tell them that they had been proceeding wrong-headedly in their own domain. Though we couldn't be sure, this second explanation had the ring of truth because it was reminiscent of a set of events that had occurred several years earlier when the first author's research team sent some challenging data to the Keep America Beautiful (KAB) organization.

KAB's principal purpose since it was founded 1953 has been to reduce the amount of litter occurring in public places. It is perhaps most famous for developing and distributing a public service announcement (PSA) called the "Crying Indian spot," which KAB claims is the single most powerful message ever sent to the American public regarding the importance of litter control in this country. It begins with a shot of a stately, buckskin-clad American Indian paddling his canoe up a river that carries various forms of industrial and individual pollution. After coming ashore near the littered side of a highway, the Indian watches as a bag of garbage is thrown, splattering and spreading along the road, from the window of a passing car. From the refuse at his feet, the camera pans up slowly to the Indian's face, where a tear is shown tracking down his cheek, and the slogan appears: "People Start Pollution, People Can Stop It." Broadcast for many years in the 1970s and 1980s, the spot won numerous awards and millions upon millions of dollars of donated airtime. Indeed, it has even been named the 16th best television commercial of all time by *TV Guide* magazine ("The Fifty Greatest," 1999).

Despite the fame and recognition value of this touching piece of public service advertising, the outcomes of our own research on the topic of littering (Cialdini et al., 1990) suggested to us that it contained features that may have been less than optimal, and perhaps even negative, in their impact on the littering actions of those who saw it. In addition to the laudable message in the ad urging viewers to stop littering, there was the underlying message that a lot of people *do* litter: Debris floats on the river, litter lies at the roadside, and trash is tossed from an automobile into the mess. Our theorizing regarding the behavioral influence of descriptive normative information indicated that this underlying message could well run counter to the purpose of the ad, and our empirical tests supported that possibility: We found the greatest littering when our participants saw an individual litter into a fully littered environment—precisely the situation depicted in the Crying Indian spot. In contrast, we found the least littering when our participants saw an individual litter into a completely clean environment (Cialdini et al., 1990).

Not so naïve to think that the KAB organization would be monitoring academic social psychology journals for relevant data sets, we sent copies of the journal article to the KAB national headquarters, along with an executive summary of our findings. We also included a recommendation that seemed warranted from our results for a small but crucial modification of any future versions of the Crying Indian spot: The scene of someone (e.g., a passing motorist) littering into the environment should stay, but the depicted environment should change from trashed to clean.

After a few months passed without an acknowledgment of receipt from KAB, we re-sent the packet of information, this time to a larger number of recipients within the organization. Again, there was no response. However, a call to the head of the local KAB affiliate revealed that there had indeed been a response but that it had been an entirely internal one—and an entirely unfavorable one, besides. She reported that our findings had been discussed at a meeting of high-level KAB personnel, who had dismissed the evidence as coming from a source that had no deep understanding of the realities of large-scale communication campaigns, of large-scale litter reduction activities, and of the operations of the KAB organization itself.

The true extent to which our data and recommendations were disregarded became obvious not long thereafter when the KAB organization released a new version of the Crying Indian spot. Because the actor, named Iron Eyes Cody, who had starred in the original version had since died, it was no longer possible to enact a live shot of him weeping at the sight of multiple litterers. Instead, the new PSA portrayed a group of citizens repeatedly littering the area around a city bus stop. After a bus carrying the litterers away departed, the camera focused on a nearby poster containing a photograph of Cody, on which viewers could see the famous tear running, wet, down his cheek once again. At fade-out, four words appeared beneath the poster, "Back by Popular Neglect." It was plain that the KAB organization had failed, adamantly, to take our research findings into account. Not only did the second-generation PSA present littering as popular, it communicated the message that new campaign ads were necessary because of a sustained neglectful attitude toward the environment (yikes!) on the part of the American public.

Being Proactive Rather Than Reactive

At this point, we gave up trying to change those policies of the KAB organization that we felt were misguided. As in the oft-used "giant oil tanker" analogy, the organization had been steaming ahead full throttle for many years, and it was not about to be turned easily or quickly, especially not by giving access to the wheel to outsiders with little knowledge of its workings.

To make a positive impact on pro-environmental behavior, it became clear that we would have to change our own direction, not KAB's. Consequently, we proposed a collaboration to the Arizona Department of Environmental Quality, designed to increase the amount of household recycling in the state through the creation of a set of PSAs that followed the implications of our earlier research. Department officials ultimately agreed and cooperated fully with us in the development, funding, production, and evaluation of three 30-second spots, each depicting an Arizona scene in which the majority of characters did recycle, approved of recycling, and distinctly disapproved of a single individual who failed to recycle. (It is possible to view those spots by visiting *www.influenceatwork.com/influenceatwork-video19.htm.*)

When in a field test these PSAs were played on the local TV and radio stations of four Arizona communities, a 25.35% net advantage in recycling tonnage was recorded over a pair of control communities not exposed to the PSAs but whose recycling was also measured during the length of the study. Moreover, just before our PSAs were distributed, one of our test communities, Flagstaff, AZ, had just completed a three-month pro-recycling advertising campaign sponsored by the Arizona Department of Environmental Quality. Yet, our PSA broadcasts produced a significant increase in recycling even there. Soon after we reported these results to the Arizona Department of Environmental Quality personnel we had been working with, they took steps to have our PSAs distributed throughout the state and, for several years afterward, pushed television station managers statewide to give them ample air time.

Whereas KAB personnel had ignored and even defied what we had to offer, the Department of Environmental Quality had embraced and promoted it. What accounts for the difference in response between the two organizations? Of course, there could be many reasons for the divergent reactions. But the one that stood out to us was our outsider versus insider status with respect to the two groups. In contrast to what happened with the KAB organization (and at the Petrified Forest National Park, too), we were at the table with the Department of Environmental Quality personnel from the formative stages of the endeavor through to its completion. Accordingly, they were able to feel a justified sense of ownership of the process and outcomes of the project as well as to feel that we were cooperating partners with them in the undertaking.

In keeping with Lesson 2, we learned that our data were unlikely to be accepted by an organization until we had been accepted by the organization. This highlights the need for behavioral scientists to be at the table when decision makers are formulating programs and policy. If we are not there with them in the way their economic and political and legal advisers traditionally are, it can be exceedingly difficult for us to get our evidence adopted after the fact. The longer we delay in forging the relationships and doing the hard work designed to reserve those critical seats at the table, the less legitimate we become as candidates for them. To paraphrase that former graduate student's fiancée, for the sake of a well-functioning society, we'd better get our seat now.

NOTES

1. At first glance, the descriptive normative approach in this study appears to have an important shortcoming. Specifically, we informed participants that a large majority (75%) of the hotel's guests participated in the towel reuse program—a number provided by the company that supplies such cards to hoteliers—yet the best-performing message yielded only a 44.1% participation rate. There are two reasons for this discrepancy that render this problem less worrisome. First, in keeping with the data reported by the towel hanger suppliers and in studies done by hoteliers themselves (Spano, 2001), the signs in our study informed the guests that the majority of individuals recycled at least one towel sometime during their stay. Because we only examined the towel reuse data for participants' first eligible day (the first day the room attendants visited their room), the compliance rate we observed is likely a fairly sizable underestimation of the number of individuals who recycle their towels at least once during their stay. Second, we used the most conservative standards for counting compliance; that is, we did not count as a reuse effort a towel that was hung on a door hook or doorknob—a very common practice for towel recyclers who misunderstand or do not thoroughly read the instructions—as we wanted to eliminate the likelihood of guests complying unintentionally with the request. Thus, we believe the overall percentage of towel reuse was artificially suppressed.

2. We included the information that the 75% figure came from an already completed study to avoid the likelihood that guests would perceive that their towel reuse was being currently monitored—a perception that could increase their tendency to comply.

REFERENCES

Burger, J. M., Messian, N., Patel, S., del Prado, A., & Anderson, C. (2004). What a coincidence! The effects of incidental similarity on compliance. *Personality and Social Psychology Bulletin, 30*, 35–43.

Burger, J. M., Soroka, S., Gonzago, K., Murphy, E., & Somervell, E. (2001). The effect of fleeting attraction on compliance to requests. *Personality and Social Psychology Bulletin, 27*, 1578–1586.

Cialdini, R. B. (1997). Professionally responsible communication with the public: Giving psychology a way. *Personality and Social Psychology Bulletin, 23*, 675–683.

Cialdini, R. B. (2003). Crafting normative messages to protect the environment. *Current Directions in Psychological Science, 12*, 105–109.

Cialdini, R. B. (2005). Don't throw in the towel: Use social influence research. *APS Observer, 18*, 33–34.

Cialdini, R. B., Reno, R. R., & Kallgren, C. A. (1990). A focus theory of normative conduct: Recycling the concept of norms to reduce littering in public places. *Journal of Personality and Social Psychology, 58,* 1015–1026.

Donaldson, S. I., Graham, J. W., Piccinin, A. M., & Hansen, W. B. (1995). Resistance-skills training and the onset of alcohol use: Evidence for beneficial and potentially harmful effects in public schools and in private Catholic schools. *Health Psychology, 14,* 291–300.

Festinger, L. (1954). A theory of social comparison processes. *Human Relations, 7,* 117–40.

Goldstein, N. J., Cialdini, R. B., & Griskevicius, V. (2007). Rooms for improvement. *Cornell Hotel and Restaurant Administration Quarterly, 48,* 145–150.

Goldstein, N. J., Cialdini, R. B., & Griskevicius, V. (2008). A room with a viewpoint: Using normative appeals to motivate environmental conservation in a hotel setting. *Journal of Consumer Research, 35,* 472–482.

Le Bon, G. (1895/1960). *Psychologie des foules* (Psychology of the crowd). New York: Viking Press.

MacKay, C. (1841/1932). *Popular delusions and the madness of crowds.* New York: Farrar, Straus, & Giroux.

Mann, T., Nolen-Hoeksema, S. K., Burgard, D., Huang, K., Wright, A., & Hansen, K. (1997). Are two interventions worse than none? *Health Psychology, 16,* 215–225.

Milgram, S., Bickman, L., & Berkowitz, L. (1969). Note on the drawing power of crowds of different size. *Journal of Personality and Social Psychology, 13,* 79–82.

Prentice, D. A., & Miller, D. T. (1993). Pluralistic ignorance and alcohol use on campus: Some consequences of misperceiving the social norm. *Journal of Personality and Social Psychology, 64,* 243–256.

Roggenbuck, J. W., Widner, C. J., & Stratton, D. W. (1997). *Reducing theft of petrified wood at Petrified Forest National Park* [final report to Petrified Forest National Park]. Petrified Forest, AZ: National Park Service.

Schultz, P. W. (1999). Changing behavior with normative feedback interventions: A field experiment on curbside recycling. *Basic and Applied Social Psychology, 21,* 25–38.

Schultz, P. W., Nolen, J. M., Cialdini, R. B., Goldstein, N. J., & Griskevicius, V. (2007). The constructive, destructive, and reconstructive power of social norms. *Psychological Science, 18,* 429–434.

Shaffer, D., Garland, A., Vieland, V., Underwood, M., & Busner, C. (1991). The impact of curriculum-based suicide prevention programs for teenagers. *Journal of the American Academy of Child and Adolescent Psychiatry, 30,* 588–596.

Sherif, M. (1936). *The psychology of social norms.* New York: Harper.

Spano, S. (2001, April 29). It's easy being green, but who benefits? *San Francisco Chronicle,* p. T10.

The fifty greatest TV commercials of all time. (1999, July 3–9). *TV Guide,* pp. 2–34.

EDITORS' CONCLUDING COMMENTS
TO CHAPTER 10

Cialdini, Goldstein, and Griskevicius explicitly identify two lessons for social psychologists from their evaluations of environmental interventions. The first is that "people underestimate the power of fundamental social influence." Neither the creators of the towel reuse, nor the authors of the Iron Eyes Cody public service announcement, nor several other intervention developers mentioned in the chapter identified the effective norm-based interventions that Cialdini and colleagues created. The authors' wonderful phrase of "turning lemonade into lemons" reflects the capacity of initiative developers to get it wrong. And their findings suggest that, at least some of the time, social psychological research and theory can help.

A second lesson that Cialdini and colleagues explicitly note is that "having research accepted by an organization often requires that the *researchers* first be accepted by the organization." The authors provide one example where the researchers collaborated with an organization that subsequently embraced the implications of their findings. They also provide two examples of findings being ignored when the researcher was an outsider.

For social psychologists interested in having their findings translated into programs, policies, and practices, there is a more general lesson expanding upon that given by Cialdini and colleagues. As summarized partly in Chapter 7, there is an extensive literature on evaluation use and influence (also see, e.g., Mark & Henry, 2004; Weiss, 1979). Some of the findings and experiences from that literature are quite consistent with Cialdini's suggestion that a collaborative process, with potential users engaged along with the evaluator, facilitates use. However, evaluators are not always able to engage collaboratively with potential users, and factors other than collaborative engagement can also facilitate use. Thus, another possible lesson, expanding on the previous chapter, is that if researchers, whether evaluators, social psychologists, or both, want to see their findings make a difference, they should become familiar with the literature on evaluation use and influence.

Yet another lesson for social psychologists can be drawn from the chapter by Cialdini et al. Their research had both theoretical and applied relevance, in part because they contrasted messages based in social psychology with other messages that were drawn from everyday practice. Social psychological researchers often construct procedures for the comparison group without explicit attention to actual real-world standards. When it is possible to ground the "control" group in real-life examples, benefits should result on both the basic and applied side of the fence.

EDITORS' INTRODUCTORY COMMENTS
TO CHAPTER 11

Many important social psychological theories focus on how groups work together and on the factors that affect such interactions. Social interdependence is one such theory. Briefly, according to this theory, positive interdependence and cooperation occur when a person perceives that reaching his or her own goals is possible only to the extent that others in the group also reach their goals. Negative interdependence and competition, in contrast, stems from the perception that one's own goals will be thwarted to the extent that others in the group reach their goals. Social interdependence theory has been applied in education and other areas, with special emphasis on the benefits of "cooperative learning" and related interventions.

The intersection between social interdependence theory and evaluation are explored in the next chapter. David Johnson, Roger Johnson, and Laurie Stevahn address the intersection in two general ways. First, they examine how evaluation studies have influenced the theory of social interdependence, especially in the section titled "Contributions of Evaluation Studies to Social Interdependence Theory." In this section and elsewhere, the authors describe several specific ways that systematic evaluation has led to theoretical modifications and refinements of social interdependence theory. Evaluation results have, for example, led to increased clarity of theoretical concepts.

The authors emphasize the often neglected role of *practice* in most discussions of the relationship between social psychological theory and research. As they point out, social interdependence theory has been translated into numerous applications and practices. But the *systematic evaluation* of such practices is necessary so that lessons can be learned about how to modify and refine the theory that guided the original practice.

Toward the end of the chapter, the authors address a second general aspect of the social psychology–evaluation relationship in the context of social interdependence theory. That is, they offer their thoughts, some provocative, about the potential benefits of applying social interdependence theory to program evaluation practice. Evaluators working with program staff, evaluation sponsors, and other stakeholders are frequently challenged as they strive to keep interactions cooperative. Likewise, evaluators meet challenges in seeking "integrative solutions" reflecting the divergent perspectives of different stakeholder groups, for example, about which things to measure and use as criteria of program success. As Johnson et al. observe, social interdependence theory offers a framework "that can guide the building of productive relationships between the evaluators and the program staff, the participants, and other stakeholders" (p. 312).

Throughout the chapter, Johnson et al. illustrate how social interdependence theory can guide programs and practices to increase cooperative interactions in different settings and among a variety of populations. Readers are encouraged to think about the potential implications of adopting similar techniques for evaluation practice, especially in the context of working with multiple stakeholder groups. Likewise, one might consider the potential implications for evaluation training and professional development. As suggested by the authors, this chapter and the broader literature on social interdependence theory may be a good place for evaluators to learn about practices that can facilitate cooperation across stakeholders—further strengthening the intersection of evaluation and social psychology.

CHAPTER 11

Social Interdependence and Program Evaluation

David W. Johnson
Roger T. Johnson
Laurie Stevahn

Cooperative learning represents one of psychology's and evaluation's success stories. From being relatively unknown and unused in the 1960s, cooperative learning is now an accepted and often the preferred instructional procedure at all levels of education throughout the world in every subject area, from preschool through graduate school and adult training programs. Its use so pervades education that it is difficult to find a textbook on instructional methods, a teacher's journal, or instructional materials that do not discuss cooperative learning. There are now Cooperative Learning Centers in such diverse places as the University of Minnesota, Hong Kong, Shanghai, Cyprus, and Norway. Our writings in cooperative learning have been translated into 16 different languages. It was not always this way.

We began training teachers in the use of cooperative learning in the mid-1960s at the University of Minnesota. At that time, schools were dominated by competitive and individualistic learning. Social Darwinism, with its premise that students must be taught to survive in a "dog-eat-dog" world, dominated educational thought in the 1960s, even as it was being challenged by individualistic learning based largely on B. F. Skinner's work on programmed learning and behavioral modification and a societal myth about "rugged individualism." There was considerable cultural resistance to the use of cooperative learning throughout the 1960s and 1970s. We continually challenged the prevailing competitive and individualistic practices, however, by carefully presenting the theory and research in cooperative learning, by creating operational procedures directly derived from social interdependence theory, and by successfully implementing cooperative learning in schools and universities and cooperative teamwork in business and industry. In doing so, we and many others conducted summative evaluations in the form of field studies of the impact of cooperative efforts on achievement and productivity and a multitude of other variables of interest to educational, business, industrial, and other organizations. By systematically evaluating cooperative learning practices, these field studies have contributed significantly to the theory underlying cooperative, competitive, and individualistic situations. That is, evaluation has contributed both to the improvement and the acceptance of social interdependence theory. The opposite direction of improvement should also operate. That is, as will be discussed later in the chapter, the field of evaluation also stands to benefit a great deal from more widespread application of social interdependence theory to the work that evaluators do.

In order to address how (1) social psychology theory and research informed the implementation of cooperative learning in schools and universities and cooperative teams in business and industry and (2) evaluations of those implementations led to modifications and refinements of social psychological theory, we review the interrelationship among theory, research, and practice. Then social interdependence theory and the validating research will be discussed, the nature of cooperative learning will be covered, and the impact of the evaluations of cooperative learning on social interdependence theory will be discussed. Of special interest is the power of practice, when systematically evaluated, to modify theory and subsequent research.

Theory, Research, Practice

Cooperative learning is an example of the ideal relationship among psychological theory, research, and (evaluated) practice. Ideally, theory guides and summarizes research, research validates or disconfirms theory (thereby leading to its refinement and modification), and effective practice is both guided by validated theory and evaluated to reveal inadequacies that lead to further refinement of the theory and new research studies (D. W. Johnson, 2003).

Social interdependence theory provides an example of how psychological theorizing and research have resulted in valuable practical applications, and of how theory, research, and practice interact in ways that enhance all three. The relationship between theory and research has long been understood (Merton, 1957). Theory identifies, clarifies, and defines the phenomena of interest and their relationships with each other. Research validates or disconfirms the theory. Deutsch (1949) formulated a strategic, profound, and powerful theory of social interdependence that has generated considerable research sufficient to test his theory (D. W. Johnson & R. Johnson, 1989). Over 97% of the studies on social interdependence have been conducted subsequent to Deutsch's development of the basic theory. The amount, quality, and generalizability of the research provide strong confirmation of the basic propositions of the theory and demonstrate the effectiveness of cooperative relative to competitive and individualistic efforts.

For the most part, the role of *carefully evaluated practice* has been neglected in discussions of the relationships among theory, research, and practice. Social interdependence theory has been applied in many diverse areas (most notably in education and business), and evaluations of these applications have had profound effects on the theory and related research. In this chapter, the focus is on the contributions of practice, specifically, practice that is subject to systematic evaluation, to the refinement and modification of social interdependence theory. One of the unique aspects of social interdependence theory is that so many of the research studies it has generated have been field evaluations of the relative effectiveness of cooperative, competitive, and individualistic situations. Conducting these studies has required that operational procedures be developed for each type of social interdependence, the procedures be implemented in applied settings (such as schools and businesses), and evaluation studies be conducted to determine the impact of the procedures on variables of interest. This process of operationalizing, implementing, and evaluating has had considerable impact on social interdependence theory and its validating research.

Social Interdependence Theory

Before turning to the role of evaluation in the study of social interdependence, we summarize the theory, define key concepts, processes, and outcomes, and discuss the strengths and weaknesses of different types of studies designed to evaluate social interdependence practices.

In the early 1900s, one of the founders of Gestalt psychology, Kurt Koffka (1935), proposed that groups were dynamic wholes in which interdependence among members could vary. One of his colleagues, Kurt Lewin (1935), refined Koffka's notion with two proposals. First, the essence of a group is the interdependence among members (created by common goals) that results in the group being a "dynamic whole," so that a change in the state of any member or subgroup changes the state of all other members or subgroups. Second, an intrinsic state of tension in group members motivates movement toward the accomplishment of the desired common goals. One of Lewin's graduate students, Morton Deutsch (1949), extended Lewin's notions to the relationship among the goals of two or more individuals. In doing so, he developed social interdependence theory.

Social interdependence exists when the accomplishment of each individual's goals is affected by the actions of others (Deutsch, 1949, 1962; D. W. Johnson, 1970; D. W. Johnson & R. Johnson, 1989). There are two types of social interdependence, positive (cooperation) and negative (competition). *Positive interdependence* exists when individuals perceive that they can reach their goals if and only if the other individuals with whom they are cooperatively linked also reach their goals and, therefore, promote each other's efforts to achieve the goals. *Negative interdependence* exists when individuals perceive that they can obtain their goals if and only if the other individuals with whom they are competitively linked fail to obtain their goals and, therefore, obstruct each other's efforts to achieve the goals. *No interdependence* results in a situation in which individuals perceive that they can reach their goal regardless of whether other individuals in the situation attain or do not attain their goals. Each type of interdependence results in certain psychological processes.

Psychological Processes

The psychological processes created by positive interdependence include *substitutability* (i.e., the degree to which actions of one person substitute for the actions of another person), *inducibility* (i.e., openness to being influenced and to influencing others), and *positive cathexis* (i.e., investment of positive psychological energy in objects outside of oneself) (Deutsch, 1949, 1962). Negative interdependence creates the psychological processes of nonsubstitutability, resistance to being influenced by others, and negative cathexis. No interdependence detaches a person from others, thereby creating nonsubstitutability, no inducibility (or resistance), and cathexis only to one's own actions.

Interaction Patterns

The basic premise of social interdependence theory is that the way in which interdependence is structured determines how individuals interact and, in turn, the interaction pattern determines the outcomes of the situation (Deutsch, 1949, 1962; D. W. Johnson, 1970; D. W. Johnson & R. Johnson, 1974, 1989, 2005a). Figure 11.1 captures this premise. Positive interdependence results in *promotive interaction* (i.e., individuals encouraging and facilitating each other's efforts to complete tasks, achieve, or produce in order to reach the group's goals). In contrast, negative interdependence results in *oppositional or contrient interaction* (i.e., may be defined as individuals discouraging and obstructing each other's efforts to complete tasks,

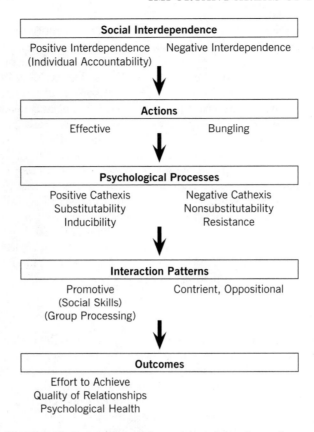

FIGURE 11.1. Overview of social interdependence theory.

achieve, or produce in order to reach their goals). And no interdependence results in *no interaction* as individuals act independently without any interchange with each other while they work to achieve their goals.

Outcomes

Promotive, oppositional, and no interaction have differential effects on the outcomes of the situation (see D. W. Johnson & R. Johnson, 1989, 1999). The research has focused on numerous outcomes, which may be subsumed within the broad and interrelated categories of effort to achieve, quality of relationships, and psychological health (D. W. Johnson & R. Johnson, 1989) (see Table 11.1 and Figure 11.2). Figure 11.2 shows the relationships among the outcomes, drawing on a meta-analysis or quantitative synthesis of the results of multiple studies.

TABLE 11.1. Mean Effect Sizes for Impact of Social Interdependence on Dependent Variables

Dependent variable	Cooperative versus competitive	Cooperative versus individualistic	Competitive versus individualistic
Achievement	0.67	0.64	0.30
Interpersonal attraction	0.67	0.60	0.08
Social support	0.62	0.70	−0.13
Self-esteem	0.58	0.44	−0.23
Time on task	0.76	1.17	0.64
Attitudes toward task	0.57	0.42	0.15
Quality of reasoning	0.93	0.97	0.13
Perspective taking	0.61	0.44	−0.13
High-quality studies			
Achievement	0.88	0.61	0.07
Interpersonal attraction	0.82	0.62	0.27
Social support	0.83	0.72	−0.13
Self-esteem	0.67	0.45	−0.25

Note. From D. W. Johnson and R. Johnson (1989). Copyright 1989 by Interaction Book Company. Reprinted by permission.

Effort to Achieve

Table 11.1 shows that cooperation promotes considerably greater effort to achieve than do competitive or individualistic efforts. "Effort exerted to achieve" includes such variables as achievement and productivity, long-term retention, on-task behavior, use of higher-level reasoning strategies, generation of new ideas and solutions, transfer of what is learned within one situation to another, intrinsic motivation, achievement motivation, continuing motivation to learn, and positive attitudes toward learning and school. Overall, cooperation tends to promote higher achievement than competitive or individualistic efforts (effect sizes = 0.67 and 0.64, respectively). An important aspect of school life is engagement in learning. One indication of engagement in learning is time on task. Cooperators spent considerably more time on task than did competitors (effect size = 0.76) or students working individualistically (effect size = 1.17). In addition, students working cooperatively tended to be more involved in activities and tasks, attach greater importance to success, and engage in more on-task behavior and less apathetic, off-task, disruptive behaviors. Finally, cooperative experiences, compared with competitive and individualistic ones, have been found to promote more positive attitudes toward the task and

FIGURE 11.2. Outcomes of cooperation. From D. W. Johnson and R. Johnson (1989). Copyright 1989 by Interaction Book Company. Reprinted by permission.

the experience of working on the task (effect sizes = 0.57 and 0.42, respectively).

Quality of Relationships

Quality of relationships includes such variables as interpersonal attraction, liking, cohesion, esprit-de-corps, and social support. The degree of emotional bonding that exists among students has a profound effect on students' behavior. Over 175 studies have investigated the relative impact of cooperative, competitive, and individualistic efforts on quality of relationships and another 106 studies on social support (D. W. Johnson & R. Johnson, 1989). As Table 11.1 shows, cooperation generally promotes greater interpersonal attraction among individuals than does competitive or individualistic efforts (effect sizes = 0.67 and 0.60, respectively). Cooperative experiences tend to promote greater social support than does competitive (effect size = 0.62) or individualistic (effect size = 0.70) efforts. Stronger effects are found for peer support than for superior (teacher) support. The high-quality studies tend to have even more powerful effects.

Psychological Health

Several studies have directly measured the relationship between social interdependence and psychological health (see D. W. Johnson & R. Johnson, 1989, 2005a). The samples studied included university students, older adults, suburban high school seniors, juvenile and adult prisoners, stepcouples, Olympic hockey players, and Chinese business executives. The results indicate that cooperative attitudes are highly correlated with a wide variety of indices of psychological health, competitiveness was in some cases positively and in some cases negatively related to indices of psychological health, and individualistic attitudes were negatively related to a wide variety of indices of psychological health.

One important aspect of psychological health is self-esteem. The studies found that cooperation promoted higher self-esteem than did competitive (effect size = 0.58) or individualistic (effect size = 0.44) efforts. Members of cooperative groups also become more socially skilled than do students working competitively or individualistically. Not only is the level of self-esteem affected by being part of a group effort, but the process by which individuals make judgments about their self-worth is also affected. Johnson and Norem-Hebeisen (1981) conducted four studies involving 821 white, middle-class, high school seniors in a midwestern suburban community. They found that cooperative experiences promoted basic self-acceptance, freedom from conditional acceptance, and positive self-image compared to peers. Competitive experiences were related to conditional self-acceptance, and individualistic attitudes were related to basic self-rejection, including anxiety about relating to other people. Cooperative, group-based experiences seem to result in (1) internalizing perceptions that one is known, accepted, and liked as one is, (2) internalizing mutual success, and (3) developing multidimensional views of self and others that allow for positive self-perceptions (D. W. Johnson & R. Johnson, 1989).

Finally, there is evidence that cooperation promotes more frequent use of higher-level reasoning strategies than do competitive (effect size = 0.93) or individualistic (effect size = 0.97) efforts. Similarly, cooperation tends to promote more accurate perspective taking than do competitive (effect size = 0.61) or individualistic (effect size = 0.44) efforts. Thus, the more cooperative learning experiences in which students are involved, the more mature their cognitive and moral decision making and the more they will tend to take other people's perspectives into account when making decisions.

Basic Elements of Cooperation

These outcomes tend to result only when cooperation is effectively structured to contain five basic elements (D. W. Johnson, 2003; D. W. Johnson & R. Johnson, 1989, 2005a). First, there must be a strong sense of *positive interdependence*, so individuals believe they are linked with others so they cannot succeed unless the others do (and vice versa). Positive interdependence may be structured through mutual goals, joint rewards, divided resources, complementary roles, and a shared identity. Second, each collaborator must be *individually accountable* to do his or her fair share of the work. Third, collaborators must have the opportunity to *promote each other's success* by helping, assisting, supporting, encouraging, and praising each other's efforts to achieve. Fourth, working together cooperatively requires *interpersonal and small group skills*, such as leadership, decision-making, trust-building, communication, and conflict-management skills. Finally, cooperative groups must engage in *group processing*, which exists when group members discuss how well they are achieving their goals and maintaining effective working relationships.

Nature of Cooperative Learning

Based on social interdependence theory, operational procedures for cooperative learning have been developed. *Cooperative learning* is the instructional use of small groups in which students work together to maximize their own and each other's learning (D. W. Johnson, R. Johnson, & Holubec, 1998, 2002). Any assignment in any curriculum for any age student can be done cooperatively. There are three types of cooperative learning—formal, informal, and base groups.

Formal cooperative learning consists of students working together, for one class period to several weeks, to achieve shared learning goals and complete jointly specific tasks and assignments (D. W. Johnson, R. Johnson, & Holubec, 1998, 2002). In formal cooperative learning groups, teachers:

1. *Make a number of preinstructional decisions.* Teachers specify the objectives for the lesson (both academic and social skills) and decide on the size of groups, the method of assigning students to groups, the roles students will be assigned, the materials needed to conduct the lesson, and the way the room will be arranged.

2. *Explain the task and the positive interdependence.* A teacher clearly defines the assignment, teaches the required concepts and strategies, specifies the positive interdependence and individual accountability criteria, gives the criteria for success, and explains the expected social skills to be used.

3. *Monitor and intervene*: Teachers monitor students' learning and intervene within the groups to provide task assistance or to increase students' interpersonal and group skills.

4. *Assess and process*: Teachers assess students' learning and structure students processing of how well their groups functioned.

Informal cooperative learning consists of having students work together to achieve a joint learning goal in temporary, ad hoc groups that last from a few minutes to one class period (D. W. Johnson, R. Johnson, & Holubec, 2002). During a lecture, demonstration, or film, informal cooperative learning can be employed in a number of ways. Informal cooperative learning can be used to focus student attention on the material to be learned, set a mood conducive to learning, help set expectations as to what will be covered in a class session, ensure that students cognitively process and rehearse the material being taught, summarize what was learned and pre-cue the next session, and provide closure to an instructional session. The procedure for using informal cooperative learning during a lecture entails having 3- to 5-minute focused discussions before and after the lecture (i.e., bookends) and 2- to 3-minute interspersing pair discussions throughout the lecture.

Cooperative base groups are long-term, heterogeneous cooperative learning groups with stable membership. Their primary responsibilities are to provide support, encouragement, and assistance to make academic progress and develop cognitively and socially in healthy ways, as well as to hold each other accountable for striving to learn (D. W. Johnson, R. Johnson, & Holubec, 2002). Typically, cooperative base groups (1) are heterogeneous in membership, (2) meet regularly (e.g., daily or biweekly), and (3) last for the duration of the semester, year, or until all members are graduated. Base groups typically consist of three to four members. They meet at the beginning and end of each class session (or week) to complete academic tasks such as checking each member's homework, routine tasks such as taking attendance, and personal support tasks such as listening sympathetically to personal problems or providing guidance for writing a paper.

These three types of cooperative learning may be used together. A typical class session may begin with a base group meeting, followed by a short lecture in which informal cooperative learning is used. A formal cooperative learning lesson is then conducted, and near the end of the class session another short lecture may be delivered with the use of informal cooperative learning. The class ends with a base group meeting.

Having outlined the essential elements of social interdependence theory, as well as the basics of cooperative learning practices, we now turn to a discussion of the nature of the research on social interdependence.

This research includes systematic evaluations of cooperative learning practices. We discuss some of the primary strengths and weaknesses of different types of evaluation studies, especially as related to informing the development and modification of social interdependence theory.

Amount and Characteristics of Research on Social Interdependence

The study of cooperative, competitive, and individualistic efforts is commonly recognized as one of the oldest fields of research in social psychology. In the late 1800s Triplett (1898) in the United States, Turner (1889, cited in Trippett, 1898) in England, and Mayer (1903) in Germany conducted a series of studies on the factors associated with competitive performance. Since then over 750 studies have been conducted on the relative merits of cooperative, competitive, and individualistic efforts and the conditions under which each is appropriate (D. W. Johnson, 2002; D. W. Johnson & R. Johnson, 1989, 2005a). This is one of the largest bodies of research within psychology.

Of the 754 studies that contained enough data to compute an effect size (there are many more studies from which an effect size cannot be computed, including numerous qualitative studies), 65% have been field evaluations (31% have been laboratory studies). It is the field evaluations that have fueled the validation and refinement of social interdependence theory. The importance of these field studies may seem unremarkable to evaluators, but it is worth highlighting for social psychologists, who often spend most of their research time in the lab.

One strength of the research on social interdependence is that it consists of both theoretical and demonstration studies. There are theory-based studies and demonstration studies on cooperative, competitive, and individualistic efforts. The theory-based studies tend to be carefully controlled laboratory or field experiments with high internal validity, random assignment of participants to conditions, careful operationalization of the independent variable, and measurement of the dependent variables with instruments both reliable and valid. These studies have focused on a wide variety of dependent variables. Theory-based studies tend to focus on internal validity. Fifty-one percent of the studies randomly assigned participants to conditions, clearly defined control conditions, controlled for an experimenter effect, and controlled for a curriculum effect (i.e., the same curricular materials were used in all conditions), and verified the successful implementation of the independent variable. There are problems, however, with theoretical studies. Many of the studies, for example, were conducted in social psychology laboratories using college students as participants. Such studies tend to lack credibility with many practitioners because, although they clarify the power of cooperative efforts, they do not demonstrate that cooperative learning could work in the "real world."

The demonstration literature is made up of field experiments, field quasi-experiments, and correlational studies, which demonstrate that cooperative efforts are effective in real-life settings such as schools, businesses, hospitals, and airplane cockpits. Most of these studies were conducted to evaluate a program without considering the potential theoretical relevance of the results. Demonstration studies tend to focus on external validity. The demonstration studies may be grouped into four categories:

Summative Evaluations

By far the largest category of demonstration studies is straightforward summative evaluations in which the central question is whether a particular cooperative, competitive, or individualistic program produces beneficial results. In education, the comparison is typically between a cooperative learning method and "traditional" classroom learning. The Johns Hopkins research on specific cooperative learning programs (Teams-Games-Tournaments [DeVries & Edwards, 1974], Student Team Achievement Divisions [Slavin, 1980], Team-Assisted Individualization [Slavin, Leavey, & Madden, 1982], and Cooperative Integrated Reading and Composition Program [Stevens, Madden, Slavin, & Farnish, 1987]) are examples. They tended to focus on achievement on lower-level learning tasks in actual classes for long periods of time. The reviews of these studies (Slavin, 1983; D. W. Johnson & R. Johnson, 2002) are organized around a particular instructional method, not a particular skill or knowledge to be learned. This serves the advocates of the method, but users of cooperative learning may not be so concerned, for example, with whether STAD works or does not work, but instead would like to know the best procedures for maximizing learning or higher-level reasoning. While these evaluation studies are of interest, the information value of their conclusions tends to be limited to the specific program evaluated.

Comparative Summative Evaluations

Less research attention has been devoted to the comparative question of which of two or more cooperative learning methods produces the most beneficial effects when compared on the same criterion measures. In education, for example, the jigsaw method might be compared with team assisted-individualization. There is an inherent problem with such studies, as it is difficult if not impossible to tell if both methods have been implemented at the same strength. The results can be inadvertently biased if one method is carefully implemented at full strength, while the other method is loosely implemented at partial strength.

Formative Evaluations

Very little research on how a cooperative, competitive, or individualistic program could be improved makes its way into the literature. Formative evaluations are aimed at improving ongoing implementations. The critical incident method seems well suited to the diagnosis of training deficiencies or unintended consequences, as does a combination of surveys with follow-up interviews of a representative subsample of respondents.

Survey Studies

A few researchers have conducted large-scale surveys of the impact of cooperative, competitive, and individualistic efforts (D. W. Johnson & R. Johnson, 1991). These studies have (1) correlated attitudes toward cooperative, competitive, and individualistic efforts with such variables as perceived social support, self-esteem, and attitudes toward the task and (2) compared the responses of individuals in high-use settings (where the type of social interdependence was frequently used) with the responses of individuals in low-use settings on a number of climate variables (e.g., D. W. Johnson, R. Johnson, & Anderson, 1983; D. W. Johnson & R. Johnson, 1983; D. W. Johnson, R. Johnson, Buckman, & Richards, 1986). These studies provide interesting data about the long-term impact of cooperative efforts on a variety of attitudinal and learning climate outcomes.

Demonstration studies have both weaknesses and strengths. First, like all case studies, demonstration studies simply indicate that a certain method worked at that time in those circumstances. Second, demonstration studies are always in danger of being biased because researchers are typically evaluating programs which they have developed themselves and in which they have a professional and sometimes financial stake. Reviews of demonstration studies, furthermore, suffer the same limitation; that is, reviews are often conducted by the researchers who invented the programs. The third problem associated with demonstration studies is that they may evaluate a cluster of procedures in a complex intervention, and some of these procedures may not be cooperative. The "cooperative method" ostensibly being evaluated may be only one element of a broader educational package, and, therefore, cooperative learning may be confounded with other variables. The original jigsaw procedure (Aronson, Blaney, Sikes, Stephan, & Snapp, 1978), for example, is a combination of resource interdependence (cooperative) and individual reward structure (individualistic). Teams-Games-Tournaments (DeVries & Edwards, 1974) and Student-Teams-Achievement-Divisions (Slavin, 1980) are mixtures of cooperation and intergroup competition. Team-Assisted-Individualization (Slavin, Leavey, & Madden, 1982) is a mixture of individualistic and cooperative learning.

It is difficult to interpret the results of studies evaluating the effectiveness of such mixtures because it is impossible to know which elements contributed to which part of the found effects. A fourth problem with demonstration studies is that they often lack methodological rigor, focusing far more on external validity (such as length of study) than on internal validity (such as experimental control). In many demonstration studies, the comparison has been with an ambiguous and unknown "traditional classroom learning." When differences are found in these cases, it is not clear what has been compared with what. The lack of methodological quality creates doubts as to the value of the results. Finally, most demonstration studies have been conducted in elementary schools. This limits their relevance.

Demonstration studies have at least three strengths. First, there is a clear value to demonstration studies when their results are viewed in combination with more controlled experimental studies. When the results of the demonstration studies agree with and support the results of the theoretical studies, the demonstration studies strengthen the validity and credibility of the theory. Second, demonstration studies provide a model for practitioners who wish to implement identical programs. Third, the high external validity of demonstration studies gives their results high credibility to practitioners.

We turn now to a more explicit discussion of one aspect of the relationship between program evaluation and social psychology. Specifically, we detail seven ways in which systematic evaluation of social interdependence practices has made important contributions to social interdependence theory.

Contributions of Evaluation Studies to Social Interdependence Theory

There is a two-way relationship between theory and practice. Validated theory guides the development of procedures to use in practical, applied situations, while practice can reveal inadequacies in or unanticipated consequences of the theory, thereby leading to its modification and refinement (which requires new research studies to validate the changes). More specifically, theory is primarily induced, modified, and refined from research results. Theory is general and, therefore, does not specify any particular actions in a given situation. Theory is used as the guide for deriving operational procedures. Practice, on the other hand, is deductive. Concrete practical procedures are deduced from theories. There should therefore be a close relationship between theorists and practitioners, but Sternberg and Lyon (2002) note that the culture of theoretical research seems to be divorcing itself from practical application, while the culture of research and evaluation in practical settings seems to be divorcing itself from theory.

Social interdependence theory is an example of how psychological theorizing and research have resulted in valuable practical applications and how theory, research, and practice interact in ways that enhance all three. The role of systematically evaluated practice has been somewhat neglected in discussions of the relationships among theory, research, and practice. Yet, evaluations of the diverse applications of social interdependence theory (most notably in education and business) have had profound effects on the theory and related research. Among other benefits, the evaluations have clarified the theory's concepts, provided a rationale for implementation, illuminated the mediating and moderating variables, expanded the dependent variables included in the theory, expanded the breadth and scope of the theory, provided external validity, and expanded the awareness of and confidence in the theory.

Clarity of Concepts

In operationalizing cooperative, competitive, and individualistic learning, the rules of correspondence between the theoretical concepts and the operational definitions clarify the adequacy of the conceptual definitions. Evaluation studies, which focus on the effectiveness of the operational definitions, tend to bring more clarity to the theoretical concepts. The operationalization of cooperative learning by so many different teachers, in so many different subject areas and settings, in preschool through adult education, with so many varied tasks and students, and in so many different countries and cultures, provides considerable evidence as to the quality of Deutsch's original conceptual definitions. The correspondence between Deutsch's (1949) theoretical definitions and the practical procedures highlights a major strength of social interdependence theory. It is noteworthy that after all the research on social interdependence and all the applications, the original definitions have not been revised or modified.

Rationale for Implementation

Operationalizing cooperative, competitive, and individualistic learning is not enough. Schools must actually implement them if their effectiveness is to be determined. In order for educators to be persuaded to implement cooperative learning, they must believe that it will be effective. This is not always easy. In the 1960s and 1970s, there was considerable cultural resistance to the use of cooperative learning due to the widespread beliefs in (1) Social Darwinism and its mistaken belief that competition was vital for the "survival of the fittest" and (2) operant conditioning and behavior modification, which emphasized the value of individualistic efforts. In order to provide a persuasive rationale for the use of cooperation, a number of comprehensive reviews of the research were conducted to organize the existing research and focus attention on the variety of the dependent variables investigated (D. W. Johnson, 1970; D. W. Johnson & R. Johnson, 1974, 1978; Johnson, Maruyama, Johnson, Nelson, & Skon, 1981; D. W. Johnson, R. Johnson, & Maruyama, 1983). These reviews tended to move the debate about the efficacy of cooperation from an ideological focus to an empirical question. In addition, they stimulated research in actual classrooms and business settings (as opposed to psychological laboratories).

Mediating and Moderating Variables

Evaluation studies can focus attention on the variables that mediate and moderate the effectiveness of cooperative, competitive, and individualistic learning. The need to increase the effectiveness of cooperative learning in dealing with a variety of educational issues such as increasing achievement, improving relationships among diverse peers, and improving self-esteem led to the examination of the internal dynamics of cooperation and the variables that mediated its effectiveness. The more the internal dynamics of cooperation are understood, the more effectively cooperative learning may be implemented. In identifying the variables that mediate cooperation's effectiveness, the theory is also extended and enhanced. The five basic elements of effective cooperation (positive interdependence, individual accountability, promotive interaction, social skills, and group processing) (D. W. Johnson & R. Johnson, 1989) were identified as the result of the efforts to understand the internal dynamics of cooperation so that it could be more effectively implemented. These mediating and moderating variables were used and refined to structure cooperative learning more effectively, solve problems students had in working together, and adapt cooperative learning to different student populations, subject areas, and conditions. Subsequently, the theory has been modified to include all five variables.

Evaluation studies of the implementation of cooperative learning have led to the expansion of the concept of positive interdependence. Lewin and Deutsch viewed interdependence as existing among individuals' goals (which individuals are committed to achieve). The day-to-day use of cooperation in settings (such as schools and businesses) in which goals were imposed revealed that in many cases, simply presenting mutual goals did not in and of itself create a perception of positive interdependence. Positive goal interdependence was supplemented and strengthened by inventive practitioners by giving rewards for group as well as individual performance, assigning group roles, dividing resources among group members, assigning each group a specific work space, and having groups develop their own name and logo. The theoretical distinctions among outcome (goals and rewards), means (roles, resources, task), and boundary (identity, environmental, outside enemy) interdependence resulted.

Social interdependence theory posits that when group members are committed to their mutual goals, responsibility forces exist which ensure that all members do their fair share of the work. The day-to-day use of cooperative learning revealed that when students are not committed to the imposed learning goals and they feel relatively anonymous, they may engage in social loafing. The importance of clear individual accountability was thus highlighted, and an important moderator was identified. Finding new ways to make each group member individually accountable for their fair share of the work strengthened the responsibility forces generated in cooperative efforts.

Social interdependence originally assumed that group members would have the necessary social skills (communication, decision making, leadership, conflict resolution skills) needed to work effectively with each other (D. W. Johnson, 2009; D. W. Johnson & F. Johnson, 2009). The day-to-day use of cooperative learning revealed that many students had very few social skills. Teachers, therefore, had to incorporate the teaching of social skills into their use of cooperative learning. Correspondingly, the theory had to be modified to take into account the necessary condition of having socially skilled group members (as part of promotive interaction).

In order continuously to improve the effectiveness of cooperative groups, it is necessary to periodically examine the processes being used to achieve the group's goals. Social interdependence theory did not discuss this issue, but practitioners highlighted the need for structured group processing. Group members discuss how well they are achieving their goals and maintaining effective working relationships, thereby identifying and solving problems in working together. This is an important addition to the nature of promotive interaction.

Expansion of Dependent Variables

The number of dependent variables included in social interdependence theory was expanded dramatically by evaluation studies of cooperative learning. Cooperative learning was proposed as a way not only to increase academic achievement, but also to solve certain social problems. One such social problem is the creation of positive relationships among students from different ethnic groups, cultural backgrounds, and handicapping conditions. Theoretically, cooperative experiences were seen as vital to building positive relationships among diverse individuals. It was only when cooperation was implemented and evaluation studies were conducted that the validity of that proposition was established (D. W. Johnson, R. Johnson, & Maruyama, 1983). Another social problem is the reduction of antisocial behavior, such as delinquency, drug abuse, sexual harassment, and bullying. In looking for ways to reduce such antisocial behaviors and increase prosocial behaviors, evaluation studies were conducted on cooperative learning that not only demonstrated reductions of antisocial behavior and increases in prosocial behavior, but also the development of related variables such as perspective-taking and empathy (D. W. Johnson & R. Johnson, 1989, 2005a). A number of other social problems have likewise been studied in actual implementations of cooperative learning (such as self-esteem, identity formation, social support, healthy socialization). Striving to solve practical problems through cooperative learning has considerably expanded the breadth and scope of social interdependence theory.

Evaluating the impact of cooperative learning on the solving of social problems has also linked social interdependence theory with other theories. Documenting the impact of cooperative and competitive experiences on students' self-esteem, for example, has linked social interdependence theory with a number of theories, such as attribution theory and social comparison theory.

Expansion of Breadth and Scope of Theory

The hundreds of evaluation studies expanded the breadth and scope of social interdependence theory. The application of social interdependence theory in education and business resulted in numerous evaluation studies using new dependent variables that extended the theory. One example involves the values inherent in social interdependence. While the laboratory research on social interdependence did not consider values as a dependent variable of interest, the implementation of cooperative, competitive, and individualistic learning revealed that each had inherent value systems (D. W. Johnson & R. Johnson, 1994, 2000). The values inherently taught by *cooperative efforts* include commitment to own and others' success and well-being, commitment to the common good, and the view that facilitating and promoting the success of others is a natural way of life. Engaging in *competitive efforts* inherently teaches the values of getting more than others, beating and defeating others, the importance of winning, and the idea that opposing and obstructing the success of others is a natural way of life. The values inherently taught by *individualistic experiences* are commitment to one's own self-interest and view of other peoples' well-being as irrelevant. Schools inculcate numerous values in students, and the instructional methods used influence the values students have developed.

Another example involves the implementation of cooperative learning focused attention on predispositions for cooperation and competition (D. W. Johnson & R. Johnson, 1991). In educational situations, some students seemed more predisposed toward cooperation, and other students seemed more comfortable with competition. Theoretically, cooperation and competition are conceptualized as opposite ends of a single continuum. Yet predisposition toward engaging in cooperation or in competition seems to be somewhat independent of each other (D. W. Johnson & Norem-Heibensen,

1977). Since both cooperative and competitive situations involve interaction with other people, it may be assumed that a person who is high on both will be a highly social person who likes to interact with others in a variety of ways, while a person who is low on both will generally be a social isolate who wishes to avoid other people no matter what the situation.

A further example is that the implementation of cooperative learning has focused attention on the relationship between cooperation and conflict. Social interdependence theorists note that both positive and negative interdependence create conflict among individuals (Deutsch, 1973; D. W. Johnson & R. Johnson, 2005b, 2007; Tjosvold, 1998). In cooperative situations, conflicts occur over how best to achieve mutual goals. In competitive situations, conflict occurs over who will win and who will lose. Two of the conflict resolution programs implemented in schools to teach students how to manage conflicts constructively are (1) the Teaching Students to Be Peacemakers Program in which students are taught how to resolve conflicts of interests constructively by engaging in integrative negotiations and peer mediation (D. W. Johnson & R. Johnson, 2003b, 2005b) and (2) the Academic Controversy Program in which students are taught how to intellectually challenge each other's ideas, reasoning, and conclusions (D. W. Johnson & R. Johnson, 2000b, 2003, 2004c, 2007). The research on both programs indicates that conflicts which occur within the context of positive (as opposed to negative) interdependence may result in a wide variety of positive outcomes (such as higher achievement, more frequent use of higher-level reasoning, more accurate perspective taking, more integrative agreements, greater liking for each other, and more positive attitudes toward conflict). These findings considerably strengthen the relationship between social interdependence theory and constructive conflict resolution.

External Validity

The evaluation studies of the implementation of cooperative learning have given social interdependence theory considerable external validity. The research on social interdependence has a generalizability rarely found in the social sciences. The more variations in places, people, and procedures the research can withstand and still yield the same findings, the more externally valid the conclusions. The research has been conducted over 12 decades by many different researchers with markedly different theoretical, methodological, and practical orientations working in different settings (e.g., educational, business, and social service organizations). A wide variety of research tasks, ways of structuring social interdependence, and measures of the dependent variables have been used. Participants in the studies varied from ages 3 to postcollege adults and have varied in economic class, age, sex, nationality, and cultural background. The studies were conducted with different durations lasting from one session to 100 sessions or more.

Research on social interdependence has been conducted in numerous cultures in North America (with Caucasian, Black American, Native American, and Hispanic populations) and countries from North, Central, and South America, Europe, the Middle East, Asia, the Pacific Rim, and Africa. The diversity of these studies gives social interdependence theorywide generalizability and considerable external validity.

Awareness of and Confidence in Theory

Drawing on the advances already described, the worldwide use of cooperative learning has spread an awareness of social interdependence theory far beyond the social psychology community. The confidence social psychologists have in social interdependence theory is strengthened by the variety of research methods used in the evaluation studies (such as observations, interviews, content analysis, and surveys) that are nonexistent or of very limited duration in the laboratory. Confidence in the theory is also increased by the generalizability of the research.

Program evaluation has helped to clarify and affirm the conceptual aspects of the theory so that a more universal language of social interdependence may be used. Convincing, positive evaluation results have also led to increased confidence in the value of social interdependence practices. Continued evaluation of such practices in different settings, with different groups of people, and different kinds of outcomes, has enhanced understanding of the nuances of social interdependence theory, while illustrating its overall value.

Importance of Implementation and Evaluation

Thus, in the interrelationships among social interdependence theory, research, and practice, carefully evaluated practice may be the most powerful link in the chain. There is nothing so important to a good theory as the convincing demonstration of its application in an effective practice.

Having examined some of the specific ways in which evaluation has contributed to the explication and refinement of social interdependence theory generally, and cooperative learning practices specifically, we now briefly examine selected findings from related research areas. These may have the potential to provide useful guidance for future evaluation practice.

Integrative Negotiations and Peer Mediation

Research areas related to social interdependence theory include constructive controversy (D. W. Johnson & R. Johnson, 1979, 1989, 1995, 2003b) and integrative negotiation. Like the more general social interdependence theory, both areas are concerned with the conditions needed to achieve cooperation and agreement among parties who have competing interests. We now examine research in the area of integrative negotiation, including the role of evaluation in the modification of theory.

Conflicts of interests exist when the actions of one person, in attempting to maximize his or her wants and benefits, prevents, blocks, or interferes with another person maximizing his or her wants and benefits (Deutsch, 1973). The Teaching Students to Be Peacemakers Program began in the 1960s (D. W. Johnson & R. Johnson, 2005b) to teach students how to engage in problem-solving negotiations and mediate their schoolmates' conflicts. When faced with a conflict of interests, a common form of conflict resolution is negotiation. *Negotiation* is a process by which persons who have shared and opposed interests, and want to come to an agreement, try to work out a settlement (D. W. Johnson & R. Johnson, 1978). Broadly, there are two approaches to negotiation: *distributive* (where the goal is to make an agreement more favorable to oneself than to the other negotiators) and *integrative* (where the goal is to make an agreement that benefits everyone involved). Of the empirical studies that have been conducted on negotiations, almost all focus on distributive negotiations (Bazerman, Curhan, Moore, & Valley, 2000). Comparatively few studies have been conducted on integrative negotiations.

In ongoing relationships, distributive negotiations tend to result in destructive outcomes, and integrative negotiations tend to lead to constructive outcomes. The steps in using problem-solving negotiations are: (1) describing what you want, (2) describing how you feel, (3) describing the reasons for your wants and feelings, (4) taking the other's perspective and summarizing your understanding of what the other person wants, how the other person feels, and the reasons underlying both, (5) inventing three optional plans to resolve the conflict that maximizes joint benefits, and (6) choosing one and formalizing the agreement with a hand shake (D. W. Johnson & R. Johnson, 2005b).

When students are unable to negotiate a resolution to their conflict, they may request help from a mediator. A *mediator* is a neutral person who helps two or more people resolve their conflict, usually by negotiating an integrative agreement. There are four steps in mediating a conflict: (1) ending hostilities, (2) ensuring disputants are committed to the mediation process, (3) helping disputants successfully negotiate with each other, and (4) formalizing the agreement (D. W. Johnson & R. Johnson, 2005b).

Each day the teacher selects two class members to serve as official mediators. Any conflicts students cannot resolve themselves are referred to the mediators. The mediators wear official T-shirts, patrol the playground and lunchroom, and are available to mediate any conflicts that occur in the classroom or school. The role of mediator is rotated so that all students in the class or school serve as mediators an equal amount of time. Initially, students mediate in pairs. This ensures that shy or less verbal students get the same amount of experience as more extroverted and verbally fluent students.

We and our colleagues have conducted over 16 evaluations of the effectiveness of the Peacemaker Program in eight different schools in two different countries (D. W. Johnson & R. Johnson, 2005b). Students involved were from kindergarten through ninth grades. The studies were conducted in rural, suburban, and urban settings. The benefits of teaching students the problem-solving negotiation and the peer mediation procedures are as follows (see Table 11.2 for a summary).

First, students and faculty tend to develop a shared understanding of how conflicts should be managed and a common vocabulary to discuss conflicts. Second, students tend to learn the negotiation and mediation procedures (effect size = 2.25), retain their knowledge throughout the school year and into the following year (effect size = 3.34), apply the procedures to their and other people's conflicts (effect size = 2.16), transfer the procedures to nonclassroom settings such as the playground and lunchroom, transfer the procedures to nonschool settings such as the home, and engage in problem solving rather than win-lose negotiations. Third, when students were involved in conflicts, trained students used more constructive strategies

TABLE 11.2. Meta-Analysis of Peacemaker Studies: Mean Effect Sizes

Dependent variable	Mean	Standard deviation	Number of effects
Academic achievement	0.88	0.09	5
Academic retention	0.70	0.31	4
Learned procedure	2.25	1.98	13
Learned procedure—retention	3.34	4.16	9
Applied procedure	2.16	1.31	4
Application—retention	0.46	0.16	3
Strategy constructiveness	1.60	1.70	21
Constructiveness—retention	1.10	0.53	10
Strategy two-concerns	1.10	0.46	5
Two-concerns—retention	0.45	0.20	2
Integrative negotiation	0.98	0.36	5
Positive attitude	1.07	0.25	5
Negative attitude	−0.61	0.37	2
Quality of solutions	0.73	0	1

Note. From D. W. Johnson and R. Johnson (2000c). Reprinted with permission from the authors.

(effect size = 1.60) such as integrative negotiations (effect size = 0.98) than did untrained students. Fourth, students' attitudes toward conflict tend to became more positive (effect size = 1.07). Students learned to view conflicts as potentially positive, and faculty and parents viewed the conflict training as constructive and helpful. Fifth, students tend to resolve their conflicts without the involvement of faculty and administrators. The number of discipline problems that teachers have to deal with decreased by about 60%, and referrals to administrators dropped about 90%. Sixth, the conflict resolution procedures tend to enhance the basic values of the classroom and school. Seventh, students generally like to engage in the procedures. A teacher states, "They never refuse to negotiate or mediate. When there's a conflict and you say it's time for conflict resolution, you never have either one say I won't do it. There are no refusals." Finally, when integrated into academic units, the conflict resolution training tends to increase academic achievement and long-term retention of the academic material (effect sizes = 0.88 and 0.70, respectively). Academic units, especially in subject areas such as literature and history, provide a setting to understand conflicts, practice how to resolve them, and use them to gain insight into the material being studied.

All of the research studies conducted to validate the theory of integrative negotiations have been field evaluations. They provide high external validity to the theory. They are some of the first studies to test a complete integrative negotiations procedure (as opposed to focusing on integrative agreements), thus providing considerable clarity as to the nature of integrative negotiations. The validation of the procedure increases the confidence social psychologists have in the theory. The number of dependent variables has expanded the breadth and scope of the theory. This is another example of how evaluations of theoretically based implementations can contribute to the theory and to the field of social psychology as a whole.

Meta-Analysis for Program and Policy Evaluations

It was not any one evaluation study that influenced social interdependence theory. Rather, it was the collective impact of hundreds of evaluation studies. The procedure through which this influence was exerted was meta-analysis. While every single evaluation study conducted has merit and is of interest, when numerous evaluations of an intervention have been conducted, a meta-analysis gives a very powerful overview of the effectiveness of the program or policy. *Meta-analysis* is a method of statistically combining the results of a set of independent studies that test the same hypothesis and using inferential statistics to draw conclusions about the overall result of the studies (Cooper & Hedges, 1994). The meta-analysis process basically consists of a literature search and the calculation of effect sizes. Meta-analysis is an important but still underutilized tool of program and policy evaluation (Johnson & Johnson, 1985).

This chapter summarizes the results of two such meta-analyses aimed at program evaluation (cooperative learning and integrative negotiations). The results of these studies provide important information about specific programs and practices rooted in social interdependence theory. It is also important to note that the results of meta-analytic studies can also be used to inform *policy* in a particular area. We use a particular education policy decision to illustrate.

In the early 2000s, the Florida State Department of Education wanted to know which types of cooperative learning should be recommended for use by Florida teachers. It commissioned a meta-analysis to determine the relative efficacy of the various methods of cooperative learning so that a recommendation could be made (D. W. Johnson & R. Johnson, 2002). An extensive search found 164 studies investigating eight cooperative learning methods. The studies yielded 194 independent effect sizes representing academic achievement. All eight cooperative learning methods had a significant positive impact on student achievement. When the impact of cooperative learning was compared with competitive learning, Learning Together (LT) promoted the greatest effect on achievement, followed by Academic Controversy (AC), Student-Team-Achievement-Divisions (STAD), Teams-Games-Tournaments (TGT), Group Investigation (GI), Jigsaw, Teams-Assisted-Individualization (TAI), and finally Cooperative Integrated Reading and Composition (CIRC). When the impact of cooperative lessons was compared with individualistic learning, LT promoted the greatest effect, followed by AC, GI, TGT, TAI, STAD, Jigsaw, and CIRC. The consistency of the results and the diversity of the cooperative learning methods provide strong validation for the effectiveness of cooperative learning and gave the Florida State Department of Education some guidance in its policy efforts regarding cooperative learning.

Social Interdependence Theory and Program/Policy Evaluation

Much of our discussion thus far has focused on the ways systematic evaluation of various cooperative practices has helped to modify and enhance social interdependence theory. That is one part of the interrelationship between social psychology and program evaluation. In our final section, we highlight the other side of the relationship. That is, we examine some of the ways in which social psychology and, more specifically, social interdependence theory can contribute to program evaluation.

Evaluating a program or a policy is typically a cooperative endeavor among the staff conducting the program, the participants in the program, the staff conducting the evaluation, and other stakeholders (King & Stevahn, 2002). For the evaluation to be conducted and to be most successful, program and evaluation staffs need to develop clear, positive goal interdependence, mutual goals that they are all committed to achieving. Positive goal interdependence also needs to be developed between the evaluation staff and the participants in the program and other stakeholders. Social interdependence theory provides a normative theory that can guide the building of productive relationships between the evaluators and the program staff, the participants, and other stakeholders.

Once clear mutual goals are established, the internal dynamics of cooperation facilitate the coordination of efforts between the program and evaluation staff. Substitutability results in a coordinated division of labor. Inducibility results in mutual influence and accommodation to each other's goals and motivations. Positive cathexis results in a bonding, liking, and friendship among the staff members. Program and evaluation staffs promote each other's success and feel pride and satisfaction when each is effective. Their coordinated effort to achieve mutual goals results in a positive relationship among program and evaluation staff that promotes a more effective evaluation of the program.

There are severe consequences for the quality of the evaluation if evaluation and program staffs develop negative goal interdependence—that is, compete with each other. Negative goal interdependence leads to nonsubstitutability, resistance to each other's influence attempts, negative cathexis to each other's actions, and dislike of each other as persons. Evaluation and program staffs will tend to obstruct and even sabotage each other's efforts as well as feel delight over each other's failures (i.e., "schadenfreude"). It is imperative that the evaluation staff develop a cooperative relationship with the program staff and that there are no competitive feelings between the two groups of professionals.

The better evaluation staff understands social interdependence theory, and the more carefully they structure positive goal interdependence among themselves and the other stakeholders, the more successful their evaluation will be (Stevahn, King, Ghere, & Minnema, 2005a, 2005b). Inevitably, however, conflicts will arise over goals between the program and evaluation staffs. Typically, the program staff wants to maximize the effectiveness and independence of the program, and the evaluation staff wants to maximize the effectiveness of the evaluation. Conflicts arise over these differences in goals, and the staffs may disagree over the best way to achieve mutual goals. How these conflicts are managed greatly influences the success of the evaluation. When conflicts of interest arise between the two staffs, for example, integrative negotiations are required. Stevahn and King (2005) have pointed out the benefits of evaluators using integrative negotiation procedures in their relationship with program staff, participants, and other stakeholders. Integrative negotiation provides a normative theory that can guide evaluators' behavior at critical times in working with the program staff (or participants and other stakeholders).

An evaluation often has several goals, one of which is to contribute to the validation of a theory. Another is to improve the effectiveness of the program (Johnson, 1966a, 1966b; Johnson & Johnson, 1985). To achieve this goal, it is imperative that program staff members feel they "own" the results of the evaluation and are motivated to implement the changes indicated. When a cooperative relationship is established with the program staff, their involvement in the process of planning and conducting the evaluation develops ownership of the results and commitment to implement the changes implied by the evaluation's results (D. W. Johnson & F. Johnson, 2009). There is no way to overemphasize the importance of such involvement.

Finally, cooperative learning, constructive controversy, and the Peacemaker procedures should be used as instructional procedures in evaluation training (Stevahn et al., 2005a, 2005b). Training programs can provide safe places for the rehearsal, reflection, and refinement of these competencies, which are essential for building and maintaining effective working relationships with program personnel, participants, decision making, and other stakeholders while conducting evaluations.

Summary

Cooperative learning demonstrates the ideal relationship among psychological theory, research, and carefully evaluated practice. Social interdependence theory has guided and summarized the research, the research has validated and modified social interdependence theory, and the validated theory has guided the development of operational procedures that educators (and others) can use to structure cooperative learning effectively. Evaluation of cooperative learning practices has revealed inadequacies in social interdependence theory, which has resulted in modification and refinement of the theory and new research studies. While all scientists recognize the relationship between theory and practice, the importance of this relationship is often underestimated, especially the value of field evaluations to the development of the theory.

Social interdependence theory defines the nature of cooperative, competitive, and individualistic situations, the psychological processes that accompany each type of interdependence, the interaction patterns that can be expected in each situation, and the probable outcomes. Hundreds of studies validate social interdependence theory, the majority of which are field evaluations of the relative efficacy of cooperative, competitive, and individualistic situations. Most of these studies have been conducted in educational settings (although many studies are conducted in business and other organizational settings). These evaluational studies have clarified the nature of cooperative, competitive, and individualistic concepts, provided a rationale for implementation of cooperative learning, expanded the dependent variables included in the theory and thereby expanded the breadth and scope of social interdependence theory, illuminated the variables mediating and moderating the effectiveness of cooperation and competition, provided considerable external validity to the theory, and expanded the awareness of and confidence in social interdependence theory.

When cooperation is structured in an applied situation, conflict is not far behind. When conflicts of interests arise, integrative negotiations are essential for constructive management. The theory of integrative negotiations was summarized, an operational procedure was developed, and students were trained. The resulting field evaluations validated both the procedure and the theory. A meta-analysis was conducted to summarize the findings. Conflict theories such as integrative negotiation supplement social interdependence theory and extend its scope and the effectiveness of its implementation.

It is not any one evaluation study that has had such influence on the theory, but rather the collective whole of hundreds of studies. The procedure through which this influence has taken place is meta-analysis. Meta-analysis has not only been a powerful influence on social interdependence theory, it has also been used to inform policy decisions.

Combining evaluation and social psychology can benefit more than social psychological theory and the selection of programs, policies, and practices based on social psychological theory. Social psychology and evaluation can be brought together for the benefit of evaluation practice. Given the potential for conflict and competition in evaluations, for example, with program staff having different goals than evaluators, there would seem to be a rich future for translating social interdependence theory and related concepts into the details of evaluation training and practice.

This chapter presents evidence that the influence of evaluation studies on social psychological theory is more far reaching and central than is commonly recognized. In the relationships among theory, research, and practice, theory and research create the validated theory necessary for practice, but once practical procedures are operationalized, implemented, and evaluated, it may be practice that has the most powerful effects on future theory and research. A true understanding of a theory may only come from its practical application and evaluation.

REFERENCES

Aronson, E., Blaney, N., Sikes, J., Stephan, C., & Snapp, M. (1978). *The jigsaw classroom.* Beverly Hills, CA: Sage.
Bazerman, M., Curhan, J., Moore, D., & Valley, K. (2000). Negotiation. In J.

Spence, J. Darley, & D. Foss (Eds.), *Annual review of psychology* (Vol. 51, pp. 279–314). Palo Alto, CA: Annual Reviews.

Cooper, H. M., & Hedges, L. V. (1994). *The handbook of research synthesis.* New York: Russell Sage Foundation.

Deutsch, M. (1949). A theory of cooperation and competition. *Human Relations, 2,* 129–152.

Deutsch, M. (1962). Cooperation and trust: Some theoretical notes. In M. R. Jones (Ed.), *Nebraska symposium on motivation* (pp. 275–319). Lincoln: University of Nebraska Press.

Deutsch, M. (1973). *The resolution of conflict.* New Haven, CT: Yale University Press.

DeVries, D., & Edwards, K. (1974). Student teams and learning games: Their effects on cross-race and cross-sex interaction. *Journal of Educational Psychology, 66*(5), 741–749.

Johnson, D. W. (1966a). Freedom school effectiveness: Changes in attitudes of Negro children. *Journal of Applied Behavioral Science, 2*(3), 325–330.

Johnson, D. W. (1966b). Racial attitudes of Negro freedom school participants and Negro and while civil rights participants. *Social Forces, 45*(2), 266–273.

Johnson, D. W. (1970). *Social psychology of education.* New York: Holt, Rinehart & Winston.

Johnson, D. W. (2003). Social interdependence: The interrelationships among theory, research, and practice. *American Psychologist, 58*(11), 931–945.

Johnson, D. W. (2009). *Reaching out: Interpersonal effectiveness and self-actualization* (10th ed.). Boston: Allyn & Bacon.

Johnson, D. W., & Johnson, F. (2009). *Joining together: Group theory and group skills* (10th ed.). Boston: Allyn & Bacon.

Johnson, D. W., & Johnson, R. (1974). Instructional goal structure: Cooperative, competitive, or individualistic. *Review of Educational Research, 44,* 213–240.

Johnson, D. W., & Johnson, R. (1978). Cooperative, competitive, and individualistic learning. *Journal of Research and Development in Education, 12,* 3–15.

Johnson, D. W., & Johnson, R. (1979). Conflict in the classroom: Controversy and learning. *Review of Educational Research, 49,* 51–70.

Johnson, D. W., & Johnson, R. (1983). Social interdependence and perceived academic and personal support in the classroom. *Journal of Social Psychology, 120,* 77–82.

Johnson, D. W., & Johnson, R. (1985). Nutrition education: A model for effectiveness, a synthesis of research. *Journal of Nutrition Education, 17* (Special supplemental issue), S1–S44.

Johnson, D. W., & Johnson, R. (1989). *Cooperation and competition: Theory and research.* Edina, MN: Interaction Book Company.

Johnson, D. W., & Johnson, R. (1991). Cooperative learning and classroom and school climate. In B. Fraser & H. Walberg, *Educational environments: Evaluation, antecedents and consequences* (pp. 55–74). New York: Pergamon Press.

Johnson, D. W., & Johnson, R. (1994). Cooperative learning and American values. *The Cooperative Link, 9*(3), 3–4.

Johnson, D. W., & Johnson, R. (2000a). Cooperative learning, values, and culturally plural classrooms. In M. Leicester, C. Modgill, & S. Modgill (Eds.), *Values, the classroom, and cultural diversity* (pp. 15–28). London: Cassell PLC.

Johnson, D. W., & Johnson, R. (2000b). Civil political discourse in a democracy: The contribution of psychology. *Peace and Conflict: Journal of Peace Psychology, 6*(4), 291–317.

Johnson, D. W., & Johnson, R. (2002). Cooperative learning methods: A meta-analysis. *Journal of Research in Education, 12*(1), 5–14.

Johnson, D. W., & Johnson, R. (2003a). Controversy and peace education. *Journal of Research in Education, 13*(1), 71–91.

Johnson, D. W., & Johnson, R. (2003b). Field testing integrative negotiations. *Peace and Conflict: Journal of Peace Psychology, 9*(1), 39–68.

Johnson, D. W., & Johnson, R. (2005a). New developments in social interdependence theory. *Genetic, Social, and General Psychology Monographs, 131*(4), 285–358.

Johnson, D. W., & Johnson, R. (2005b). *Teaching students to be peacemakers* (4th ed.). Edina, MN: Interaction Book Company.

Johnson, D. W., & Johnson, R. (2005c). Democratic decision making, political discourse, and constructive controversy. *The Cooperative Link, 20*(1), 3.

Johnson, D. W., & Johnson, R. (2007). *Creative controversy: Intellectual challenge in the classroom* (4th ed.). Edina, MN: Interaction Book Company.

Johnson, D. W., Johnson, R., & Anderson, D. (1983). Social interdependence and classroom climate. *Journal of Psychology, 114*, 135–142.

Johnson, D. W., Johnson, R., Buckman, L., & Richards, P. (1986). The effect of prolonged implementation of cooperative learning on social support within the classroom. *Journal of Psychology, 119*, 405–411.

Johnson, D. W., Johnson, R., & Holubec, E. (2008). *Cooperation in the classroom* (7th ed.) Edina, MN: Interaction Book Company.

Johnson, D. W., Johnson, R., & Holubec, E. (2009). *Circles of learning* (6th ed.) Edina, MN: Interaction Book Company.

Johnson, D. W., Johnson, R., & Maruyama, G. (1983). Interdependence and interpersonal attraction among heterogeneous and homogeneous individuals: A theoretical formulation and a meta-analysis of the research. *Review of Educational Research, 53*, 5–54.

Johnson, D. W., Maruyama, G., Johnson, R., Nelson, D., & Skon, L. (1981). Effects of cooperative, competitive, and individualistic goal structures on achievement: A meta-analysis. *Psychological Bulletin, 89*, 47–62.

Johnson, D. W., & Norem-Hebeisen, A. (1977). Attitudes toward interdependence among persons and psychological health. *Psychological Reports, 40*, 843–850.

Johnson, D. W., & Norem-Hebeisen, A. (1981). The relationship between cooperative, competitive, and individualistic attitudes and differentiated aspects of self-esteem. *Journal of Personality, 49*, 415–426.

King, J. A., & Stevahn, L. (2002). Three frameworks for considering evaluator role. In K. E. Ryan & T. A. Schwandt (Eds.), *Exploring evaluator role and identity* (pp. 1–16). Greenwich, CT: Information Age Publishing.

Koffka, K. (1935). *Principles of Gestalt psychology.* New York: Harcourt, Brace.

Lewin, K. (1935). *A dynamic theory of personality.* New York: McGraw Hill.

Mayer, A. (1903). Uber einzel-und gesamtleistung des scholkindes. *Archiv fur die Gesamte Psychologie, 1*, 276–416.

Merton, R. K. (1957). *Social theory and social structure.* New York: Free Press.

Slavin, R. (1980). Cooperative learning. *Review of Educational Research, 50*, 315–342.

Slavin, R. (1983). *Cooperative learning.* New York: Longman.

Slavin, R., Leavey, M., & Madden, N. (1982). *Team-assisted individualization: Mathematics teacher's manual.* Baltimore, MD: Johns Hopkins University, Center for Social Organization of Schools.

Sternberg, R., & Lyon, R. (2002, July/August). Making a difference to education: Will psychology pass up the chance? *Monitor on Psychology, 33*(8), 74–78.

Stevahn, L., & King, J. A. (2005). Managing conflict constructively in program evaluation. *Evaluation, 11*(4), 415–427.

Stevahn, L., King, J. A., Ghere, G., & Minnema, J. (2005a). Establishing essential competencies for program evaluators. *American Journal of Evaluation, 26*(1), 43–59.

Stevahn, L., King, J. A., Ghere, G., & Minnema, J. (2005b). Evaluator competencies in university-base evaluation training programs. *Canadian Journal of Program Evaluation, 20*(2), 101–123.

Stevens, R. J., Madden, N. A., Slavin, R. E., & Farnish, A. M. (1987). Cooperative integrated reading and composition: Two field experiments. *Reading Research Quarterly, 22*(4), 433–454.

Tjosvold, D. (1998). Cooperative and competitive goal approach to conflict: Accomplishments and challenges. *Applied Psychology: An International Review, 47*(3), 285–342.

Triplett, N. (1898). The dynamogenic factors in pacemaking and competition. *American Journal of Psychology, 9*, 507–533.

EDITORS' CONCLUDING COMMENTS
TO CHAPTER 11

To varying degrees, all the contributors to this volume inhabit the intersection between social psychology and evaluation. Still, many lean at least somewhat more in one direction or the other. This point comes into focus with an observation about the previous chapter.

When discussing research on social interdependence, the authors describe different kinds of evaluative studies (demonstration studies), pointing out some of the strengths and weaknesses of each kind. In contrast to theory-based studies, Johnson and colleagues describe demonstration studies as conducted, not to evaluate a theory (or aspects of a theory), but to evaluate a program that may consist of a cluster of practices derived from multiple theories. For Johnson et al., the major problem with this is the inability to tease apart a cluster of "cooperative procedures" in order to say with any degree of confidence "which elements contributed to which part of the found effects" (p. 301). For these authors, an important goal in using evaluation to evaluate social interdependence theory is to clearly explicate and test parts of the theory, moving toward improving and proving the theory.

Consider the sharp contrast to the perspective advanced by Riemer and Bickman (Chapter 4, this volume), who are less interested in the relatively clean tests of any one theory. For Riemer and Bickman, the important question is whether program developers can create a cluster of practices that solve the problem addressed by the program, regardless of the theoretical origins or conceptual purity of the intervention. This comparison highlights an interesting difference between the interests of different researchers at the intersection of social psychology and evaluation.

Some researchers tend to ascribe primacy to the theory that is operationalized in an intervention, viewing evaluation as a tool for testing that theory in real-world contexts that facilitate external validity. In our experience this position is more likely for those who identify more strongly with mainstream social psychology. For others, the specific theory—and indeed the conceptually clean testing of a given theory—is secondary. These researchers give primacy to developing and testing a potentially effective solution to the problem, no matter the theory. In our experience, this position is more likely to be held by those who identify more strongly with evaluation or with a very applied approach to social psychology. Of course, theory-driven evaluation approaches can provide a way of reducing the gulf between these two perspectives. But different perspectives exist nonetheless. Ideally, the best rapprochement may occur if one adopts varying perspectives across studies in a series of investigations, or if the people working in a given topical area (education, the environment, etc.) stake out different but complementary positions.

EDITORS' INTRODUCTORY COMMENTS
TO CHAPTER 12

Johnson, Dove, and Boynton explore the intersection between social psychology and a very specific type of evaluation research—the evaluation of health behavior programs. They point out that health psychology focuses largely on how behavior affects health and illness, and unlike social psychology, historically has predominantly been an applied field. Evaluations of programs designed to change behavior and improve health and well-being are also commonplace in the evaluation literature, often drawing on social psychology theories, principles, and methods. This chapter explores the intersection between social psychology and the evaluation of health psychology programs, and suggests ways to make this intersection more fruitful to both social and health psychologists.

The authors argue that while health psychology has benefited greatly from social psychology theory and research, the influence has been rather unidirectional to date. That is, a number of social psychological theories such as social cognitive theory, the theory of reasoned action, the theory of planned behavior, and the information–motivation–behavioral skills model, among others, have played an important role in the development of health psychology and successful health promotion and disease prevention programs. Johnson and colleagues describe why, in contrast, social psychologists have profited much less than they should have from health behavior research and evaluation. The authors provide compelling arguments for why social psychologists should learn more from the evaluation of health behavior programs, as well as for why good social science takes advantage of the best of both basic and applied research studies. This chapter provides readers with an excellent discussion and clear examples of how the intersection between social psychology and evaluation is important to the future success of both disciplines. It also provides many helpful suggestions for expanding the intersection to better benefit society. As we note in the comments following the chapter, although the chapter focuses on the mutual improvement of social psychology and the evaluation of health behavior programs, the points could be generalized to many other types of programs based on social psychological theory, principles, and research.

CHAPTER 12

On Being Basic and Applied at the Same Time

Intersections between Social and Health Psychology

Blair T. Johnson
Natalie L. Dove
Marcella H. Boynton

Scholars from a host of subfields and backgrounds have brought their experience to bear on the issue of health promotion and change, among them are neuroscientists, public health researchers, clinicians, and social psychologists. Emerging from this multidisciplinary convergence is *health psychology*, a field that focuses on promoting positive health behaviors and preventing negative health behaviors. Understanding health behavior change has become so essential that health psychology has developed from a rarefied specialization into an entire subfield of psychology, complete with its own doctoral degree (Kuhlberg, 2000) and specialized journals (Kaplan, 2007). Traditionally, health psychology is a field defined as including "any aspect of psychology that bears upon the existence of health and illness and the behavior that affects health status" (Rodin & Stone, 1987, pp. 15–16). Because this definition invites contributions from researchers in many psychological subfields, health psychologists frequently find themselves juggling dual identities. One very common pairing combines "social psychology," which has historically been a predominately theoretical field, with "health psychology," which has historically been a predominately applied field.

Just as social psychologists' training informs their approach to understanding health behavior, in turn, what they learn doing health research—

including evaluations of programs related to health behavior—should inform their approach to social psychology. Yet, as we shall see, to date, the influence has been largely unidirectional, with social psychology profiting less than it should from health behavior research and evaluations of health behavior programs. This chapter explores the intersections between social and health psychology. We will examine ways that social psychology as a field can benefit from the experience and knowledge of health psychologists. In our view, applied and basic interests are *not* opposed, as some have argued, but complementary. Basic and applied perspectives, and more specifically, the subfields of social and health psychology, ought to cooperate better than they have to date, and much is potentially lost when they do not. In short, social psychology, as a predominately theoretical field, can profit from a consideration of the real-world implications that health psychology offers, and health psychology, as a predominately applied field, can increasingly profit from a consideration of the theoretical principles that social psychology offers. In this chapter, we consider some social psychological research that has influenced health psychology to date and will discuss ways for social psychology to have an even greater impact on health psychology. We will then consider how health behavior research and evaluation has impacted social psychology and how it can continue to influence this field.

A Bit of Social Psychological History

Many scholars have marked the birth of social psychology as a scientific field in its own right with the publication of Floyd Henry Allport's (1924) seminal volume, *Social Psychology* (cf. Johnson & Nichols, 1998; Post, 1980; Watson & Evans, 1991). The field remained a relatively small discipline for some time afterward, but, like many other sciences, social psychology experienced a huge growth spurt during World War II when policy makers called on social psychologists and their students to develop the means of gauging and improving morale among the Allies, focusing both on civilians and members of armed forces, and reducing morale in Axis nations (Harris, 1986; Johnson & Nichols, 1998). U.S. citizens, for example, needed to maintain high spirits in order to defeat Hitler and his allies by keeping work productivity high and contributing more to war-related campaigns. On the other side of the ocean, social psychologists found the means to gauge morale in enemy nations. For example, social psychologists assessed how residents in these nations reacted to Allied bombings in their neighborhoods and examined whether bombing techniques could be altered in such a way as to demoralize these people, reduce their support for the war, and, better still, lobby their leaders to surrender. If surrender could be encouraged, more lives could be saved (Morale Division, 1946,

1947). Their focus on understanding social behavior aptly equipped social psychologists not only for assessing war-related attitudes, but also potentially for changing them.

In the decades after the war, social psychologists spent much of their efforts attempting to understand the atrocities that became fully known only after Germany's surrender (e.g., Asch, 1952; Milgram, 1963). Despite pointed successes in World War II, the place for social psychologists in the academic enterprise remained minimal until the mid- to late 1950s. Instead, scholars who focused on learning and memory processes held the primary place of prestige in psychology because of the recognition they received for their theoretical tomes (e.g., C. L. Hull, 1943; Spence, 1956), buttressed by clear demonstrations of reinforcement learning curves in rats and pigeons (e.g., Skinner, 1938). Meanwhile, social psychologists were typically considered token members of their departments or curiosities added only to entertain college undergraduates with their lectures about attitudes, social perception, and group processes (Berscheid, 1992). Learning and memory theorists maintained that concepts such as attitudes and social perception were a mere epiphenomenon of behavior. As such, they did not theorize about these constructs, but social psychologists such as Leon Festinger provided compelling theoretical statements about central concepts such as social comparison (1954) and cognitive dissonance (1957). These early theories still form the basis for much of contemporary social and health psychology. In sum, the Zeitgeist of psychology during that time period emphasized theory far more than application, an emphasis that has continued to the present day.

Behavior as Crucial to Health

Health psychology as a field has become increasingly important as scientists, medical professionals, and policy makers have come to a fuller realization that health and illness are more than mere biomedical issues. All concerned realize that contact with viruses and other microorganisms can result in disease, but until the mid-1970s, it was commonly believed that individuals' genetic makeup would guide their patterns of health or illness. In other words, if one's family's genes included heart disease, one would get heart disease. This fated perspective left little room for behavioral contributors to health, and likewise, there was believed to be little need for behavioral intervention. Meanwhile, the leading causes of death shifted substantially in the last 100 years. In 1900, for example, tuberculosis, influenza, and pneumonia were among the leading causes of death. None of these illnesses involves any obvious role for behavior; instead the causative agent was incidental exposure to the germs that spread these diseases. Fortunately, there are now many vaccinations and medications to curb the illnesses that historically posed a major threat to health and well-being, and sanitation in developed nations has also greatly improved.

In the 21st century, in sharp contrast, the leading causes of death in developed nations include cardiovascular disease and various types of cancer. These illnesses have a very distinct behavioral component. Poor eating habits and a lack of exercise contribute substantially to both. Because the types of illnesses that are the leading causes of death in developed nations are largely based on lifestyle choices, most can be prevented. For example, if smokers stop smoking, they can expect longer and healthier lives. If children consume no lead (e.g., from paint), their mental functioning is much higher. If people exercise more and maintain healthier diets, they will have longer, higher quality lives. If people limit their exposure to the sun, they will have less skin cancer. Despite such knowledge, people still smoke tobacco, live in toxic environments, exercise too little, eat fatty foods, and sunbathe excessively. In sum, many people continue behaviors that lead to illnesses such as cardiovascular disease and cancer. Consequently, health psychologists examine what psychological determinants lead to unhealthy behaviors and what techniques may be used to change them. Typically, scholars focus on how knowledge, positive attitudes, skills, and motivation to engage in healthy behavior can be increased, thereby increasing positive health behaviors and decreasing negative health behaviors.

To illustrate this principle more fully, consider the HIV/AIDS pandemic, which has devastated entire nations and drained communities of life and other resources. First, note that because there is no cure for HIV or AIDS once contracted, and no effective vaccine to prevent acquiring HIV, behavior change is currently the only option to prevent its transmission. At its outset, prevention of the spread of HIV was seriously hampered by a lack of understanding of the virus and its transmission routes (Centers for Disease Control, 2007). Twenty-five years later, an enormous amount is known about the prevention of HIV transmission, with the exchange of bodily fluids between individuals as the key vector of transmission. The two primary ways that bodily fluids are exchanged is during unprotected sexual interactions and when hypodermic syringes are shared without first properly cleaning them. Consequently, people need to engage in safe sex, or abstain from sex altogether, if they are to avoid contracting HIV from others, and if they are injection drug users, they either need to refrain from sharing needles or else to clean or use a new syringe each time, safely discarding it afterward. Thus, the behaviors necessary to avoid this deadly and debilitating disease would seem quite easy to perform for most individuals. Nonetheless, HIV continues to spread at an alarming rate. Adding to the complexity of HIV transmission are the new medications available to control HIV. These medications are helping those living with the disease to have longer, more productive, and higher quality lives than they would without the drugs, but high adherence to the medications is crucial and cannot be assumed (e.g., due to difficult schedules or the drugs' side effects). Indeed, behaviorally oriented interventions can improve adherence to these medications, as systematic summative evaluations have shown (Amico, Harman, & Johnson, 2006; De Bruin et al., 2010).

More specifically, although most people now increasingly realize that consistent condom use is the only way to curb sexual transmission of HIV, consistent condom use is far from the norm in most populations. If a sizable majority of people have the requisite knowledge to prevent their seroconversion and still engage in risky behaviors, then clearly there is more to HIV prevention than education alone. In fact, many reviews have demonstrated that information alone is typically insufficient for instigating lasting behavior change. Albarracín et al.'s (2003) meta-analysis of evaluations of HIV prevention campaigns found that interventions that tried simply to persuade audiences without also providing other communication components (e.g., skill building) had, on average, minimal impact on condom use. On the surface, this finding may seem to contradict lay wisdom, which contends that to know better means to do better. Nonetheless, "knowing better" is not as simple as possessing basic knowledge about a given topic. Human beings are motivated by many factors, and these motivations sometimes run directly counter to what one's knowledge base would dictate. Furthermore, the influence of culture, society, and social networks often readily trump a single individual's wisdom. Due to these conflicts of individual knowledge with other drives and social factors, it is often the case that people knowingly make unhealthy and risky decisions. As a consequence, social psychology has much to offer in terms of illuminating and impacting health behaviors.

Because social psychologists commonly focus on attitude and behavior change in other domains, they are well equipped theoretically and methodologically to contribute to health behavior change research. In the remainder of this subsection, we briefly survey social psychological research and theories that are relevant to these concerns. Indeed, social psychologists have examined a myriad of health concerns. One of the fathers of modern social psychology, Kurt Lewin, is often given credit for advancing the mission of social psychology into health-related problems. During World War II, better cuts of meat, rationed for the war effort, were often unavailable to civilians. Lewin examined how to use positive social models to encourage Americans to supplement their diets with greater consumption of organ meats and other "unrestricted meats" (Lewin, 1943; Wansink, 2002). This trend has continued, as more recently, a host of social psychologists have studied health-related issues such as obesity and eating habits (Rodin, 1977; Schachter, 1968), condom use (e.g., Albarracín, Johnson, Fishbein, & Muellerleile, 2001), blood donation (Breckler & Wiggins, 1989; Godin et al., 2005; Pittman, Pallak, Riggs, & Gotay, 1981), cancer screening (Orbell, Hagger, Brown, & Tidy, 2006), smoking (Higgins & Conner, 2003), and exercise (Hagger, 2006; Jessor, Turbin, & Costa, 1998), to name a few. In short, many social psychologists have realized the critical nature of changing health behavior.

A number of social psychologically based theories have already played a role in the development of the field of health psychology, namely, via the development of social cognitive theories of health promotion and change. A number of these theories directly address the issue of health promotion and have been widely applied, including social cognitive theory (Bandura, 1989, 1997), the theory of reasoned action (TRA; Fishbein & Ajzen, 1975), the theory of planned behavior (TPB; Ajzen, 1985), and the information–motivation–behavioral skills (IMB) model (Fisher & Fisher, 1992). Many psychological constructs that are central to health behavior change have been extracted from these theoretical perspectives. First, self-efficacy (Bandura, 1986, 1997), defined as perceptions of control over the environment with respect to behavior, has been linked to many health behaviors (Conner & Norman, 1995). For example, Johnson, Carey, Marsh, Levin, and Scott-Sheldon's (2003) meta-analysis of evaluations of HIV prevention interventions for adolescents showed that condom use increased more to the extent that the interventions trained condom skills, logically increasing the adolescents' efficacy in using them.

Second, the TRA and TPB conceptualize behaviors as driven by deliberative, thoughtful processes, namely, behavioral intentions. In the case of the TRA (Fishbein & Ajzen, 1977), behavioral intentions are influenced by two factors. The first of these factors is attitudes, or a person's evaluations of a behavior. For example, in the case of getting a mammogram, a particular person may feel positively or negatively about that behavior, which then affects how "good" or "bad" that behavior is perceived to be. Behavioral intentions are also driven by subjective norms, which refer to how a person believes that important others would view a particular behavior. If people believe that close others would not want them to perform a specific behavior, it is less likely that they will perform that behavior. In the case of getting a mammogram, the norm may be positive toward being screened (e.g., "Others in my family would like me to get a mammogram"). To the extent that people have positive attitudes and subjective norms about the behavior in question, they will be more likely to intend to perform the behavior.

Ajzen's (1980) TPB adds the construct of perceived behavioral control, similar to Bandura's self-efficacy construct. Perceived behavioral control (PBC) relates to how real or imagined outside factors are *perceived* to affect an individual's ability to perform a given behavior. If a person has a positive attitude toward obtaining a mammogram and believes that close others would like her to obtain one, but has neither medical insurance nor the financial means to pay for the service directly, the behavior is unlikely to be performed because the control over obtaining the mammogram is minimal in that case. The TRA and TPB have been widely applied across health behaviors, and meta-analyses of these studies have provided useful summaries (see also Johnson & Boynton, 2010). Two recent meta-analyses, one on condom use (Albarracín et al., 2001) and another on exercise (Hagger, Chatzisarantis, & Biddle, 2002), have concluded that the TRA and TPB provide good depictions of behavior (for a review of the meta-analytic method, see Johnson & Boynton, 2008).

Combining aspects of the models outlined in the preceding paragraph, the information-motivation-behavioral skills (IMB) model (Fisher & Fisher, 1992) asserts that interventions are most effective when they include (1) information about the health behavior of interest. More specifically, regarding a specific health behavior like condom use, do individuals know that condom use arrests the spread of sexually transmitted infections and HIV? Do they know where condoms are sold? (2) Motivation is a key component. Do individuals personally desire to use a condom? Do they want to take the steps necessary to enact the behavior? (3) Behavioral skills are the final, necessary piece of both the intervention content and the theoretical framework. Do individuals know how to purchase a condom and more importantly, how to use it properly and to negotiate its use with a sexual partner?

Recent meta-analytic work from studies that have evaluated the HIV prevention intervention strategies has provided strong support for the IMB model. Johnson, Carey, Chaudoir, and Reid (2006) reviewed the relatively small literature of studies evaluating interventions for people living with HIV and found that the studies were more successful in increasing condom use if they included all three IMB components. Similarly, Smoak, Scott-Sheldon, Johnson, and Carey (2006) quantitatively reviewed the 100-plus studies that had evaluated HIV prevention intervention strategies designed to impact frequencies of sexual interactions, including number of sexual occasions, number of sexual partners, and sexual activity status. They found that when interventions included information, motivation, *and* behavioral skills, they were more successful at reducing the number of sexual occasions and the number of sexual partners (see also Albarracín et al., 2005). Interestingly, many of the studies included in this review predated the IMB, suggesting that Fisher and Fisher drew from existing, efficacious interventions as they crafted the model. Conversely, many of the more recently conducted studies included interventions that were specifically designed based on the recommendations of the IMB model, suggesting that the IMB model has also informed intervention efforts with increasing facility.

Thus, it is clear that health psychology and public health have profited from the work of scholars who have applied social psychological theory to health behavior. Indeed, some have even encouraged health researchers to become more theoretical (Rothman, 2000), suggesting the field would profit from even more social psychological theory. Health research on behaviors that are co-acted (e.g., condom use, diet) may also profit greatly from incorporating statistical techniques developed by social psychologists to analyze dyadic data structures (Kenny, Kashy, & Cook, 2006).

It is clear that health psychology has benefited enormously from social psychological theory and methods. What of the reverse direction? Has social psychology learned anything from health-related research and evaluations of health behavior interventions? What are the challenges faced by social-health psychologists? In the next section, we discuss what, if anything, social psychology has gleaned from health psychology research, and we provide some recommendations for how social psychology could benefit in the future by borrowing the lessons learned from health psychology.

Why Knowledge Flows Slowly from Health Research to Social Psychology

Unfortunately, in our opinion, to date social psychology has learned little directly from health behavior research. Instead, as we have noted, the pathway has been more from the theoretical side to the applied. As we have argued, it is a worthwhile challenge to apply social psychological theory to "real-world" behaviors. Doing so means maximizing the value social psychology offers to the largest set of possible stakeholders. When researchers publish in journals widely read by policy wonks, their findings have a greater chance at widespread application in particular countries or regions of the world. The problem is that for too long, social psychologists who have moved to publishing their real-world-relevant research in nonsocial psychological journals have rarely returned to social psychology journals in order to tell other social psychologists what they have discovered and how it affects social psychological principles of behavior.

Three interrelated reasons for this pattern seem clear: (1) Academic social psychologists are typically hired and rewarded to do social psychology per se rather than to contribute to other fields. A tenured post and bigger raises are more likely to the extent that an assistant professor contributes basic research in the field's best journals, which, as mentioned, emphasize theoretical content. (2) Social psychologists that move to health psychology or public health research are typically rewarded more for publishing their work in applied outlets than in social psychology outlets per se. These outlets often have much larger audiences than those for social psychologists and have a greater chance of influencing policy because the audiences more often include policy makers. Consequently, the work has a better chance of improving public health. Publishing in prestigious, high-impact applied outlets, in turn, makes it more likely that the research can successfully compete for large external grants. Thus, social-health psychologists are less likely to return to social psychology outlets with their research. And (3), related to the prior two reasons, understandably, those who remain researchers in basic social psychology view those who are not publishing in social psychology journals as producing knowledge that is largely irrelevant to theoretical social psychology (Cialdini, 2009). They may well suspect that, while the research may help improve public health, it is too uncontrolled to have produced valid knowledge that has bearing on key principles of social behavior. The result is an increasing difficulty in changing social psychology per se. These pressures imply that social psychology journals will continue a spiral into increasingly narrow slices of reality defined as basic science. Nonetheless, just as World War II moved social psychologists into applied research, larger structural changes can impact whole scientific fields. NIH's recent emphasis on translation of basic research into applications (Sussman, Valente, Rohrbach, Skara, & Pentz, 2006) promises to move some mainstream social psychologists into applied research.

What Should Social Psychology Learn from Health Behavior Change Research?

Health behavior research can inform many aspects of social behavior that have to date largely eluded social psychologists, including both methodological and substantive contributions. First, for better or worse, the bulk of social psychological research has focused on a convenience sample, the college undergraduate, a sample that often poorly matches much of society (Sears, 1986). Social psychological research is often greeted skeptically by outsiders who trivialize the samples it uses to make its points. In contrast, health-behavior change trials routinely get into the field and sample people who are actually at risk for obtaining a certain condition, or who already have it, in order to evaluate an intervention with controlled or relatively controlled trials. This research may not rest on truly representative samples from defined populations (though some does), but at least it rests on samples that are very relevant for the public health problem under consideration. Consequently, the research is received by outside audiences with greater respect. Although the reputation of social psychological research would rise if its sampling were more representative in scope, it would be foolish to conclude that this research is without merit. For example, basic psychological research with undergraduates is what started Kahneman and Tversky (e.g., 1979) on the road to international acclaim with their prospect theory, which has been shown to have numerous useful applications. Indeed, some of the basic principles of prospect theory have even been shown to apply to our primate cousins (e.g., Chen, Lakshminaryanan, & Santos, 2006). Recently, these findings have found their way into larger policies that, among other benefits, help people to save for retirement (Leonhardt, 2007).

Its theoretical and applied implications make prospect theory a modern success, both for scientific and the public good.

Second, although social psychology has made numerous forays into the nature of private versus public behavior, including phenomena such as the social facilitation effect (e.g., Zajonc, 1965), deindividuation (Zimbardo, 1970), and the bystander effect (Latané & Darley, 1970), it has paid less attention to the behaviors that are routinely performed in private, such as sexual interactions. The HIV epidemic forced a focus on sexual risk outcomes as crucial to health research. Research on sexual risk outcomes promises to contribute rich knowledge to a behavior that is fundamental to evolutionary psychology and biology, among other fields. The number of relevant studies that have been conducted around the world over the last 25 years has become truly impressive and touch on cultures and contexts that basic social psychology has rarely examined. Future meta-analyses of such literatures will have the potential to address a number of fascinating questions: Does private behavior differ across diverse cultures and times? Is it easier to change sexual risk patterns in developed societies than in non-developed societies? In the West versus the East? In societies dominated by polygyny versus monogamy? It could well be that what functions as "private" behavior in one culture is not so private in another, with implications for how the behaviors function and are understood.

Third, in contrast to most social psychological laboratory research, where measured behaviors tend to be of little applied interest, real-world measures such as those used by health psychologists are often instrumental to functioning. Indeed, they often relate to mortality or quality of life. More importantly, whereas social psychologists nearly always take measures in a laboratory setting at one thin slice in time, health researchers have been obtaining measures 3, 6, even 60 months after an intervention's end. In the areas of obesity reduction and smoking cessation, much progress has been made in terms of examining how to prevent relapses and maintain healthy behavior (for a review, see Rothman & Salovey, 2007). Given the tendency for behavior changes to abate, evidence that behavior change can be demonstrated so long after an intervention's implementation is truly noteworthy and would be relevant to social psychological research in the areas of consumer behavior and prejudice reduction, to name but a few. In sum, although social psychological theory has addressed maintenance of behavior change in the form of habit (e.g., Neal, Wood, & Quinn, 2006; Ouellette & Wood, 1998) and attitude change (e.g., Johnson, Maio, & Smith-McLallen, 2005), social psychology research on these topics has seldom examined long-term change such as is the goal of many evaluations of health behavior programs.

Fourth, social psychology could benefit from expanding its theory and research on social structure and culture—considerations that are already influencing health research (Rothman & Salovey, 2007). Individuals in HIV prevention and other types of health promotion trials typically experience health disparities, being at high risk for other health problems, such as obesity or illicit drug use. They generally are economically challenged, residing in low-income neighborhoods as members of subordinate groups within the locale and society at large (Kelly, 1995). Affected disproportionately by the HIV pandemic, members of these groups share many myths about HIV, such that it has been perpetrated by the dominant group in an effort to eliminate their own group (e.g., Crocker, Luhtanen, Broadnax, & Blaine, 1999). Blacks often are suspect of government-sponsored condom distribution programs and distrust whites generally (e.g., Dovidio et al., 2008). Relatedly, blacks tend to distrust their health care providers more than whites do (Doescher, Saver, Franks, & Fiscella, 2000). Quite possibly, distrust results from the fact that three-quarters of blacks' interactions with health care providers are interethnic encounters (Chen, Fryer, Phillips, Wilson, & Pathman, 2005). The distrust may also be related to the fact that physicians perceive their black patients as less intelligent, less likely to conform to the physician's instructions, and more prone to drug abuse (Van Ryn & Burke, 2000). Physicians in an experimental study were less likely to give referrals for supplementary testing to blacks than to whites (Schulman et al., 1999), and patients belonging to minority groups were also less likely to be given sufficient information or to arouse empathic reactions from their physicians than whites (Ferguson & Candib, 2002). In addition, HIV-infected persons belonging to ethnic minorities receive less care than do others (Cunningham, Hays, & Duan, 2005).

Potentially compounding these problems, most members of high-risk groups see the media as regularly portraying their fellow group members as villainous and the dominant group members as heroic. In short, most groups at high risk for HIV and other health problems live without empowerment within their social milieu. Intensive HIV prevention and other health promotion efforts often do empower their recipients to live safer lives, but once the intervention ends, these individuals encounter an unfriendly environment that challenges their new, health-promoting behaviors. Safety and survival often outrank concern for acquiring (or transmitting) HIV. Such factors are likely to have an important impact on the sustainability of behavior change.

An example from our research group will illustrate this concept. Huedo-Medina et al. (2010) showed that three indices of economic development related to HIV prevention success in Latin American countries: Human Development Index (HDI), the gender-related development index (GDI), and the Gini coefficient of income inequality. Although to date it has been almost completely ignored in an HIV prevention literature dominated by individual-level (i.e., psychological) interventions, it is growing increasingly clear that social structure is a key consideration for the efficacy of behavioral HIV prevention interventions and relates to short- and long-term behavior change (e.g., Logan, Cole, & Leukefeld, 2002). Thus, broader economic and social structures can be highly important to health behavior change. For many reasons, not the least of which is convenience, social psychological studies are often examined in the absence of the larger social context, most frequently within an artificial laboratory setting. It would seem that these larger, contextual variables have great potential to illuminate social psychological phenomena. Johnson and colleagues (2010) have developed a perspective that weaves such factors into a cohesive framework in which individuals exchange resources with networks with which they are connected.

Work on social structure also highlights the role of status in human functioning. People who are low on the proverbial totem pole seem like magnets for most of the problems in the world. For example, for a host of reasons, poverty is associated with significantly higher rates of disease. Studies in this domain provide an important counterpoint to the laboratory-based undergraduate research that largely dominates the field of social psychology. Consensual ideologies, such as the Protestant work ethic or the belief that America is a land of opportunity, which can be held by members of both economically advantaged and economically disadvantaged groups, feed into the perception that poverty is a personally controllable factor (e.g., Ellis, 1999). Then, if consensual stereotypes of the poor reflect the notion that the poor are responsible for their condition, greater levels of stigmatization may result (Jones et al., 1984). These ideologies ignore the reality that the capitalistic economic structure in the United States makes upward intergenerational class mobility very difficult (Wright, 2000). People inherit a social class and all of the situations associated with it; any social mobility that is achieved is typically attained only through long-term educational mechanisms (e.g., Ceci & Williams, 1997). In addition, racial and sexist beliefs also tend to coincide across gender and racial groups (Sidanius & Pratto, 1999), and status-related beliefs are often shared between lower and higher status groups (e.g., Glick & Fiske, 2001). The mere salience of a person's lower social class also acts as a stereotype threat that can lower his or her intellectual performance (Croizet & Claire, 1998).

Although this research to some extent suggests that the behaviors of economically disadvantaged people are implicated in perpetuating their lower status, it in no way absolves those with higher status of responsibility (Harman & Johnson, 2003). Indeed, higher status people participate in inculcating these reinforcing beliefs and behaviors in lower status individuals. Rather, for any realistic hope to effect social change, psychologists need (1) a balanced perspective that accounts for both sides of the status coin and (2) recognition of the fact that earned status is often acknowledged as legitimate and deserved by those in both lower and higher status positions. Because health research and evaluation often focuses on those who are lower in status, it has the potential to contribute to a fuller understanding of human functioning. Social psychology stands to gain much if status variables are more fully considered during its theory construction and testing (see Johnson et al., 2010, for one such effort).

Are Basic and Applied Goals at Odds?

It is fair to say that most of the Zeitgeist within social psychology has focused on a more basic approach to psychological issues. As noted earlier, the resulting perception is that most of the information within social psychology originates from basic, theoretically driven studies, which then later lead to more applied contexts. The migration of classically trained social psychologists into health research demonstrates this perception. Still, sociologists of science have argued that the more common pathway is the reverse. Of particular note, Don Stokes, in his classic 1997 book *Pasteur's Quadrant*, argued that application generally precedes basic science. Thus, industry often capitalizes on a phenomenon that has been discovered serendipitously with little understanding of what drives the phenomenon. As a key exemplar of the applied strategy, Stokes cited Thomas Alva Edison, the genius who invented so many useful devices (Figure 12.1, *applied* quad-

Applied Science (Purely Technological)	Basic Science (Purely Conceptual)	
	Low	High
High	**Applied** Important knowledge serves the public interest, but underlying mechanisms are ignored or unknown. Key exemplar: Thomas Alva Edison	**Basic–Applied** Important knowledge serves both the public interest and explicates the underlying mechanisms. Key exemplar: Louis Pasteur
Low	**Serendipitous** Knowledge is important only for arcane purposes, and underlying mechanisms are ignored or unknown. Key exemplar: Charles Darwin	**Basic** Knowledge is important only to explicate underlying mechanisms and does not need to serve the public interest. Key exemplar: Niels Henrik David Bohr

FIGURE 12.1. The intersection of applied and basic goals. Based on Stokes (1997).

rant), such as the phonograph and the incandescent light bulb. Scholars who emphasize application in such a single-minded fashion are probably rare in any field, yet the inspiration for much of social psychology's rich history has indeed stemmed from observations of real-world phenomena. The holocaust in Nazi Germany motivated many investigations into human nature to determine how otherwise-normal people could act in such heinous ways. Another key example is the 1964 murder of Kitty Genovese, which was witnessed by many individuals who failed to help, and inspired Bibb Latané and John Darley's (e.g., 1970) research on bystander apathy. Real-world inspiration need not require loss of life. Famed social psychologist Robert Cialdini, for example, went "under cover" to learn what social influence tactics successful companies taught their salespeople. He then conducted research to demonstrate the efficacy of these strategies and to determine why the strategies worked. A book that chronicled these experiences and the related research became an instant classic and is a standard text for both marketing and psychology students (Cialdini, 1985).

These examples all started with inspiration from application but then yielded later, more deliberate examination of the topic within laboratory and field settings. When research seeks to discover a deeper theoretical understanding of the problem, and not its applications, it best matches Figure 12.1's *basic* quadrant. As a key exemplar of this basic science strategy, Stokes (1997) described the work of Niels Bohr, the physicist whose research on the structure of atoms won him great acclaim. As we have discussed in this chapter, much of the contemporary social psychological approach rewards this type of theoretical, basic scientific endeavor. Consequently, when they design their studies, social psychologists tend to focus on subject matter that may have little chance of application. By "little chance," we do not mean to imply that there are *no* applications that may result from the research: No matter how artificial the subject matter may be, it still may have important implications for application in some domain. It is just that the domain may be a relatively small niche. For example, attitude researchers commonly study how persuaded undergraduate students are to messages recommending that comprehensive examinations be instituted as a requirement for graduation at their university (for a review, see Johnson et al., 2005). Although the results of the research may seem to have narrow application to political campaigns and the like, one can imagine administrators of any college or university taking keen interest in these results, particularly if they really want to institute such a policy.

While it may seem impossible for a scientist to have relatively low interest in both applied and basic goals, Stokes actually placed one of the world's most impressive scientists in this quadrant (Figure 12.1, *serendipitous* quadrant), Charles Darwin, whose descriptive work documented evolutionary pressures at work in the subject matter of a wide array of disciplines. Darwin's work made it plausible that evolution has happened and still does, but he could not provide the exact underlying mechanism—genetics. Nonetheless, his two main concepts, natural selection and sexual selection anticipated later genetic discoveries. Although we have labeled Darwin's quadrant *serendipitous*, another apt label would be *inductive*, in the spirit of Baconian scientific method (D. L. Hull, 1988).

Although the research and scientific expression represented by each of the three aforementioned quadrants is valid and useful in certain circumstances, Stokes (1997) maintained that in its ideal form, science makes basic and applied advances simultaneously. As a key exemplar, Stokes provided Louis Pasteur, who discovered and explicated basic phenomena (e.g., germ theory, as illustrated by biological activity in milk), while simultaneously inventing applications that the public could quickly and efficiently use to avoid health hazards (e.g., pasteurization of milk; see Figure 12.1, *basic-applied* quadrant). Stokes argued that either linear flow of information (i.e., from basic to applied or applied to basic) is usually less than ideal; at its best, science should maximize both applied and basic goals simultaneously. Government-based funding agencies have stressed applied ends because these have the most immediate impact on the public good and because these are ends that the public easily understands. Scientists, meanwhile, typically aim to acquire deeper understanding of their chosen topics of investigation, to the point that the public may have great difficulty understanding the nuances of the resulting research and potentially even greater difficulty supporting public funding of said research.

The implications of Stokes's arguments for the intersection of social and health psychology are quite profound. Social psychologists should look more often toward the research's applied value to the public, which may at times be at odds with the priorities of basic scientists. Then, perhaps, scientific research may become more palatable to and more widely used by the public. More active attempts to mesh the applied with the basic can be boosted in part via collaborations among scholars from multiple disciplines, in the fashion that noted biologist Edward O. Wilson (1998) labeled *consilience*. Because any phenomenon can be understood from a multitude of disciplines that offer different perspectives on it (Johnson, 1983), such collaborations ought to routinely afford deeper knowledge that is less subject to revision. Thus, forging interdisciplinary ties is another way to maximize the basic and applied benefits of this research. Scholars from different disciplines bring different training that can enlighten how the research can benefit basic or applied aims. In this fashion, the research can maximize its value to multiple quarters.

One advantage of melding basic with applied goals in an interdisciplinary fashion is that doing so results in "big science" and a way to maximize the benefits of the research we conduct. In much the same fashion, a two-way exchange of information and ideas between basic and applied research can and should exist, and the notion that a zero-sum competition exists between basic and applied interests should be, in fact, considered false. In effect, social psychological theory and research should inform health psychology and vice versa. This conclusion becomes intuitive upon the realization that many of the best examples of current research in health psychology cannot be easily classified as basic *or* applied. Rather, as Stokes (1997) maintained, it is often the case that the most contributory research simultaneously develops the theoretical underpinnings of health behavior and the associated practical implications.

Conclusion

In this chapter, we have argued that the applied and basic concerns of health and social psychology need not conflict, but in fact can go hand in hand, when practiced optimally. Unfortunately, to date, the influence of health psychology and evaluation research on social psychology has been largely unidirectional, with social psychology profiting less than it should from the other disciplines. We maintain that social psychology as a field can benefit greatly from the experience and knowledge gained in these other fields, and much is potentially gained when they do. By the same token, health psychology and public health can increasingly profit by greater incorporation of theoretical principles that social psychology offers. Thus, although there are significant barriers to social and health psychology maintaining close theoretical and collaborative ties, the potential benefits to both fields are well worth the effort.

ACKNOWLEDGMENTS

The preparation of this chapter was supported by U.S. Public Health Service Grant Nos. F31-MH079759 to Marcella H. Boynton and R01-MH58563 to Blair T. Johnson.

REFERENCES

Ajzen, I. (1980). Emotional conservatism: The basis of social behavior? *PsycCRITIQUES, 25,* 775–776.
Ajzen, I. (1985). From intentions to actions: A theory of planned behavior. In J. Kuhl & J. Beckmann (Eds.), *Action control: From cognition to behavior* (pp. 11–39). Heidelberg: Springer.
Albarracín, D., Gillette, J. C., Earl, A. N., Glasman, L. R., Durantini, M. R., & Ho, M. (2005). A test of major assumptions about behavior change: A comprehensive look at the effects of passive and active HIV-prevention interventions since the beginning of the epidemic. *Psychological Bulletin, 131,* 856–897.

Albarracín, D., Johnson, B. T., Fishbein, M., & Muellerleile, P. (2001). Theories of reasoned action and planned behavior as models of condom use: A meta-analysis. *Psychological Bulletin, 127,* 142–161.

Albarracín, D., McNatt, P. S., Klein, C. T. F., Ho, R. M., Mitchell, A. L., & Kumkale, G. T. (2003). Persuasive communications to change actions: An analysis of behavioral and cognitive impact in HIV prevention. *Health Psychology, 22,* 166–177.

Allport, F. H. (1924). *Social psychology.* Boston: Houghton Mifflin.

Amico, K. R., Harman, J. J., & Johnson, B. T. (2006). Efficacy of ART adherence interventions: A research synthesis of trials, 1996–2004. *Journal of Acquired Immune Deficiency Syndromes, 41,* 285–297.

Asch, R. S. E. (1952). *Social Psychology.* Englewood Cliffs, NJ: Prentice-Hall.

Bandura, A. (1986). *Social foundations of thought and action: A social cognitive theory.* Englewood Cliffs, NJ: Prentice-Hall.

Bandura, A. (1989). Human agency in social cognitive theory. *American Psychologist, 44,* 1175–1184.

Bandura, A. (1997). *Self-efficacy: The exercise of control.* New York: Freeman/ Times Books/ Henry Holt.

Berscheid, E. (1992). A glance back at a quarter century of social psychology. *Journal of Personality and Social Psychology, 63,* 525–533.

Breckler, S. J., & Wiggins, E. C. (1989). Affect versus evaluation in the structure of attitudes. *Journal of Experimental Social Psychology, 25,* 253–271.

Ceci, S. J., & Williams, W. M. (1997). Schooling, intelligence, and income. *American Psychologist, 52,* 1051–1058.

Centers for Disease Control. (2007). HIV/AIDS Basic Information. Retrieved on June 22, 2007 from *www.cdc.gov/hiv/topics/basic/index.htm.*

Chen, F. M., Fryer, G. E. J., Phillips, R. L. J., Wilson, E., & Pathman, D. E. (2005). Patients' beliefs about racism, preferences for physician race, and satisfaction with care. *Annals of Family Medicine, 3,* 138–143.

Chen, M. K., Lakshminaryanan, V., & Santos, L. R. (2006). The evolution of our preferences: Evidence from capuchin monkey trading behavior. *Journal of Political Economy, 114,* 517–537.

Cialdini, R. B. (1985). Setting fractures in the bones of social interaction. *PsycCRITIQUES, 30,* 324.

Conner, M., & Norman, P. (1995). *Predicting health behaviour: Research and practice with social cognition models.* Buckingham, UK: Open University Press.

Crocker, J., Luhtanen, R., Broadnax, S., & Blaine, B. E. (1999). Belief in U.S. government conspiracies against Blacks among Black and White college students: Powerlessness or system blame? *Personality and Social Psychology Bulletin, 25,* 941–953.

Croizet, J. C., & Claire, T. (1998). Extending the concept of stereotype threat to social class: The intellectual underperformance of students from low socioeconomic background. *Personality and Social Psychology Bulletin, 24,* 588–594.

Cunningham, W. E., Hays, R. D., & Duan, N. (2005). The effect of socioeconomic status on the survival of people receiving care for HIV infection in the United States. *Journal of Health Care for the Poor and Underserved, 16,* 655–676.

De Bruin, M., Viechtbauer, W., Schaalma, H. P., Kok, G., Abraham, C., & Hospers, H. J. (2010). Standard care impacts intervention effects in HAART adherence RCTs: A meta-analysis. *Archives of Internal Medicine, 170,* 240–250.

Doescher, M. P., Saver, B. G., Franks, P., & Fiscella, K. (2000). Racial and ethnic disparities in perceptions of physician style and trust. *Archives of Family Medicine, 9,* 1156–1163.

Dovidio, J. F., Penner, L. A., Albrecht, T. L., Norton, W. E., Gaertner, S. L., & Shelton, J. N. (2008). Disparities and distrust: The implications of psychological processes for understanding racial disparities in health and health care. *Social Science and Medicine, 67,* 478–486.

Ellis, D. G. (1999). *Crafting society: Ethnicity, class, and communication theory.* Mahwah, NJ: Erlbaum.

Ferguson, W. J., & Candib, L. M. (2002). Culture, language, and the doctor–patient relationship. *Family Medicine, 34,* 353–361.

Festinger, L. (1954). A theory of social comparison processes. *Human Relations, 7,* 117–140.

Festinger, L. (1957). *A theory of cognitive dissonance.* Stanford, CA: Stanford University Press.

Fishbein, M., & Ajzen, I. (1975). *Belief, attitude, intention and behavior.* Reading, MA: Addison-Wesley.

Fisher, J. D., & Fisher, W. A. (1992). Changing AIDS-risk behavior. *Psychological Bulletin, 111,* 455–474.

Glick, P., & Fiske, S. T. (2001). Ambivalent stereotypes as legitimizing ideologies: Differentiating paternalistic and envious prejudice. In J. T. Jost & B. Major (Eds.), *The psychology of legitimacy: Emerging perspectives on ideology, justice, and intergroup relations* (pp. 278–306). Cambridge, England: Cambridge University Press.

Godin, G., Sheeran, P., Conner, M., Germain, M., Blondeau, D., Gagné, C., et al. (2005). Factors explaining the intention to give blood among the general population. *Vox Saguinis, 89,* 140–149.

Hagger, M. S. (2006). Meta-analysis in sport and exercise research: Review, recent developments, and recommendations. *European Journal of Sport Science, 6,* 103–115.

Hagger, M. S., Chatzisarantis, N. L. D., & Biddle, S. J. H. (2002). A meta-analytic review of the theories of reasoned action and planned behavior in physical activity: Predictive validity and the contribution of additional variables. *Journal of Sports and Exercise Psychology, 24,* 3–32.

Harris, B. (1986). Reviewing 50 years of the psychology of social issues. *Journal of Social Issues, 42,* 1–20.

Higgins, A., & Conner, M. (2003). Understanding adolescent smoking: The role of the theory of planned behavior and implementation intentions. *Psychology, Health and Medicine, 8,* 173–186.

Huedo-Medina, T. B., Boynton, M. H., Warren, M. R., LaCroix, J. M., Carey, M. P., & Johnson, B. T. (2010). Efficacy of HIV prevention interventions in Latin America and Carribean nations, 1995–2008: A meta-analysis. *AIDS and Behavior, 14*(6), 1237–1251.

Hull, C. L. (1943). *Principles of behavior: An introduction to behavior theory.* Oxford, UK: Appleton-Century.

Hull, D. L. (1988). *Science as a process: An evolutionary account of the social and conceptual development of science.* Chicago: University of Chicago Press.

Jessor, R., Turbin, M. S., & Costa, F. M. (1998). Protective factors in adolescent health behavior. *Journal of Personality and Social Psychology, 75,* 788–800.

Johnson, B. T. (1983). A dialogue on epistemology between René Descartes and Henri Poincaré. *Dialogue, 25,* 41–47.

Johnson, B. T., & Boynton, M. H. (2008). Cumulating evidence about the Social Animal: Meta-analysis in social-personality psychology, *Personality and Social Psychology Compass, 2,* 1–25.

Johnson, B. T., & Boynton, M. B. (2010). Putting attitudes in their place: Behavioural prediction in the face of competing variables. In J. P. Forgas, J. Cooper, & W. Crano (Eds.), *Attitudes: Sydney Symposium of Social Psychology* (pp. 19–38). London: Cambridge University Press.

Johnson, B. T., Carey, M. P., Chaudoir, S., & Reid, A. E. (2006). Sexual risk reduction for persons living with HIV: Research synthesis of randomized controlled trials, 1993 to 2004. *Journal of Acquired Immune Deficiency Syndromes, 41,* 642–650.

Johnson, B. T., Carey, M. P., Marsh, K. L., Levin, K. D., & Scott-Sheldon, L. A. J. (2003). Interventions to reduce sexual risk for the Human Immunodeficiency Virus in adolescents, 1985–2000: A research synthesis. *Archives of Pediatrics and Adolescent Medicine, 157,* 381–388.

Johnson, B. T., Maio, G. R., & Smith-McLallen, A. (2005). Communication and attitude change: Causes, processes, and effects. In D. Albarracín, B. T. Johnson, & M. P. Zanna (Eds.), *The handbook of attitudes* (pp. 617–670). Mahwah, NJ: Erlbaum.

Johnson, B. T., & Nichols, D. R. (1998). Social psychologists' expertise in the public interest: Civilian morale research during World War II. *Journal of Social Issues, 54,* 53–77.

Johnson, B. T., Redding, C. A., DiClemente, R. J., Dodge, B. M., Mustanski, B. S., Sheeran, P., et al. (2010). A network–individual–resource model for HIV prevention. *AIDS and Behavior, 14,* 204–221.

Jones, E. E., Farina, A., Hastorf, A. H., Markus, H., Miller, D. T., & Scott, R. A. (1984). *Social stigma: The psychology of marked relationships.* New York: Freeman.

Kahneman, D., & Tversky, A. (1979). On the interpretation of intuitive probability: A reply to Jonathan Cohen. *Cognition, 7,* 409–411.

Kaplan, R. M. (2007). Health psychology: Continuity and change. *Health Psychology, 26,* 133–135.

Kelly, J. A. (1995). *Changing HIV risk behavior: Practical strategies.* New York: Guilford Press.

Kenny, D. A., Kashy, D. A., & Cook, W. L. (2006). *Dyadic data analysis.* New York: Guilford Press.

Kuhlberg, J. (2000). *Careers in Health Psychology.* Retrieved on June 13, 2007 from   *www.wcupa.edu/_ACADEMICS/sch_cas.psy/Career_Paths/Health/Career02.htm*.

Latané, B., & Darley, J. M. (1970). *The unresponsive bystander: Why doesn't he help?* New York: Appleton-Century-Crofts.

Leonhardt, D. (2007, May 2). Your plate is bigger than your stomach. *New York Times*, C1.

Lewin, K. (1943). Forces behind food habits and methods of change. In *The Problem of Changing Food Habits*, Bulletin of the National Research Council, Washington, DC: National Research Council and National Academy of Sciences, 108, 35–65.

Logan, T. K., Cole, J., & Leukefeld, C. (2002). Women, sex, and HIV: Social and contextual factors, meta-analysis of published interventions, and implications for practice and research. *Psychological Bulletin, 128*, 851–885.

Milgram, S. (1963). Behavioral study of obedience. *Journal of Abnormal and Social Psychology, 67*, 371–378.

Morale Division. (1946). *The effects of strategic bombing on German morale* (Vol. 2). Washington, DC: Author.

Morale Division. (1947). *The effects of strategic bombing on German morale* (Vol. 1). Washington, DC: Author.

Neal, D. T., Wood, W., & Quinn, J. M. (2006). Habits: A repeat performance. *Current Directions in Psychological Science, 15*, 198–202.

Orbell, S., Hagger, M., Brown, V., & Tidy, J. (2006). Comparing two theories of health behavior: A prospective study of noncompletion of treatment following cervical cancer screening. *Health Psychology, 25*, 604–615.

Ouellette, J. A., & Wood, W. (1998). Habit and intention in everyday life: The multiple processes by which past behavior predicts future behavior. *Psychological Bulletin, 124*, 54–74.

Pittman, T. S., Pallak, M. S., Riggs, J. M., & Gotay, C. C. (1981). Increasing blood donor pledge fulfillment. *Personality and Social Psychology Bulletin, 7*, 195–200.

Post, D. L. (1980). Floyd H. Allport and the launching of modern social psychology. *Journal of the History of the Behavioral Sciences, 16*, 369–376.

Rodin, J. (1977). Research on eating behavior and obesity: Where does it fit in personality and social psychology? *Personality and Social Psychology Bulletin, 3*, 333–355.

Rodin, J., & Stone, G. C. (1987). Historical highlights in the emergence of the field. In G. C. Stone, F. Cohen, & N. E. Adler (Eds.), *Health Psychology* (pp. 15–26). Chicago: University of Chicago Press.

Rothman, A. J. (2000). Toward a theory-based analysis of behavioral maintenance. *Health Psychology, 19*, 64–69.

Rothman, A. J., & Salovey, P. (2007). Shaping perceptions to motivate healthy behavior: The role of message framing. *Psychological Bulletin, 121*, 3–19.

Schachter, S. (1968). Obesity and eating. *Science, 161*, 751–756.

Schulman, K. A., Berlin, J. A., Harless, W., Kerner, J. F., Sistrunk, S., Gersh, B. J., et al. (1999). The effect of race and sex on physicians' recommendations for cardiac catheterization. *The New England Journal of Medicine, 340*, 618–626.

Sears, D. O. (1986). College sophomores in the laboratory: Influences of a narrow data base on social psychology's view of human nature. *Journal of Personality and Social Psychology, 51*, 515–530.

Sidanius, J., & Pratto, F. P. (1999). *Social dominance.* Cambridge, UK: Cambridge University Press.

Skinner, B. F. (1938). *The behavior of organisms: An experimental analysis.* Oxford, UK: Appleton-Century.

Smoak, N. D., Scott-Sheldon, L. A. J., Johnson, B. T., & Carey, M. P. (2006). Sexual risk reduction interventions do not inadvertently increase the overall frequency of sexual behavior: A meta-analysis of 174 studies with 116,735 participants. *Journal of Acquired Immune Deficiency Syndromes, 41*, 374–384.

Spence, K. W. (1956). *Behavior theory and conditioning.* New Haven, CT: Yale University Press.

Stokes, D. E. (1997). *Pasteur's quadrant: Basic science and technological innovation.* Washington, DC: Brookings Institution Press.

Stone, G. C. (1982). Psychology in the health system. In G. C. Stone, F. Cohen, & N. E. Adler (Eds.), *Health Psychology* (pp. 47–75). Chicago: University of Chicago Press.

Sussman, S., Valente, T. W., Rohrbach, L. A., Skara, S., & Pentz, M. A. (2006). Translation in the health professions: Converting science into action. *Evaluation and the Health Professions, 29*, 7–32.

Van Ryn, M., & Burke, J. (2000). The effect of patient race and socio-economic status on physicians' perceptions of patients. *Social Science and Medicine, 50*, 813–828.

Wansink, B. (2002). Changing eating habits on the home front: Lost lessons from World War II research. *Journal of Public Policy and Marketing, 21*, 90–99.

Watson, R. I., Sr., & Evans, R. B. (1991). *The great psychologists: A history of psychological thought* (5th ed.). New York: HarperCollins.

Wilson, E. O. (1998). *Consilience: The unity of knowledge.* New York: Knopf.

Wright, E. O. (2000). *Class counts.* Cambridge, UK: Cambridge University Press.

Zajonc, R. B. (1965). Social facilitation. *Science, 149*, 269–274.

Zimbardo, P. G. (1970). The human choice: Individuation, reason, and order versus deindividuation, impulse, and chaos. In W. J. Arnold & D. Levine (Eds.), *1969 Nebraska Symposium on Motivation* (pp. 237–307). Lincoln: University of Nebraska Press.

EDITORS' CONCLUDING COMMENTS
TO CHAPTER 12

Johnson, Dove, and Boynton describe the intersection between social psychology and health psychology, including especially the evaluation of health behavior programs, throughout the preceding chapter. They argue that health psychology is predominately an applied field and argue that traditional social psychology could gain more by attending more closely to the lessons of health psychology.

The intersection with social psychology that Johnson and colleagues chose to examine is rich with examples that extend well beyond health psychology and health behavior program evaluation. For example, one of their main points, that social psychology has probably given more and profited less than it should from the health behavior area, can be generalized to many other areas of programming and evaluation such as education, human services, the environment, and the like. Their call for social psychologists to pay more attention to the benefits of applied research and evaluation for enhancing social psychology also reaches beyond the health psychology domain. What is clear in this chapter is that social psychology has been a major player in providing theory, principles, and methods to improve programs and policies. We hope that what is also clear is that the next generation of social psychologists will be better off if they take advantage of the benefits that applied research and evaluation have to offer social psychology. We invite the reader to consider how the issues discussed throughout this chapter, related to the mutual improvement of social psychology and the evaluation of health behavior programs, could also be applied to many other types of programs based on social psychological theory, principles, and research.

PART V

Expanding the Intersection between Social Psychology and Evaluation

EDITORS' INTRODUCTORY COMMENTS
TO CHAPTER 13

In the next chapter, Bernadette Campbell and April L. McGrath explore the notion of middle-range theory at the intersection of social psychology and evaluation. After explaining what they mean by middle-range theory, they apply it to the components of an influential model from Shadish, Cook, and Leviton (1991). Shadish and his colleagues suggested that a good evaluation theory should include five components: (1) a theory of social programming, that is, a model of the thing being evaluated, how it operates, what its constraints are; (2) a theory of knowledge construction, with guidance as to what counts as good evidence; (3) a theory of valuing, which specifies where the values come from that are imbued at various points in the evaluation, including in the choice of measures and the way mixed findings are combined (if at all); (4) a theory of evaluation use, indicating what kinds of use are to be sought when, and what the evaluator's role is in facilitating use; and (5) a theory of evaluation practice, which emphasizes a range of practice issues that draw in part on other components of the theory.

Campbell and McGrath illustrate the development of middle-range theory for each of these five components. Drawing on literature from both social psychology and evaluation, they sketch out middle-range theory for social programming and the other four components. They do not attempt to provide a complete and comprehensive theory for any of the components, nor to deliver a grand theory of evaluation. Middle-range theory pushes in another direction, that is, for conceptual models intended to describe a portion of one of Shadish et al.'s components, drawing on extant knowledge, offering a potential guide for evaluation practice, and perhaps most importantly stimulating further empirical tests and subsequent conceptual refinement.

Campbell and McGrath's approach appears to hold considerable promise as a model for reducing the distance that remains between social psychology and evaluation.

CHAPTER 13

Where the Rubber Hits the Road

*The Development of Usable Middle-Range
Evaluation Theory*

Bernadette Campbell
April L. McGrath

In this chapter, we take up the issue of middle-range theory as it might apply to the field of evaluation. We will answer such questions as, "What *is* middle-range theory? What might middle-range evaluation theory look like? What kinds of phenomena would such theories attempt to explain? How might social psychology help us to construct middle-range evaluation theory?" We suggest some middle-range themes—topics that lie at the intersection of social psychology and evaluation and that are, in our estimation, worthy candidates for more developed middle-range theory. Two of these themes are explored in detail, including suggestions for middle-range theoretical propositions and testable hypotheses. We close the chapter with some of the potential benefits of middle-range evaluation theory and a discussion of what it will take to realize our vision for middle-range evaluation theory. But first we turn to a modern parable that provides an interesting parallel to middle-range theory (Weick, 1980) and its benefits for evaluation theory specifically. A story of two watchmakers, it was written to illustrate important lessons about the evolution (and survival) of complex systems (Simon, 1962). We believe that this parable also holds critical lessons for the evolution (and survival) of evaluation theory. Specifically, the image of building blocks, or stable subassemblies, offers a powerful analogy for the central role of middle-range theories in the development of a stable, more comprehensive evaluation theory.

Once there were two watchmakers, Hora and Tempus, who manufactured very fine watches which consisted of 1,000 parts each. Both watchmakers were highly regarded. The phones in their workshops rang constantly with new orders for their famous watches. Hora prospered while Tempus became poorer and poorer and finally lost his shop. It seems that the two men used very different strategies when building their watches. Tempus built his watches one piece at a time. He needed a great deal of uninterrupted time to build one of his watches. If one of his watches was partially assembled and Tempus had to put it down to answer the phone, the watch fell to pieces and had to be reassembled one piece at a time. Of course, the more his customers liked his watches, the more phone calls Tempus received, and the more difficult it became for him to finish a watch. The watches Hora handled were equally complex, and he received just as many phone calls as Tempus. But Hora had designed his watches so that he could put together subassemblies of about 10 pieces each. Ten of these subassemblies could be put together into a larger subassembly; and a system of 10 of the latter subassemblies constituted the whole watch. When Hora had to put down a partially assembled watch in order to answer the phone, he lost only a small part of his work. So, Hora was able to assemble his watches in only a fraction of the time that it took Tempus.

What can evaluation theorists learn from the story of Hora and Tempus? One lesson is that interruptions in the development of any complex system are inevitable. Be it the ringing phone of a watchmaker or the waxing and waning of theoretical work in evaluation, progress toward a larger goal will inevitably be plagued by interruptions. The second, perhaps more important lesson, is that if complex systems (such as watches, and theoretical systems) are built with a series of stable *subassemblies*, the effect of interruptions will be negligible. The appropriate subassembly for evaluation theory is, we believe, middle-range theory.

Through this chapter, we hope to stimulate a greater commitment to developing middle-range theories for evaluation. Further, we intend to show that exploiting some of the intersections between evaluation theory and social psychological theory will both hasten the development of usable, middle-range evaluation theory and add to existing social psychological theories. Others before us have alluded to the potential benefits of a similar approach to evaluation theorizing, calling for more usable, testable, evaluation theories (Cousins, 2003; Greene, 2001; Mark & Henry, 2004). Still others have suggested the potential benefits to evaluation theory of drawing on the intellectual capital of existing fields of study such as psychology (Donaldson, Gooler, & Scriven, 2002; Taut & Brauns, 2003; Thorngate, 2001), organizational learning (Preskill & Torres, 1999), knowledge utilization (Cousins & Shulha, 2006), industrial engineering (Morell, 2000), and nursing (Rogers, 2001). Potential benefits for social psychology have also been enumerated (Mark, Donaldson, & Campbell, Chapter 14, this volume). We hope to take this discussion even further, and to plant the seeds for thinking more specifically about ways in which social psychology in particular can contribute to the development and testing of middle-range evaluation theory. In turn, results from this kind of work can be used to enhance and expand many of social psychology's theories. But first, what exactly *is* middle-range theory?

What *Is* Middle-Range Theory?

Middle-range theory has generally been viewed as a solution to the problem of overly general, abstract theoretical statements on one hand and overly specific, blind empiricism on the other hand. First elaborated by sociologist Robert Merton, the idea of middle-range theory was in large part a reaction to grand sociological theories of the day which attempted to explain all of human behavior. In Merton's (1968) words, middle-range theories "lie between the minor but necessary working hypotheses that evolve in abundance during day-to-day research and the all-inclusive, systematic efforts to develop a unified theory that will explain all the observed uniformities of social behaviour, social organization and social change" (p. 39). Merton's original treatment of middle-range theory is detailed and extensive. Since its beginnings in sociology, the core principles of middle-range theory have been adopted in many diverse disciplines including nursing (Smith & Liehr, 2003), organizational behaviour and industrial relations (Bourgeois, 1979; Kochan, 1992), and archaeology (Raab & Goodyear, 1984), to name just a few.

For our purposes, certain features of middle-range theory are notable. First, middle-range theories are somewhat narrow in scope. They maintain a focus on one or two limited phenomena or processes of interest within a field. Second, middle-range theories are abstract enough to transcend simple description but are concrete enough to generate empirically testable inferences or hypotheses (Pinder & Moore, 1980). Middle-range theories usually begin with a simple idea or proposition. From this seemingly simple idea emerges empirically testable inferences, some of which may be at odds with commonly held, perhaps unexamined, assumptions or expectations. According to Merton (1968), "If the simple idea has theoretical worth, it should generate distinctive problems for [*sociological*] inquiry" (p. 42). Finally, middle-range theories can be linked to other, related, middle-range theories. Because middle-range theories tend to be (ultimately) linkable to each other, they can appropriately be viewed as building blocks for wider-ranging theories within a discipline. At the core of Merton's definition of middle-range theory is a clear parallel with Hora's methods for managing complexity (Simon, 1962). That is, middle-range theory is essentially a subassembly—a stable, intermediate step in the construction of a more complex, comprehensive evaluation theory.

Any middle-range evaluation theory must incorporate key features of Merton's (1968) definition described above. That is, it should be narrow in scope, empirically testable, and linkable to other middle-range theories. We also believe that many candidates for middle-range evaluation theory would be strengthened by focusing on conceptual similarities found in the social psychology literature. In our view, by mining the intersection between important evaluation phenomena and the rich body of social psychological research, the development of usable middle-range evaluation theory will be hastened. As most of the chapters in this volume illustrate, there are many areas of theoretical overlap between evaluation phenomena and social psychological phenomena. Indeed, each chapter has itself provided some of the necessary scaffolding to build stable middle-range evaluation theories. In a later section, we offer more specific suggestions about exactly how middle-range evaluation theories might be constructed. But first, we try to put our vision for middle-range evaluation theory into context.

Contemporary Evaluation Theory: Some Context

Contemporary sociological theory consists of general orientations toward data, suggesting types of variables which theories must somehow take into account, rather than clearly formulated, verifiable statements of relationships between specified variables. We have many concepts but fewer confirmed theories; many points of view, but few theorems; many "approaches" but few arrivals. Perhaps some further changes in emphasis would be all to the good.
—ROBERT K. MERTON (1968, p. 52)

Merton's lament about the state of sociological theory rings all too true for the state of contemporary evaluation theory. Most current evaluation *theories* might be more accurately labeled as evaluation *approaches* or *models*—prescriptive theories. We have many unique concepts, but are missing the essential theoretical glue that holds them together, specifying the nature of relationships among concepts or variables.

Generally speaking, evaluation theories lay out prescriptions or guiding frameworks that specify what a good or proper evaluation is or how to conduct an evaluation (Alkin, 2004). By a strict definition of the term, however, evaluation has no established *empirical* theories.

The dominance of prescriptive evaluation theory has come under scrutiny in recent (and not so recent) years, resulting in calls from the field to develop more *descriptive*, empirically supported evaluation theory (Alkin, 2003; Cousins & Shulha, 2006; Greene, 2001; Henry & Mark, 2003a; Rogers, 2001; Shadish, 1997; Shadish, Cook, & Leviton, 1991; Smith, 1979, 1993; Worthen, 2001). The distinction between *prescriptive* and *descrip-*

tive evaluation theory has become a rallying cry for those in the evaluation field advocating for more empirically based evaluation theory relative to experience- and ideology-based prescriptions for evaluation. Middle-range theories, we argue, represent a critical starting point in the development of descriptive, empirically based contingency theories for evaluation. Rather than entirely replace existing evaluation theories, a middle-range orientation to evaluation theory would aim to strengthen and enhance the work that has begun in evaluation theory development.

In the next section, we show that basic social psychology is present in many aspects of evaluation work, making it an ideal discipline for informing evaluation theory. Following this, we offer some preliminary ideas for tying together evaluation concepts and social psychological research in an attempt to more clearly specify important evaluation phenomena.

Social Psychology and Evaluation: Natural Partners

There are countless conceptual links between the issues and processes important for evaluation and topics studied in social psychology (Campbell & Mark, 2006; Donaldson et al., 2002; Taut & Brauns, 2003; Thorngate, 2001). Indeed, as the chapters in this volume illustrate, the potential intersections between social psychology and evaluation are many and fruitful. In recent years, we have witnessed a "revival" of the identification and development of theoretical connections between evaluation practice phenomena and phenomena studied in other social science disciplines. For instance, Donaldson and his colleagues (2002) discuss the issue of evaluation anxiety as it relates to the way this construct is studied in clinical psychology (Beck, 1989). Taut and Brauns (2003) have drawn theoretical connections between resistance to evaluation as observed in practice and relevant social psychological constructs such as reactance (Brehm & Brehm, 1981), and competition and conflict (Pruitt & Rubin, 1986). Similarly, Geva-May and Thorngate (2003) use a sociopsychological analysis to illustrate some of the ways that collaboration may be enhanced within the practice of evaluation. Campbell and Mark (2006) draw on similarities between negotiation and conflict resolution as studied in social psychology (Pruitt, 1998) and the practice of stakeholder dialogue in program evaluation. Similarly, Stevahn and King (2005) draw on conflict strategies theory (Johnson & Johnson, 2003) to suggest theoretical directions for evaluation in the area of conflict management. As these examples suggest, social psychology holds much promise as a source of conceptual insight into issues of theoretical and practical relevance to evaluation.

In addition to offering a conceptual head start for many of the theoretical issues that evaluation must grapple with, partnering with social psychology also offers a much needed empirical foundation to build upon. When we draw on existing theories about general social psychological processes such as the way people process persuasive communications, we can be reasonably assured that our initial theories or models are grounded in empirical support (see Fleming, Chapter 8, this volume). In addition to buying us the security of empirical grounding, social psychological theory tends to be much more detailed and developed relative to evaluation theories. Existing theories in social psychology can serve as models for the kind of evaluation theory that we might develop and test ourselves. What is needed now, we believe, is a strengthening of theoretical frameworks specific to evaluation and a move toward empirically testable hypotheses. Middle-range evaluation theory, informed in part by social psychological research, is an essential step in building evaluation's much needed theoretical subassemblies.

Keeping the "Evaluation" in Middle-Range Evaluation Theory

We have discussed some of the benefits of drawing on social psychology as we endeavor to build usable middle-range theories for evaluation. But social psychology is only part of the marriage we propose. Indeed, in order for our middle-range theories to be relevant and useful, they must be rooted in the unique realities of evaluation, many of which are not represented in the social psychological literature. The task of mining the intersection between evaluation and social psychology is not so simple as to test an existing social psychology theory in an evaluation context. To be sure, while many parallels exist between the kinds of topics studied in social psychology and phenomena of interest in evaluation, many critical differences exist as well. For example, a significant majority of social psychological theory is based on experimentally manipulated laboratory tests conducted with undergraduate students (Cook & Groom, 2004; Higbee, Millard, & Folkman, 1982; Sherman, Buddie, Dragan, End, & Finney, 1999). Most of the processes and phenomena of interest to evaluation, on the other hand, take place in settings where experimental manipulation is impossible, the research participants are much more diverse, and very little is under the researchers' control. Theories of evaluation must necessarily incorporate evaluation realities, and many of these realities will mean that an exact fit or one-to-one correspondence with existing research findings in social psychology will be impossible. We must, rather, do the difficult work of thinking through the conceptual parallels and the conceptual differences, including the ways in which processes might unfold differently in an evaluation setting compared to what is often a laboratory setting. Doing this work is a nontrivial part of the job of constructing middle-range evaluation theories. But such efforts are sure to yield benefits for evaluation theory and social psychology theory alike.

Middle-Range Evaluation Theory:
Sketching Out Theoretical Subassemblies

As we start to envision middle-range theory for evaluation, one of the first questions to emerge is "What should middle-range evaluation theories be about?" "What processes or phenomena are appropriate for middle-range evaluation theory?" The answers to these questions essentially boil down to those evaluation topics that are worthy of describing and explaining. For any discipline, that can be a lot of territory to cover. To simplify our task, we begin with one of the few formal classifications of evaluation theory. According to this framework, good evaluation theory should include (1) theories of social programming, or the things that we evaluate, (2) theories of knowledge construction, (3) theories of valuing, (4) theories of evaluation use, and (5) theories of evaluation practice (Shadish et al., 1991). To be sure, the evaluation literature has contributed volumes to various aspects of these domains; but comprehensive, empirically tested (or testable) theories remain elusive. Yet, for each of these domains, we can imagine the beginnings of a variety of middle-range evaluation theories.

After briefly defining each dimension, we suggest some potential middle-range themes as an early step in sketching out some of evaluation's theoretical subassemblies. Of those themes suggested, two are examined in particular detail—stakeholder dialogue and decision-making processes and evaluator–stakeholder communications to foster evaluation use. Here, our goal is to begin fleshing out in more detail selected middle-range evaluation theories. Fitting with the spirit of middle-range theorizing, for each topic we begin with a simple idea. From these simple ideas we suggest inferences or questions that seem to follow. If the simple idea has theoretical worth, it should generate distinctive problems for *empirical* inquiry. We hope to demonstrate the theoretical worth of our ideas by suggesting some empirically testable hypotheses that flow from the initial propositions. The value of this exercise is enhanced by drawing on both evaluation realities and conceptually similar social psychology research and findings. This is an early attempt to plant the seeds for middle-range theory development, but, we hope, an exercise that will stimulate much more thought and research activity.

As we approached this exercise, we first asked ourselves, "What might a middle-range evaluation theory look like?" Theories are empirically supported models that describe regularities in the way a particular process or phenomenon operates. Any middle-range evaluation theory would, at a minimum, include a definition of the core processes or phenomena of interest. For evaluation, core topics might include evaluation resistance, stakeholder selection and participation, perceptions of objectivity and credibility in evaluation, evaluation utilization or influence, conflict and collaboration in evaluation, decision making in evaluation, constructing and presenting persuasive communications, organizational learning from evaluation, program and/or social change, and many more. In order to describe or explain these and other evaluation phenomena in more detail, a middle-range evaluation theory would also begin to specify key antecedents of the process or phenomenon of interest (e.g., characteristics of the evaluation context that might contribute to evaluation resistance). Having specified the kinds of variables that are likely to influence the process of interest, it is appropriate for a theory to also propose the mechanisms through which the antecedents exert their influence on the evaluation topic. Finally, by including potential moderating variables, or factors that may change the direction or strength of the relationships proposed above, the middle-range theory begins to specify important contingencies affecting the process or phenomenon described. We draw on the theoretical dimensions of evaluation practice and evaluation use to illustrate precisely how we might begin to sketch out selected middle-range evaluation theories.

Middle-Range Theories of Evaluation Practice

This dimension relates to the work that evaluators do, and hence, is probably the broadest of all the dimensions of evaluation theory. Good theories of evaluation practice should provide guidance for evaluators, including suggestions for general strategies and practical methods within the constraints of evaluation settings (Shadish et al., 1991). Middle-range theories within the domain of evaluation practice might cover relatively narrow phenomena such as evaluation anxiety and resistance, conflict in evaluation, (e.g., among stakeholders, between evaluator and client), and decision-making processes in evaluation, to name just a few.

We use the phenomenon of stakeholder dialogue processes to illustrate some of the important issues and questions that will ultimately arise in the course of middle-range theory development. Indeed, the twin issues of conflict and cooperation in stakeholder interactions have received a good deal of attention recently, including by those who have drawn parallels with social psychological research (Campbell & Mark, 2006; Geva-May & Thorngate, 2003; Stevahn & King, 2005). Many evaluators invite participation by diverse stakeholder groups to contribute to key evaluation decisions (such as which of many possible outcomes to measure or how to interpret a set of evaluation findings). The details of how these issues get sorted out vary from situation to situation, but it is widely known that these interactions can be quite difficult, primarily because of competing interests (Greene, 2000; Ryan & DeStefano, 2000). Stakeholder dialogue processes can reasonably be viewed as a special case of intergroup conflict, a topic studied extensively by social psychologists (Dovidio & Gaertner, 2010).

A middle-range theory of stakeholder dialogue processes would, at a minimum, specify (1) the nature of possible stakeholder dialogue processes (e.g., conflict, cooperation, withdrawal, compromise), (2) the antecedents of different types of dialogue processes (e.g., group composition, level of self-interest in the group, expectations going into the interaction, personality, how big is the *stake?*), (3) the mechanisms or likely process through which the antecedents exert their influence on the interaction process (e.g., Trust: when self-interest is high, trust of other group members is low, ultimately resulting in conflictive interactions), and (4) potential moderating variables, or factors that may change the direction or strength of the relationships proposed in (1), (2), and (3) (e.g., Interest in Others: high self-interest will *not* lead to low trust of others and, ultimately, conflict, when group members also have a high level of interest in the outcomes of others). Within each of these requirements for a middle-range theory of dialogue processes, there remain many unknowns. To begin to flesh out some of the gaps in our knowledge (and hence, our theory as it were), we begin with a simple idea related to stakeholder dialogue processes:

A high level of self-interest among individual stakeholders can lead to contentious interactions when faced with a group discussion or decision-making task.

This simple idea has been stated in various ways by many evaluation practitioners (Greene, 2000; House & Howe, 1999; Ryan & Johnson, 2000). Conceptually similar ideas have been examined by social psychologists for decades (Ben-Yoav & Pruitt, 1984; O'Connor, 1997; Thompson, 1995; Thompson, Wang, & Gunia, 2010). While there is a good base to go on in the social psychology literature, certain important variables are unique to evaluation settings that must be clarified and examined if a truly usable middle-range evaluation theory is to emerge. For instance, a long-standing finding in the negotiation literature is that negotiators who are accountable to a constituency tend to be much more confrontational in their interactions compared with negotiators who bargain as solos (Druckman, 1994; Kramer, Pommerenke, & Newton, 1993). Yet this particular conception of accountability makes no sense in most evaluation contexts. Stakeholder representatives are, by definition, accountable to a larger constituency. Moreover, it is not possible to manipulate this variable in a real evaluation setting. Interesting areas for inquiry, then, may involve posing questions about whether there can be different *kinds* of accountability or whether accountability might be experienced as less of an us-versus-them phenomenon. For example, research on social identity theory suggests that creating a common goal among stakeholders (e.g., social betterment) and a superordinate group identity may aid in resolving intergroup conflicts (Brewer, 1996; Dovidio, Gaertner, & Validzic, 1998; Tajfel, 1982). Viewed in the context of middle-range evaluation theory, we might propose the following testable hypothesis:

> *H1: Explicit commitments to fostering a superordinate group identity and goals may lessen the severity of stakeholder conflicts.*

Still many other areas of a middle-range theory of stakeholder interaction processes are in need of clarification and testing. For example, with respect to the issue of stakeholder expectations going in to a discussion, one can imagine another testable hypothesis, based at least in part, on existing research. A good deal of research on bargaining and negotiation suggests that the quality of interaction between negotiators tends to be more cooperative to the extent that they do not perceive the negotiation task as a "fixed-pie" (Bazerman & Carroll, 1987; deDreu, Koole, & Steinel, 2000). Specifically, "fixed-pie" perceptions refer to the expectation that a concession won on one side of the table is an automatic loss on the other side of the table (Thompson & Hastie, 1990). Applied to the case of stakeholder interactions, we might draw inferences about the potential effect of "framing" on stakeholder interactions. For example:

> *H2: Framing a decision task as a fixed-pie scenario will lead to more contentious interactions than if the task is framed as having win–win potential.*

By implementing a simple set of instructions prior to a stakeholder discussion, we may be able to examine the impact of framing on stakeholder interaction processes and outcomes. Moreover, the results from such an examination could certainly contribute to existing social psychological theories of negotiation, offering insights into the generalizability of framing effects across different contexts.

The testable hypotheses suggested here are by no means exhaustive. Volumes have been written by social psychologists on topics related to group decision making and conflict resolution (deDreu, 2010). Similarly, evaluation practitioners have offered many speculations about how stakeholder interactions might be improved. Our intent here is simply to illustrate how the integration of evaluation realities and social psychological research can suggest fruitful directions for the development of more comprehensive evaluation theories. Starting with a relatively narrow focus and a simple idea, empirically testable hypotheses emerge. With a commitment to systematically testing various aspects of middle-range evaluation theory, piece by piece, we will develop our much-needed theoretical subassemblies. We now turn our attention to middle-range theories of evaluation use.

Middle-Range Theories of Evaluation Use

This dimension relates to the utilization of findings from evaluation research, and it has arguably received the most empirical research attention among all five of the theoretical dimensions (Alkin, Daillak, & White, 1979; Feinstein, 2002; Johnson, Greenseid, Toal, King, Lawrenz, & Volkov, 2009; Leviton & Hughes, 1981). Good theories of evaluation use would provide not only guidelines for implementing evaluation results, but such theories would also account for the varying climates of acceptance of evaluation results (e.g., due to entrenched interests, the incremental nature of policy change, or time and budgetary constraints). Middle-range themes within the domain of evaluation use might cover relatively narrow phenomena such as communication with stakeholders, the role of trust and credibility in the acceptance of evaluative outcomes, and the format or presentation of findings to various audiences, to suggest a few.

Recently, several researchers have proposed extending beyond our current understandings of use and moving into the more complex, but potentially more empirically fruitful, construct of evaluation influence (Henry & Mark, 2003b; Kirkhart, 2000; Mark & Henry, 2004). Rather than focusing on the different types of use that exist, these researchers focus on the underlying mechanisms and pathways by which evaluation exerts its influence on individuals, interpersonal interactions, and organizations (Henry & Mark, 2003b). Many of the proposed mechanisms originate from the social psychology literature. Developing middle-range theories within the domain of use, or influence, will necessarily involve creating and empirically testing pathway models that result in outcomes (e.g., attitudinal or behavioral changes), which may ultimately lead to the use of evaluation findings. Social psychological theories of influence and persuasion may in turn benefit from hypothesis tests that are conducted in evaluation settings. Such research may reveal the need for additions to or revisions in an existing theory (Mark et al., Chapter 14, this volume).

We use the phenomenon of communication with stakeholders to illustrate some of the important issues and questions that will arise in the course of developing middle-range theories of evaluation influence. For the past several decades, evaluators have lamented the ineffective use, or complete lack of use, of evaluation findings. The political realities of evaluation contexts, dominated by self-interest and organizational inertia, stimulated the development of strategies aimed at increasing the utilization of evaluation findings. Some of these suggestions recommend incorporating persuasive techniques during the evaluation process (e.g., engendering a commitment to the evaluation and to use) (Patton, 1997), and as such, communication with stakeholders can be viewed as a special case of persuasion.

A middle-range theory of communication with stakeholders would, at a minimum, specify (1) the nature of the communication with stakeholders (e.g., high or low levels of communication, persuasive or unconvincing communication), (2) the antecedents of the different types of communication (e.g., stakeholder involvement, commitments from stakeholders, perceived credibility of the evaluator, and personal characteristics such as need for cognition), (3) the mechanisms or likely process through which the antecedents exert their influence on the communication process (e.g., thoughtful process: high involvement among stakeholders may lead to issue-relevant thinking (i.e., a thoughtful communication process), which may ultimately result in strong persuasive communication), and (4) potential moderating variables, or factors that may change the direction or strength of the relationships proposed in (1), (2), and (3) (e.g., the type of commitment chosen: public written commitments may increase persuasion more than personal verbal commitments, or the timing of a commitment: requesting a commitment at an appropriate time will lead to more persuasive communication).

To illustrate the development of a middle-range theory of communication with stakeholders, we begin with a simple idea related to utilization:

Involving key stakeholders in evaluation decision making from the beginning will increase primary intended use by primary intended users.

A significant literature on communication and persuasion exists within social psychology, and there is little question that the extant research from this literature can be useful to evaluators interested in fostering the utilization of results. Specifically, research within social psychology has identified a number of factors (e.g., source credibility, argument strength, medium of presentation, etc.) that facilitate persuasive communication. A key finding for the discipline of evaluation is the fact that high involvement in a process can lead people to engage in issue-relevant thinking, which means that individuals are more likely to be persuaded by the content of an argument rather than peripheral cues (Fleming, Chapter 8, this volume; Perloff, 2003). When arguments are considered through an involved and thoughtful process, attitudes and behaviors are more likely to be influenced. Furthermore, involvement can increase the amount of effort expended on a task and one's level of comprehension of the task, both of which are factors that can increase an individual's susceptibility to persuasion (Rosnow & Robinson, 1967). Clearly, this is especially useful knowledge for the discipline of evaluation, and it has already been suggested as a strategy (i.e., involving stakeholders in an evaluation should increase their use of the evaluation) to increase utilization. Yet, involvement is only one of many factors that may contribute to the persuasiveness of a communication. Another factor for evaluators to consider is the time at which they request a commitment to utilization from stakeholders.

> *H1: A commitment to the evaluation and to utilization*
> *should be sought only after individuals adjust*
> *to the evaluation process and express interest in*
> *the activity.*

Effective commitments are freely chosen and sought when people express interest in, and engagement with, an activity (Cialdini, 2009). Given stakeholders' initial reluctance to begin an evaluation, it may be important to consider when and how a commitment to utilization is fostered. Specifically, it may be in the evaluator's best interest not to solicit commitments to the evaluation process and to use until some of the initial hesitation held by stakeholders wanes. That is, employing voluntary commitments, as opposed to more coercive attempts, should result in more persuasive communication. In addition to timing considerations, the social psychology literature on persuasion also provides information on the types of commitments that are likely to be the most effective.

> *H2: Obtaining written commitments from an entire*
> *group of stakeholders will lead to increased levels*
> *of evaluation utilization.*

While the evaluation literature suggests increasing utilization by obtaining a commitment to use from stakeholders, social psychology research also suggests different ways in which a meaningful, and potentially more effective, commitment can be obtained. Specifically, commitments obtained from an entire group of people tend to increase the effectiveness of the commitment because group members wish to be perceived as consistent in front of their peers (Dickerson, Thibodeau, Aronson, & Miller, 1992). Essentially, group or public commitments place normative pressure on individuals to follow through on their commitments with action.

Research on persuasion also emphasizes the importance of written commitments over verbal commitments (Cialdini, 2009). Written commitments provide evidence that an agreement was reached, and they again remind people of the social pressure placed upon them to act consistently with their previous claims. The simple act of writing out a statement can even influence the internal state of individuals, such that they come to perceive themselves as truly believing in the commitment (Schlenker, Dlugolecki, & Doherty, 1994). In summary, incorporating written commitments to use from a group of stakeholders during the evaluation process may be one way to create a more persuasive dialogue between stakeholders and evaluators.

Ideally, persuasive communication between an evaluator and stakeholders would lead to measurable outcomes such as attitudinal or behavioral changes on the part of stakeholders. Yet even if such changes were to occur, utilization is certainly not assured. Weiss (1970, 1976) pioneered efforts to bring to light the inherently political nature of evaluation, illuminating how social programs really operate and change in political and organizational environments. Her work dispelled evaluators' wishful thinking for a rational decision maker, unimpeded by political and organizational concerns and constraints, willing to make radical program changes in response to a single evaluation report. Consequently, even if persuasive communication techniques are employed, there is certainly no guarantee that such effects would be strong enough to overcome powerful realities such as organizational inertia and the incremental nature of program and policy change. Yet at the same time, we can see no reason to throw the baby out with the bath water. Persuasive communication techniques are one potential way to influence stakeholder decisions, and coupled with other factors they may well lead to evaluation use in certain contexts. Indeed, sorting through such contingencies is a central purpose for middle-range theory development.

Having provided some (albeit limited) direction for middle-range theory development in the domains of evaluation practice and evaluation use, we turn now to the remaining domains of evaluation theory. For each we try to identify some potentially rich middle-range themes and general areas that may benefit from more middle-range thinking.

Middle-Range Theories of Social Programming

Theories of social programming should help us to achieve a better understanding of the things that we evaluate, whether small-scale interventions, large-scale social programs, policies, or products. Middle-range theories within the domain of social programming might describe how social programs (or other evaluands) work, how they change, the impact of external constraints on the operation of programs, and perhaps, generally, how programs contribute to larger social change (Shadish et al., 1991). For insight into how particular social interventions work, evaluators could, for example, look to the work of Ajzen on the theory of planned behavior (Ajzen, Chapter 3, this volume). Research on the realities of program implementation, adoption, and adaptation, particularly as they relate to evaluating programs, would also contribute to a more complete, usable middle-range theory of social programming for evaluation (Castro, Barrera, & Martinez, 2004; Pentz, 2004). While researchers in many areas have contributed a good deal to our understanding of such issues, evaluation has been slow to weigh in on these topics that are clearly relevant to a theory of social programming.

The work of Weiss has contributed a great deal to our current understanding of program change. Incidentally, many of the concepts discussed here are potentially linkable to theories of utilization. We have long known that the complexity of a program (e.g., simple vs. complex) impacts the quality of program change that can be expected (e.g., incremental change vs. radical change) following an evaluation. Program change is also impacted by characteristics of the organizational context (e.g., whether the decision makers are amenable to program change; or their level of trust in the evaluation process) (Weiss, 1973). A wealth of research on topics such as organizational culture (Denison & Mishra, 1995) and organizational change and development (Detert, Schroeder, & Mauriel, 2000) may be brought to bear on questions relevant to social programming and program change. In our existing knowledge about social programming are possibilities for sketching out more elaborate middle-range theories of social programming. Many of the pieces are there. We must continue to assemble them.

Middle-Range Theories of Knowledge Construction

This dimension of evaluation theory concerns the content of the knowledge that evaluators construct, the methods they use to get to that knowledge, and factors that influence an evaluator's method choices. Middle-range theories in the domain of knowledge construction would address purposes, strengths, and limitations of different methods (broadly defined) and the links between methods and the resulting knowledge. A middle-range theory of knowledge construction might draw on research on the "logic of conversation" (Schwarz & Oyserman, 2001, and Chapter 9, this volume) to begin to describe and explain the link between method choices, participant interpretations, and the implications for an evaluation's results. A theory of method choice, for example, might include contingencies describing external pressures to adopt certain "types" of methods, as with the U.S. Department of Education's policy of promoting randomized field trials. Theories of knowledge construction might revisit some of the questions raised during the qualitative–quantitative debates, including, "What are the real and perceived benefits of quantitative methods, qualitative methods or mixed methods for an evaluation? What mechanisms explain such real and/or perceived benefits?" As evaluators, we aim for accuracy and credibility with our methods choices. A middle-range theory of knowledge construction may begin to tell us whether, when, and how certain choices lead to these desired outcomes.

Middle-Range Theories of Valuing

The valuing dimension of evaluation theory concerns the ways in which values are handled in an evaluation. It is widely accepted that values are an inevitable part of the work we do. Middle-range theories within the domain of valuing might cover phenomena such as stakeholder participation and perceived fairness, perceptions of objectivity and trust in evaluation, and values inquiry and synthesis in evaluation, to suggest a few. A middle-range theory in the valuing domain may, for example, address issues surrounding representation of different viewpoints and perceptions of fairness. Evaluators have long known that when multiple perspectives or interests are represented in an evaluation, the evaluation process will be perceived as fairer than when a particular perspective is given preference (Chelimsky, 1998; Datta, 2001). A theory of representation and fairness in evaluation must take this idea further and flesh out the key concepts, the key processes operating, and the key contingencies. Social psychologists have addressed questions like these extensively (Azzi, 1993; Blader & Tyler, 2003; Tyler, Degoey & Smith, 1996; VanDenBos, Wilke & Lind, 1998), but rarely outside of the laboratory. Empirical examinations of group representation and perceived fairness within evaluation settings could contribute valuable information to both the evaluation and the social psychology literatures.

In summary, there are many potential middle-range themes for evaluation theory, and many of these themes share a significant conceptual overlap with issues studied by social psychologists. Drawing on our knowledge of our own discipline, together with the accumulated wisdom from other fields, will only serve evaluation well. The more we push ourselves to think deeply about any number of evaluation phenomena, the more questions are raised—questions that may ultimately lead to hypotheses, tests of hypotheses, and more stable connections in our theoretical subassemblies.

Adopting a Middle-Range Frame of Mind: Benefits and Challenges

Having sketched out some fruitful starting points for the development of middle-range evaluation theory, we now discuss some of the primary benefits of adopting a middle-range orientation to evaluation research. Together with the benefits, we examine some of the challenges that must be overcome to realize them.

Strengthening Empirical Norms

In order for middle-range evaluation theory to develop and flourish, empirical research on evaluation must become a common practice. It is only by testing individual inferences and propositions that each theoretical subassembly will be built and strengthened. Given its practical beginnings, the field of evaluation has focused primarily on *doing* evaluations, with far less emphasis on empirically studying evaluation processes and phenomena (King, 2003). Theory-building has not traditionally been a major focus of the work of evaluators, and the dearth of empirical research on evaluation is attributable in part to the practice origins of the field.

We suspect another factor that has contributed to a lack of theoretically driven empirical research on evaluation is that many of us find the prospect rather daunting. In a field that has many unknowns and very little empirical work to build on, it can be difficult to know where precisely to start. By providing that much-needed sketch of evaluation processes, even preliminary middle-range evaluation theories may help us to better focus our theoretical questions and our empirical energies. Indeed, all the complexity of evaluation theory can be handled much more efficiently, and perhaps approached more eagerly, when the task is broken down into manageable parts. With a broader commitment to developing and testing middle-range evaluation theories, we believe that empirical norms will be strengthened, providing a much needed response to the call for descriptive evaluation theory.

In order to fully realize the benefits of an empirical shift in evaluation research, we will need to have an open mind about appropriate ways to do evaluation and research on evaluation. Single-case studies are one of the most commonly reported empirical evaluation study methods, but there are many other, underutilized methods that may breathe new life into the empirical program of research on evaluation (Henry & Mark, 2003a). A more variable distribution of study types used to examine and test aspects of evaluation theory would benefit us all. Overcoming the inertia of "the way things are done around here" will take time and persuasion. Researchers and practitioners alike must see the value in theory development and must also be provided with guidance and direction about how they can accomplish it. Recent simulation studies (Azzam, 2010; Campbell & Mark, 2006; Christie, 2007), comparative research (Christie, 2003), and empirical reviews (Miller & R. Campbell, 2006) represent a positive trend. As this type of research becomes more commonplace, empirical norms will be strengthened.

Forcing a Focus on the Issues

In addition to fostering empirical norms, a middle-range orientation will help us to move away from purely prescriptive, "brand-name" evaluation theories, and toward a focus on more general evaluation issues that cut across evaluations of all stripes. In his day, Merton (1968) was concerned about the potential negative effects of "brand-named" theories, worried that "the road to effective general schemes in sociology will only become clogged if ... each charismatic sociologist tries to develop his own general system of theory" (p. 51). A similar concern has been voiced in the field of evaluation, with a push to reframe theoretical debates to those surrounding theoretical issues rather than the positions of a few prominent grand theorists. Indeed, a focus on brand names rather than on the theoretical issues underlying them has been viewed by some as a significant barrier to progress in the development of evaluation theory (Miller & Campbell, 2006; Schwandt, Mark, Hopson, & Cooksy, 2003).

Shifting to a middle-range theoretical orientation addresses this concern in at least two ways. First, rather than our theories being overarching prescriptive approaches to evaluation practice (e.g., empowerment evaluation, utilization-focused evaluation), narrower, more manageable middle-range theories would focus on key evaluation issues and processes that are common across many evaluation orientations, such as issues of stakeholder group composition and implications for decision making. By focusing on issues we may go a longer way toward consolidating evaluation theory (i.e., by avoiding duplication of efforts). Second, and perhaps more importantly, we believe, with others (Schwandt et al., 2003), that a shift of focus would help more would-be theorists to overcome the psychological barriers imposed by brand-named theories. When evaluation theory is about issues, and not about labels, the work of theory development and testing becomes anyone's territory. Such a shift in mindset, we believe, will result in a more inclusive approach to research on evaluation, generating more theory development, testing, and consolidation.

Making Our Theories and Assumptions More Explicit

Contemporary evaluation theory operates with an abundance of unexamined or even unstated assumptions. Approaches, methods, and techniques, are frequently recommended for evaluation practice, but without explicit theories about the mechanisms through which such practices are likely to have an impact on the desired outcomes. If we approach the act of evaluation as an intervention in its own right, as others have done (Henry & Mark, 2003b), we will be faced with the need to clearly explicate our theories. By forcing ourselves to make our assumptions clear and explicit (as many of us do when we encourage clients to create logic models), we will be better prepared to show convincing support for the theoretical propositions that we already have. Although some of our taken-for-granted assumptions will be found untenable, many others will be supported. Because, by definition, middle-range theories must be empirically testable, they must also be specified at a level that lends itself to empirical inquiry. With many current evaluation theories, we are left with more questions than answers about critical evaluation processes and practice decisions. Some of these problems will be addressed with a shift toward middle-range theorizing.

When middle-range theories become the norm in evaluation, we will all find ourselves being a bit more thoughtful and explicit when discussing our theories and assumptions. We will ask ourselves "why" and "how" more often. The very structure of theories requires us to think through and explicate our concepts and theoretical assumptions. We will have to be able to justify our reasons for drawing a particular inference or testing a particular proposition. In the course of drawing analogies between evaluation phenomena and social psychological research, we come face to face with the issue of conceptual compatibility (e.g., how is this evaluation construct similar to/different from its counterpart in social psychology), and we are forced to think through our definitions, assumptions, and proposed mechanisms (Johnson, Johnson, & Stevahn, Chapter 11, this volume). This will be both a benefit and a challenge. The very act of carefully thinking through the implied logic of our theories should force us to be specific about the details of the statements and assumptions we make and the ways in which the theory may be supported or not. In the end, our theories will be stronger and less subject to criticism based in ideology alone. A thoughtful, systematic approach will only contribute positively to middle-range theory development and testing.

Adding to Evaluation's Knowledge Base: Theory and Practice

As the discipline of evaluation grows, it is becoming more imperative for us to move away from a knowledge base predominated by the experiences and opinions of a few (Worthen, 2001). The institutionalization of evaluation, in part, depends on legitimizing our field through empirically supported processes. In addition to the benefits outlined above, the development of middle-range theories is one way to answer the call for more cumulative knowledge about evaluation (Mark, 2001). As the evidence for specific middle-range theories grows and as links between theories are strengthened, a cumulative, comprehensive knowledge base for evaluation becomes within reach. The potential of evaluation as a tool for social betterment is great, but we must be prepared for this call with sound theories.

Surely, the development and consolidation of middle-range evaluation theories will contribute to "academic," theoretical goals. But such theories will also contribute to practical goals, yielding a great deal more practice guidance than is currently available (Donaldson & Lipsey, 2006). This has been a challenge since the emergence of evaluation as a profession. As Shadish et al. (1991) pointed out in their seminal work, a good theory of evaluation practice will "help evaluators sort through the discrepant advice that different theorists give about practice" (p. 63). An illustrative example shows that for any given challenge an evaluator faces, different and in fact, conflicting, advice may be given by different evaluators. Without a clearer basis on which to choose, practicing evaluators will be left to use more biased judgments and decisions. Middle-range theorizing can provide useful guidance to practice, while steering the field of evaluation away from the popular trend of best practices. According to Patton (2001), best practices often lack meaning and standards, and they tend to oversimplify contexts. Middle-range theories necessarily value context and can take us beyond best practices by providing a basis in which to systematically examine evaluation processes.

Summary

We have proposed the development of usable, middle-range evaluation theory that draws on evaluation realities and a large body of social psychological research. Middle-range theories are relatively narrowly focused, empirically testable models intended to describe the way in which particular processes or phenomena operate. The potential benefits of adopting a middle-range orientation to evaluation are many. First, by serving as a series of subassemblies, middle-range theories will act as important placeholders in the overall development of evaluation theory. Second, with middle-range theories, we will move away from evaluation's "grand" theories, perhaps reducing some of the psychological barriers to participating in theoretical activities, while focusing our efforts on the real issues that define evaluation theory. Third, a commitment to developing and testing middle-range theories will force us to clarify and explicate many evaluation phenomena, which, at present, are discussed at a level entirely too abstract. Finally, focusing on narrow, manageable issues that can be empirically investigated will encourage the development of descriptive evaluation theory that will add to evaluation's cumulative knowledge base.

In order to realize the benefits of middle-range evaluation theory, we must be willing to do the work necessary to build our theoretical subassemblies. Despite the inevitable challenges, it is, we believe, a worthy undertaking, but one that will require thought, patience, perseverance, and, most importantly, humility. Indeed,

the middle-range orientation involves the specification of ignorance. Rather than pretend to knowledge where it is in fact absent, it expressly recognizes what must still be learned in order to lay the foundation for still more knowledge. It does not assume itself to be equal to the task of providing theoretical solutions to all the urgent practical problems of the day but addresses itself to those problems that might now be clarified in the light of available knowledge. (Merton, 1968, p. 69)

It is our hope that a trend of middle-range theorizing will take hold in the field of evaluation—a trend that will encourage targeted, empirical research on important evaluation themes and that will ultimately produce a comprehensive base of empirically tested, relevant, evaluation theory.

REFERENCES

Alkin, M. C. (2003). Evaluation theory and practice: Insights and new directions. In C. A. Christie (Ed.), *The practice-theory relationship in evaluation* (New Directions for Evaluation, No. 97, pp. 81–89). San Francisco: Jossey-Bass.

Alkin, M. C. (2004). Comparing evaluation points of view. In M. C. Alkin (Ed.), *Evaluation roots* (pp. 3–11).Thousand Oaks, CA: Sage.

Alkin, M. C., Daillak, R., & White, P. (1979). *Using evaluations: Does evaluation make a difference?* Beverly Hills, CA: Sage.

Azzam, T. (2010). Evaluator responsiveness to stakeholders. *American Journal of Evaluation, 31*(1), 45–65.

Azzi, A. E. (1993). Group representation and procedural justice in multigroup decision-making bodies. *Journal of Social Issues, 6*(2), 195–218.

Bazerman, M. H., & Carroll, J. S. (1987). Negotiator cognition. *Research in Organizational Behavior, 9*, 247–288.

Beck, A. T. (1989). Evaluation anxieties. In C. Lindemann (Ed.), *Handbook of phobia therapy* (pp. 89–112). Northvale, NJ: Aronson.

Ben-Yoav, O., & Pruitt, D. G. (1984). Resistance to yielding and the expectation of cooperative future interactions in negotiation. *Journal of Experimental Social Psychology, 20*, 323–335.

Blader, S. L., & Tyler, T. R. (2003). A four-component model of procedural justice: Defining the meaning of a "fair" process. *Personality and Social Psychology Bulletin, 29*(6), 747–758.

Bourgeois, L. J. (1979). Toward a method of middle-range theorizing. *Academy of Management Review, 4*(3), 443–447.

Brehm, S. S., & Brehm, J. W. (1981). *Psychological Reactance.* New York: Academic Press.

Brewer, M. B. (1996). When contact is not enough: Social identity and intergroup cooperation. *International Journal of Intercultural Relationships, 20*(3/4), 291–303.

Campbell, B., & Mark, M. M. (2006). Toward more effective stakeholder dialogue: Applying theories of negotiation to policy and program evaluation. *Journal of Applied Social Psychology, 36*(12), 2834–2863.

Castro, F. G., Barrera, M., Jr., & Martinez, C. R. (2004). The cultural adaptation of prevention interventions: Resolving tensions between fidelity and fit. *Prevention Science, 5*(1), 41–45.

Chelimsky, E. (1997). The political environment of evaluation and what it means for the development of the field. In E. Chelimsky & W. R. Shadish (Eds.), *Evaluation for the 21st century: A handbook* (pp. 53–68). Thousand Oaks, CA: Sage.

Christie, C. A. (2003). What guides evaluation? A study of how evaluation practice maps onto evaluation theory. In C. A. Christie (Ed.), *The practice-theory relationship in evaluation* (New Directions for Evaluation, No. 97, pp. 7–35). San Francisco: Jossey-Bass.

Christie, C. A. (2007). Reported influence of evaluation data on decision makers' actions: An experimental examination. *American Journal of Evaluation, 28*(1), 8–25.

Cialdini, R. B. (2009). *Influence: Science and practice.* New York: Pearson.

Cook, T. D., & Groom, C. (2004). The methodological assumptions of social psychology: The mutual dependence of substantive theory and method choice. In C. Sansone, C. C. Morf, & A. T. Panter (Eds.), *The Sage handbook of methods in social psychology* (pp. 19–44). Thousand Oaks, CA: Sage.

Cousins, J. B. (2003). Utilization effects of participatory evaluation. In T. Kellaghan, D. L. Stufflebeam, & L. A. Wingate (Eds.), *International handbook of educational evaluation* (pp. 245–265). Boston: Kluwer.

Cousins, J. B. (2004). Crossing the bridge: Toward understanding use through systematic inquiry. In M. C. Alkin (Ed.), *Evaluation roots* (pp. 319–330). Thousand Oaks, CA: Sage.

Cousins, J. B., & Shulha, L. M. (2006). A comparative analysis of evaluation utilization and its cognate fields. In B. Staw, M. M. Mark, & J. Greene (Eds.), *International handbook of evaluation.* Thousand Oaks, CA: Sage.

Datta, L-e. (2001). Seriously seeking fairness: Strategies for crafting non-partisan evaluations in a partisan world. *American Journal of Evaluation, 21*(1), 1–14.

deDreu, C. K. W. (2010). Social conflict: The emergence and consequences of struggle and negotiation. In S. T. Fiske, D. T. Gilbert, & G. Lindzey (Eds.), *Handbook of social psychology* (5th ed., pp. 983–1023). Hoboken, NJ: Wiley.

deDreu, C. K. W., Koole, S. L., & Steinel, W. (2000). Unfixing the fixed pie: A motivated information-processing approach to integrative negotiation. *Journal of Personality and Social Psychology, 79*(6), 975–987.

Denison, D. R., & Mishra, A. K. (1995). Toward a theory of organizational culture and effectiveness. *Organization Science, 6,* 204–223.

Detert, J. R., Schroeder, R. G., & Mauriel, J. J. (2000). A framework for linking culture and improvement initiatives in organizations. *Academy of Management Review, 25,* 850–963.

Dickerson, C., Thibodeau, R., Aronson, E., & Miller, D. (1992). Using cognitive dissonance to encourage water conservation. *Journal of Applied Social Psychology, 22,* 841–854.

Donaldson, S. I., Gooler, L. E., & Scriven, M. (2002). Strategies for managing evaluation anxiety: Toward a psychology of program evaluation. *American Journal of Evaluation, 23,* 261–273.

Donaldson, S. I., & Lipsey, M. W. (2006). Roles for theory in contemporary evaluation practice: Developing practical knowledge. In I. F. Shaw, J. C. Greene, & M. M. Mark (Eds.), *The Sage handbook of evaluation* (pp. 56–75). Thousand Oaks, CA: Sage.

Dovidio, J. F., & Gaertner, S. L. (2010). Intergroup bias. In S. T. Fiske, D. T. Gilbert, & G. Lindzey (Eds.), *Handbook of social psychology* (5th ed., pp. 1084–1121). Hoboken, NJ: Wiley.

Dovidio, J. F., Gaertner, S. L., & Validzic, A. (1998). Intergroup bias: Status, differentiation, and a common in-group identity. *Journal of Personality and Social Psychology, 75,* 109–120.

Druckman, D. (1994). Determinants of compromising behavior in negotiation: A meta-analysis. *Journal of Conflict Resolution, 38*(3), 507–556.

Feinstein, O. N. (2002). Use of evaluations and the evaluation of their use. *Evaluation, 8*(4), 433–439.

Geva-May, I., & Thorngate, W. (2003). Reducing anxiety and resistance in policy and programme evaluations: A socio-psychological analysis. *Evaluation, 9*(2), 205–227.

Greene, J. C. (2000). Challenges in practicing deliberative democratic evaluation. In K. E. Ryan & L. DeStefano (Eds.), *Evaluation as a democratic process: Promoting inclusion, dialogue, and deliberation* (New Directions for Evaluation, No. 85, pp. 13–26). San Francisco: Jossey-Bass.

Greene, J. C. (2001). Evaluation extrapolations. *American Journal of Evaluation, 22,* 397–402.

Henry, G. T., & Mark, M. M. (2003a). Toward an agenda for research on evaluation. In C. A Christie (Ed.), *The practice-theory relationship in evaluation* (New Directions for Evaluation, No. 97, pp. 69–80). San Francisco: Jossey-Bass.

Henry, G. T., & Mark, M. M. (2003b). Beyond use: Understanding evaluation's influence on attitudes and actions. *American Journal of Evaluation, 24,* 293–314.

Higbee, K. L., Millard, R. J., & Folkman, J. R. (1982). Social psychology research during the 1970's: Predominance of experimentation and college students. *Personality and Social Psychology Bulletin, 8*(1), 180–183.

House, E. R., & Howe, K. R. (1999). *Values in evaluation.* Thousand Oaks, CA: Sage.

Johnson, D. W., & Johnson, F. P. (2003). *Joining together: Group theory and group skills* (8th ed.). Boston: Allyn & Bacon.

Johnson, K., Greenseid, L. O., Toal, S. A., King, J. A., Lawrenz, F., & Volkov, B. (2009). Research on evaluation use: A review of the empirical literature from 1986 to 2005. *American Journal of Evaluation, 30*(3), 377–410.

King, J. A. (2003). The challenge of studying evaluation theory. In C. A. Christie (Ed.), *The practice-theory relationship in evaluation* (New Directions for Evaluation, No. 97, pp. 57–67). San Francisco: Jossey-Bass.

Kirkhart, K. (2000). Reconceptualizing evaluation use: An integrated theory of influence. In V. Caracelli & H. Preskill (Eds.), *The expanding scope of evaluation use* (New Directions for Evaluation, No. 88, pp. 5–24). San Francisco: Jossey-Bass.

Kochan, T. A. (1992). Teaching and building middle range industrial relations theory. In R. J. Adams & N. Meltz (eds.), *Industrial relations theory: Its nature, scope and pedagogy.* Melbourne, Australia: Longman-Cheshire.

Kramer, R. M., Pommerenke, P., & Newton, E. (1993). The social context of negotiation: Effects of social identity and interpersonal accountability on negotiator decision making. *Journal of Conflict Resolution, 37*(4), 633–654.

Leviton, L. C., & Hughes, E. F. X. (1981). Research on the utilization of evaluations: A review and synthesis. *Evaluation Review, 5*(4), 525–548.

Mark, M. M. (2001). Evaluation's future: Furor, futile or fertile? *American Journal of Evaluation, 22*, 457–479.

Mark, M. M., & Henry, G. T. (2004). The mechanisms and outcomes of evaluation influence. *Evaluation, 10*(1), 35–57.

Merton, R. K. (1968). *Social Theory and Social Structure.* New York: Free Press.

Miller, R. L., & Campbell, R. (2006). Taking stock of empowerment evaluation: An empirical review. *American Journal of Evaluation, 27*(3), 296–319.

Morell, J. A. (2000). Internal evaluation: A synthesis of traditional methods and industrial engineering. *American Journal of Evaluation, 21*(1), 41–52.

O'Connor, K. M. (1997). Groups and solos in context: The effects of accountability on team negotiation. *Organizational Behavior and Human Decision Processes, 72*, 384–407.

Patton, M. Q. (1997). *Utilization focused evaluation: The new century text* (3rd ed.). London: Sage.

Patton, M. Q. (2001). Evaluation, knowledge management, best practices, and high quality lessons learned. *American Journal of Evaluation, 22*(3), 329–336.

Pentz, M. A. (2004). Form follows function: Designs for prevention effectiveness and diffusion research. *Prevention Science, 5*(1), 23–29.

Perloff, R. M. (2003). *The dynamics of persuasion: Communication and attitudes in the 21st century.* Englewood Cliffs, NJ: Erlbaum.

Pinder, C. C., & Moore, L. F. (1980). The resurrection of taxonomy to aid the development of middle range theories of organizational behaviour. In C. C. Pinder & L. F. Moore (Eds.), *Middle range theory and the study of organizations* (pp. 187–211). Boston: Martinus Nijhoff.

Preskill, H. S., & Torres, R. T. (1999). Building capacity for organizational learning through evaluative inquiry. *Evaluation, 5*(1) 42–60.

Pruitt, D. G. (1998). Social conflict. In Daniel T. Gilbert, Susan T. Fiske, & Gardner Lindzey (Eds.), *The handbook of social psychology* (pp. 470–503). Boston: McGraw-Hill.

Pruitt, D. G., & Rubin, J. Z. (1986). *Social conflict: Escalation, stalemate, and settlement.* New York: Random House.

Raab, L. M., & Goodyear, A. C. (1984). Middle-range theory in archaeology: A critical review of origins and applications. *American Antiquity, 49*(2), 255–268.

Rogers, P. J. (2001). The whole world is evaluating half-full glasses. *American Journal of Evaluation, 22*(3), 431–435.

Rosnow, R. L., & Robinson, E. J. (1967). Active versus passive participation. In R. L. Rosnow & E. J. Robinson (Eds.), *Experiments in persuasion* (pp. 347–352). New York: Academic Press.

Ryan, K. E., & DeStefano, L. (2000). Disentangling dialogue: Issues from practice. In K. E. Ryan & L. DeStefano (Eds.), *Evaluation as a democratic process: Promoting inclusion, dialogue, and deliberation* (New Directions for Evaluation, No. 85, pp. 63–76). San Francisco: Jossey-Bass.

Ryan, K. E., & Johnson, T. D. (2000). Democratizing evaluation: Meanings and methods from practice. In K. E. Ryan & L. DeStefano (Eds.), *Evaluation as a democratic process: Promoting inclusion, dialogue, and deliberation* (New Directions for Evaluation, No. 85, pp. 39–50). San Francisco: Jossey-Bass.

Schlenker, B. R., Dlugolecki, D. W., & Doherty, K. (1994). The impact of self-presentations on self-appraisals and behavior. The power of public commitment. *Personality and Social Psychology, 20*, 20–33.

Schwandt, T. A., Mark, M. M., Hopson, R. K., & Cooksy, L. (2003). *From theories, brand names, and "great men" to fundamental issues and challenges: Reframing debates about evaluation theory.* Paper presented at the annual meeting of the American Evaluation Association, Reno, NV.

Schwarz, N., & Oyserman, D. (2001). Asking questions about behaviour: Cognition, communication, and questionnaire construction. *American Journal of Evaluation, 22*(2), 127–160.

Shadish, W. R. (1997). Evaluation theory is who we are. *American Journal of Evaluation, 19*(1), 1–19.

Shadish, W. R., Cook, T. D., & Leviton, L. C. (1991). *Foundations of program evaluation: Theories of practice.* Newbury Park, CA: Sage.

Sherman, R. C., Buddie, A. M., Dragan, K. L., End, C. M., & Finney, L. J. (1999). Twenty years of PSPB: Trends in content, design, and analysis. *Personality and Social Psychology Bulletin, 25*(2), 177–187.

Simon, H. A. (1962). The architecture of complexity. *Proceedings of the American Philosophical Society, 160*(6), 467–482.

Smith, M. J., & Liehr, P. (Eds.). (2003). *Middle range theory for nursing.* New York: Springer.

Smith, N. L. (1979). Requirements for a discipline of evaluation. *Studies in Educational Evaluation, 5*(1), 5–12.

Smith, N. L. (1993). Improving evaluation theory through the empirical study of evaluation practice. *Evaluation Practice, 14*(3), 237–242.

Stevahn, L., & King, J. A. (2005). Managing conflict constructively in program evaluation. *Evaluation, 11*(4), 415–427.

Tajfel, H. (Ed.). (1982). *Social identity and intergroup relations.* New York: Cambridge University Press.

Taut, S., & Brauns, D. (2003). Resistance to evaluation: A psychological perspective. *Evaluation, 9*, 247–264.

Thompson, L. (1995)."They saw a negotiation": Partisanship and involvement. *Journal of Personality and Social Psychology, 68*(5), 839–853.

Thompson, L., & Hastie, R. (1990). Social perception in negotiation. *Organizational Behavior and Human Decision Processes, 47*(1), 98–123.

Thompson, L. L., Wang, J., & Gunia, B. C. (2010). Negotiation. *Annual Review of Psychology, 61*, 491–515.

Thorngate, W. (2001). The social psychology of policy analysis. *Journal of Comparative Policy Analysis: Research and Practice, 3*, 85–112.

Tyler, T. R., Degoey, P., & Smith, H. J. (1996). Understanding why the justice of group procedures matters. *Journal of Personality and Social Psychology, 70*, 913–930.

VanDenBos, K., Wilke, H. A. M., & Lind, E. A. (1998). When do we need procedural fairness? The role of trust in authority. *Journal of Personality and Social Psychology, 75,* 1449–1458.

Weick, K. E. (1980). Middle range themes in organizational theorizing. In C. C. Pinder & L. F. Moore (Eds.), *Middle range theory and the study of organizations* (pp. 392–407). Boston: Martinus Nijhoff.

Weiss, C. H. (1970). The politicization of evaluation research. *Journal of Social Issues, 26,* 57–68.

Weiss, C. H. (1973). Where politics and evaluation research meet. *Evaluation, 1,* 37–45.

Weiss, C. H. (1976). Using research in the policy process: Potential and constraints. *Policy Studies Journal, 4,* 224–228.

Worthen, B. R. (2001). Whither evaluation? That all depends. *American Journal of Evaluation, 22,* 409–418.

EDITORS' CONCLUDING COMMENTS
TO CHAPTER 13

Campbell and McGrath covered a great deal of territory in considering the use of middle-range theory in the intersection between social psychology and evaluation. At the same time, far more territory remains to be examined. We invite the reader to consider either of two large exercises at this point. In one of the exercises, you would review one or more of the previous chapters, especially those in the penultimate section of the book. Do the authors present a middle-range theory? On which of Shadish et al.'s five components do they focus?

A second exercise would be more ambitious. It would involve drawing on the social psychological and the evaluation literature to sketch out another middle-range theory beyond those presented by Campbell and McGrath and others in this book. If you have been reading this book as part of a course on evaluation or applied social psychology, either of these exercises might make a good final project. If you are reading this volume outside of a class, we believe there are opportunities for publishing strong products, especially those of the second exercise.

CHAPTER 14

Building a Better Future

Melvin M. Mark
Stewart I. Donaldson
Bernadette Campbell

This volume has examined the relationship between social psychology and the evaluation of programs, policies, and practices. As indicated in Chapter 1, there was a something of an influx of social psychologists into evaluation in the first heyday of modern evaluation, at the time of the Great Society of the 1960s. These social psychologists, along with colleagues from related disciplines, brought skills in research methods to the work of planning and doing evaluation. These skills included familiarity with experimental and quasi-experimental designs, which were used to assess the effects of programs, and relevant forms of measurement such as questionnaires, which were used to measure outcomes of interest.

More recently, the application of social psychological theory in evaluation has increased. As illustrated throughout the book, but especially in Part II, social psychological theory can provide a guide to the design and evaluation of a wide range of programs and policies. This is particularly true for the many programs and policies that involve efforts to change human behavior (see also Donaldson, 2007).

As the chapters in Part III highlight, there are numerous opportunities for research and theory in social psychology to offer guidance for the challenges that arise in evaluation practice. For example, multiple areas of social psychology can inform evaluators about how best to involve stakeholder groups in evaluation planning and evaluation practice. Literature on attitude change and persuasion, as well as other areas of social psychological research, can likewise inform efforts to facilitate the appropriate use of evaluation findings.

In addition, as has been alluded to throughout the book, especially in Part IV, considerable potential exists for evaluation to serve as a testbed for conceptualization and research that enriches social psychology (see also Campbell & Mark, 2006). Findings from theory-driven evaluations and from research on evaluation can offer several advantages for social psychologists. Such findings could increase the external validity of social psychological research, improve construct validity with real-world procedures and refined conceptualizations, and identify and help fill gaps in theory that has largely been built on laboratory research (see also Tashiro & Mortensen, 2006).

A Completely Unique Relationship? No.

Although the focus of this book is on evaluation and social psychology, we would be remiss if we failed to point out that social psychology is not unique among the social and behavioral sciences in having a relationship with evaluation. Indeed, there are other fields that overlap with social psychology to which we could apply many of the general points made in this book. These include related parts of sociology and certain other subareas of psychology, such as developmental, cognitive, and organizational psychology. Most of this book's points about the social psychology–evaluation relationship could also be applied to a more recent cousin of social psychology, behavioral economics. In recent years behavioral economics has generated considerable excitement regarding applications to policy and program design (e.g., Thaler & Sunstein, 2008).

We will not go into detail here, but there are various shared intellectual precursors across many of these fields. For example, Kurt Lewin, discussed in Chapter 1 as an historical figure in social psychology and evaluation, also had influence in multiple other disciplines and subareas. Another notable example involves cognitive psychologists such as Herbert Simon and Daniel Kahneman, who have had striking influence on social psychology and on behavioral economics. In fact, Simon and Kahneman each received the Nobel Prize in economics as well as various honors in psychology.

More generally, Vaessen and Leeuw (2010) have edited a book examining the relationship between evaluation and several disciplines or fields. These include sociology, economics, public management, international development, and criminology.

To point out that the social psychology–evaluation relationship is not wholly unique is not, however, to diminish either the historical linkage or the potential future connection between the two. To the contrary. Social psychology has a strong historical linkage to evaluation, involving figures such as Lewin, Campbell, and Rossi (see Chapter 1, this volume). Social psychological theory has repeatedly been the point of origin for the program theory of theory-based evaluations (see, e.g., Donaldson, 2007). And the wide scope of social psychological theory and research, with topics ranging from social power to inter- and intragroup processes to persuasion and behavior change, provide an especially rich base for attempts to solve the practice challenges of evaluation (see Campbell & Mark, 2006). Moreover, much of evaluation practice is hard if not impossible to distinguish from instances of applied social psychology (see, e.g., Oskamp & Schultz, 1999). Though not unique, the social psychology–evaluation relationship certainly merits special attention.

Plan for the Chapter

In this concluding chapter, we address two general issues. First, we take the opportunity to point to future directions that we think would be beneficial for one or both sides of the social psychology–evaluation relationship. For example, we describe what we think is fertile ground for expanding and enhancing the application of social psychological theory in theory-driven program design and evaluation. Second, we explore a very pragmatic professional concern, that is, employment opportunities at the intersection of social psychology and evaluation. Relative to evaluation, there are far more graduate programs that train far more social psychologists. Accordingly, we emphasize employment opportunities for social psychologists in evaluation, rather than the other way around.

Program Theory from Social Psychology: New Directions

As was noted in Chapter 1 and illustrated throughout the volume, evaluation, especially in the form of theory-driven program design and evaluation, already has benefited by drawing on theory and findings from social psychology. The chapters of Part II especially illustrate the use of social psychological theory for the development of sound program theory. More extensive linkages between the two fields should increase this importation of social psychological theory into program theory-driven design and evaluation in the future.

As illustrated throughout this book, especially in Parts II and IV, social psychological theory and its evidence base can substantially benefit in return. For example, when social psychological theory is the basis of theory-driven program design, one can better assess the scope, range, and limits of the original theory. When the social psychological theory is translated into real program operations, it is easier to see its strength and limits. Chapter 11 on cooperative learning and related interventions illustrates this process, as well as the theoretical refinement that can result. In addition, findings from theory-driven evaluation can provide tests of key aspects of social psychological theory, while also providing relatively strong construct and external validity.

In short, there will be benefits if an even stronger connection is built between social psychological theory and theory-driven program design and evaluation. At the same time, the chapters in this book, as well as other experiences with theory-driven evaluation, suggest future directions for improvement. We turn to these now.

Expand the Scope of Program Theory

At present, theory-driven evaluation focuses on theories of the program (or policy, or practice, or whatever is being evaluated). The evaluator, typically working with program stakeholders, builds and then tests a model of the mediation and moderation of program effects. The mediational model is typically represented graphically, with arrows connecting aspects of program operations that are expected to trigger change in one or more mediator, and with other arrows connecting mediators to expected outcomes. Metaphorically, the program theory specifies one or more lines of dominoes standing on edge, with one domino expected to knock over the next in line. Program activities are the first domino(es), anticipated mediators the next domino(es), and the desired outcomes the last domino(es). In other words, the theories of today's theory-driven evaluations describe the expected process(es) whereby program operations help bring about improvements in long-term outcomes. For example, social psychologically based theories involving norms, intentions, anticipated outcomes, and the like have supplied potential mediators for a program aimed at changes in health behavior (see, e.g., Figures 3.1 and 4.3 in Chapters 3 and 4).

Again, the way that social psychological theory connects with evaluation is by helping specify a theory of the *program*, of the way program activities are expected to translate into the outcomes of interest. Drawing in part on the chapters in this volume, we suggest that there are several other directions on which social psychologists and evaluators could fruitfully collaborate in the future. These include what can be called translational theory, theory knitting theory, sustainability theory, and generalizability theory.

Translational Theory

One area for future attention involves translational theory. The concept of translational research and theory has received a great deal of attention in recent years, arising largely from the focus on translational work by the U.S. National Institutes of Health (NIH). The NIH's general idea was to facilitate the translation of science "from bench to bedside." That is, translational research and science is intended to ensure that discoveries from the research lab (i.e., the bench) move expeditiously to direct application in health care (i.e., the bedside) (Woolf, 2008). Starting with this predominantly medical origin, the concept of translational research has generated considerable attention in psychology (Breckler, 2008; Tashiro & Mortensen, 2006; Vernig, 2007). In an important sense, the use of social psychology in evaluation represents a notable example of translational research.

Nevertheless, the theory of translational research and theory itself can be strengthened in important ways. One aspect of translational research seems straightforward: How can a given theoretical construct from social psychology be translated effectively into the specific activities employed in a social program? For example, suppose the relevant social psychological theory says that, in order to change the target behavior, the program needs to modify program participants' perception of social norms. In this case, a key translational question is, "What activities can the program implement that will effectively modify perceived norms in the specific circumstances in which the program is being implemented?"

Answering this question may in turn require effective theories of culture and local context. For example, it may not suffice to understand how to change perceived norms among first-year college students, if the program is to be implemented in elementary schools in the United States or in small African villages. Moreover, many programs are implemented across a wide range of program participants and settings. For example, mass media campaigns typically broadcast the same message for the heterogeneous subgroups that comprise the U.S. population. Can a single message effectively trigger perceived social norms across these subgroups, or must a narrowcasting strategy be applied?

These are the kinds of questions that translational theory could help answer better in the future. As social psychology continues to expand its focus on culture and local context (e.g., Heine, 2010), social psychological theory should be better able to address such questions of translation. Decades ago, there was considerable attention to the social psychology of the social psychology (lab) experiment (e.g., Orne, 1962). Here we call for the development and testing of social psychological models of the translation of social psychology, especially into program design.

Theory Knitting

Riemer and Bickman (Chapter 4, this volume) apply Kalmar and Sternberg's (1988) concept of theory knitting to capture their efforts to integrate concepts from multiple theories and research areas in developing a program design. Kalmar and Sternberg focused on theory knitting as an integrative approach to theory development, one that "seeks to identify those facets of competing theories that can provide a unified explanation of a given problem area" (1988, p. 153). In Riemer and Bickman's case, theory knitting involves drawing on multiple (and not necessarily competing) theories and research literatures in an effort to build a more comprehensive, unified, and effective program theory for use in program design and evaluation.

The idea of theory knitting for program design and evaluation is attractive. Individual social psychological theories are likely to provide some insight into the problem a program or policy is designed to address. But any individual theory is unlikely to address all the relevant issues. As attractive as the general idea of theory knitting is, however, much is yet to be learned about how to do it well. For example, how should the theory knitter select the presumably complementary theories? How does one match each theory to the distinct pieces of the puzzle of program design? How does the knitter try to ensure that the result is a seamless cloth rather than a collection of knots and loose ends? We invite those who are involved in the future of the social psychology–evaluation intersection to explore theory knitting explicitly, and to see if their work can contribute to better understanding of this as an aspect of practice and theory building. For advancement to occur, articles and chapters would have to be published on the process of theory knitting and on the quality of the programs that result.

Despite the potential benefits of improved theory knitting, there is a downside as well. When program design draws on a single theoretical perspective, then the evaluation results provide a test of that theory in a real-world setting. If the evaluation shows that the program works, this finding offers support for the theory on which the program was based. In contrast, if strands from various theories have been knitted together, then the implication of evaluation findings for the theories will often be unclear. The program is a theoretical hodge-podge, rather than a clear representation of one theory's constructs. Any given aspect of the program may not have mattered in terms of the program's success.

To reiterate, a key advantage of a program theory knit from multiple strands is that it may be more likely to address the complexities of real problems and of program implementation. However, a potentially important disadvantage is that the payoff may be less for social psychology. Many would accept such a tradeoff. Fortunately, there may also be ways to avoid or at least reduce the tradeoff in some evaluations. That is, strands from several theories could be knit together, potentially increasing the odds of the program working. At the same time, mediational models could be used in the evaluation to assess the unique contribution of each strand to program effectiveness (Donaldson, 2007), thus feeding the results back into social psychology.

Sustainability

Yet another potentially important direction for future expansion of program theory involves sustainability. The concept of sustainability is familiar in environmental contexts, involving, for example, whether certain farming practices can be maintained in the long run. Sustainability is also often an important consideration for programs. Not every new program is implemented universally. Nor is there always a strong likelihood for continued funding if the program is found to work. Instead, a program often starts in a pilot fashion, implemented in a set of sites. A funder such as a private foundation may provide initial funding for a new program offering, on the hope that if found effective the program will be integrated into regular organizational processes and receive other ongoing funding. For example, in numerous cases foundations have funded services for children (along with funding for an evaluation), with the idea that schools or local governments will provide long-term support if the services are shown to be effective. In such instances, the concern about sustainability includes the general question of whether the program continues to exist after the initial period of funding and evaluation, as well as the more specific question of what precisely the program consists of if it continues in name (Scheirer, 2005).

At present, program theory typically addresses program operations in general, especially how program activities are expected to effect change in program clients. Program theory generally does little, if anything, to address how the program might act to increase the likelihood of being continued. Social psychological research and theory could be applied to this issue, probably knitted together with organizational theory, the literature on coalition formation, and other fields related to program sustainability. Moving into the future, then, we would like to see an expansion of theory to include the social psychology of program sustainability.

Generalizability of Effectiveness

Program evaluations by necessity have limited timeframes and scopes. An evaluation may examine a program's effectiveness for a few years, but at some point the evaluation ends. Thus, questions remain about whether similar effects will continue in the future. Evaluations usually also take place in limited settings, with a particular group of participants. Resource constraints typically prohibit examining all potential program locations, or even gathering a truly representative sample of respondents. Even if a random sample of all settings and participants were observed, the nature of these could change in the future.

Circumstances could change in ways that make the program more, or less, effective. For example, a job training program that is found to be effective at one point in the business cycle may have a different effect later, when unemployment is drastically different than at the time of the evaluation. In addition, the program may change over time in ways that alter its effectiveness. The highly motivated and conscientious staff may burn out or turn over, for instance, resulting in less effective implementation of the program. Effectiveness may also change because people come to respond differently to the intervention over time, even if the intervention itself is fixed. For example, consider the cards in hotel rooms that ask customers to reuse towels and sheets (see Chapter 10, this volume). We can speculate about whether the effectiveness of this simple intervention would change over time. Perhaps initially these cards are novel, thus garnering attention, generating thought, and creating compliance with the suggestion of reusing towels and sheets. Perhaps over time the cards gather less attention from travelers, thereby generating less compliance. The example is hypothetical, but the point is simple: Evaluation findings from one point in time may not hold in the future.

Evaluation findings may also not hold across different settings and different types of individuals. A program that works in suburban schools may not work in urban schools. A treatment that works for mild anxiety might not be effective for individuals with chronic severe anxiety. A workplace health intervention shown to be effective at a company with high worker morale might not work equally well in companies with less cohesion and morale. And so on.

As is the case in social psychology and elsewhere, replication is the primary means of assessing the generalizability of evaluation findings. In fact, meta-analysis—that is, the quantitative synthesis of multiple studies—has been advocated as a key way to extend the generalizability of evaluation and other findings (e.g., Shadish et al., 2001). However, in many cases, any action triggered by evaluation will take place before the accumulation of multiple evaluation studies required for meta-analysis. Thus it might be profitable to attempt to build theory that addresses the likely persistence and generalizability of effects of different kinds of interventions. For example, are interventions based on theories like Bandura's and Ajzen's relatively stable across time and individuals? Or are there predictable variations in effects that could inform predictions about generalizability, even without the multiple evaluations required for an evaluation. In the long run, greater attention to theory about the generalizability of findings could have major benefits. It could lead to programs that are more effective across time and circumstances, and to social psychological theory that expands beyond the short-term evidence of the typical social psychological study (Cook & Groom, 2004).

Interesting and potentially valuable integrations exist whereby social psychology could help address efforts to learn more about generalizability in program evaluation. For example, it has been suggested that external validity could be enhanced in evaluation if more attention were paid to key stakeholders' implicit theories of moderating forces (Chen, Donaldson, & Mark, in press). Program staff may have valuable insights into the conditions under which the program is more or less effective. Social psychologists have skills that should aid in uncovering and systematizing these kinds of implicit theories, which in turn can guide further work, meta-analytic or otherwise, to probe the limits of a programs; effects.

Conclusion

Social psychological theory has been a valuable source of program theory for program design and evaluation. Strengthening this link between the two fields should increase this benefit. In addition, there are several ways that program theory and its application can be expanded in the future. These include attention to theory involving translation, theory knitting, sustainability theory, and generalizability. Expanding the social psychology–evaluation link to include more attention to these factors holds promise of benefits to both fields. Such expansion will also inform efforts to transfer pilot programs to more widespread implementation, a concern commonly referred to as "going to scale." Scaling up a program would benefit greatly from insights from better translation and generalizability theory, in particular.

Social Psychology and the Practice Challenges of Evaluation

In addition to serving as a wellspring for program theory, social psychology contains a wealth of research and theory that are relevant to the challenges that arise in the practice of evaluation. Examples of the practice challenges of evaluation include questions about how to guide interactions among stakeholders who vary in power and in their views and interests; gather information about stakeholders' views about such matters as the relative importance of various possible program outcomes; seek consensus across stakeholders with different interests; develop and maintain trust with stakeholders, while also eliciting continued participation; alleviate anxiety about the evaluation; maintain compliance with data collection protocols; make sure that evaluation procedures address cross-cultural issues and meet cultural competency standards; measure behaviors that take place repeatedly over time; make sense of mixed patterns of results, whereby a program that does well on one outcome does poorly on another; and facilitate use of evaluation findings.

The research and theory of social psychology can be applied to address some of these and other practice-based challenges of evaluation, as illustrated in the chapters of Part III. The potential sources of practice lessons for evaluation can come from numerous areas of social psychology. Examples include areas of research and theory such as interpersonal and intergroup processes, social power, stereotyping, biases in inference, persuasion and attitude change, cooperation and negotiation, affect and judgment, and many others.

Moving into the future, then, evaluation practice could be strengthened by additional importation of hypotheses from social psychological research and theory. The object of these hypotheses is to suggest better ways to address the challenges that arise in the conduct of evaluation. This might involve drawing on a single literature from social psychology (e.g., negotiation), or it could involve theory knitting across multiple areas (e.g., negotiation, affect and judgment, and biases in inference). The notion of middle-range theory is one promising general model for how to undertake such efforts (see Campbell & McGrath, Chapter 13, this volume).

Rather than simply export social psychological concepts to program evaluators, we encourage social psychologists interested in evaluation also to respond to calls for more systematic study of evaluation (e.g., Mark, 2008). For instance, social psychologists might be well positioned to study evaluation influence and use (Mark & Henry, 2004), leading to a better knowledge base to guide evaluators' actions. As another example, rather than simply import lessons from social psychology about how to engender trust, an experiment could be conducted to study the effectiveness of the social psychological suggestion in an evaluation context.

Doing so would provide tests of the social psychologically based hypotheses in the real-world context of evaluations. Much of social psychology research still takes place in research labs at universities, typically with introductory psychology students as participants. This is a cause for criticism, both historically (e.g., Orne, 1972) and more recently (e.g., Cook & Groom, 2004). The criticism involves both construct validity (i.e., concern about whether the lab experiment is studying the real phenomenon, such as cooperation) and external validity (i.e., concern about whether the findings, however labeled, can be generalized elsewhere). Tests of social psychological hypotheses in real evaluation contexts would go a long way toward addressing such criticism.

If the future includes increased testing of social psychological hypotheses in evaluation practice contexts, the potential advantages go beyond strengthening construct and external validity. Attempts to apply social psychology to evaluation challenges may help identify gaps in existing theory and research, thus pointing the way to improved theory. For example, Campbell and Mark (2006) applied aspects of the literatures on negotiation and accountability to challenges in reaching agreement among stakeholders with differing views about an intervention. In reviewing the social psychological literature on accountability, they observed that this construct had generally been treated as an either/or phenomenon, with the person either being accountable or not. In contrast, in stakeholder situations in actual evaluation, the key issue instead seemed to be *to whom* each stakeholder felt accountable. As this example illustrates, applications of social psychology to real-world settings can identify gaps to be addressed in subsequent research and theory.

Professional Matters

Throughout this chapter we have issued a call for a future with a stronger integration of social psychology and evaluation. This includes increased use of social psychological theory for program design and evaluation; expansion of theory to include notions of translation, theory knitting theory, program sustainability, and generalizability of effects; increased importation of social psychology to address the practice challenges of evaluation; and more testing of social psychological hypotheses in the context of evaluation. For any or all of this to occur, professional arrangements need to be developed in such a way as to facilitate rather than inhibit these proposed changes.

Publication Options

One important professional matter involves opportunities for publication. There would be little incentive for social psychologists to test hypotheses in the applied setting of evaluation practice, for example, if the results could not be published in respectable journals. In addition, if the results of such studies could not be published, then it would be difficult to see increased benefits for social psychology of the social psychology–evaluation relationship. Our assessment is that, fortunately, opportunities exist for publications that lie at the intersection of social psychology and evaluation.

Not surprisingly, theory-driven evaluations can and have been published in both the evaluation literature and in social psychology as well as in journals related to the content area of the program (e.g., health, education, the environment). Examples are present throughout this volume. See for instance the D.A.R.E. work cited in Chapter 5 of this volume, which includes papers published in *Health Psychology* and *The Journal of Behavioral Medicine*.

Past efforts to apply social psychological theory to the practice challenges of evaluation have found outlets in top-tier evaluation journals. For example, Donaldson, Gooler, and Scriven (2002) and Taut and Brauns (2003) both addressed practice challenges that arise because of the anxiety that stakeholders often have about an evaluation. These authors published articles in different evaluation journals, drawing on the social psychological literature about evaluation apprehension and test anxiety, and discussing ways to try to alleviate stakeholder anxiety about participating in evaluation. As another example, Mark and Henry (2004) have published a model of the potential mediators of evaluation use and influence, drawing heavily on the social psychological literature. In our experience, demand exists for guidance for evaluation that can come from social psychology.

For research on social psychologically derived solutions to challenges from evaluation practice, opportunities exist for publication in both the social psychological and evaluation literature. For instance, Campbell and Mark (2006), drawing on the social psychological literatures on negotiation and accountability, conducted a simulation study to test hypotheses about how to engender effective stakeholder processes in evaluation. They published the results in a psychology journal, the *Journal of Applied Social Psychology*. Almost certainly they could have published a report about this study in the evaluation literature instead.

In short, there are publication opportunities for the scholarly work that would result from a stronger future linkage between social psychology and evaluation. Other professional considerations that could affect—and we believe, benefit from—this linkage involve training and employment opportunities. We turn to these issues next.

Training and Employment

The image and impact of psychology have changed dramatically over the past three decades, with a large increase in the number of research psychologists seeking careers in a wide variety of applied settings (Romero, 2007). Donaldson and Berger (2006) have documented these trends using data from the National Center for Education Statistics in the U.S. Department of Education. To further understand the specific training and employment opportunities for applied scientific psychologists, the American Psychological Association produced a series of projects to identify (1) the various skills sets and expertise that are valued by employers and (2) the university-based training programs that prepare psychologists for these careers (APA, 2005a, 2005b). Social psychology turns out to have the largest number of applied training programs and to be a subarea of psychology that is particularly well suited for making an impact in this rapidly growing employment domain (Crano, 2006).

DeAngelis (2008) identified program evaluation as one particularly hot growth area for applied psychologists. Social psychologists have the potential to make a major difference in education, public health, community settings, private business, and the like by applying social psychological theory, research, and evaluation to assess the strengths and weaknesses of programs, policies, and organizations in order to improve their effectiveness. The rich intersection of social psychology and evaluation has proven to provide many social psychologists with lucrative and rewarding careers outside of traditional academic settings (see APA, 2005; Donaldson & Berger, 2006). This has been especially important in recent times as the economic downturn has led to a serious shortage of academic jobs (Romero, 2007). Looking toward the future, both fields—social psychology and evaluation—could be significantly strengthened by increasing the opportunities for joint training. For example, a social psychology PhD program could be strengthened by making an evaluation minor available. Undergraduates with interests related to evaluation can be guided to applied social psychology training programs. More generally, recently trained social psychologists, especially those with a good grounding in evaluation, can help meet what appears to be a rapidly expanding market for evaluation (Donaldson & Christie, 2006).

Conclusion

This book has illustrated several kinds of connections between social psychology and evaluation, and this chapter specifically has offered several directions for strengthening that relationship. The advantages of a strengthened social psychology–evaluation relationship will accrue, not only to each of those fields, but also to future beneficiaries of the programs, policies, and practices that would benefit from better program design and evaluation. What will determine whether the future sees a strengthened relationship between these two fields? To a large extent, the future of the social psychology–evaluation relationship is in the hands of the readers of this book.

REFERENCES

American Psychological Association. (2005a). *Non-academic careers for scientific psychologists: Interesting careers in psychology*. Retrieved October 15, 2010, from *www.apa.org/science/nonacad_careers.html*.

American Psychological Association. (2005a). *Non-academic careers for scientific psychologists: Graduate program in applied psychology*. Retrieved October 15, 2010, from *www.apa.org/science/nonacad-grad.html*.

Breckler, S. J. (2008). The NIH Roadmap: Are psychologists in or out? *Journal of Clinical Psychology in Medical Settings, 15*(1), 60–64.

Campbell, B. C., & Mark, M. M. (2006). Toward more effective stakeholder dialogue: Applying theories of negotiation to policy and program evaluation. *Journal of Applied Social Psychology*, 2834–2863.

Chen, H-t., Donaldson, S., & Mark, M. M. (in press). *Validity in Outcome Evaluation*. San Francisco: Jossey-Bass.

Cook, T. D., & Groom, C. (2004). The methodological assumptions of social psychology: The mutual interdependence of substantive theory and method choice. In C. Sansone, C. C. Morf, & A. T. Panter (Eds.), *The Sage handbook of methods in social psychology*. Thousand Oaks, CA: Sage.

Crano, W. D. (2006). Social psychology: Applications and careers. In S. I. Donaldson, D. E. Berger, & K. Pezdek (Eds.), *Applied psychology: New frontiers and rewarding careers*. Mahwah, NJ: Erlbaum.

DeAngelis, T. (2008). Psychology's growth careers: Psychologists' expertise in human behavior is increasingly welcomed in many nontraditional career settings. *APA Monitor, 39*(4), 64.

Donaldson, S. I. (2007). *Program theory-driven evaluation science: Strategies and applications*. Mahwah, NJ: Erlbaum.

Donaldson, S. I., & Berger, D. E. (2006). The rise and promise of applied psychology in the 21st century. In S. I. Donaldson, D. E. Berger, & K. Pezdek (Eds.), *Applied psychology: New frontiers and rewarding careers*. Mahwah, NJ: Erlbaum.

Donaldson, S. I., & Christie, C. A. (2006). Emerging career opportunities in the transdiscipline of evaluation science. In S. I. Donaldson, D. E. Berger, & K. Pezdek (Eds.), *Applied psychology: New frontiers and rewarding careers*. Mahwah, NJ: Erlbaum.

Donaldson, S. I., Gooler, L. E., & Scriven, M. (2002). Strategies for managing evaluation anxiety: Toward a psychology of program evaluation. *American Journal of Evaluation, 23*, 261–273.

Heine, S. J. (2010). Cultural psychology. In S. T. Fiske, D. T. Gilbert, & G. Lindzey (Eds.), *Handbook of social psychology* (5th ed., Vol. 2). Hoboken, NJ: Wiley.

Kalmar, D. A., & Sternberg, R. J. (1988). Theory knitting: An integrative approach to theory development. *Philosophical Psychology, 1*(2), 153–170.

Mark, M. M. (2008). Building a better evidence-base for evaluation theory. In P. R. Brandon & N. L. Smith (Eds.), *Fundamental issues in evaluation* (pp. 111–134). New York: Guilford Press.

Mark, M. M., & Henry, G. T. (2004). The mechanisms and outcomes of evaluation influence. *Evaluation, 10*(1), 35–57.

Orne, M. T. (1962). On the social psychology of the psychological experiment: With particular reference to demand characteristics and their implications. *American Psychologist, 17*, 776–783.

Oskamp, S., & Schultz, W. (1999). *Applied social psychology*. Englewood Cliffs, NJ: Prentice Hall.

Romero, V. L. (2007). The changing image of psychology: The rise of applied psychology. *Observer, 16*(7), 27–30.

Scheirer, M. A. (2005). Is sustainability possible? A review and commentary on empirical studies of program sustainability. *American Journal of Evaluation, 26*(3), 320–347.

Shadish, W. R., Cook, T. D., & Campbell, D. T. (2002). *Experimental and quasi-experimental designs for generalized causal inference*. Boston: Houghton Mifflin.

Tashiro, T., & Mortensen, L. (2006). Translational research: How social psychology can improve psychotherapy. *American Psychologist, 61*, 959–966.

Taut, S., & Brauns, D. (2003). Resistance to evaluation: A psychological perspective. *Evaluation, 9*, 247–264.

Thaler, R. H., & Sunstein, C. R. (2008). *Nudge: Improving decisions about health, wealth, and happiness*. New Haven, CT: Yale University Press.

Vaessen, J., & Leeuw, F. L. (Eds.). (2010). *Mind the gap: Perspectives on policy evaluation and the social sciences*. New Brunswick, NJ: Transaction Publishers.

Vernig, P. M. (2007). From science to practice: Bridging the gap with translational research. *APS Observer, 20*, 29–30.

Woolf, S. H. (2008). The meaning of translational research and why it matters. *Journal of the American Medical Association, 299*(2), 211–213.

Author Index

Subject Index

Page numbers followed by *t* indicate tables, by *f* indicate figures.

About the Editors

Melvin M. Mark, PhD, is Professor and Head of Psychology at The Pennsylvania State University in University Park, Pennsylvania. He has served as President of the American Evaluation Association and as Editor of the *American Journal of Evaluation* (for which he is now Editor Emeritus). Dr. Mark's interests include the theory, methodology, and practice of program and policy evaluation, as well as the application of social psychology. Among his books are *Evaluation: An Integrated Framework for Understanding, Guiding, and Improving Policies and Programs*; *The SAGE Handbook of Evaluation*; *What Counts as Credible Evidence in Applied Research and Evaluation Practice?*; *Evaluation in Action: Interviews With Expert Evaluators*; *Evaluation Policy and Evaluation Practice*; and *Advancing Validity in Outcome Evaluation: Theory and Practice*.

Stewart I. Donaldson, PhD, is Professor and Chair of Psychology, Director of the Institute of Organizational and Program Evaluation Research, and Dean of the School of Behavioral and Organizational Sciences at Claremont Graduate University in Claremont, California. Dr. Donaldson continues to develop and lead one of the most extensive and rigorous graduate programs specializing in applied social psychology and evaluation. He is serving a 3-year elected term on the Board of the American Evaluation Association. Among his recent books are *Applied Positive Psychology: Improving Everyday Life, Health, Schools, Work, and Society*; *Advancing Validity in Outcome Evaluation: Theory and Practice*; *What Counts as Credible Evidence in Applied Research and Evaluation Practice?*; *Program Theory-Driven Evaluation Science: Strategies and Applications*; *Applied Psychology: New Frontiers and Rewarding Careers*; and *Evaluating Social Programs and Problems: Visions for the New Millennium*. Dr. Donaldson has been honored with Early Career Achievement Awards from the Western Psychological Association and the American Evaluation Association.

Bernadette Campbell, PhD, is Assistant Professor of Psychology at Carleton University in Ottawa, Ontario, Canada. Her research interests are in the area of applied social psychology. In particular, Dr. Campbell is interested in the many ways that social psychology and its theories can be used to empirically examine assumptions and claims made in the field of program and policy evaluation. Funded by the Social Science and Humanities Research Council of Canada, her research applies social psychological theories of negotiation, persuasion, and attitude change to achieve a better practical and theoretical understanding of evaluation activities and concepts such as stakeholder dialogue and evaluation influence.

Contributors

Icek Ajzen, Department of Psychology, University of Massachusetts, Amherst, Massachusetts

Albert Bandura, Department of Psychology, Stanford University, Stanford, California

Leonard Bickman, Department of Psychology, Vanderbilt University, Nashville, Tennessee

Marcella H. Boynton, Center for Child and Family Policy, Duke University, Durham, North Carolina

Bernadette Campbell, Department of Psychology, Carleton University, Ottawa, Ontario, Canada

Robert B. Cialdini, Department of Psychology and Marketing, Arizona State University, Tempe, Arizona

Taya R. Cohen, Tepper School of Business, Carnegie Mellon University, Pittsburgh, Pennsylvania

William D. Crano, Department of Psychology, Claremont Graduate University, Claremont, California

Stewart I. Donaldson, School of Behavioral and Organizational Sciences, Claremont Graduate University, Claremont, California

Natalie L. Dove, Department of Psychology, Eastern Michigan University, Ypsilanti, Michigan

Monique A. Fleming, Department of Psychology, University of Southern California, Los Angeles, California

Noah J. Goldstein, Department of Human Resources and Organizational Behavior, Anderson School of Management, University of California at Los Angeles, Los Angeles, California

Vladas Griskevicius, Department of Marketing, Carlson School of Management, University of Minnesota, Minneapolis, Minnesota

Blair T. Johnson, Department of Psychology, University of Connecticut, Storrs, Connecticut

David W. Johnson, Department of Educational Psychology, University of Minnesota, Minneapolis, Minnesota

Roger T. Johnson, Department of Educational Psychology, University of Minnesota, Minneapolis, Minnesota

Lindsay A. Kennedy, Department of Psychology, University of North Carolina at Chapel Hill, Chapel Hill, North Carolina

Melvin M. Mark, Department of Psychology, The Pennsylvania State University, University Park, Pennsylvania

April L. McGrath, Department of Psychology, Carleton University, Ottawa, Ontario, Canada

Daphna Oyserman, Department of Psychology, University of Michigan, Ann Arbor, Michigan

A. T. Panter, Department of Psychology, University of North Carolina at Chapel Hill, Chapel Hill, North Carolina

Emil J. Posavac, Department of Psychology, Loyola University Chicago, Chicago, Illinois

Manuel Riemer, Department of Psychology, Wilfrid Laurier University, Waterloo, Ontario, Canada

Lawrence J. Sanna, Department of Psychology, University of North Carolina at Chapel Hill, Chapel Hill, North Carolina

Norbert Schwarz, Department of Psychology, University of Michigan, Ann Arbor, Michigan

Laurie Stevahn, College of Education, Seattle University, Seattle, Washington

R. Scott Tindale, Department of Psychology, Loyola University Chicago, Chicago, Illinois